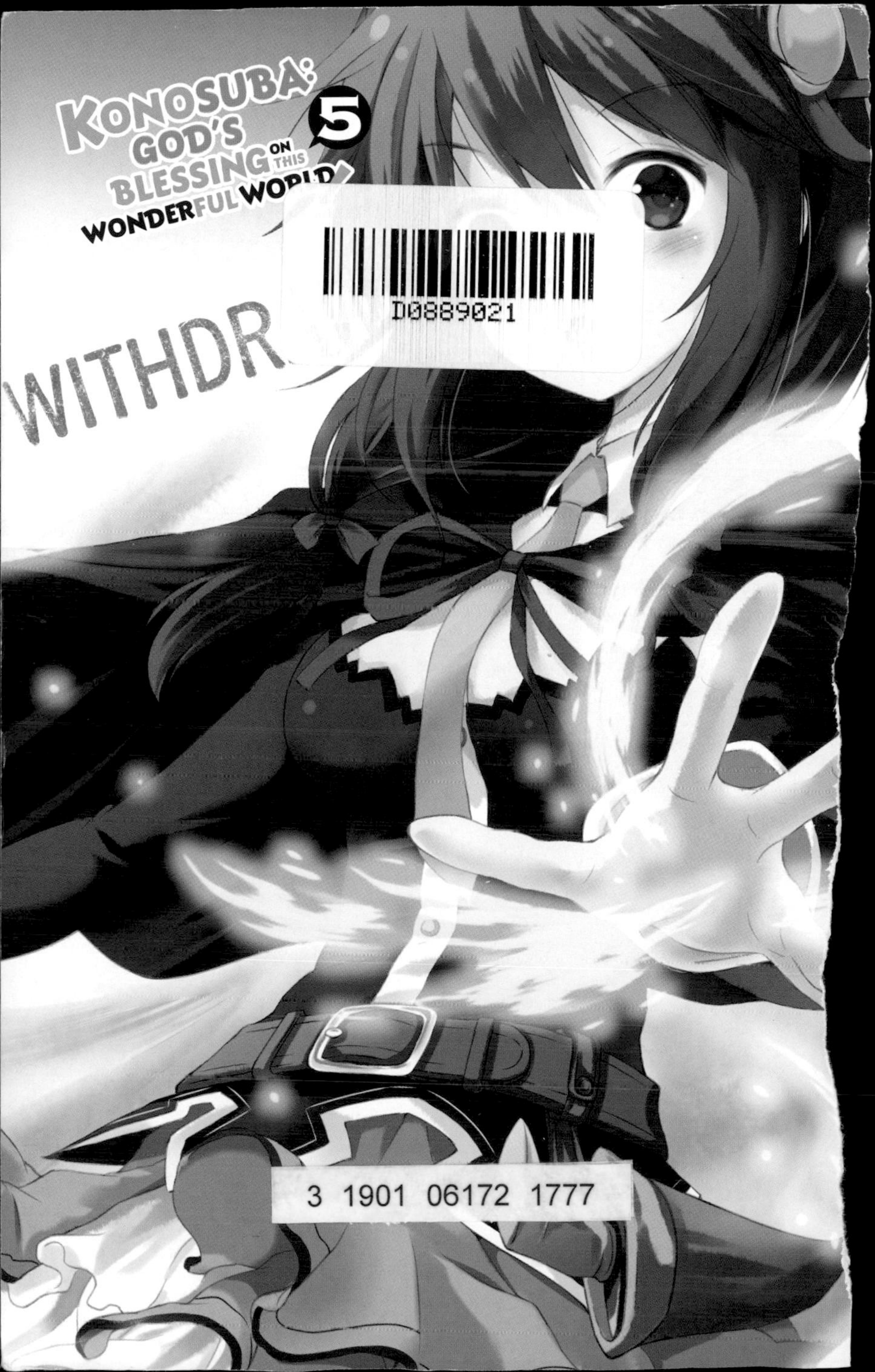
KONOSUBA: GOD'S BLESSING ON THIS WONDERFUL WORLD!
5

5

GOD'S BLESSING ON THIS WONDERFUL WORLD!

CONTENTS

Chapter 25 May Friendship Come to This Crimson Magic Girl! (1) 3

Chapter 26 May Friendship Come to This Crimson Magic Girl! (2) 29

Chapter 27 May There Be a Good Match for This Noble Daughter! (1) 61

Chapter 28 May There Be a Good Match for This Noble Daughter! (2) 85

Chapter 29 May This Masked Knight Submit! (1) 109

Chapter 30 May This Masked Knight Submit! (2) 135

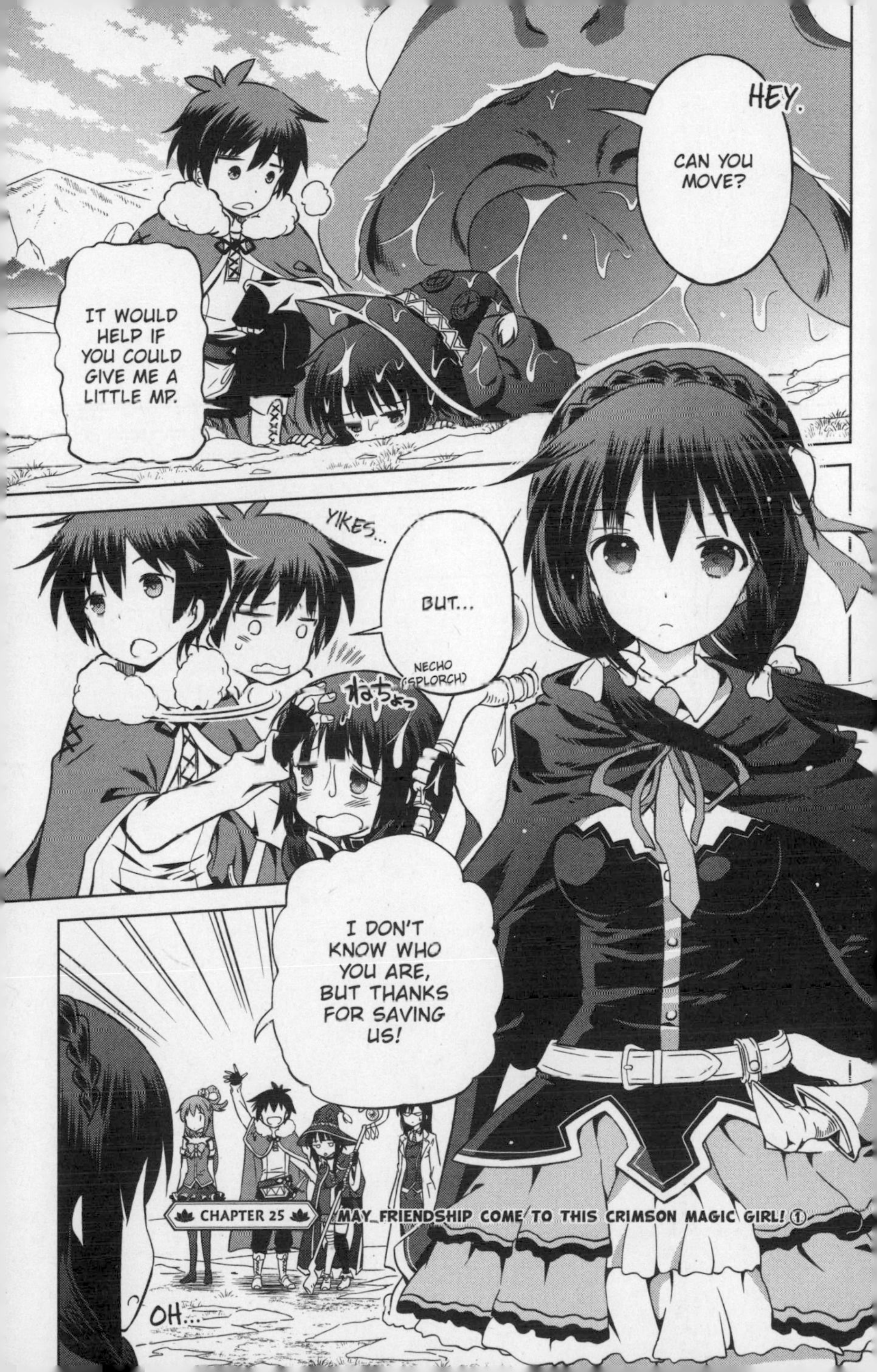
HEY.
CAN YOU MOVE?
IT WOULD HELP IF YOU COULD GIVE ME A LITTLE MP.
BUT...
YIKES...
ねちょっ
NECHO (SPLORCH)
I DON'T KNOW WHO YOU ARE, BUT THANKS FOR SAVING US!
CHAPTER 25
MAY FRIENDSHIP COME TO THIS CRIMSON MAGIC GIRL! ①
OH...

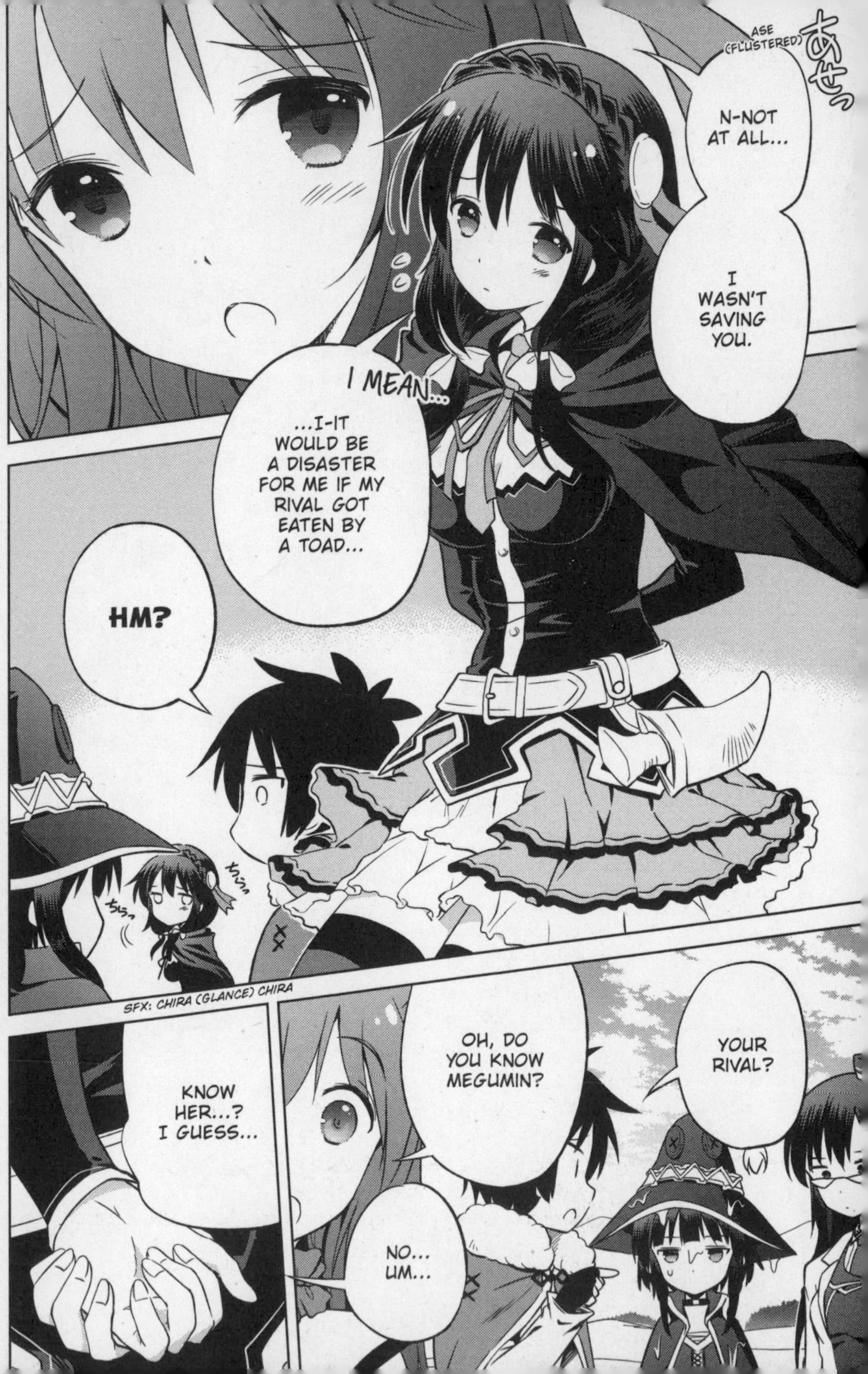

あせっ
ASE (FLUSTERED)
N-NOT AT ALL...
I WASN'T SAVING YOU.
I MEAN...
...I-IT WOULD BE A DISASTER FOR ME IF MY RIVAL GOT EATEN BY A TOAD...
HM?
ちらっ
ちらっ
SFX: CHIRA (GLANCE) CHIRA
YOUR RIVAL?
OH, DO YOU KNOW MEGUMIN?
NO... UM...
KNOW HER...? I GUESS...

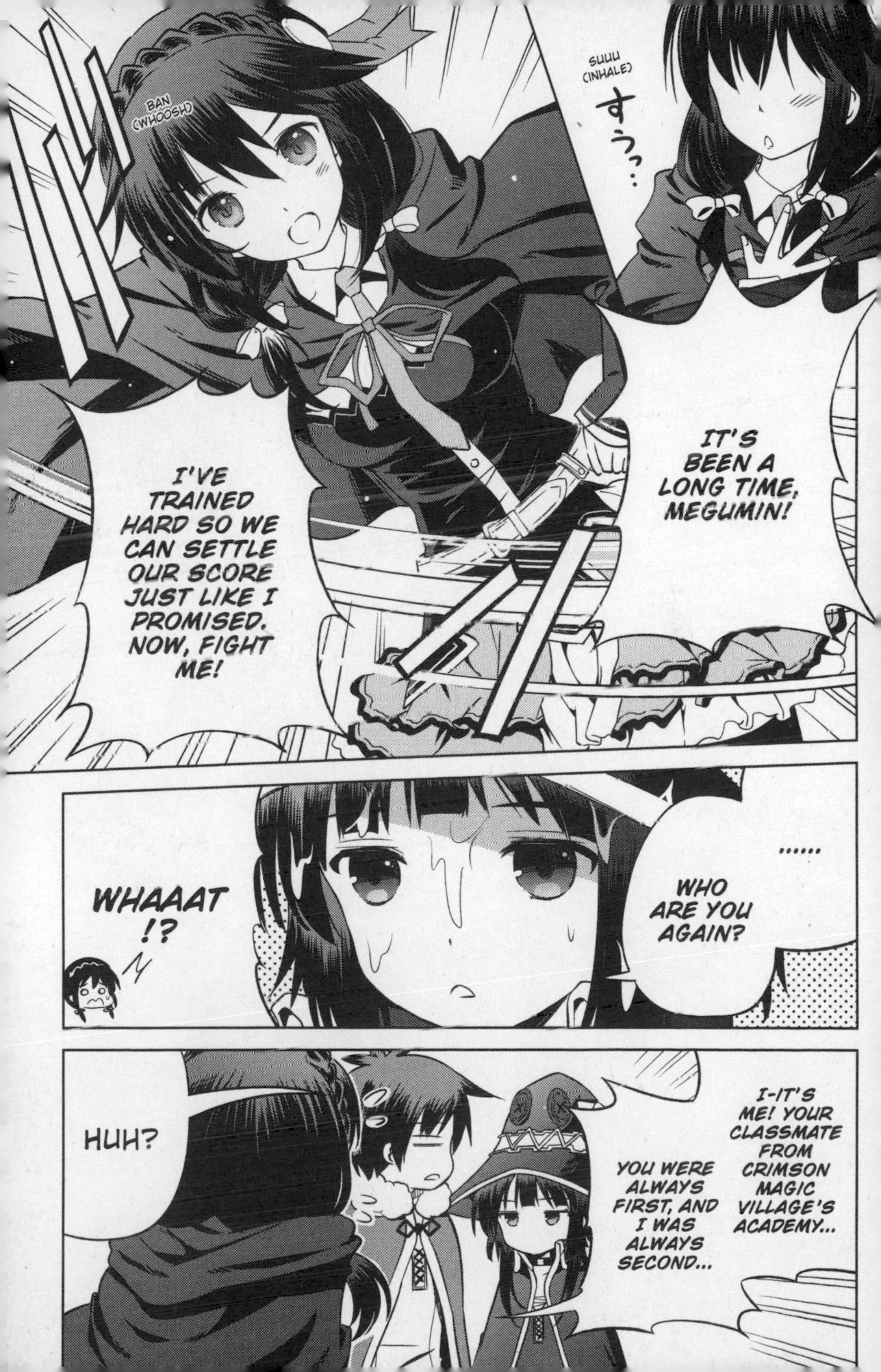
SUUU (INHALE)
すぅ…
BAN (WHOOSH)
IT'S BEEN A LONG TIME, MEGUMIN!
I'VE TRAINED HARD SO WE CAN SETTLE OUR SCORE JUST LIKE I PROMISED. NOW, FIGHT ME!
......
WHO ARE YOU AGAIN?
WHAAAT !?
I-IT'S ME! YOUR CLASSMATE FROM CRIMSON MAGIC VILLAGE'S ACADEMY...
YOU WERE ALWAYS FIRST, AND I WAS ALWAYS SECOND...
HUH?

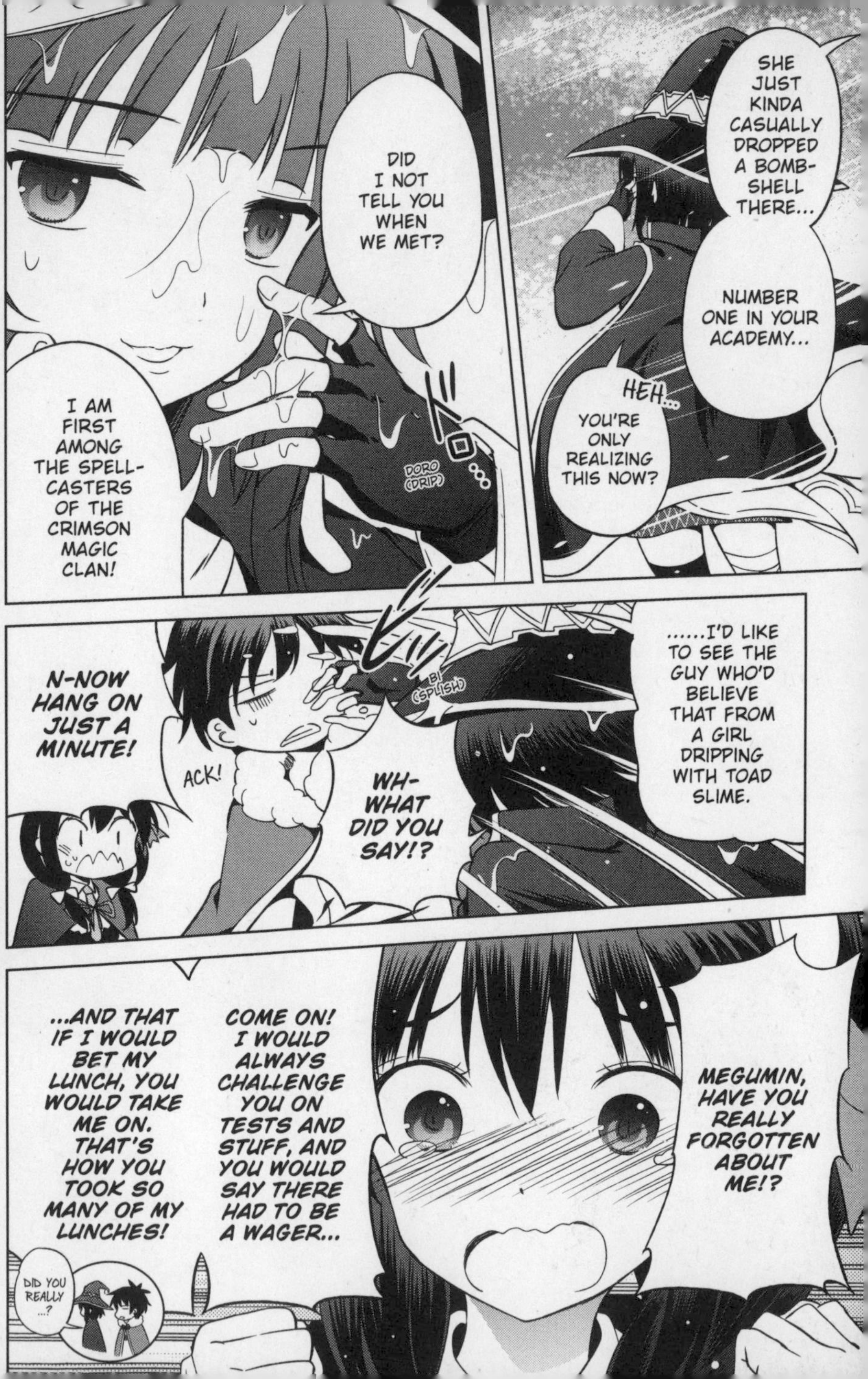
SHE JUST KINDA CASUALLY DROPPED A BOMB-SHELL THERE...
NUMBER ONE IN YOUR ACADEMY...
HEH...
YOU'RE ONLY REALIZING THIS NOW?
DID I NOT TELL YOU WHEN WE MET?
I AM FIRST AMONG THE SPELL-CASTERS OF THE CRIMSON MAGIC CLAN!
DORO (DRIP)
......I'D LIKE TO SEE THE GUY WHO'D BELIEVE THAT FROM A GIRL DRIPPING WITH TOAD SLIME.
BI (SPLISH)
WH-WHAT DID YOU SAY!?
ACK!
N-NOW HANG ON JUST A MINUTE!
MEGUMIN, HAVE YOU REALLY FORGOTTEN ABOUT ME!?
COME ON! I WOULD ALWAYS CHALLENGE YOU ON TESTS AND STUFF, AND YOU WOULD SAY THERE HAD TO BE A WAGER...
...AND THAT IF I WOULD BET MY LUNCH, YOU WOULD TAKE ME ON. THAT'S HOW YOU TOOK SO MANY OF MY LUNCHES!
DID YOU REALLY ...?

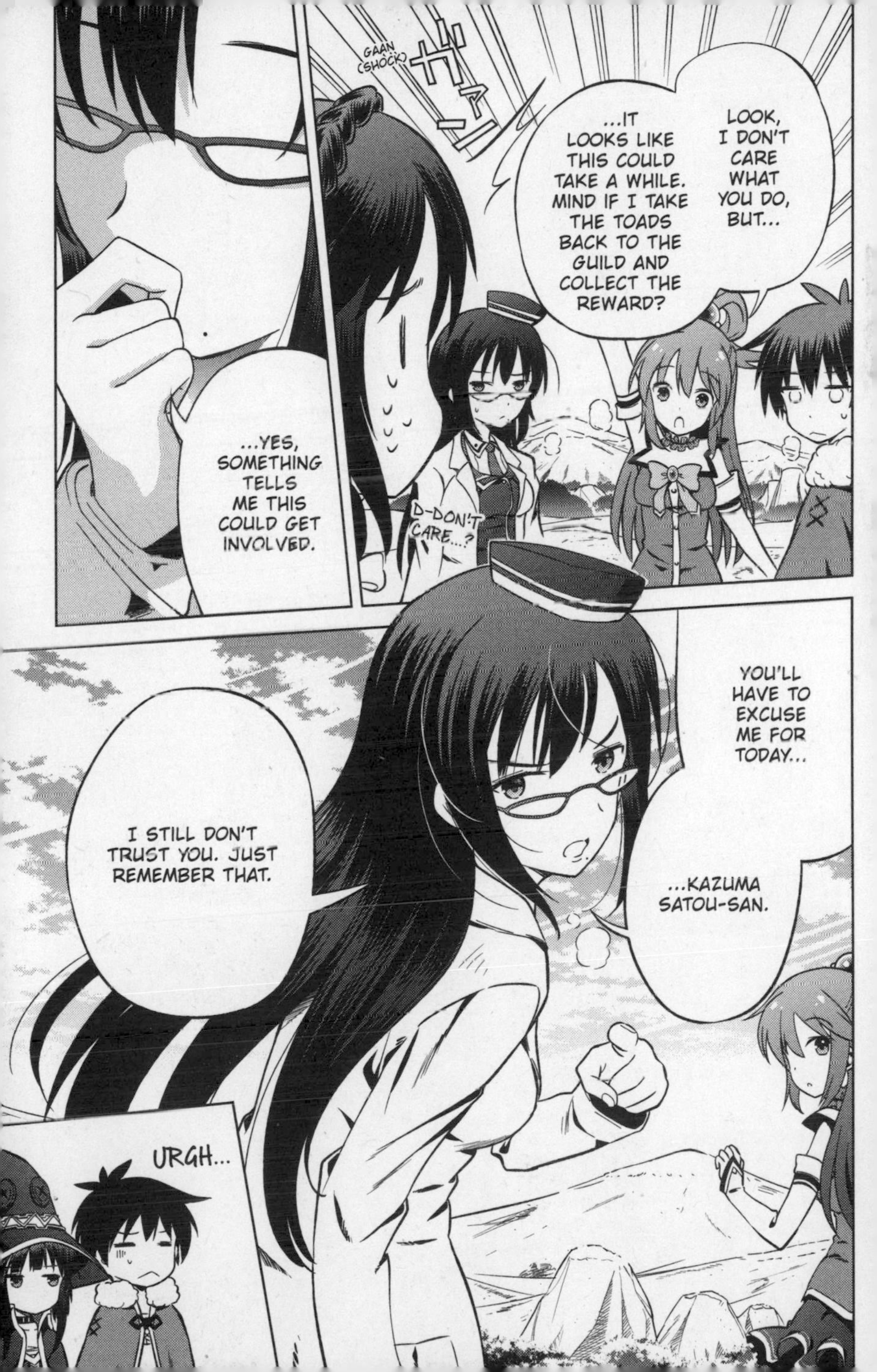
LOOK, I DON'T CARE WHAT YOU DO, BUT...
...IT LOOKS LIKE THIS COULD TAKE A WHILE. MIND IF I TAKE THE TOADS BACK TO THE GUILD AND COLLECT THE REWARD?
GAAN (SHOCK)
D-DON'T CARE...?
...YES, SOMETHING TELLS ME THIS COULD GET INVOLVED.
YOU'LL HAVE TO EXCUSE ME FOR TODAY...
...KAZUMA SATOU-SAN.
I STILL DON'T TRUST YOU. JUST REMEMBER THAT.
URGH...

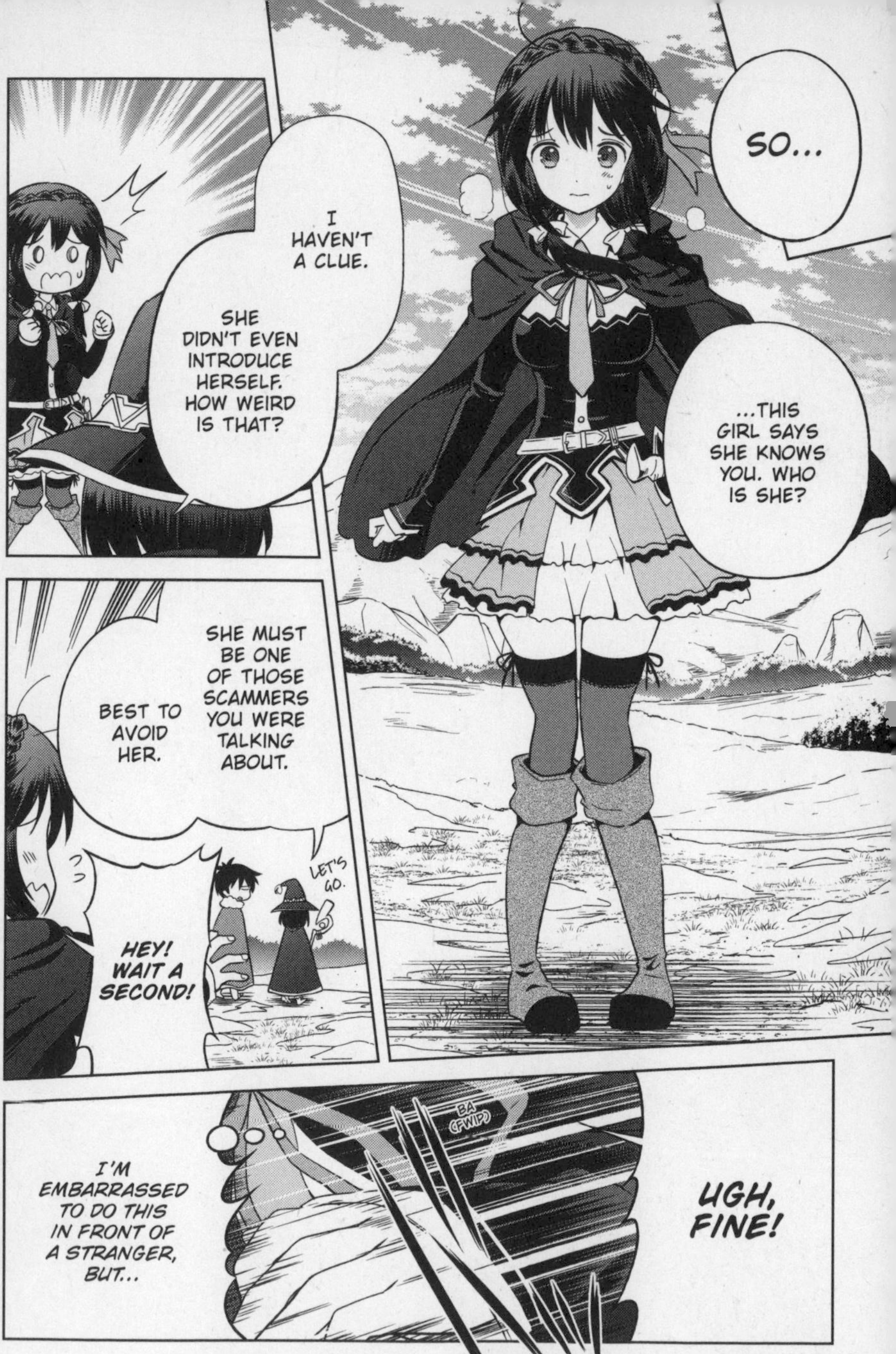
SO...
...THIS GIRL SAYS SHE KNOWS YOU. WHO IS SHE?
I HAVEN'T A CLUE.
SHE DIDN'T EVEN INTRODUCE HERSELF. HOW WEIRD IS THAT?
SHE MUST BE ONE OF THOSE SCAMMERS YOU WERE TALKING ABOUT.
BEST TO AVOID HER.
LET'S GO.
HEY! WAIT A SECOND!
UGH, FINE!
BA (FWIP)
I'M EMBARRASSED TO DO THIS IN FRONT OF A STRANGER, BUT...

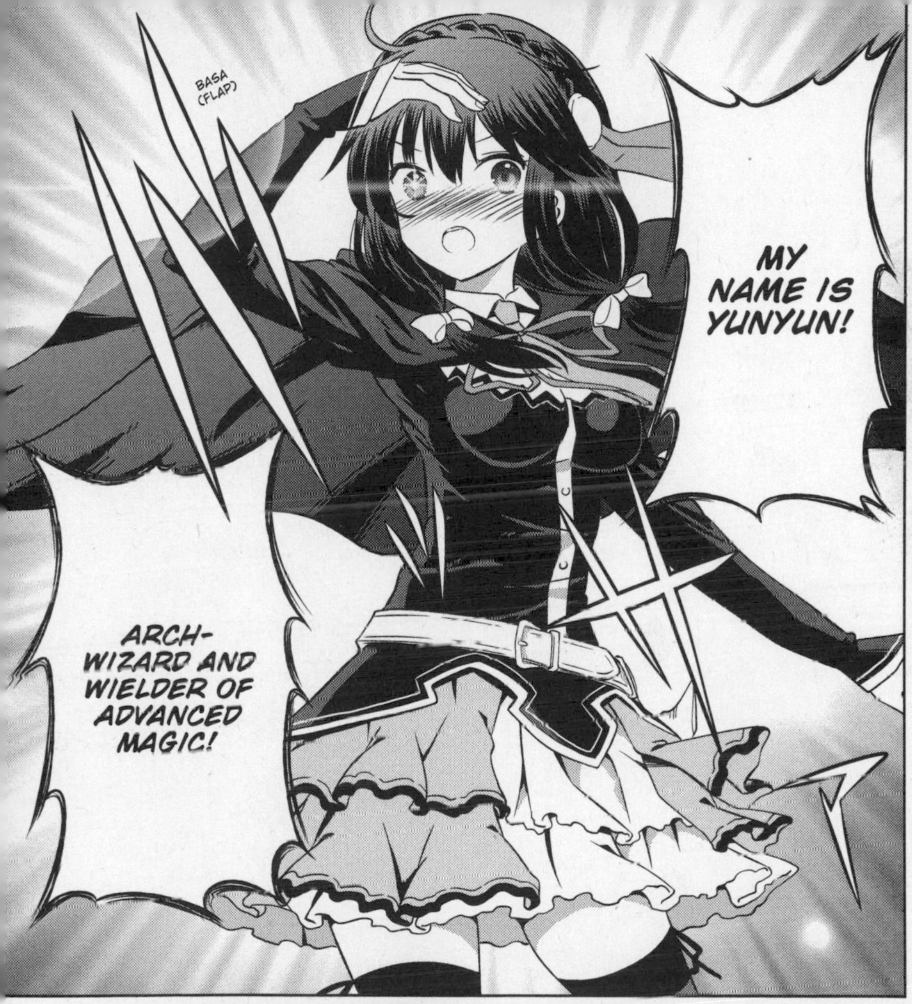
BASA (FLAP)
MY NAME IS YUNYUN!
ARCH-WIZARD AND WIELDER OF ADVANCED MAGIC!
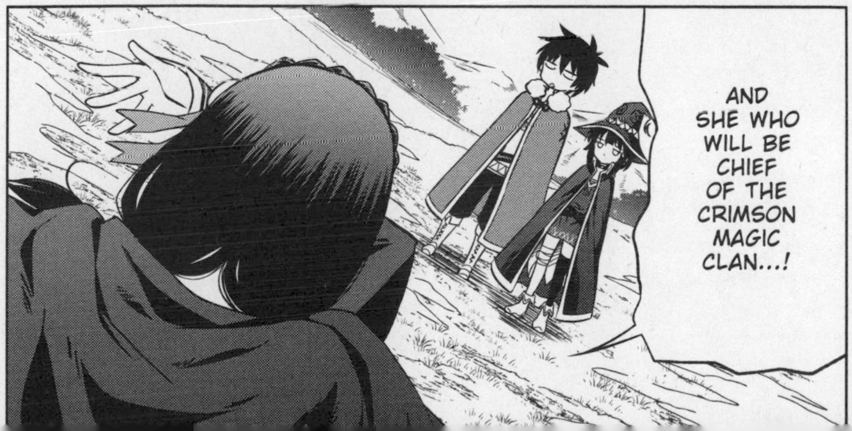
AND SHE WHO WILL BE CHIEF OF THE CRIMSON MAGIC CLAN...!

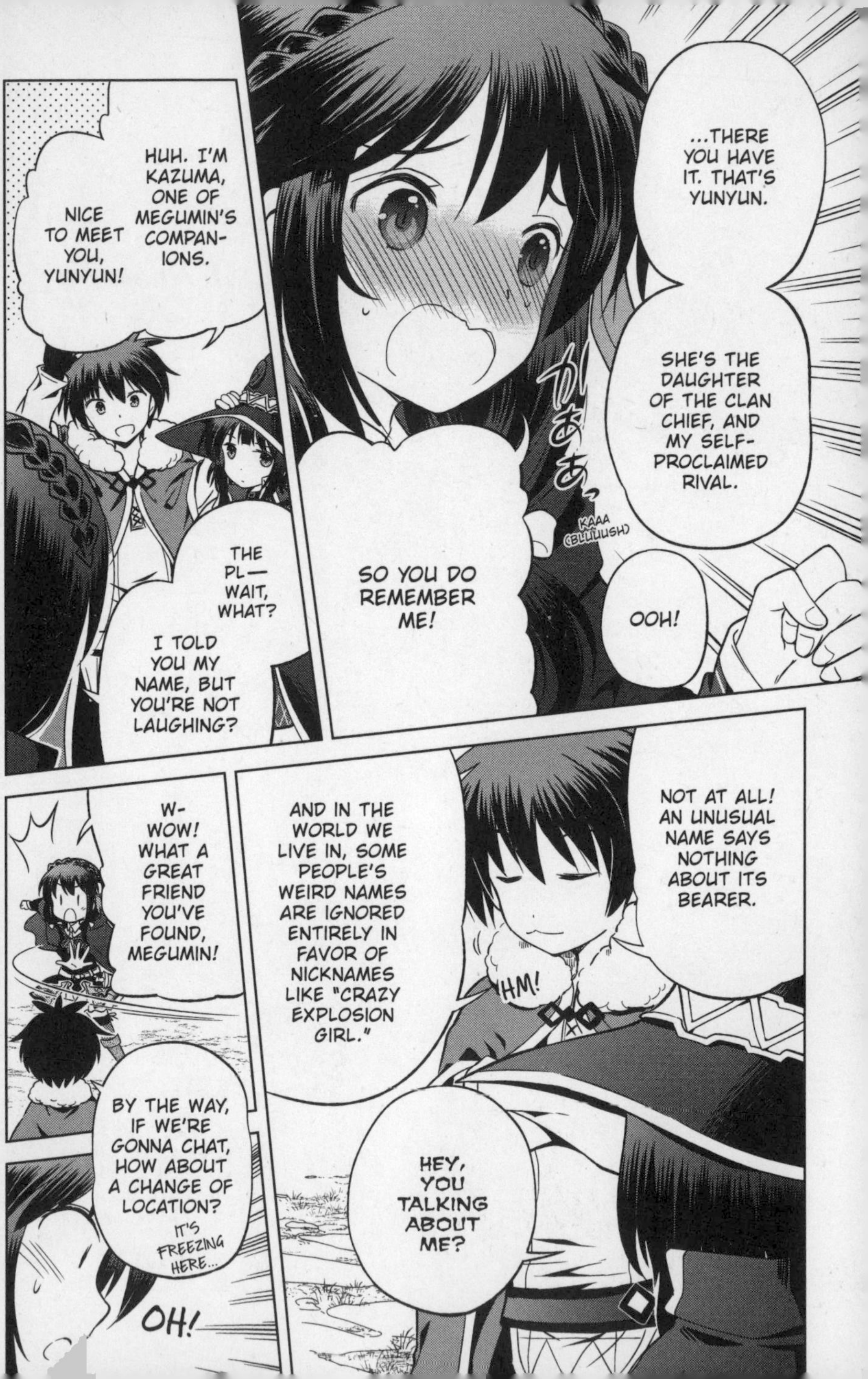
...THERE YOU HAVE IT. THAT'S YUNYUN.
SHE'S THE DAUGHTER OF THE CLAN CHIEF, AND MY SELF-PROCLAIMED RIVAL.
OOH!
かあぁ
KAAA (BLUUUSH)
SO YOU DO REMEMBER ME!
HUH. I'M KAZUMA, ONE OF MEGUMIN'S COMPANIONS.
NICE TO MEET YOU, YUNYUN!
THE PL— WAIT, WHAT?
I TOLD YOU MY NAME, BUT YOU'RE NOT LAUGHING?
NOT AT ALL! AN UNUSUAL NAME SAYS NOTHING ABOUT ITS BEARER.
HM!
AND IN THE WORLD WE LIVE IN, SOME PEOPLE'S WEIRD NAMES ARE IGNORED ENTIRELY IN FAVOR OF NICKNAMES LIKE "CRAZY EXPLOSION GIRL."
W-WOW! WHAT A GREAT FRIEND YOU'VE FOUND, MEGUMIN!
HEY, YOU TALKING ABOUT ME?
BY THE WAY, IF WE'RE GONNA CHAT, HOW ABOUT A CHANGE OF LOCATION?
IT'S FREEZING HERE...
OH!

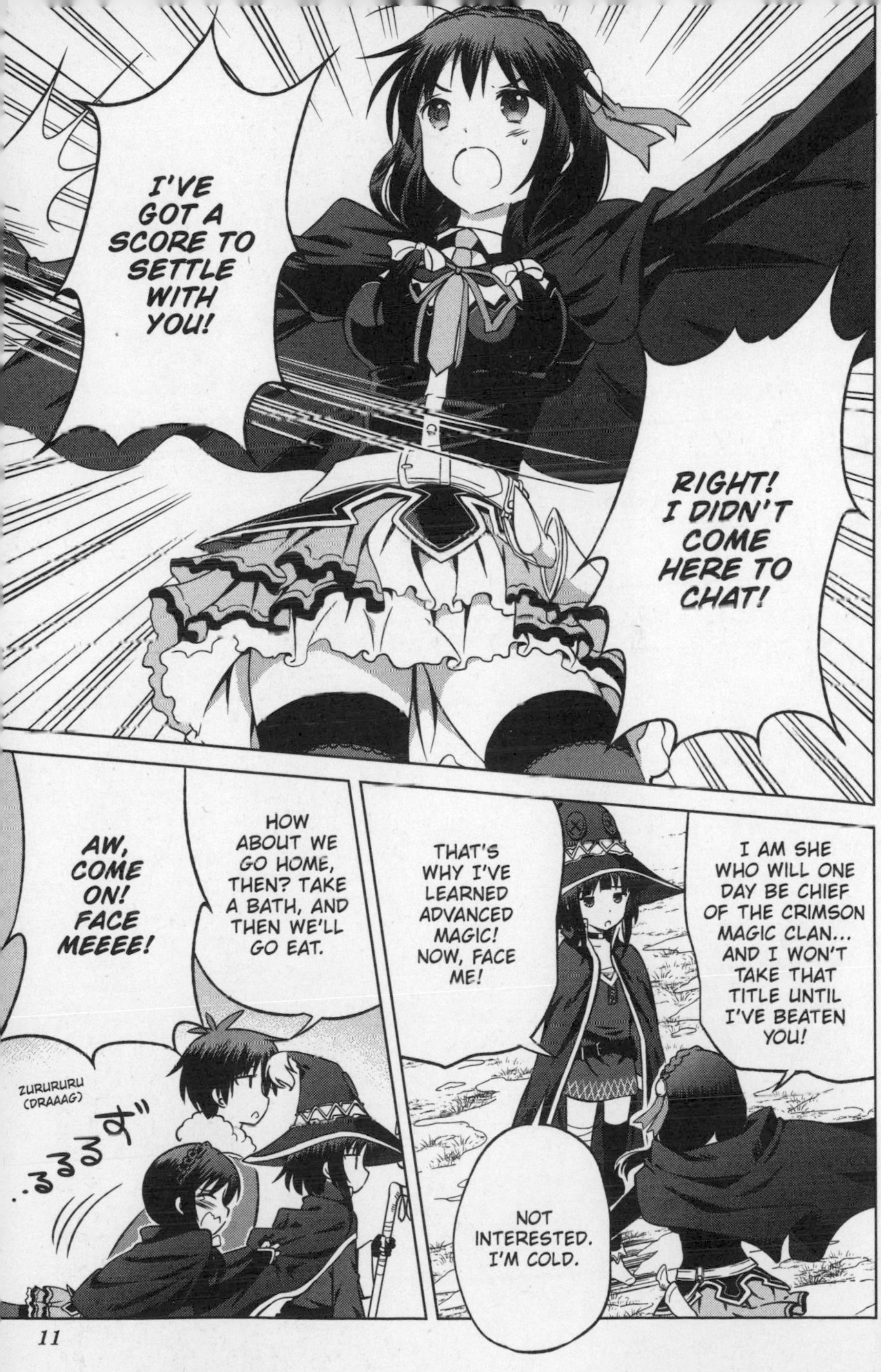
RIGHT! I DIDN'T COME HERE TO CHAT!
I'VE GOT A SCORE TO SETTLE WITH YOU!
I AM SHE WHO WILL ONE DAY BE CHIEF OF THE CRIMSON MAGIC CLAN... AND I WON'T TAKE THAT TITLE UNTIL I'VE BEATEN YOU!
THAT'S WHY I'VE LEARNED ADVANCED MAGIC! NOW, FACE ME!
NOT INTERESTED. I'M COLD.
HOW ABOUT WE GO HOME, THEN? TAKE A BATH, AND THEN WE'LL GO EAT.
AW, COME ON! FACE MEEEE!
ずるるる..
ZURURURU (DRAAAG)

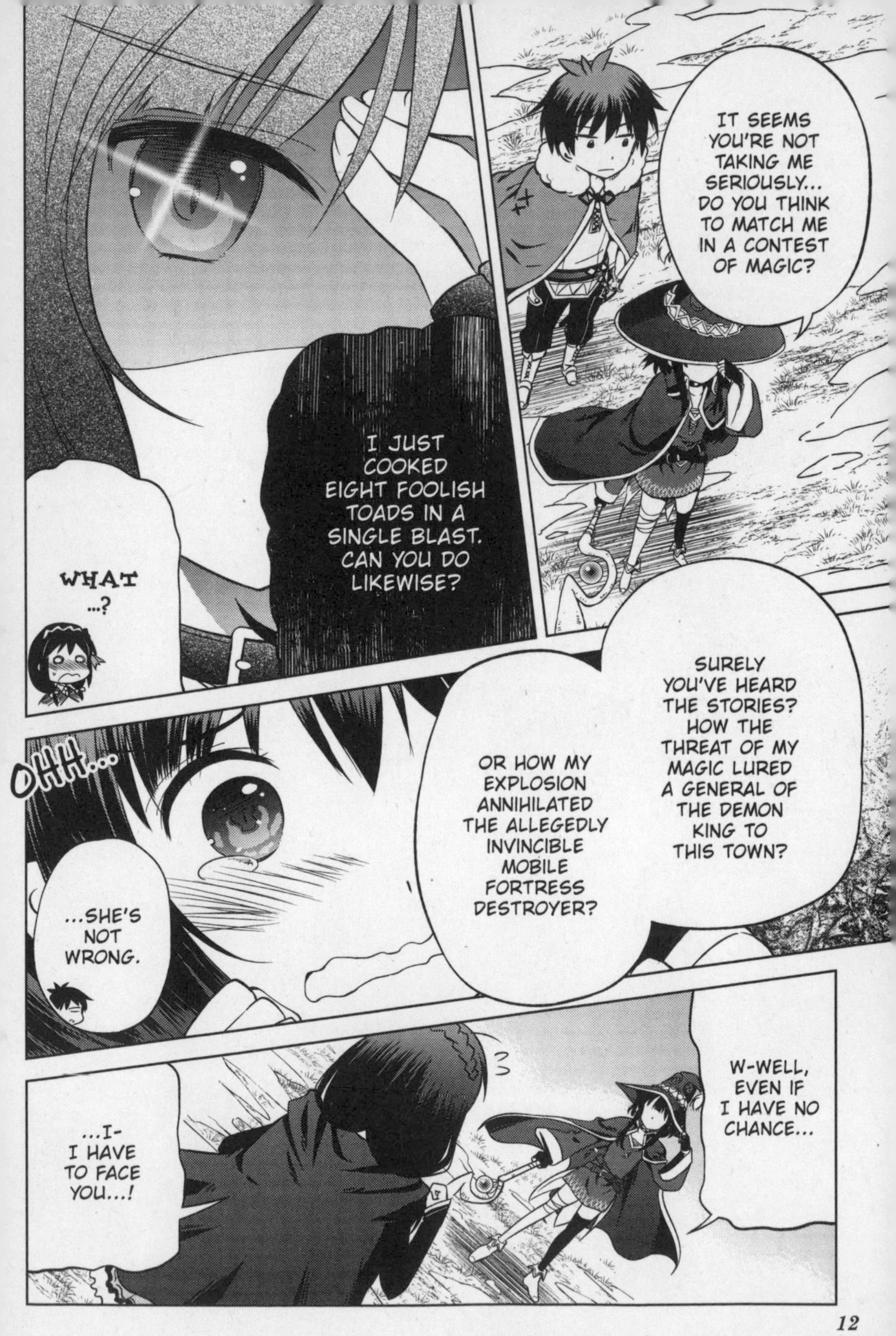
IT SEEMS YOU'RE NOT TAKING ME SERIOUSLY... DO YOU THINK TO MATCH ME IN A CONTEST OF MAGIC?
I JUST COOKED EIGHT FOOLISH TOADS IN A SINGLE BLAST. CAN YOU DO LIKEWISE?
WHAT ...?
SURELY YOU'VE HEARD THE STORIES? HOW THE THREAT OF MY MAGIC LURED A GENERAL OF THE DEMON KING TO THIS TOWN?
OR HOW MY EXPLOSION ANNIHILATED THE ALLEGEDLY INVINCIBLE MOBILE FORTRESS DESTROYER?
OHH...
...SHE'S NOT WRONG.
W-WELL, EVEN IF I HAVE NO CHANCE...
...I- I HAVE TO FACE YOU...!

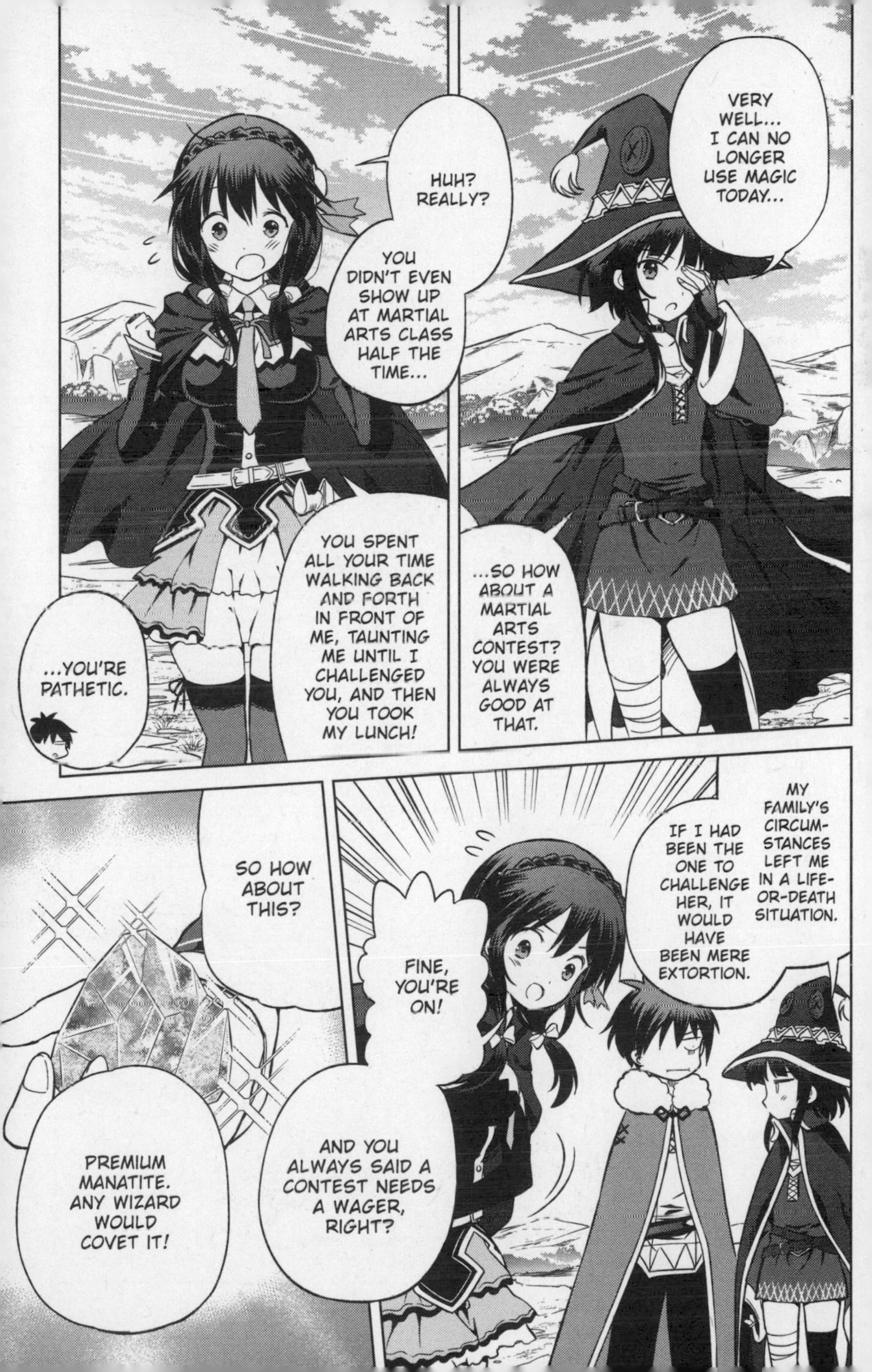
VERY WELL... I CAN NO LONGER USE MAGIC TODAY...
...SO HOW ABOUT A MARTIAL ARTS CONTEST? YOU WERE ALWAYS GOOD AT THAT.
HUH? REALLY?
YOU DIDN'T EVEN SHOW UP AT MARTIAL ARTS CLASS HALF THE TIME...
YOU SPENT ALL YOUR TIME WALKING BACK AND FORTH IN FRONT OF ME, TAUNTING ME UNTIL I CHALLENGED YOU, AND THEN YOU TOOK MY LUNCH!
...YOU'RE PATHETIC.
MY FAMILY'S CIRCUM-STANCES LEFT ME IN A LIFE-OR-DEATH SITUATION.
IF I HAD BEEN THE ONE TO CHALLENGE HER, IT WOULD HAVE BEEN MERE EXTORTION.
FINE, YOU'RE ON!
SO HOW ABOUT THIS?
AND YOU ALWAYS SAID A CONTEST NEEDS A WAGER, RIGHT?
PREMIUM MANATITE. ANY WIZARD WOULD COVET IT!

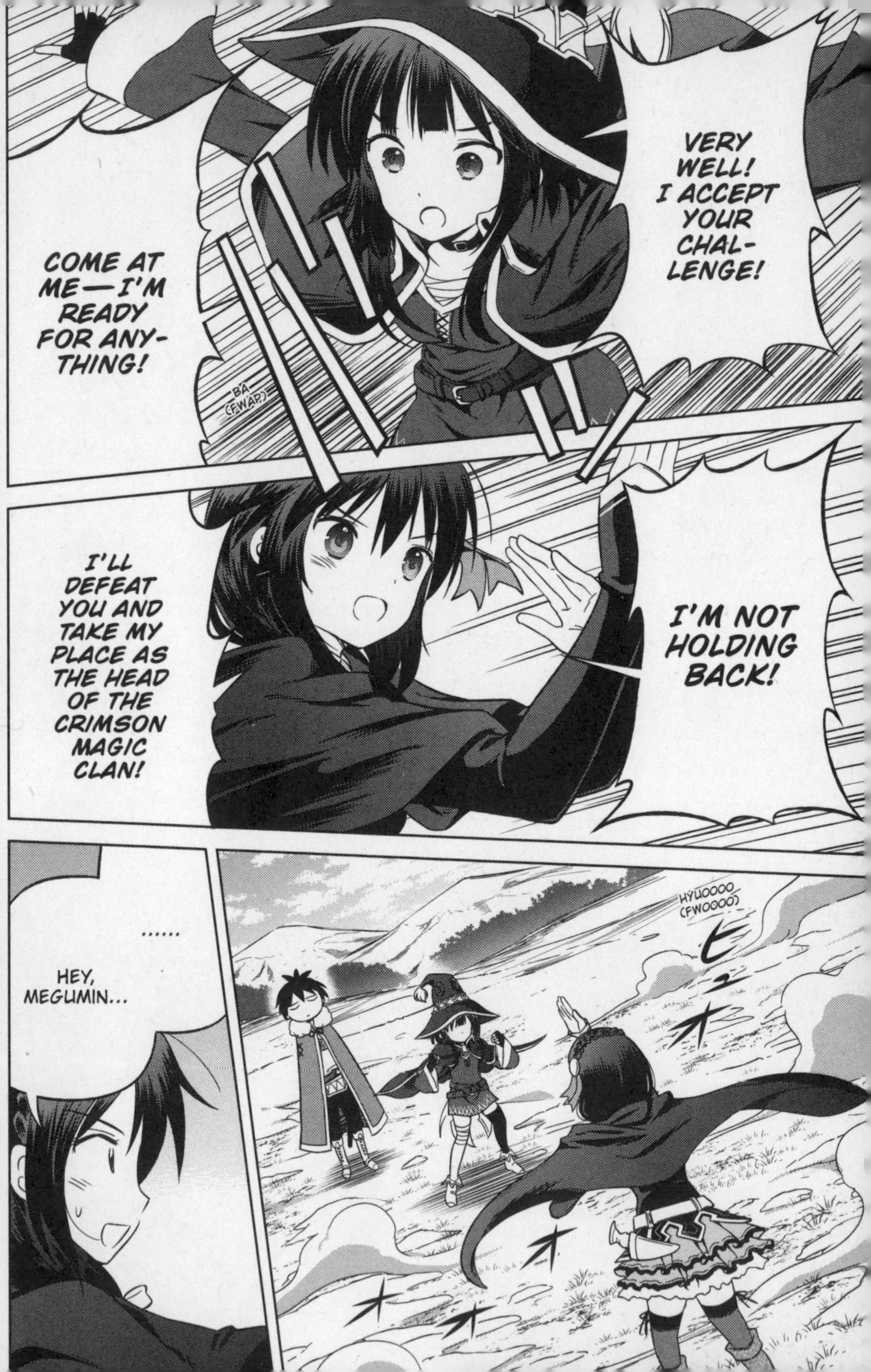
VERY WELL! I ACCEPT YOUR CHAL-LENGE!
COME AT ME—I'M READY FOR ANY-THING!
BA (FWAP)
I'M NOT HOLDING BACK!
I'LL DEFEAT YOU AND TAKE MY PLACE AS THE HEAD OF THE CRIMSON MAGIC CLAN!
HYUOOOO (FWOOOO)
......
HEY, MEGUMIN...

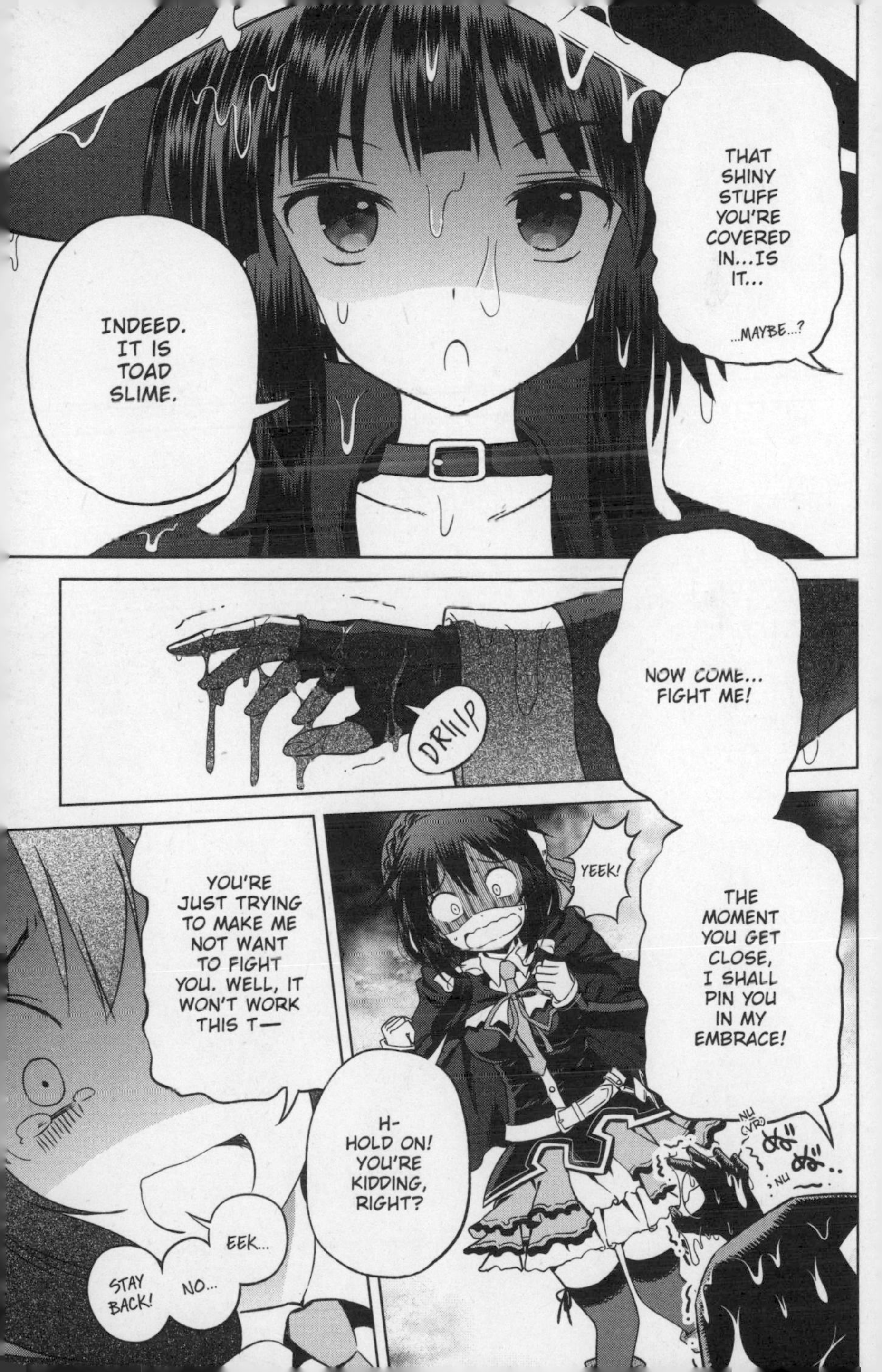
THAT SHINY STUFF YOU'RE COVERED IN...IS IT...
...MAYBE...?
INDEED. IT IS TOAD SLIME.
NOW COME... FIGHT ME!
DRIIIP
THE MOMENT YOU GET CLOSE, I SHALL PIN YOU IN MY EMBRACE!
YEEK!
NU (VR)
ぬ
ぬ
NU
H- HOLD ON! YOU'RE KIDDING, RIGHT?
YOU'RE JUST TRYING TO MAKE ME NOT WANT TO FIGHT YOU. WELL, IT WON'T WORK THIS T—
EEK...
NO...
STAY BACK!

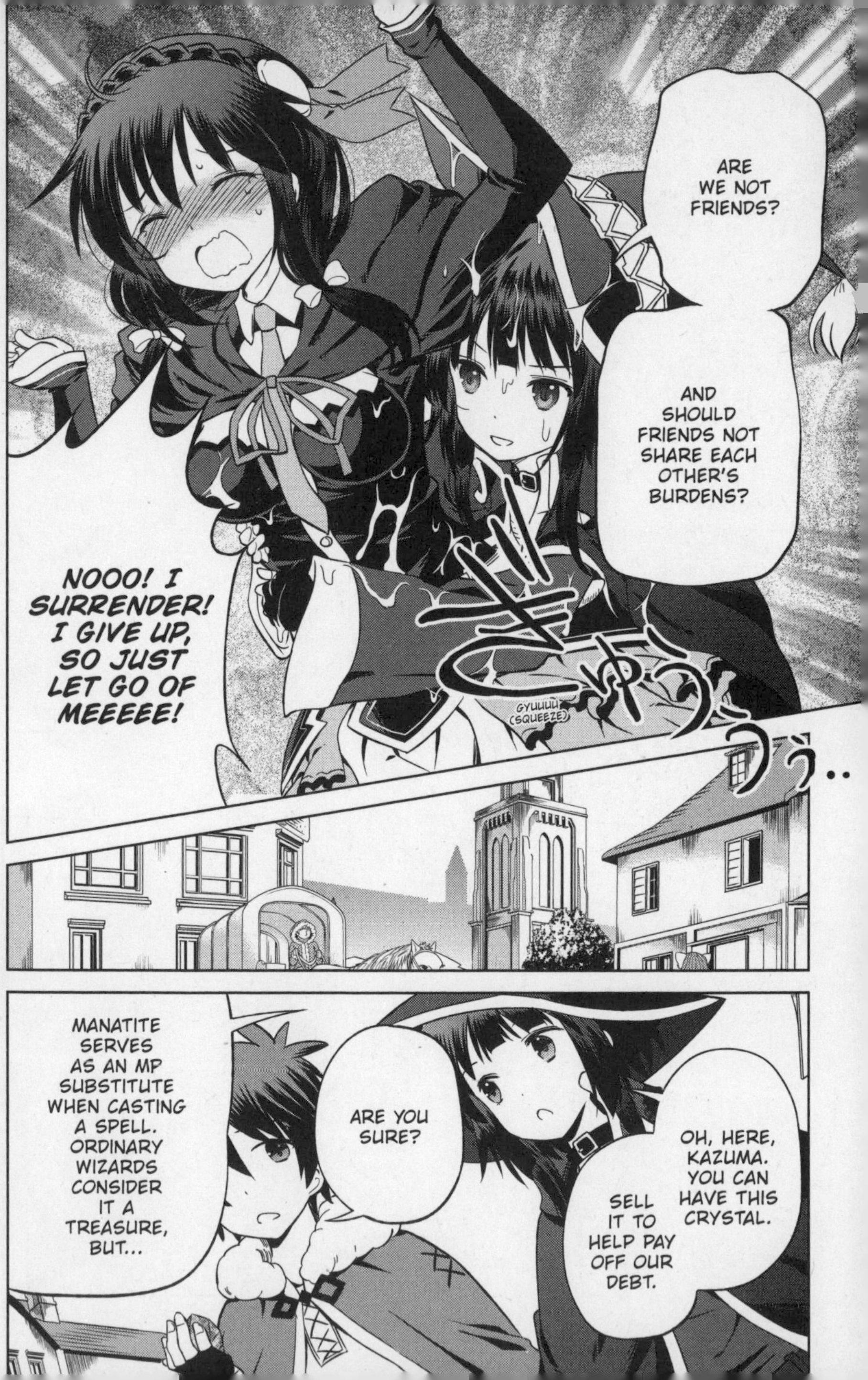
ARE WE NOT FRIENDS?
AND SHOULD FRIENDS NOT SHARE EACH OTHER'S BURDENS?
GYUUUU (SQUEEZE)
NOOO! I SURRENDER! I GIVE UP, SO JUST LET GO OF MEEEEE!
OH, HERE, KAZUMA. YOU CAN HAVE THIS CRYSTAL.
SELL IT TO HELP PAY OFF OUR DEBT.
ARE YOU SURE?
MANATITE SERVES AS AN MP SUBSTITUTE WHEN CASTING A SPELL. ORDINARY WIZARDS CONSIDER IT A TREASURE, BUT...

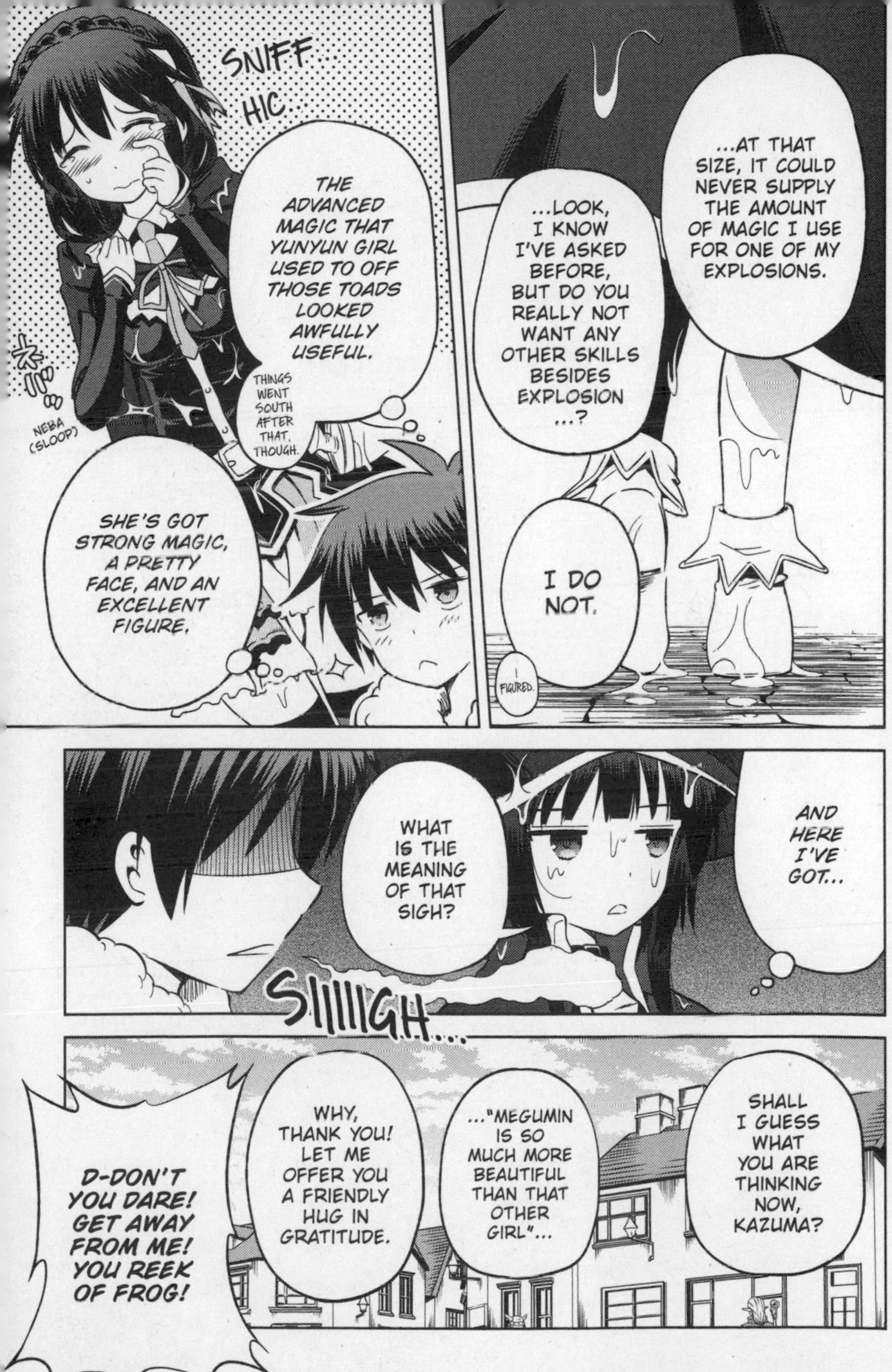

...AT THAT SIZE, IT COULD NEVER SUPPLY THE AMOUNT OF MAGIC I USE FOR ONE OF MY EXPLOSIONS.
...LOOK, I KNOW I'VE ASKED BEFORE, BUT DO YOU REALLY NOT WANT ANY OTHER SKILLS BESIDES EXPLOSION ...?
I DO NOT.
I FIGURED.
SNIFF
HIC
THE ADVANCED MAGIC THAT YUNYUN GIRL USED TO OFF THOSE TOADS LOOKED AWFULLY USEFUL.
THINGS WENT SOUTH AFTER THAT, THOUGH.
ネバ
NEBA (SLOOP)
SHE'S GOT STRONG MAGIC, A PRETTY FACE, AND AN EXCELLENT FIGURE.
AND HERE I'VE GOT...
SIIIIIGH....
WHAT IS THE MEANING OF THAT SIGH?
SHALL I GUESS WHAT YOU ARE THINKING NOW, KAZUMA?
..."MEGUMIN IS SO MUCH MORE BEAUTIFUL THAN THAT OTHER GIRL"...
WHY, THANK YOU! LET ME OFFER YOU A FRIENDLY HUG IN GRATITUDE.
D-DON'T YOU DARE! GET AWAY FROM ME! YOU REEK OF FROG!

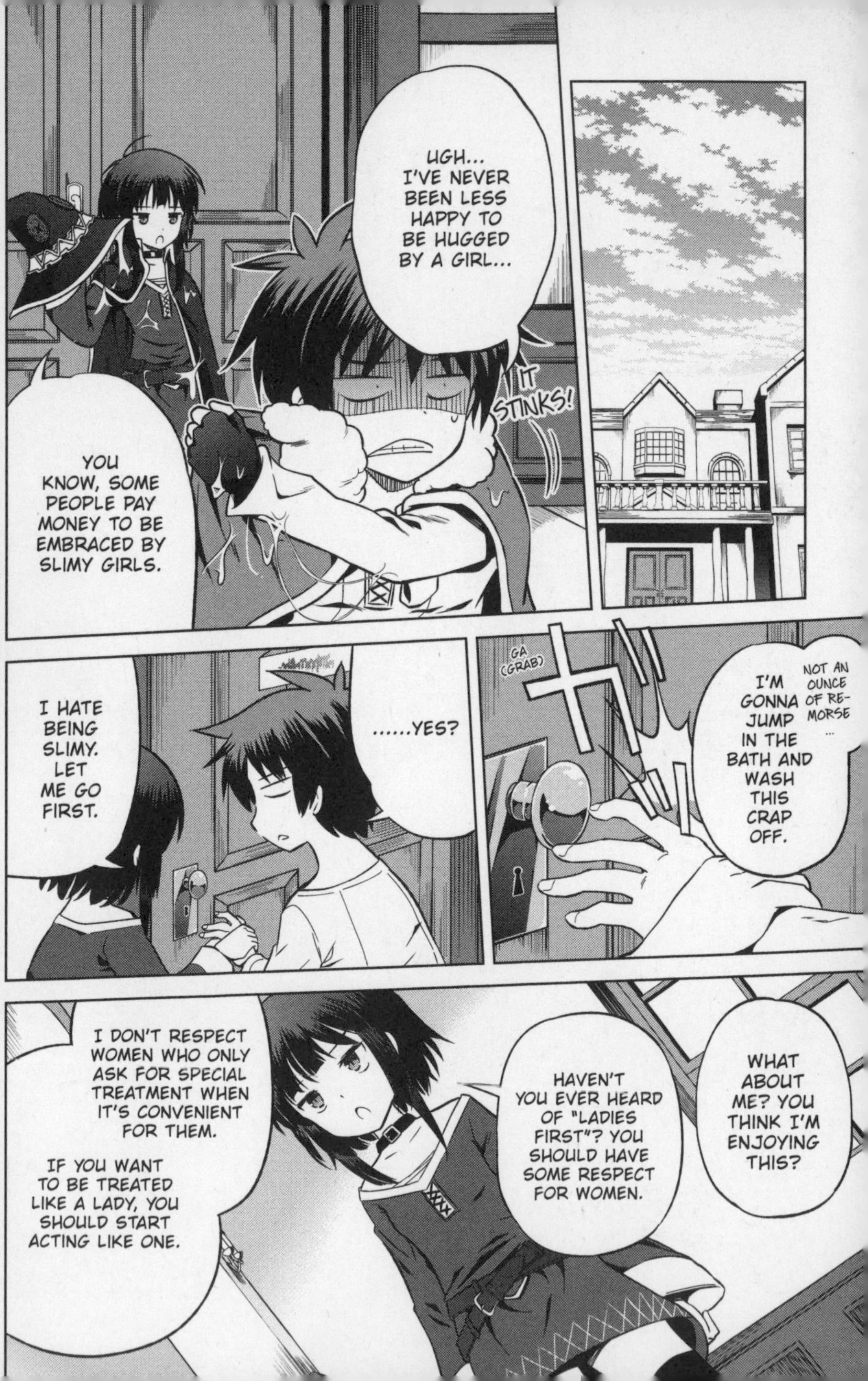
UGH... I'VE NEVER BEEN LESS HAPPY TO BE HUGGED BY A GIRL...
IT STINKS!
YOU KNOW, SOME PEOPLE PAY MONEY TO BE EMBRACED BY SLIMY GIRLS.
I'M GONNA JUMP IN THE BATH AND WASH THIS CRAP OFF.
NOT AN OUNCE OF RE-MORSE ...
GA (GRAB)
......YES?
I HATE BEING SLIMY. LET ME GO FIRST.
WHAT ABOUT ME? YOU THINK I'M ENJOYING THIS?
HAVEN'T YOU EVER HEARD OF "LADIES FIRST"? YOU SHOULD HAVE SOME RESPECT FOR WOMEN.
I DON'T RESPECT WOMEN WHO ONLY ASK FOR SPECIAL TREATMENT WHEN IT'S CONVENIENT FOR THEM.
IF YOU WANT TO BE TREATED LIKE A LADY, YOU SHOULD START ACTING LIKE ONE.

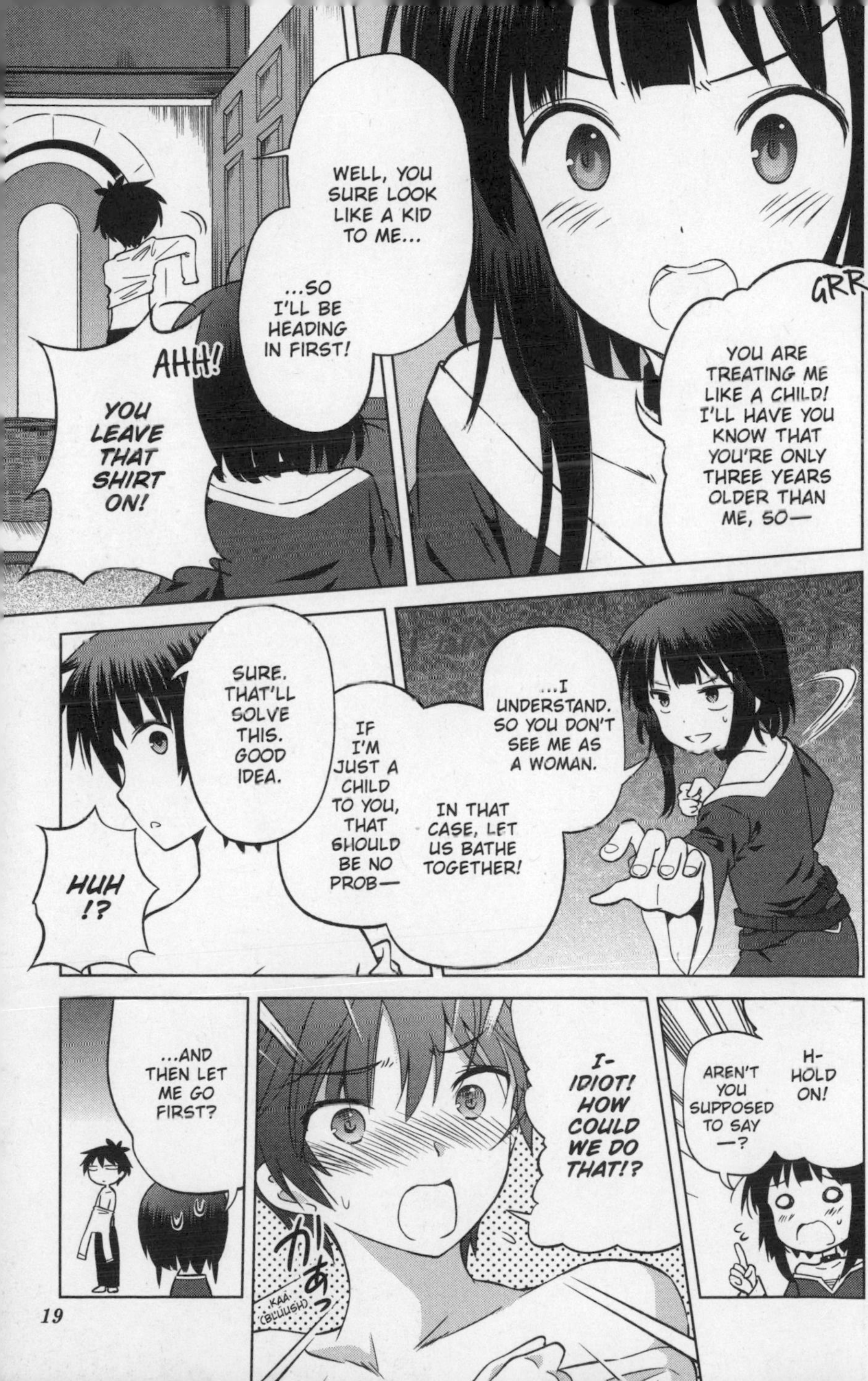
GRR!
YOU ARE TREATING ME LIKE A CHILD! I'LL HAVE YOU KNOW THAT YOU'RE ONLY THREE YEARS OLDER THAN ME, SO—
WELL, YOU SURE LOOK LIKE A KID TO ME...
...SO I'LL BE HEADING IN FIRST!
AHH!
YOU LEAVE THAT SHIRT ON!
...I UNDERSTAND. SO YOU DON'T SEE ME AS A WOMAN.
IN THAT CASE, LET US BATHE TOGETHER!
IF I'M JUST A CHILD TO YOU, THAT SHOULD BE NO PROB—
SURE. THAT'LL SOLVE THIS. GOOD IDEA.
HUH!?
H-HOLD ON!
AREN'T YOU SUPPOSED TO SAY —?
I-IDIOT! HOW COULD WE DO THAT!?
かあっ
KAA (BLUUSH)
...AND THEN LET ME GO FIRST?

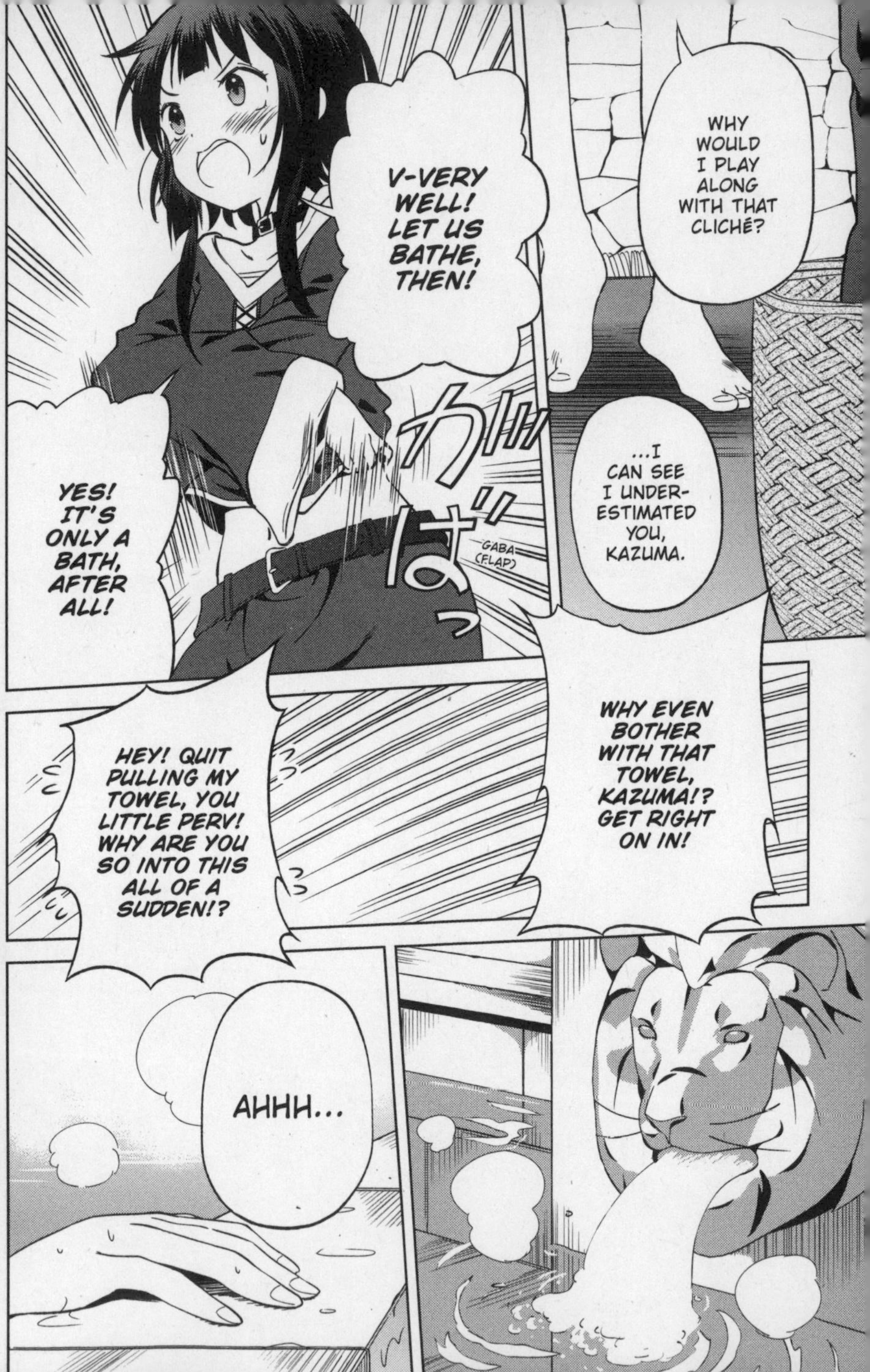
WHY WOULD I PLAY ALONG WITH THAT CLICHÉ?
...I CAN SEE I UNDER-ESTIMATED YOU, KAZUMA.
V-VERY WELL! LET US BATHE, THEN!
GABA (FLAP)
YES! IT'S ONLY A BATH, AFTER ALL!
WHY EVEN BOTHER WITH THAT TOWEL, KAZUMA!? GET RIGHT ON IN!
HEY! QUIT PULLING MY TOWEL, YOU LITTLE PERV! WHY ARE YOU SO INTO THIS ALL OF A SUDDEN!?
AHHH...

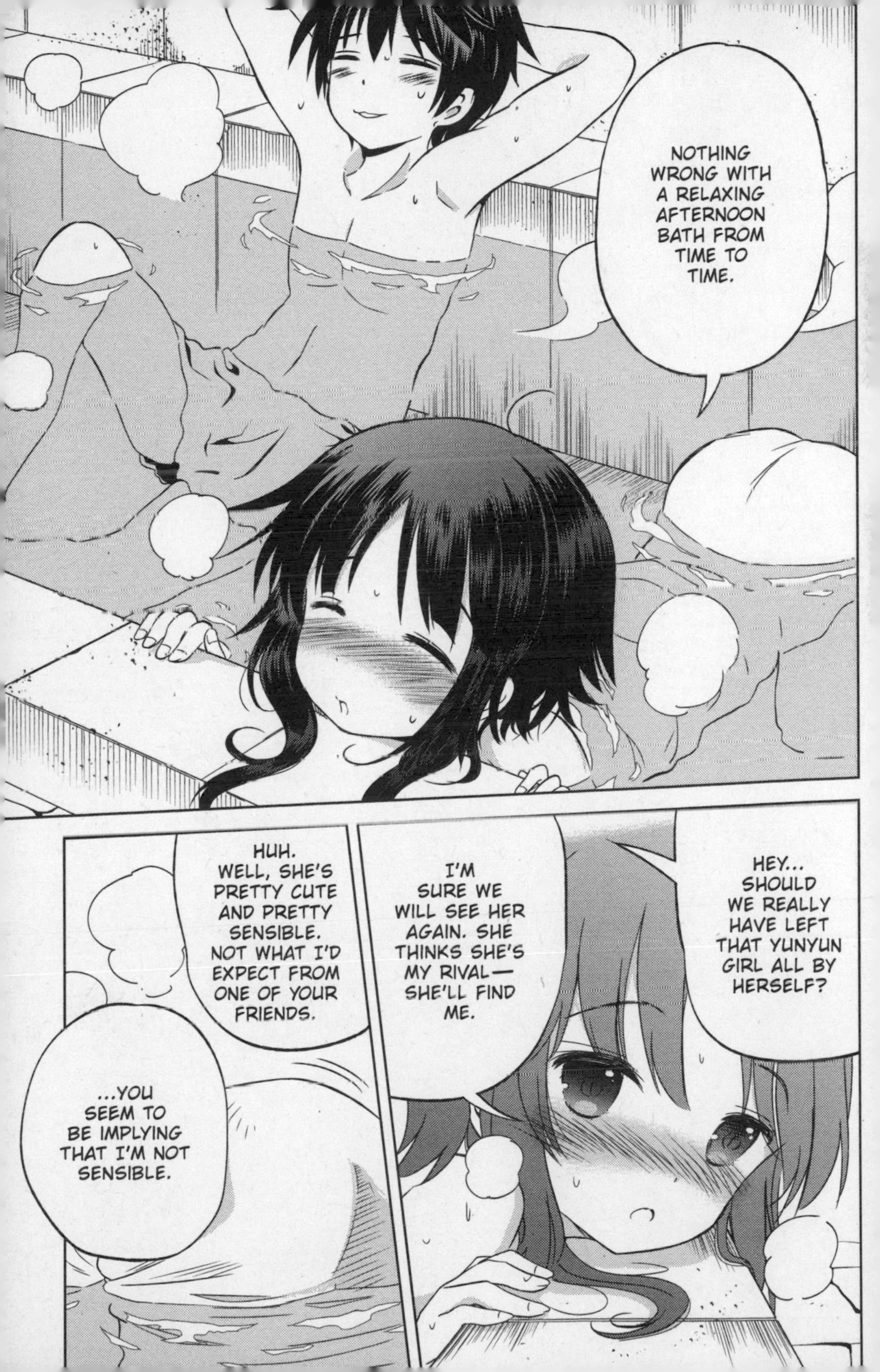
NOTHING WRONG WITH A RELAXING AFTERNOON BATH FROM TIME TO TIME.
HEY... SHOULD WE REALLY HAVE LEFT THAT YUNYUN GIRL ALL BY HERSELF?
I'M SURE WE WILL SEE HER AGAIN. SHE THINKS SHE'S MY RIVAL— SHE'LL FIND ME.
HUH. WELL, SHE'S PRETTY CUTE AND PRETTY SENSIBLE. NOT WHAT I'D EXPECT FROM ONE OF YOUR FRIENDS.
...YOU SEEM TO BE IMPLYING THAT I'M NOT SENSIBLE.

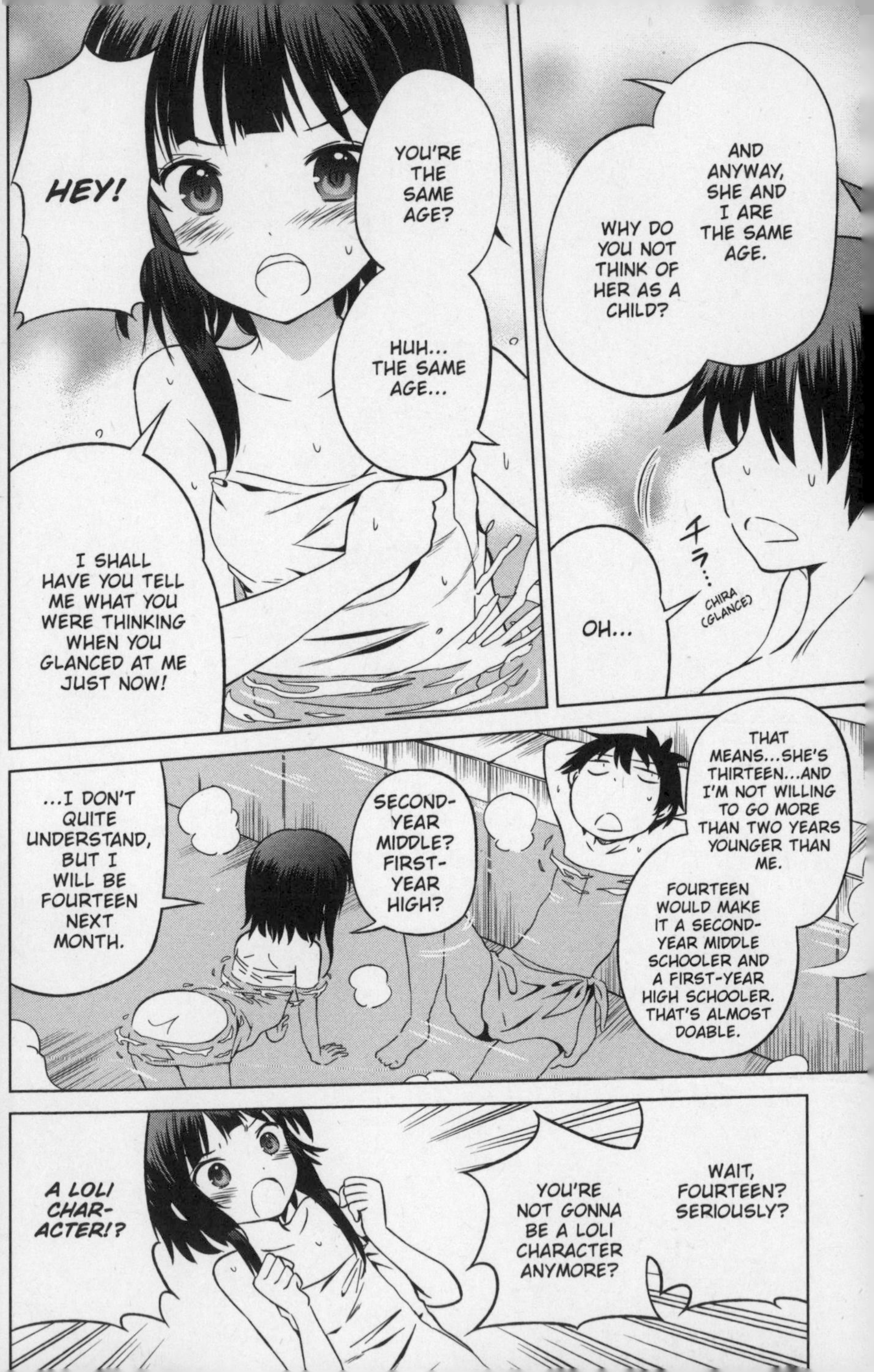
AND ANYWAY, SHE AND I ARE THE SAME AGE.
WHY DO YOU NOT THINK OF HER AS A CHILD?
チラ…
CHIRA (GLANCE)
OH...
YOU'RE THE SAME AGE?
HEY!
HUH... THE SAME AGE...
I SHALL HAVE YOU TELL ME WHAT YOU WERE THINKING WHEN YOU GLANCED AT ME JUST NOW!
THAT MEANS...SHE'S THIRTEEN...AND I'M NOT WILLING TO GO MORE THAN TWO YEARS YOUNGER THAN ME.
FOURTEEN WOULD MAKE IT A SECOND-YEAR MIDDLE SCHOOLER AND A FIRST-YEAR HIGH SCHOOLER. THAT'S ALMOST DOABLE.
SECOND-YEAR MIDDLE? FIRST-YEAR HIGH?
...I DON'T QUITE UNDERSTAND, BUT I WILL BE FOURTEEN NEXT MONTH.
WAIT, FOURTEEN? SERIOUSLY?
YOU'RE NOT GONNA BE A LOLI CHARACTER ANYMORE?
A LOLI CHAR-ACTER!?

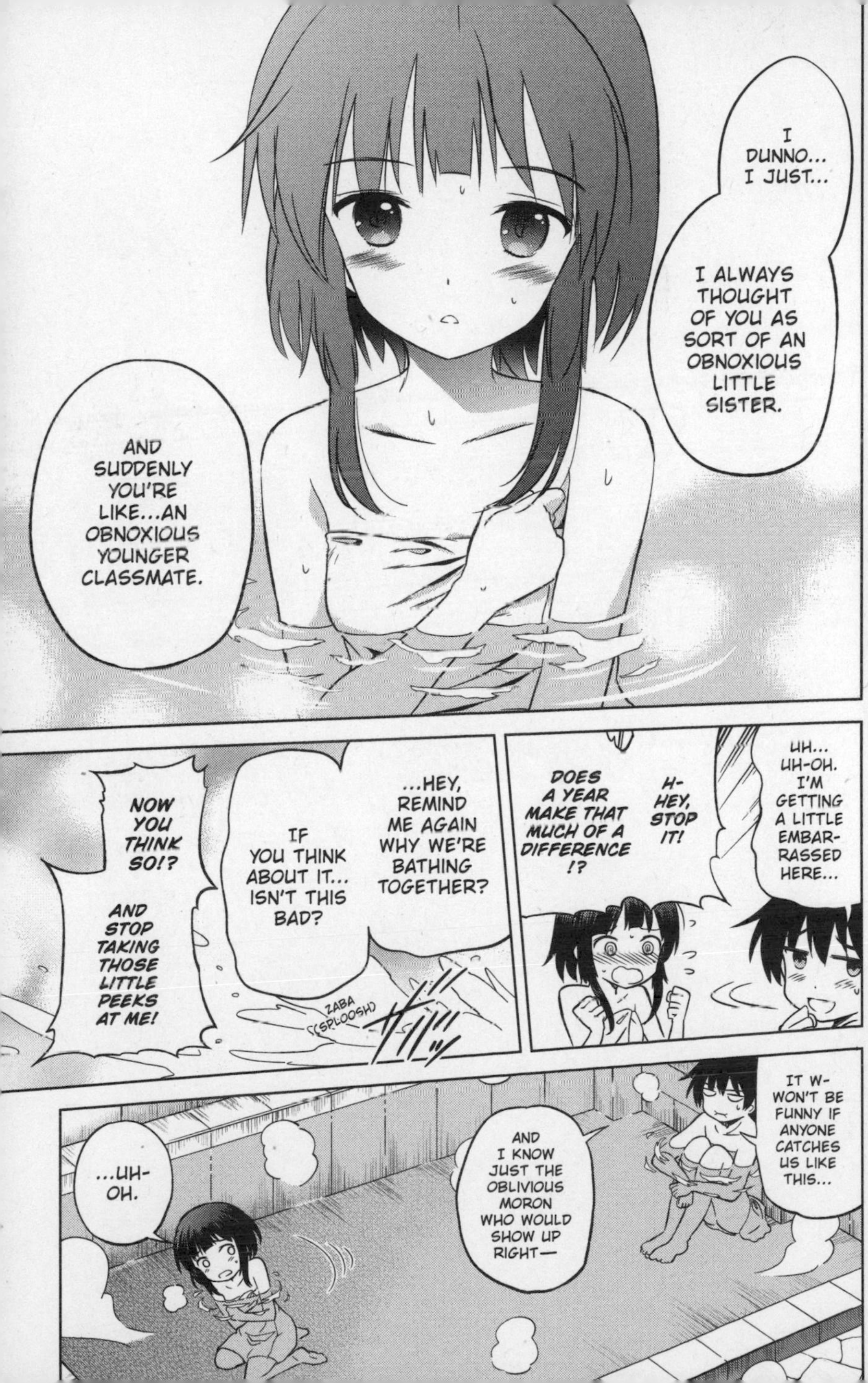
I DUNNO... I JUST...
I ALWAYS THOUGHT OF YOU AS SORT OF AN OBNOXIOUS LITTLE SISTER.
AND SUDDENLY YOU'RE LIKE...AN OBNOXIOUS YOUNGER CLASSMATE.
UH... UH-OH. I'M GETTING A LITTLE EMBARRASSED HERE...
H-HEY, STOP IT!
DOES A YEAR MAKE THAT MUCH OF A DIFFERENCE!?
...HEY, REMIND ME AGAIN WHY WE'RE BATHING TOGETHER?
IF YOU THINK ABOUT IT... ISN'T THIS BAD?
ZABA ((SPLOOSH))
NOW YOU THINK SO!?
AND STOP TAKING THOSE LITTLE PEEKS AT ME!
IT W-WON'T BE FUNNY IF ANYONE CATCHES US LIKE THIS...
AND I KNOW JUST THE OBLIVIOUS MORON WHO WOULD SHOW UP RIGHT—
...UH-OH.

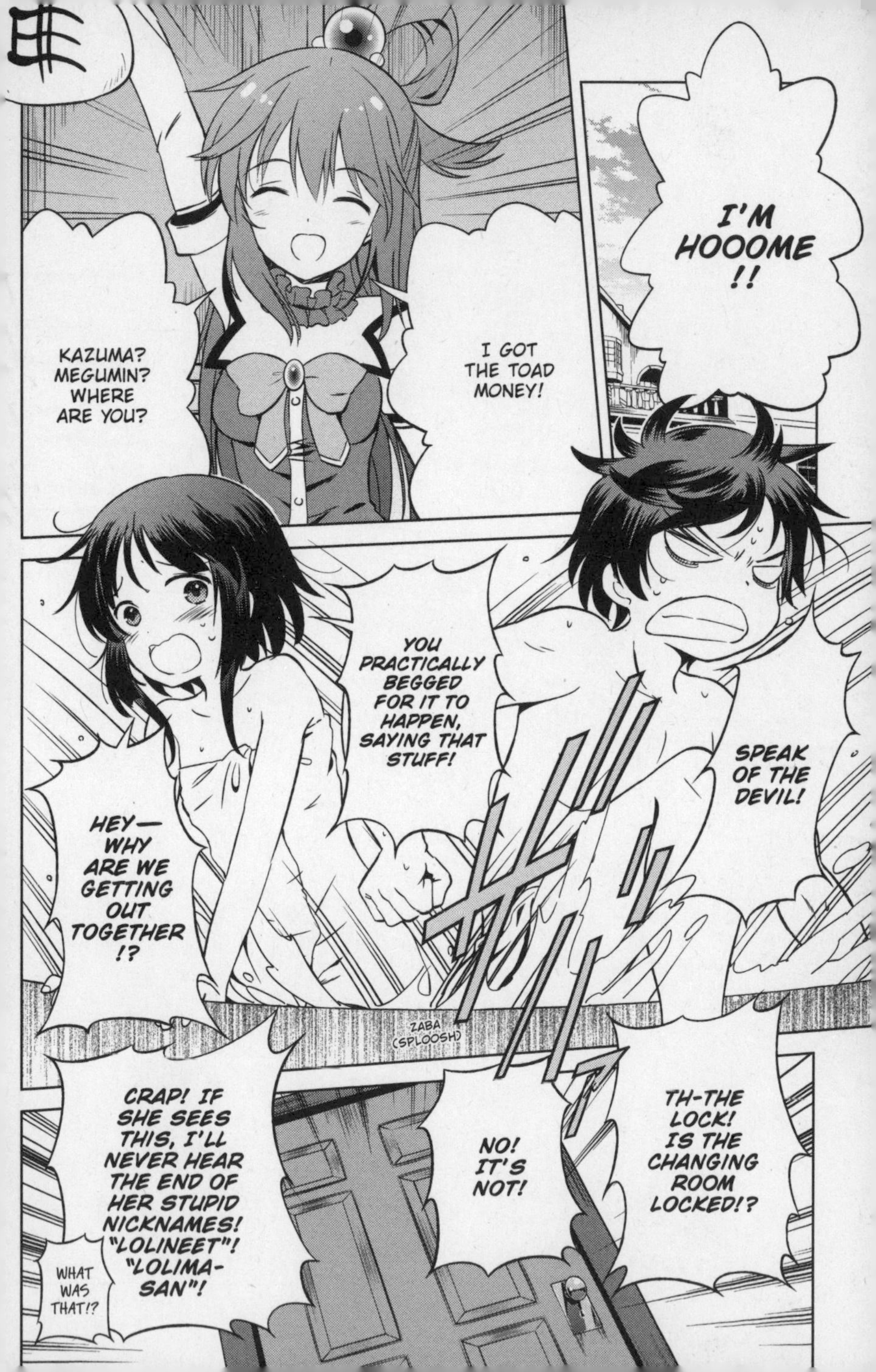
I'M HOOOME!!
I GOT THE TOAD MONEY!
KAZUMA? MEGUMIN? WHERE ARE YOU?
SPEAK OF THE DEVIL!
YOU PRACTICALLY BEGGED FOR IT TO HAPPEN, SAYING THAT STUFF!
HEY— WHY ARE WE GETTING OUT TOGETHER!?
ZABA (SPLOOSH)
TH-THE LOCK! IS THE CHANGING ROOM LOCKED!?
NO! IT'S NOT!
CRAP! IF SHE SEES THIS, I'LL NEVER HEAR THE END OF HER STUPID NICKNAMES! "LOLINEET"! "LOLIMA-SAN"!
WHAT WAS THAT!?

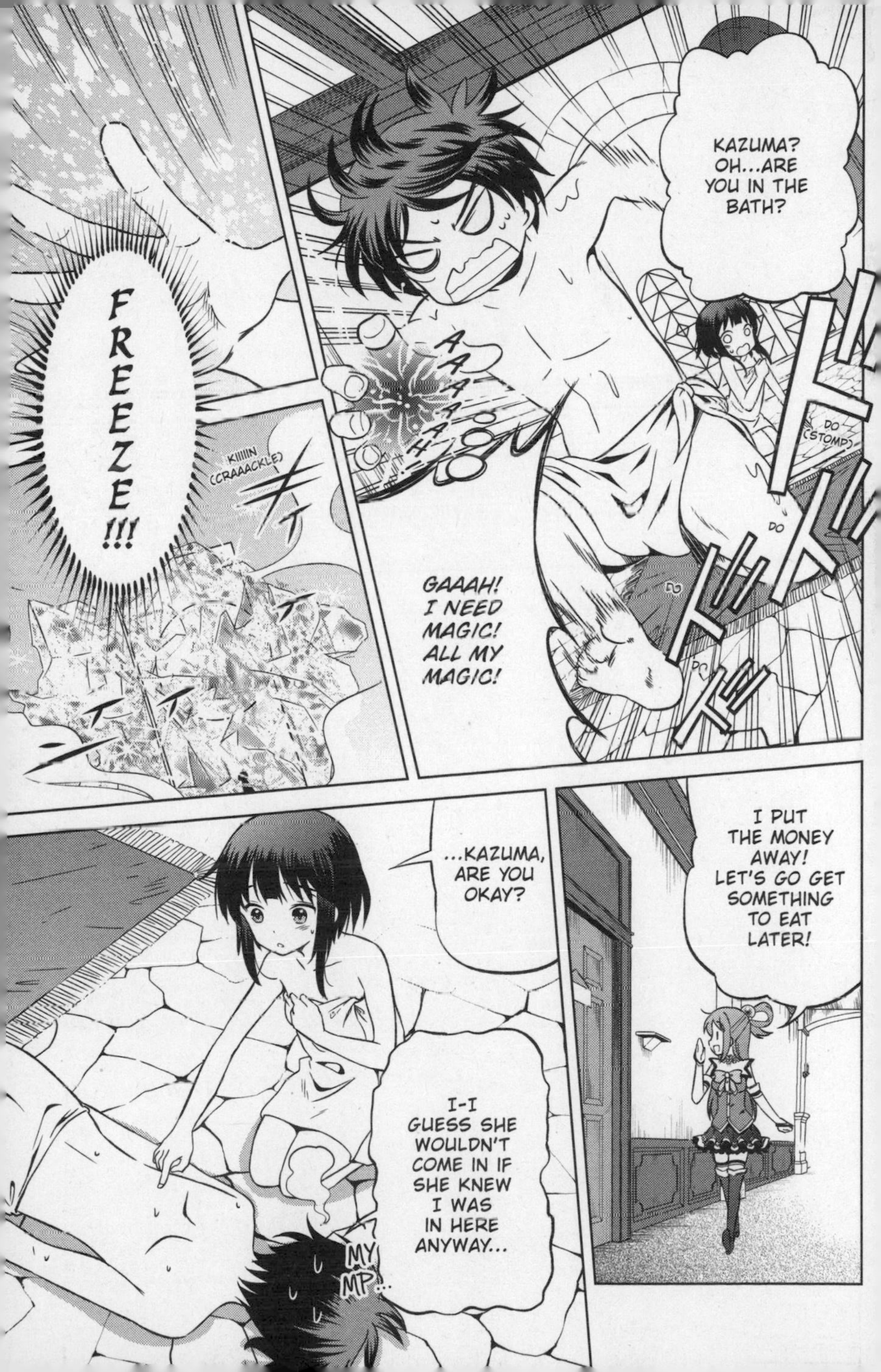
KAZUMA? OH...ARE YOU IN THE BATH?
DO (STOMP)
DO
DO
AAAAAAAH!
GAAAH! I NEED MAGIC! ALL MY MAGIC!
FREEZE!!!
KIIIIN (CRAAACKLE)
I PUT THE MONEY AWAY! LET'S GO GET SOMETHING TO EAT LATER!
...KAZUMA, ARE YOU OKAY?
I-I GUESS SHE WOULDN'T COME IN IF SHE KNEW I WAS IN HERE ANYWAY...
MY MP...

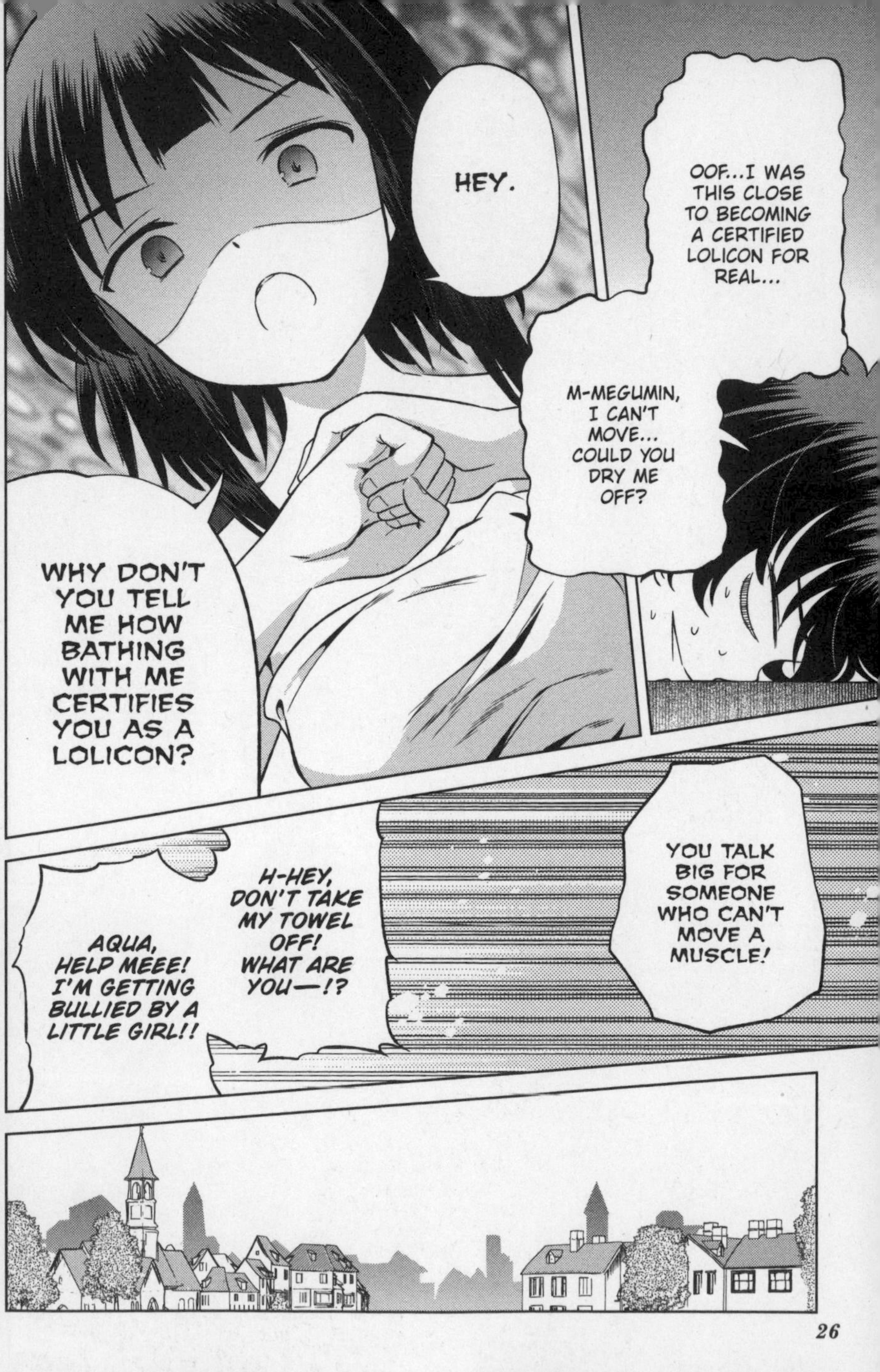
OOF...I WAS THIS CLOSE TO BECOMING A CERTIFIED LOLICON FOR REAL...
M-MEGUMIN, I CAN'T MOVE... COULD YOU DRY ME OFF?
HEY.
WHY DON'T YOU TELL ME HOW BATHING WITH ME CERTIFIES YOU AS A LOLICON?
YOU TALK BIG FOR SOMEONE WHO CAN'T MOVE A MUSCLE!
H-HEY, DON'T TAKE MY TOWEL OFF! WHAT ARE YOU—!?
AQUA, HELP MEEE! I'M GETTING BULLIED BY A LITTLE GIRL!!

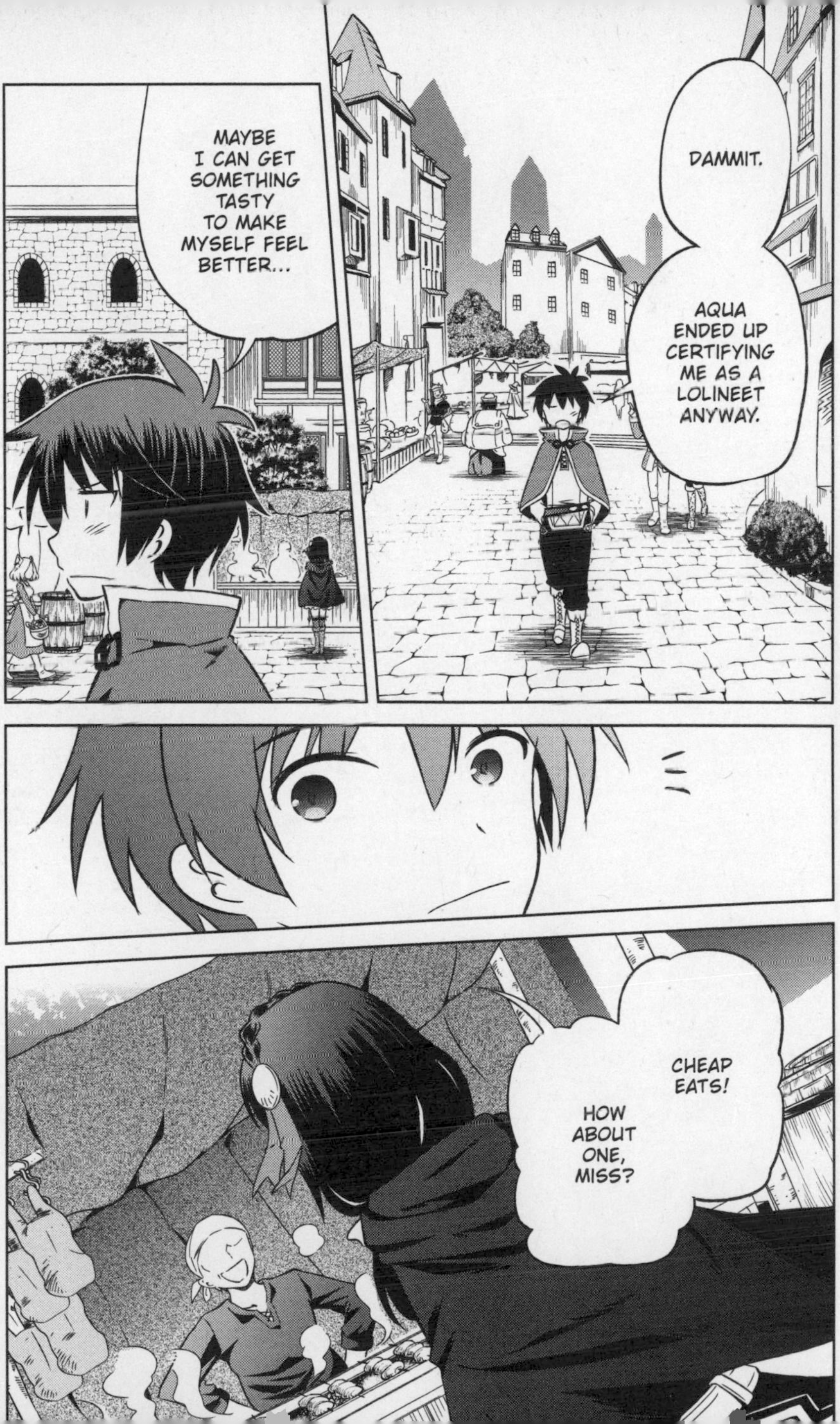
DAMMIT.
AQUA ENDED UP CERTIFYING ME AS A LOLINEET ANYWAY.
MAYBE I CAN GET SOMETHING TASTY TO MAKE MYSELF FEEL BETTER...
CHEAP EATS!
HOW ABOUT ONE, MISS?

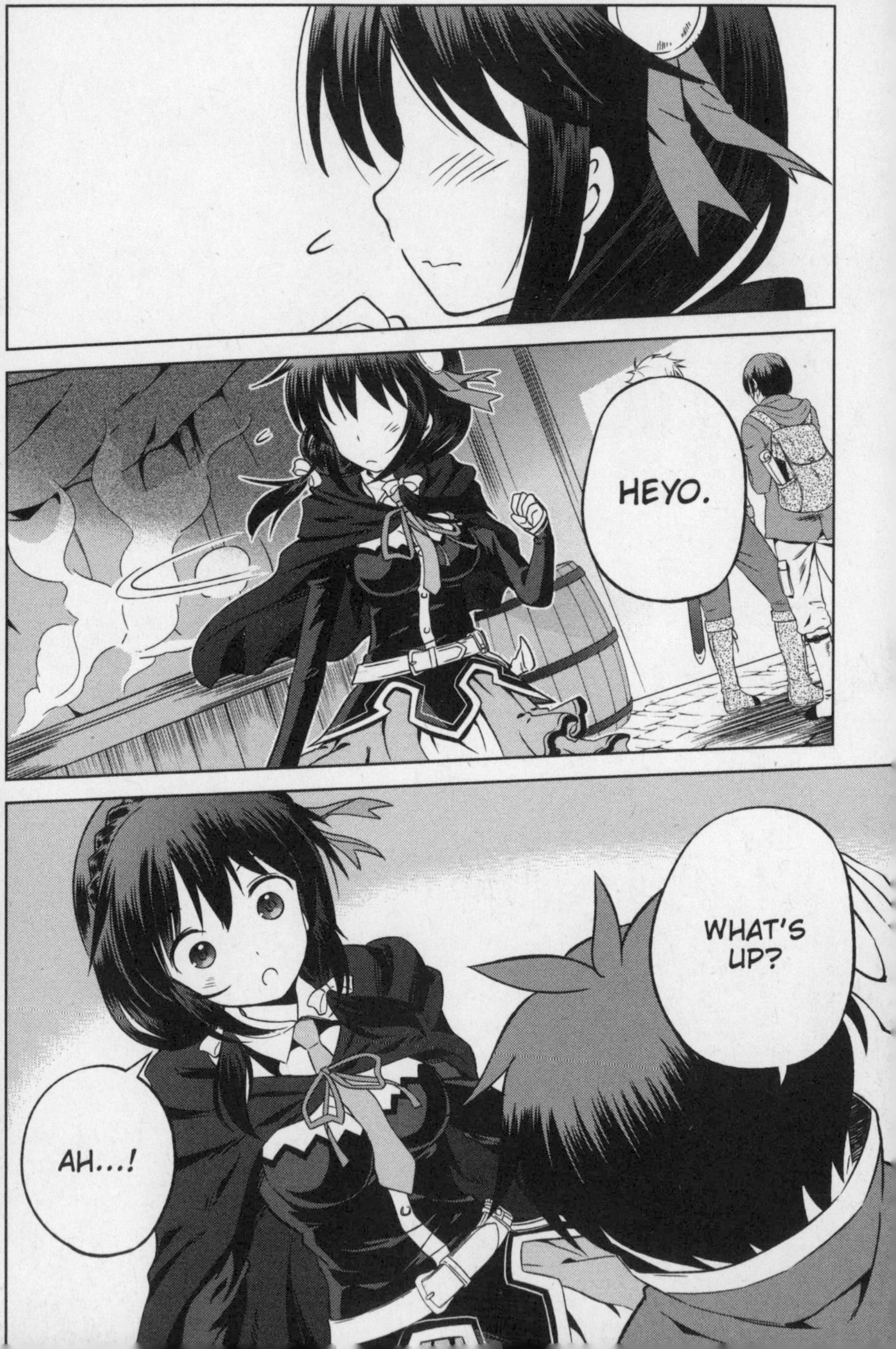
HEYO.
WHAT'S UP?
AH...!

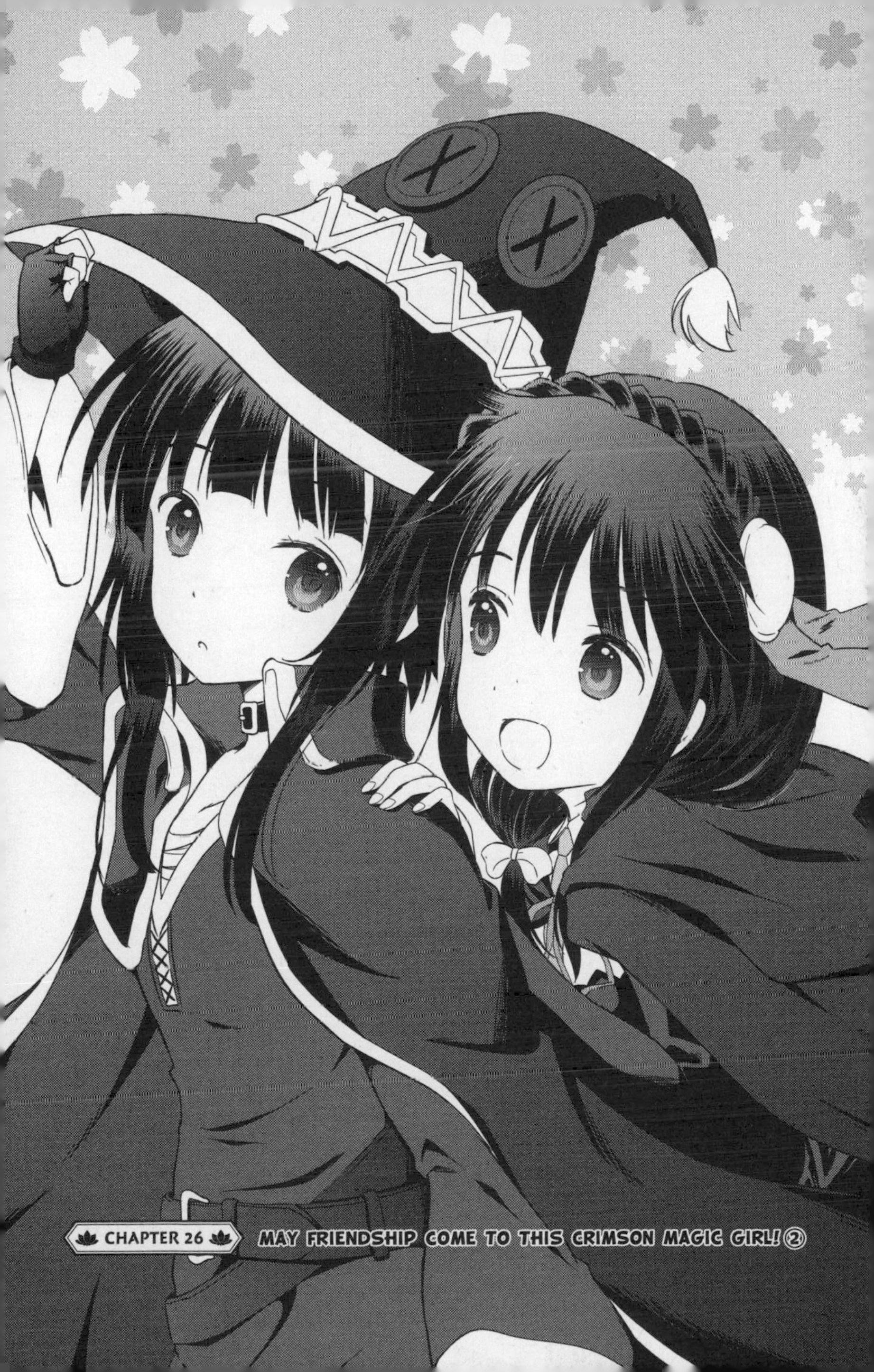

CHAPTER 26 MAY FRIENDSHIP COME TO THIS CRIMSON MAGIC GIRL! ②

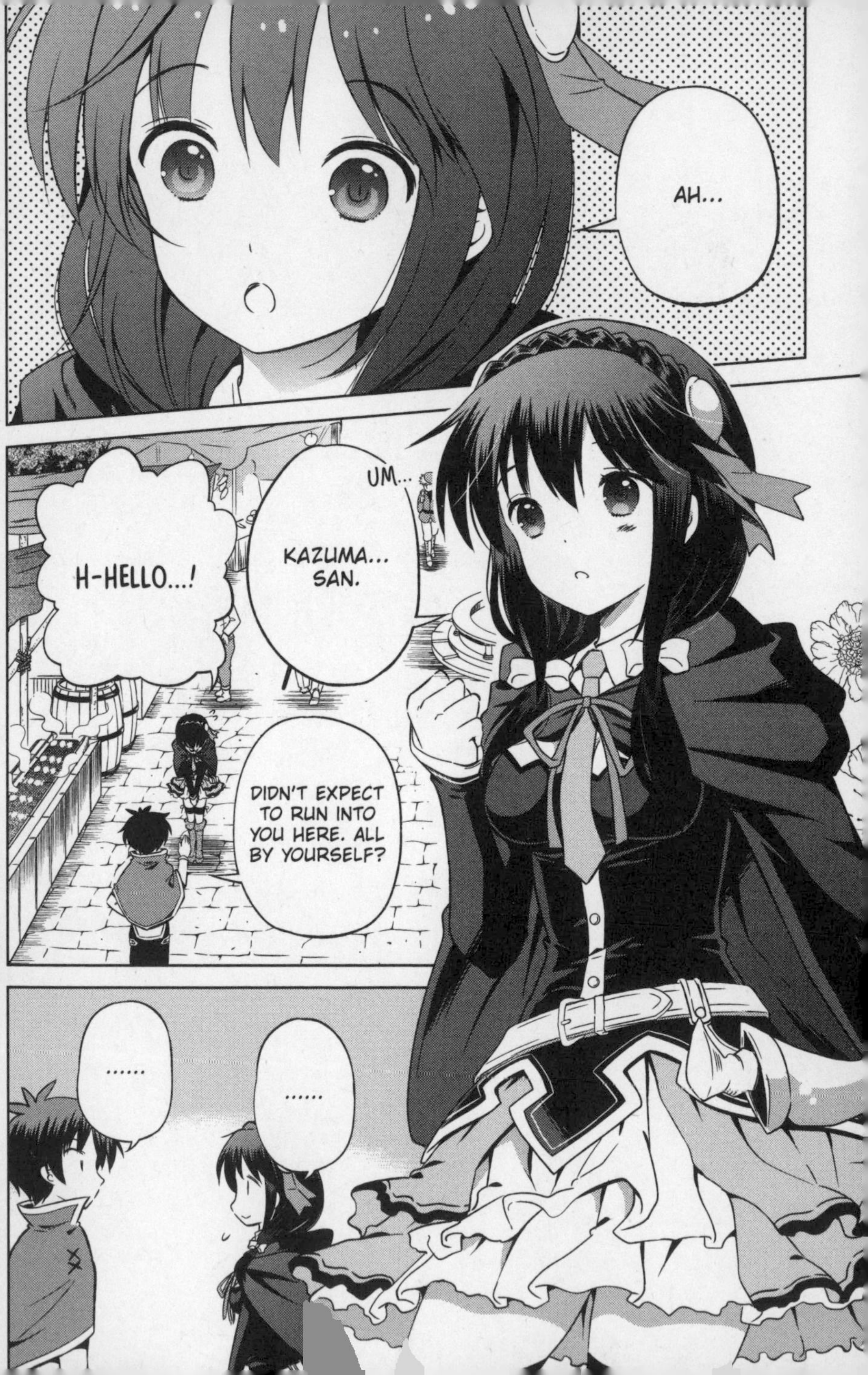
AH...
UM...
KAZUMA... SAN.
H-HELLO...!
DIDN'T EXPECT TO RUN INTO YOU HERE. ALL BY YOURSELF?
......
......

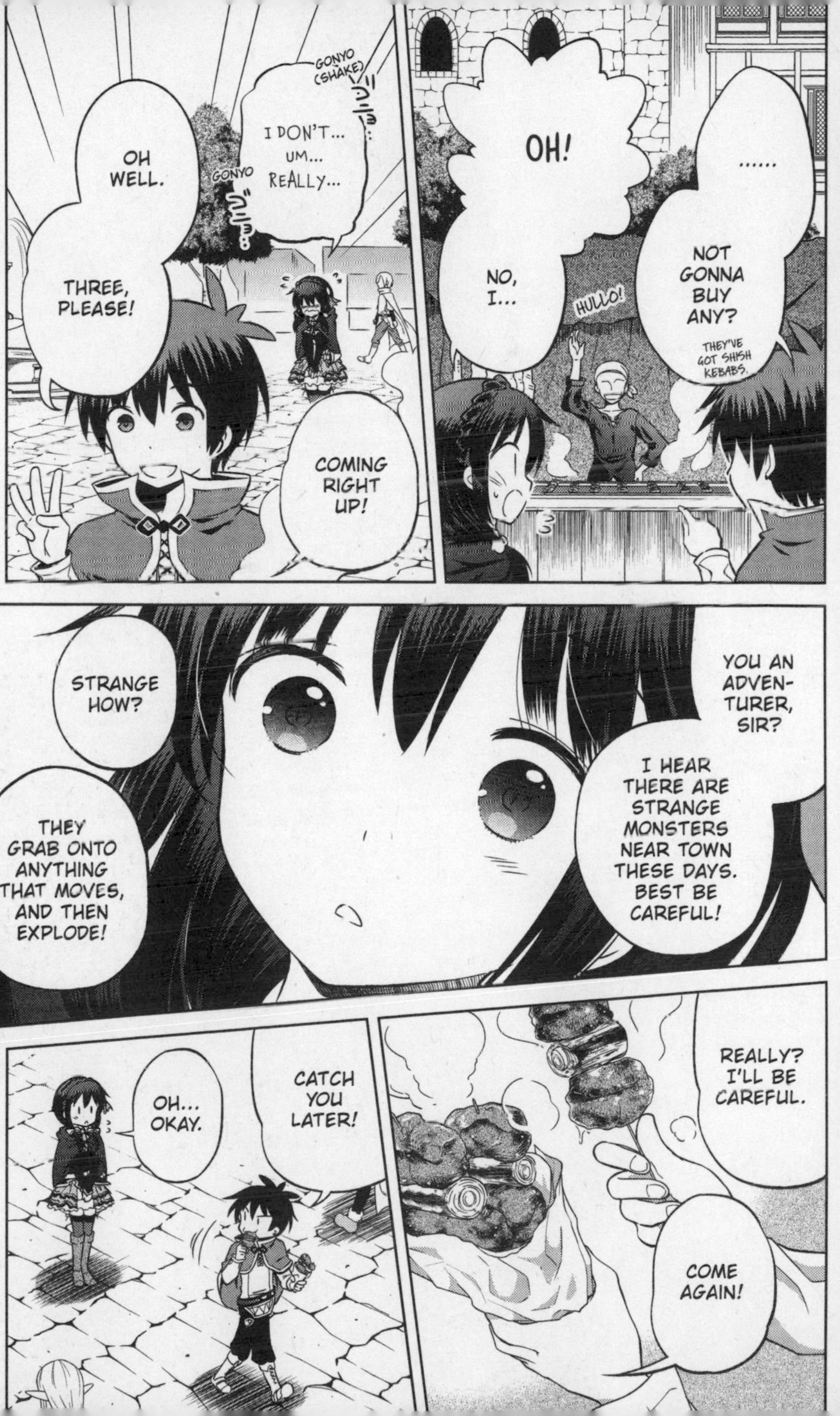
......
OH!
NOT GONNA BUY ANY?
THEY'VE GOT SHISH KEBABS.
HULLO!
NO, I...
GONYO (SHAKE)
I DON'T... UM... REALLY...
GONYO
OH WELL.
THREE, PLEASE!
COMING RIGHT UP!
YOU AN ADVENTURER, SIR?
I HEAR THERE ARE STRANGE MONSTERS NEAR TOWN THESE DAYS. BEST BE CAREFUL!
STRANGE HOW?
THEY GRAB ONTO ANYTHING THAT MOVES, AND THEN EXPLODE!
REALLY? I'LL BE CAREFUL.
COME AGAIN!
CATCH YOU LATER!
OH... OKAY.

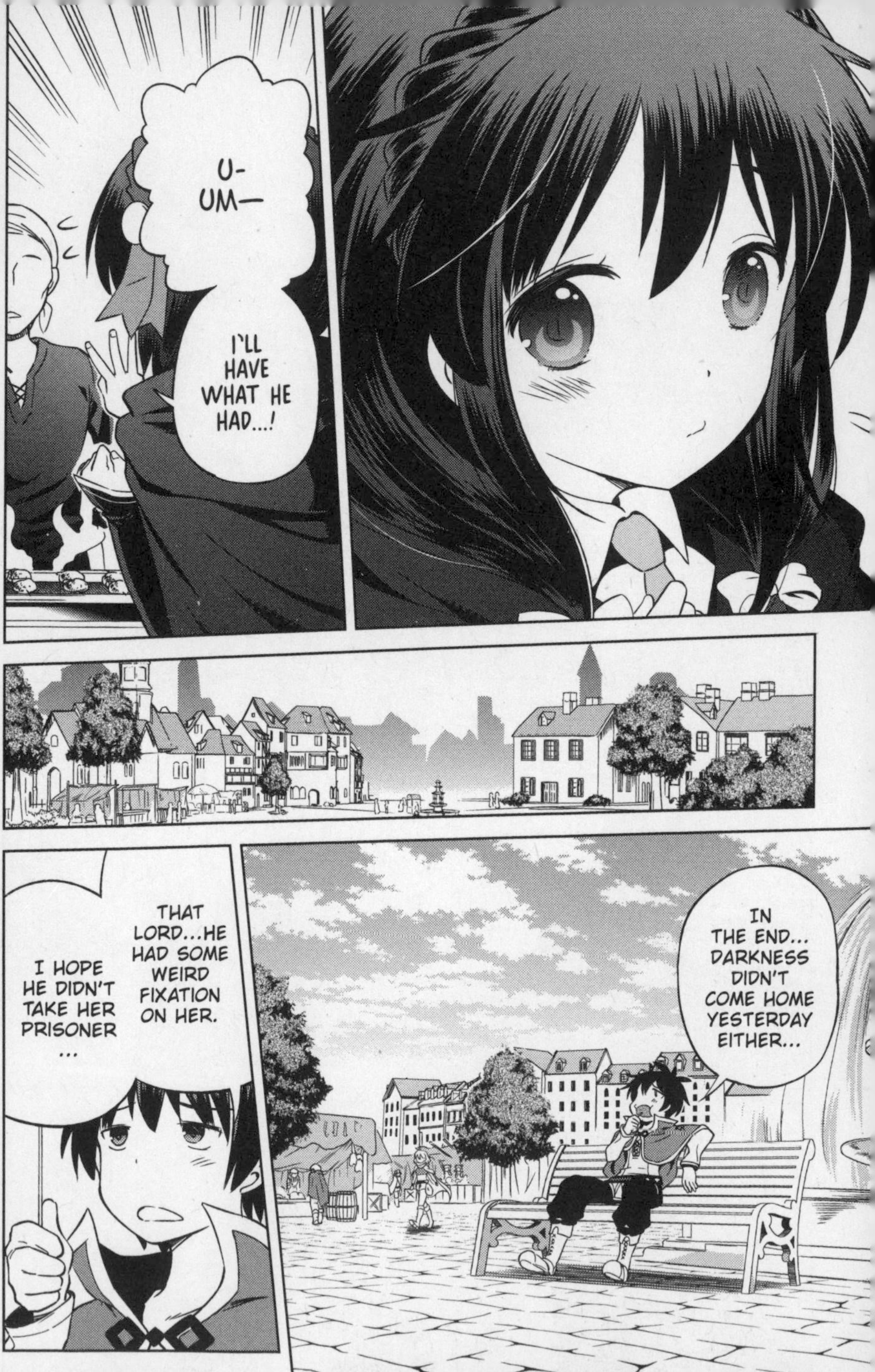
U-UM—
I'LL HAVE WHAT HE HAD...!
IN THE END... DARKNESS DIDN'T COME HOME YESTERDAY EITHER...
THAT LORD...HE HAD SOME WEIRD FIXATION ON HER.
I HOPE HE DIDN'T TAKE HER PRISONER...

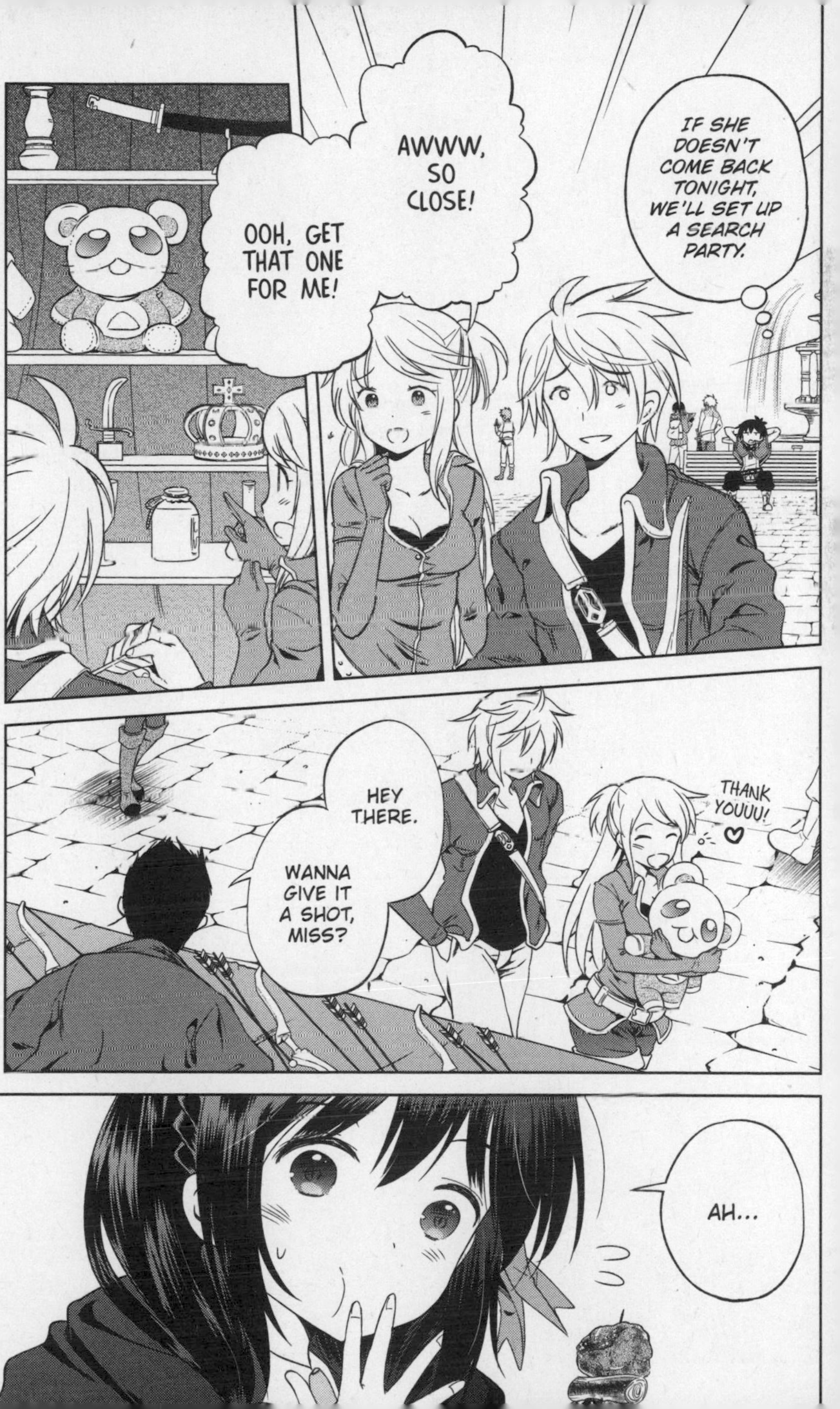
IF SHE DOESN'T COME BACK TONIGHT, WE'LL SET UP A SEARCH PARTY.
AWWW, SO CLOSE!
OOH, GET THAT ONE FOR ME!
THANK YOUUU!
HEY THERE.
WANNA GIVE IT A SHOT, MISS?
AH...

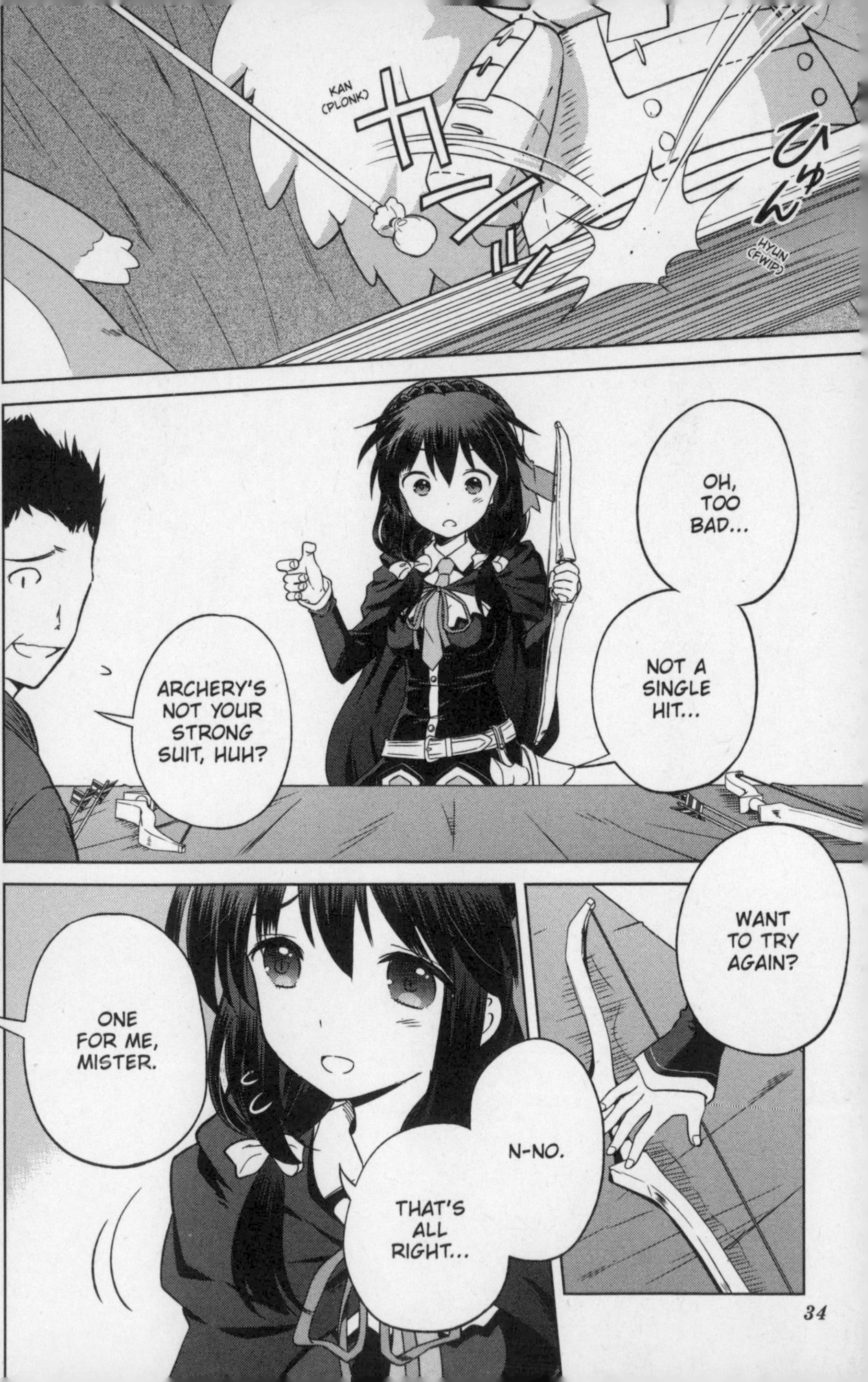
ひゅん
HYUN (FWIP)
カーン
KAN (PLONK)
OH, TOO BAD...
NOT A SINGLE HIT...
ARCHERY'S NOT YOUR STRONG SUIT, HUH?
WANT TO TRY AGAIN?
N-NO.
THAT'S ALL RIGHT...
ONE FOR ME, MISTER.

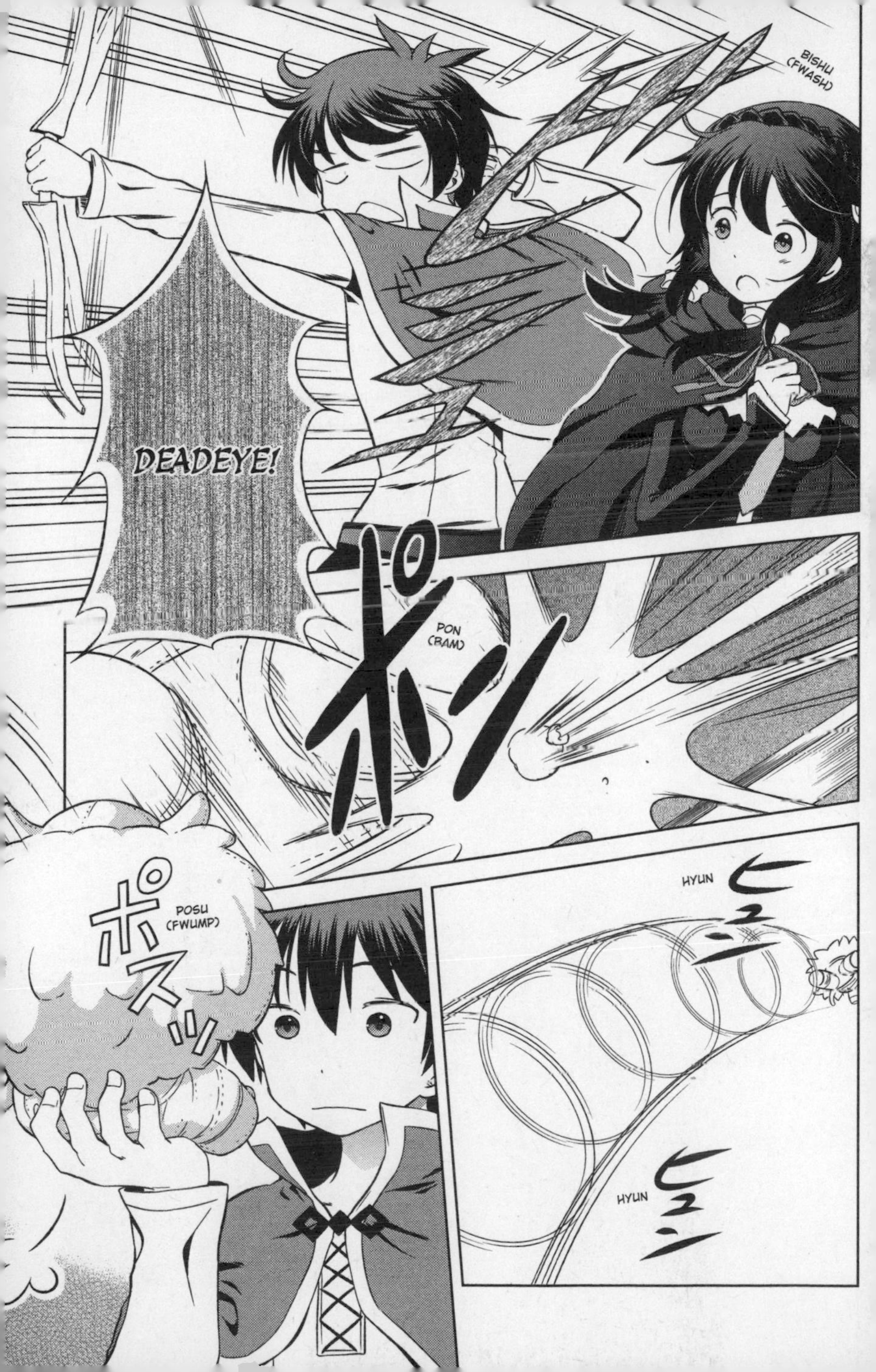
BISHU (FWASH)
DEADEYE!
ポン
PON (BAM)
ヒュン
HYUN
ヒュン
HYUN
ポスッ
POSU (FWUMP)

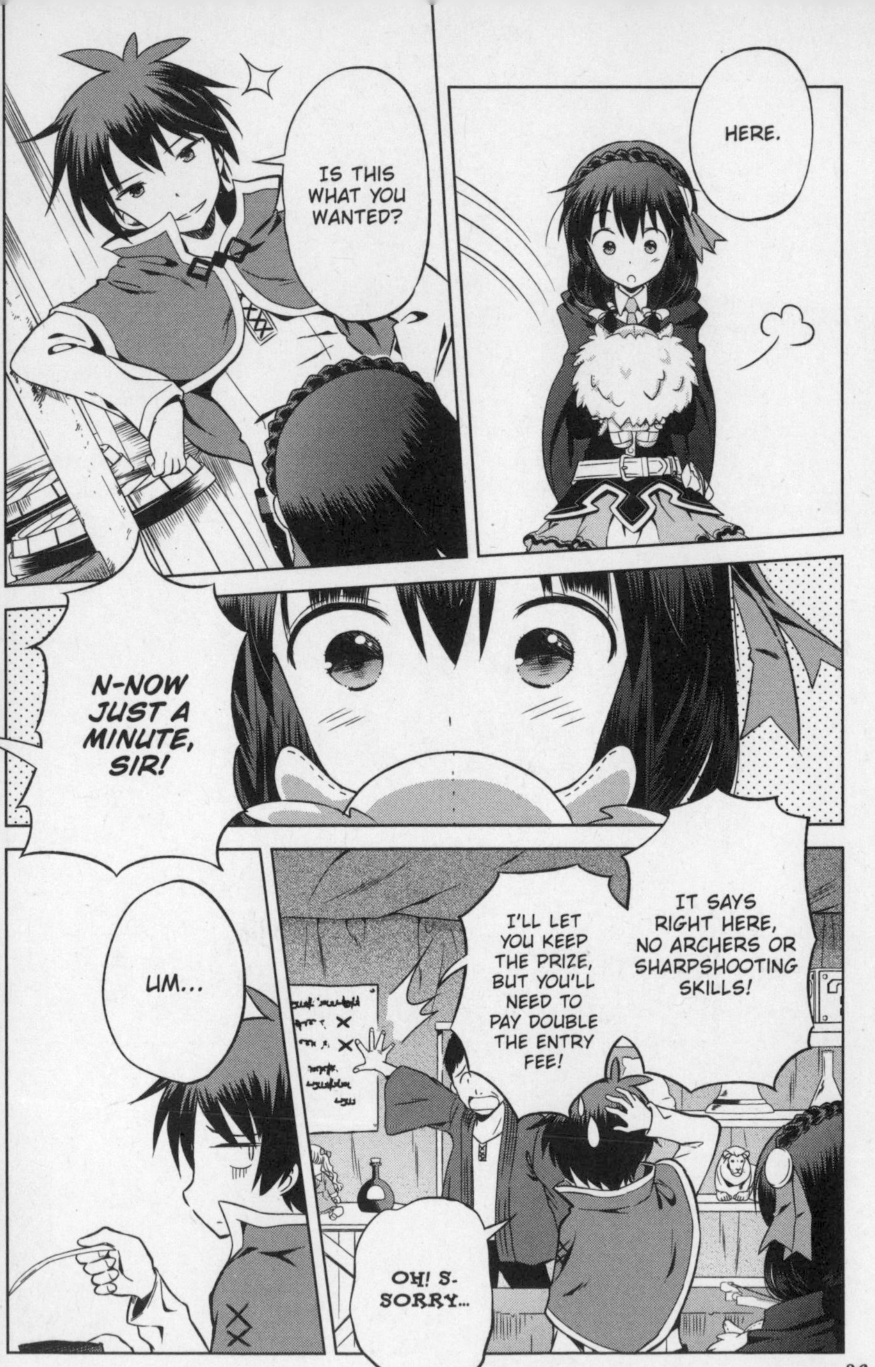
HERE.
IS THIS WHAT YOU WANTED?
N-NOW JUST A MINUTE, SIR!
IT SAYS RIGHT HERE, NO ARCHERS OR SHARPSHOOTING SKILLS!
I'LL LET YOU KEEP THE PRIZE, BUT YOU'LL NEED TO PAY DOUBLE THE ENTRY FEE!
OH! S-SORRY...
UM...

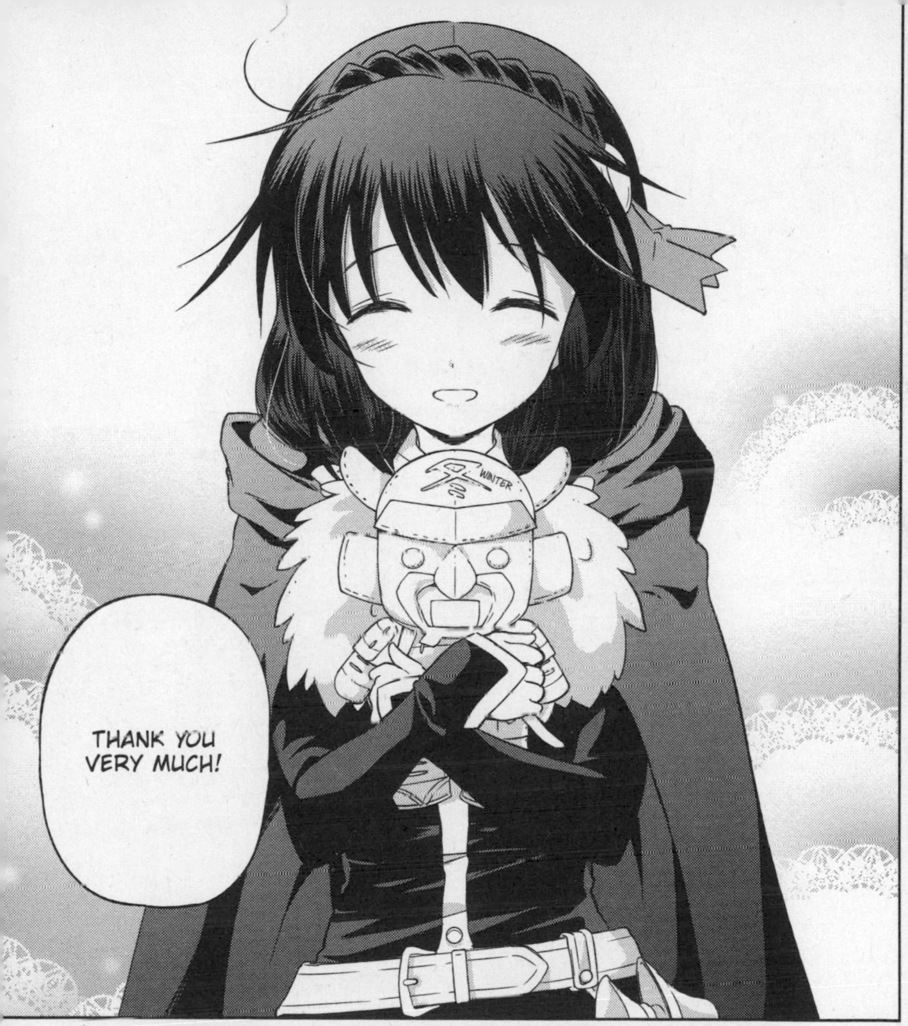
WINTER
THANK YOU VERY MUCH!

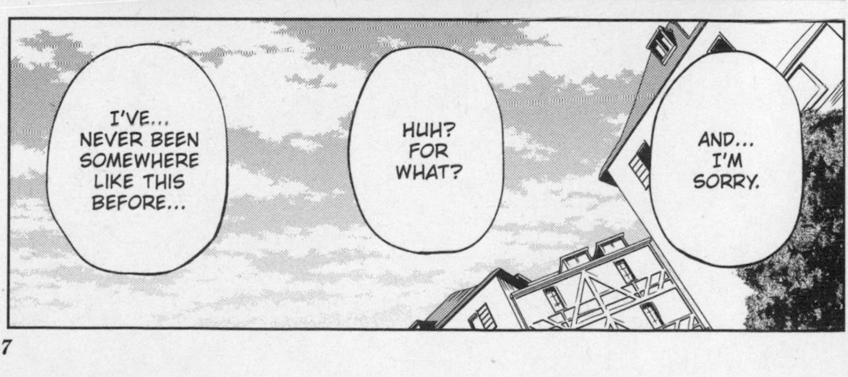
AND... I'M SORRY.
HUH? FOR WHAT?
I'VE... NEVER BEEN SOMEWHERE LIKE THIS BEFORE...

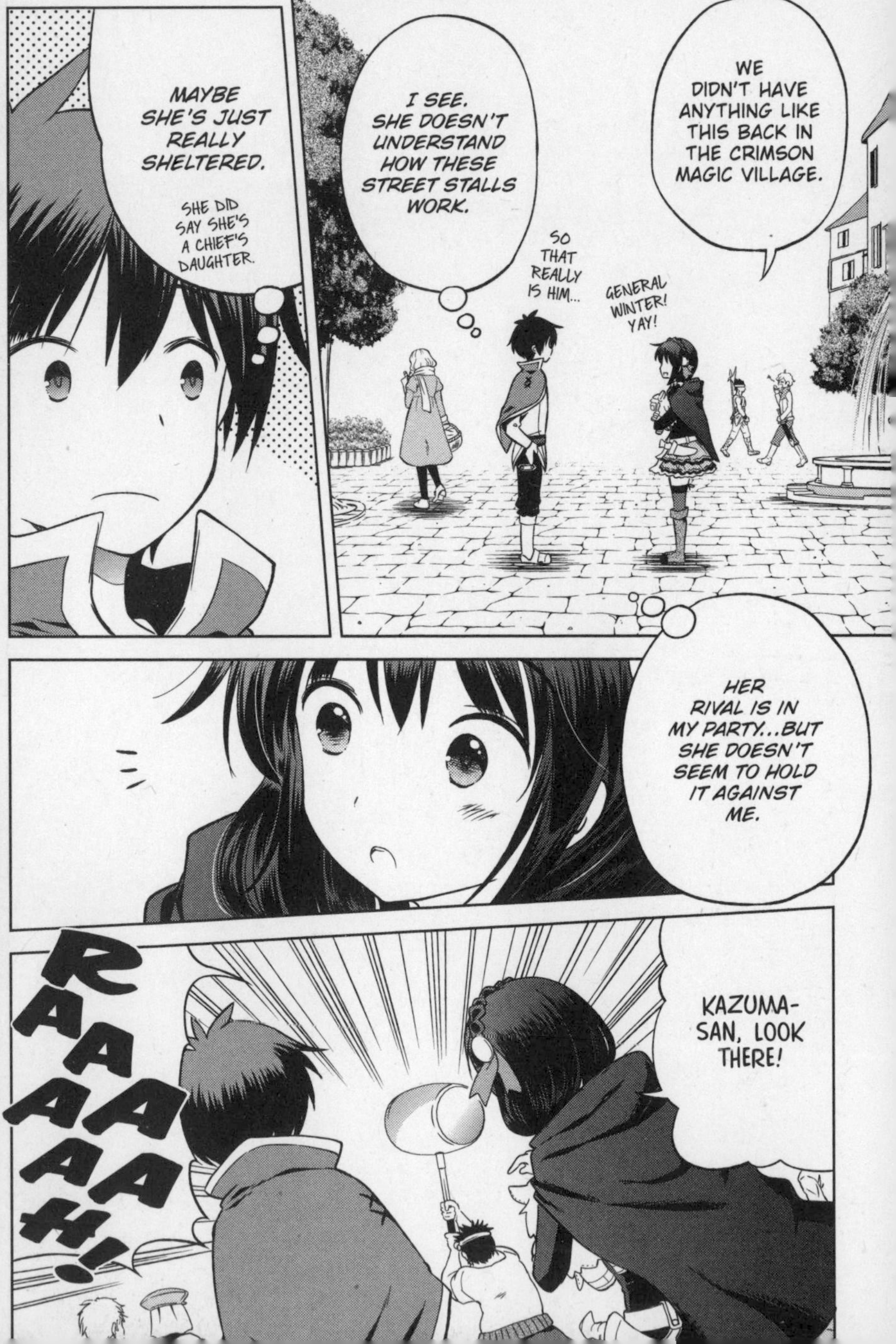
WE DIDN'T HAVE ANYTHING LIKE THIS BACK IN THE CRIMSON MAGIC VILLAGE.
I SEE. SHE DOESN'T UNDERSTAND HOW THESE STREET STALLS WORK.
GENERAL WINTER! YAY!
SO THAT REALLY IS HIM...
MAYBE SHE'S JUST REALLY SHELTERED.
SHE DID SAY SHE'S A CHIEF'S DAUGHTER.
HER RIVAL IS IN MY PARTY...BUT SHE DOESN'T SEEM TO HOLD IT AGAINST ME.
KAZUMA-SAN, LOOK THERE!
RAAAAAAAH!!

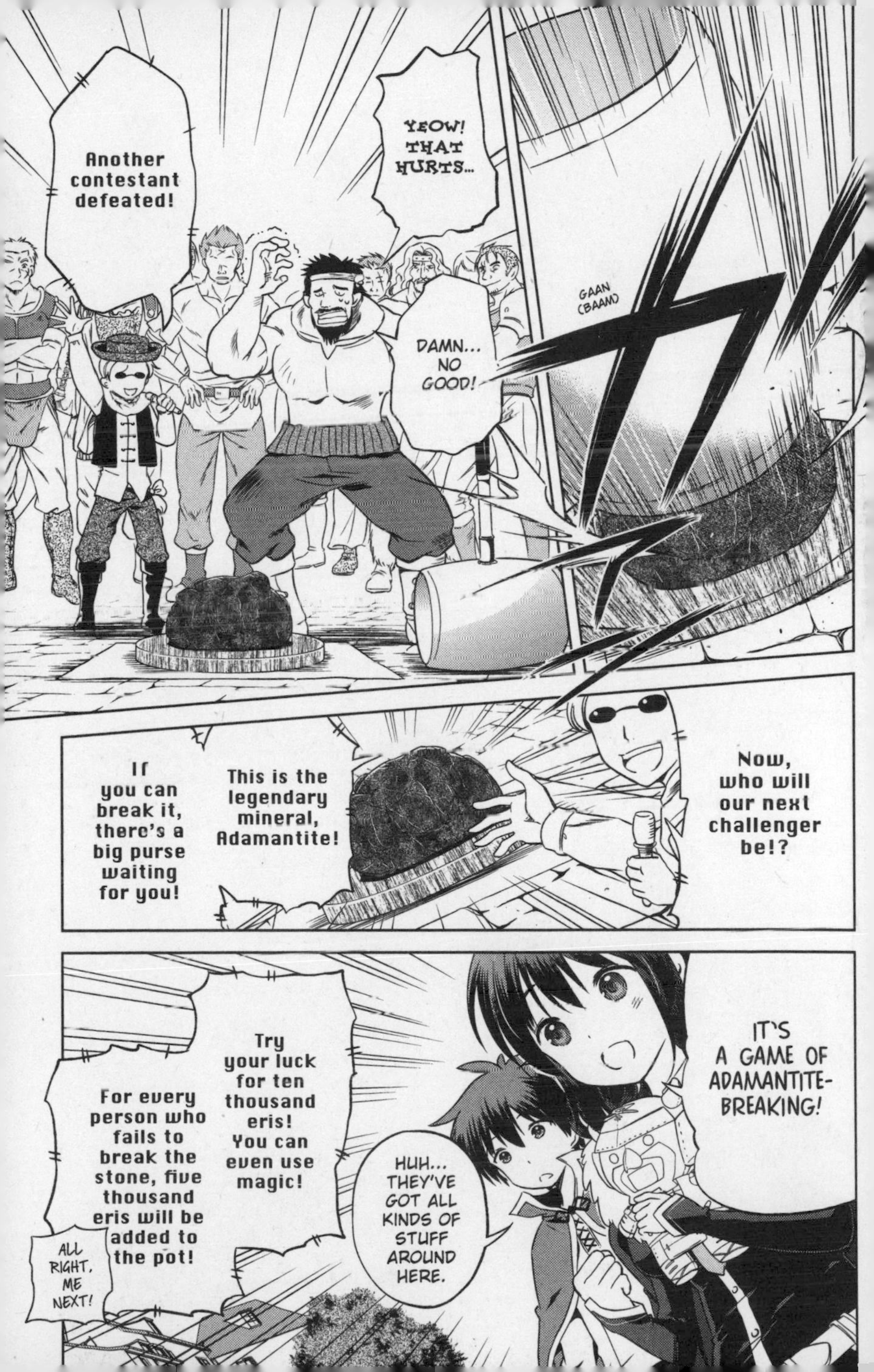
GAAN (BAAM)
YEOW! THAT HURTS...
DAMN... NO GOOD!
Another contestant defeated!
Now, who will our next challenger be!?
This is the legendary mineral, Adamantite!
If you can break it, there's a big purse waiting for you!
IT'S A GAME OF ADAMANTITE-BREAKING!
HUH... THEY'VE GOT ALL KINDS OF STUFF AROUND HERE.
Try your luck for ten thousand eris! You can even use magic!
For every person who fails to break the stone, five thousand eris will be added to the pot!
ALL RIGHT, ME NEXT!

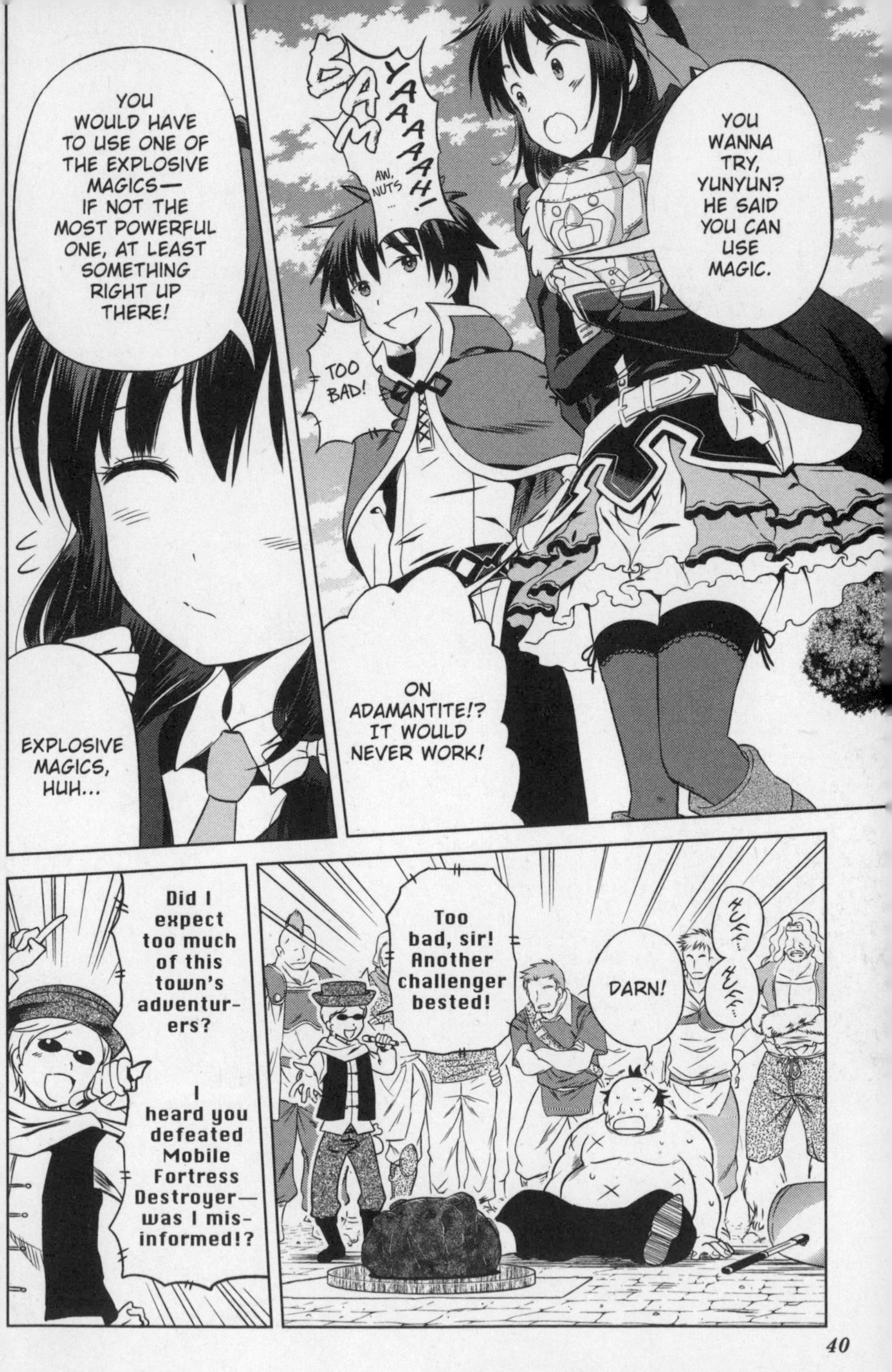
YOU WANNA TRY, YUNYUN? HE SAID YOU CAN USE MAGIC.
YAAAAAAH!
BAM
AW, NUTS...
TOO BAD!
ON ADAMANTITE!? IT WOULD NEVER WORK!
YOU WOULD HAVE TO USE ONE OF THE EXPLOSIVE MAGICS— IF NOT THE MOST POWERFUL ONE, AT LEAST SOMETHING RIGHT UP THERE!
EXPLOSIVE MAGICS, HUH...
HUFF... HUFF...
DARN!
Too bad, sir! Another challenger bested!
Did I expect too much of this town's adventur-ers?
I heard you defeated Mobile Fortress Destroyer— was I mis-informed!?

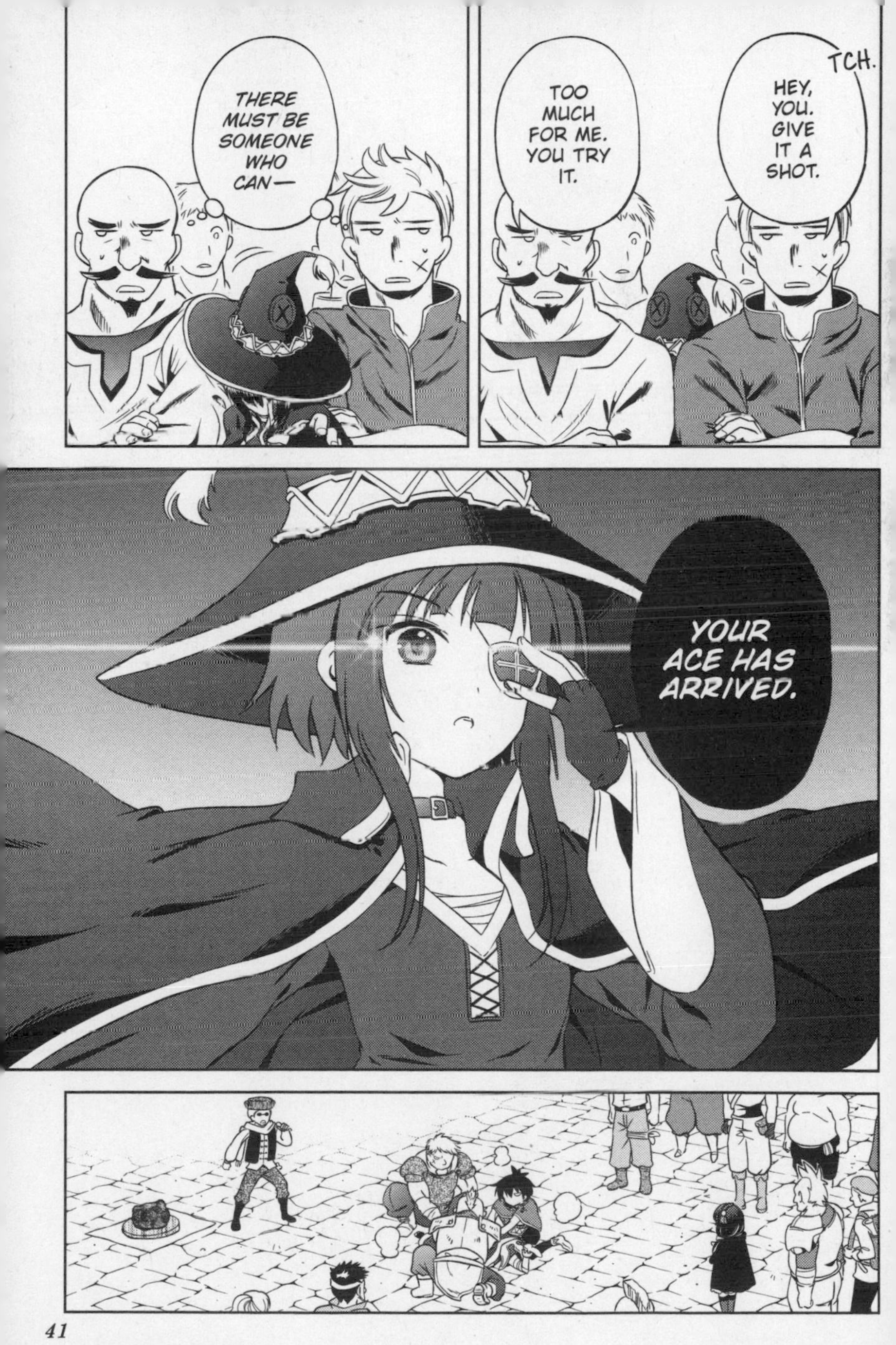
TCH.
HEY, YOU. GIVE IT A SHOT.
TOO MUCH FOR ME. YOU TRY IT.
THERE MUST BE SOMEONE WHO CAN—
YOUR ACE HAS ARRIVED.

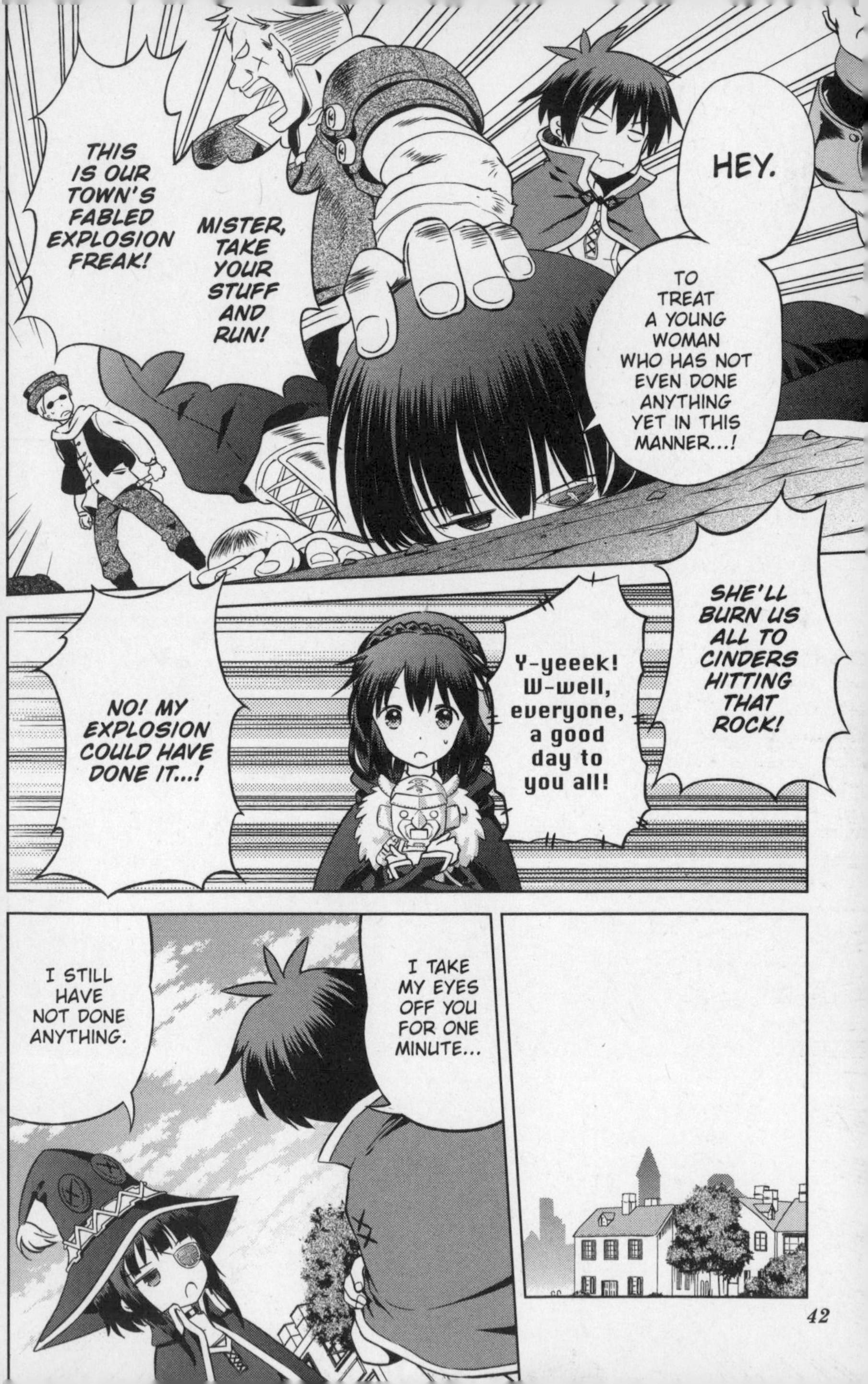
HEY.
TO TREAT A YOUNG WOMAN WHO HAS NOT EVEN DONE ANYTHING YET IN THIS MANNER...!
MISTER, TAKE YOUR STUFF AND RUN!
THIS IS OUR TOWN'S FABLED EXPLOSION FREAK!
SHE'LL BURN US ALL TO CINDERS HITTING THAT ROCK!
Y-yeeek! W-well, everyone, a good day to you all!
NO! MY EXPLOSION COULD HAVE DONE IT...!
I TAKE MY EYES OFF YOU FOR ONE MINUTE...
I STILL HAVE NOT DONE ANYTHING.

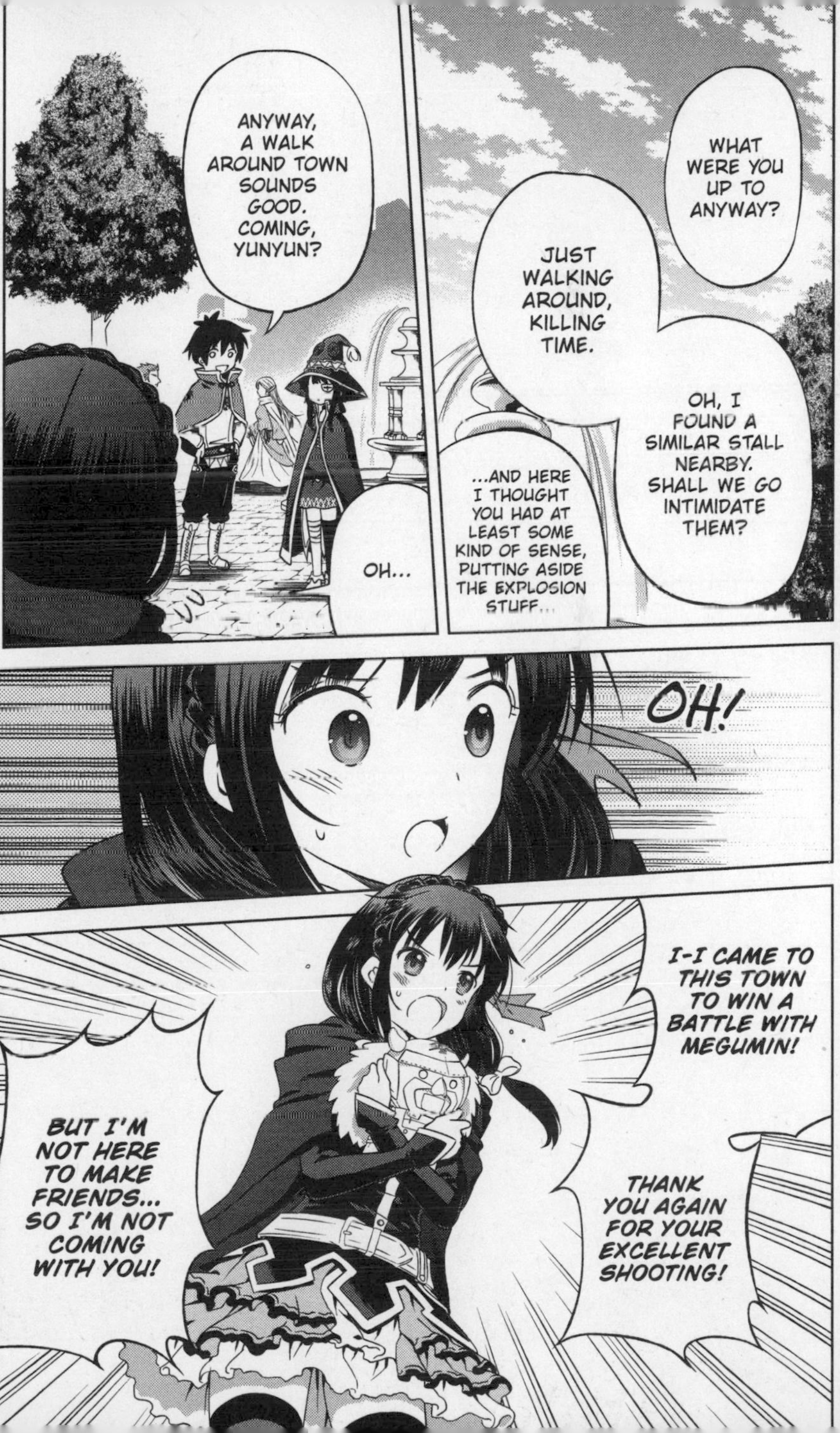
WHAT WERE YOU UP TO ANYWAY?
JUST WALKING AROUND, KILLING TIME.
OH, I FOUND A SIMILAR STALL NEARBY. SHALL WE GO INTIMIDATE THEM?
...AND HERE I THOUGHT YOU HAD AT LEAST SOME KIND OF SENSE, PUTTING ASIDE THE EXPLOSION STUFF...
ANYWAY, A WALK AROUND TOWN SOUNDS GOOD. COMING, YUNYUN?
OH...
OH!
I-I CAME TO THIS TOWN TO WIN A BATTLE WITH MEGUMIN!
THANK YOU AGAIN FOR YOUR EXCELLENT SHOOTING!
BUT I'M NOT HERE TO MAKE FRIENDS... SO I'M NOT COMING WITH YOU!

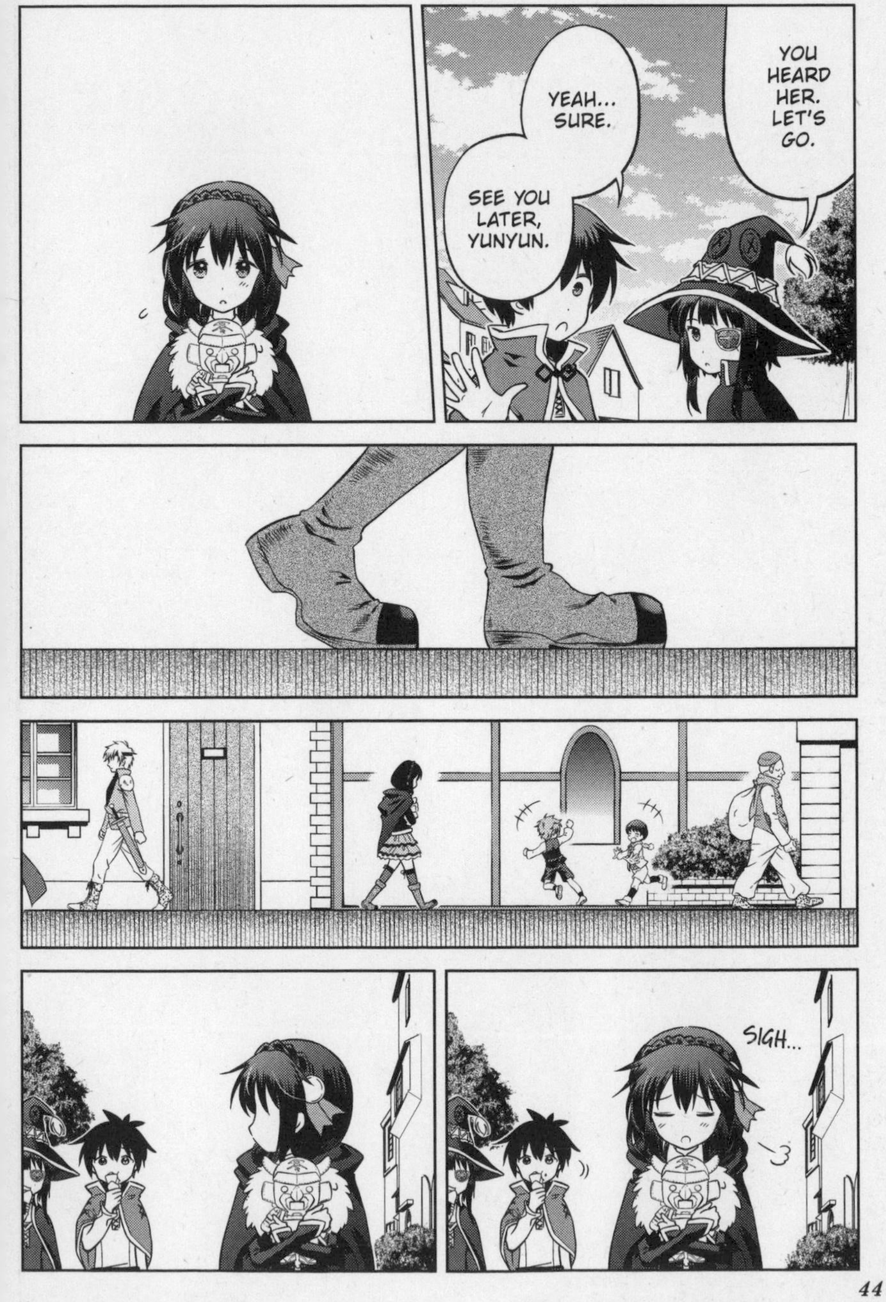
YOU HEARD HER. LET'S GO.
YEAH... SURE.
SEE YOU LATER, YUNYUN.
SIGH...

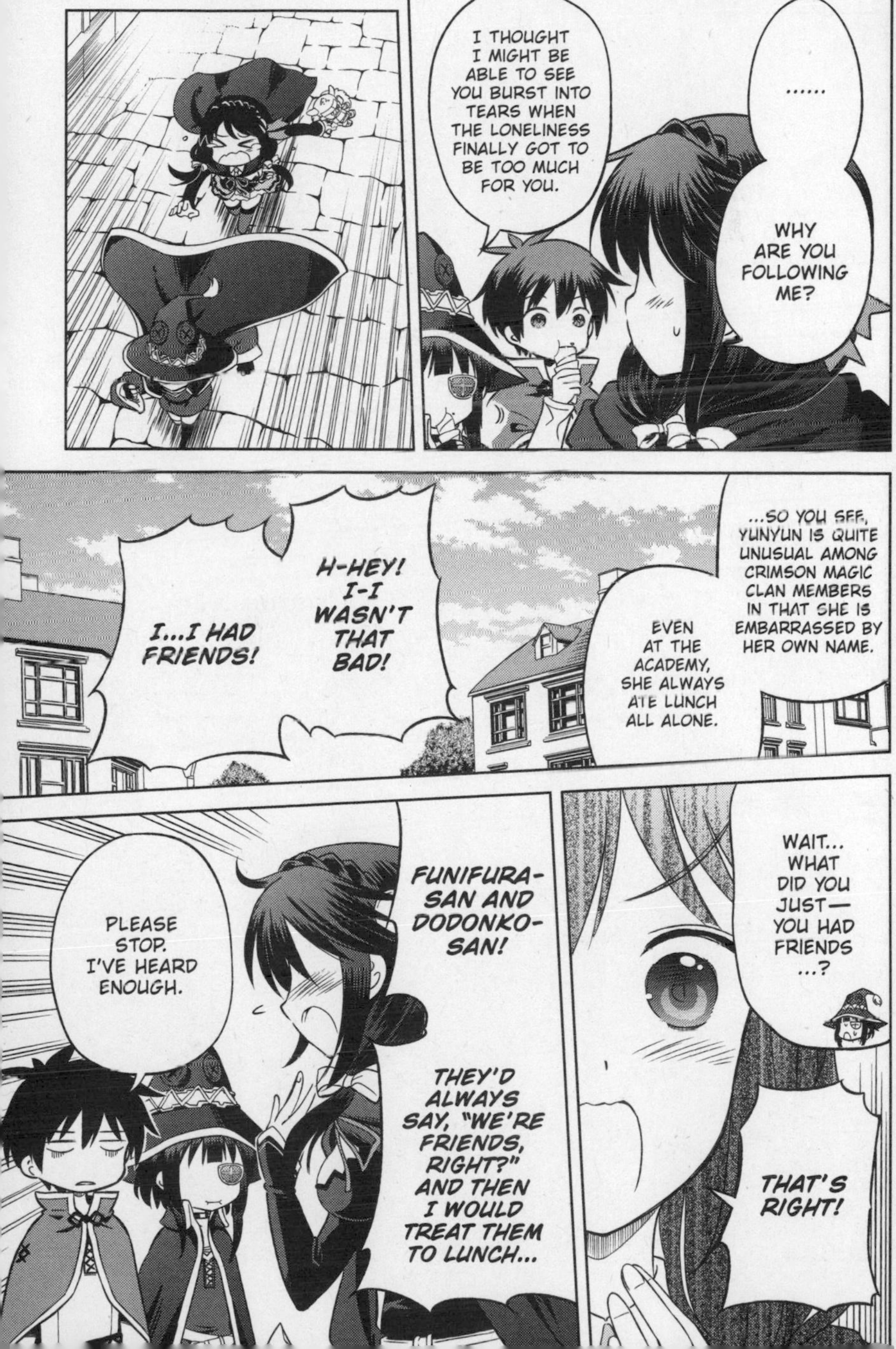
......
WHY ARE YOU FOLLOWING ME?
I THOUGHT I MIGHT BE ABLE TO SEE YOU BURST INTO TEARS WHEN THE LONELINESS FINALLY GOT TO BE TOO MUCH FOR YOU.
...SO YOU SEE, YUNYUN IS QUITE UNUSUAL AMONG CRIMSON MAGIC CLAN MEMBERS IN THAT SHE IS EMBARRASSED BY HER OWN NAME.
EVEN AT THE ACADEMY, SHE ALWAYS ATE LUNCH ALL ALONE.
H-HEY! I-I WASN'T THAT BAD!
I...I HAD FRIENDS!
WAIT... WHAT DID YOU JUST— YOU HAD FRIENDS ...?
THAT'S RIGHT!
FUNIFURA-SAN AND DODONKO-SAN!
THEY'D ALWAYS SAY, "WE'RE FRIENDS, RIGHT?" AND THEN I WOULD TREAT THEM TO LUNCH...
PLEASE STOP. I'VE HEARD ENOUGH.

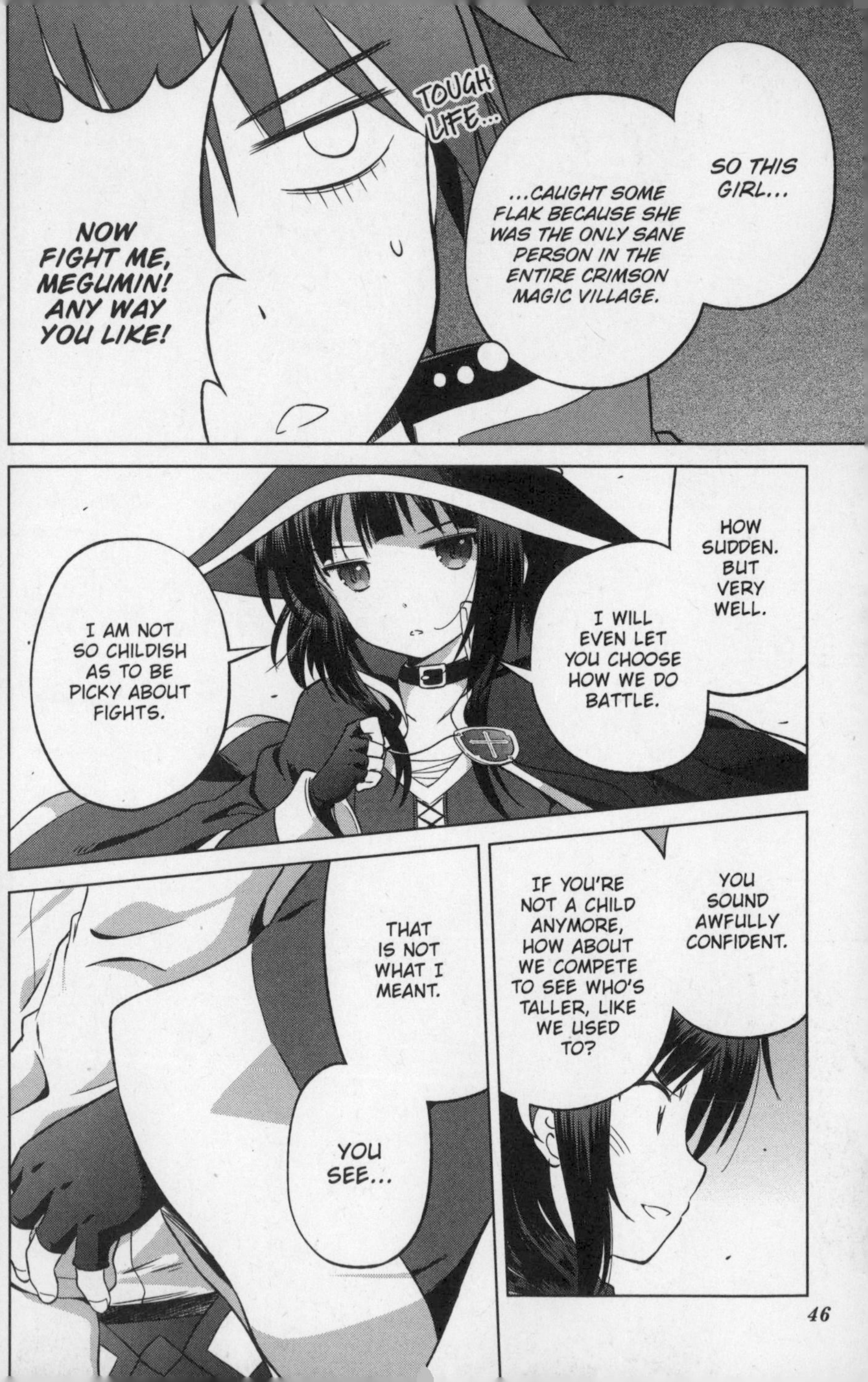
SO THIS GIRL...
...CAUGHT SOME FLAK BECAUSE SHE WAS THE ONLY SANE PERSON IN THE ENTIRE CRIMSON MAGIC VILLAGE.
TOUGH LIFE...
NOW FIGHT ME, MEGUMIN! ANY WAY YOU LIKE!
HOW SUDDEN. BUT VERY WELL.
I WILL EVEN LET YOU CHOOSE HOW WE DO BATTLE.
I AM NOT SO CHILDISH AS TO BE PICKY ABOUT FIGHTS.
YOU SOUND AWFULLY CONFIDENT.
IF YOU'RE NOT A CHILD ANYMORE, HOW ABOUT WE COMPETE TO SEE WHO'S TALLER, LIKE WE USED TO?
THAT IS NOT WHAT I MEANT.
YOU SEE...

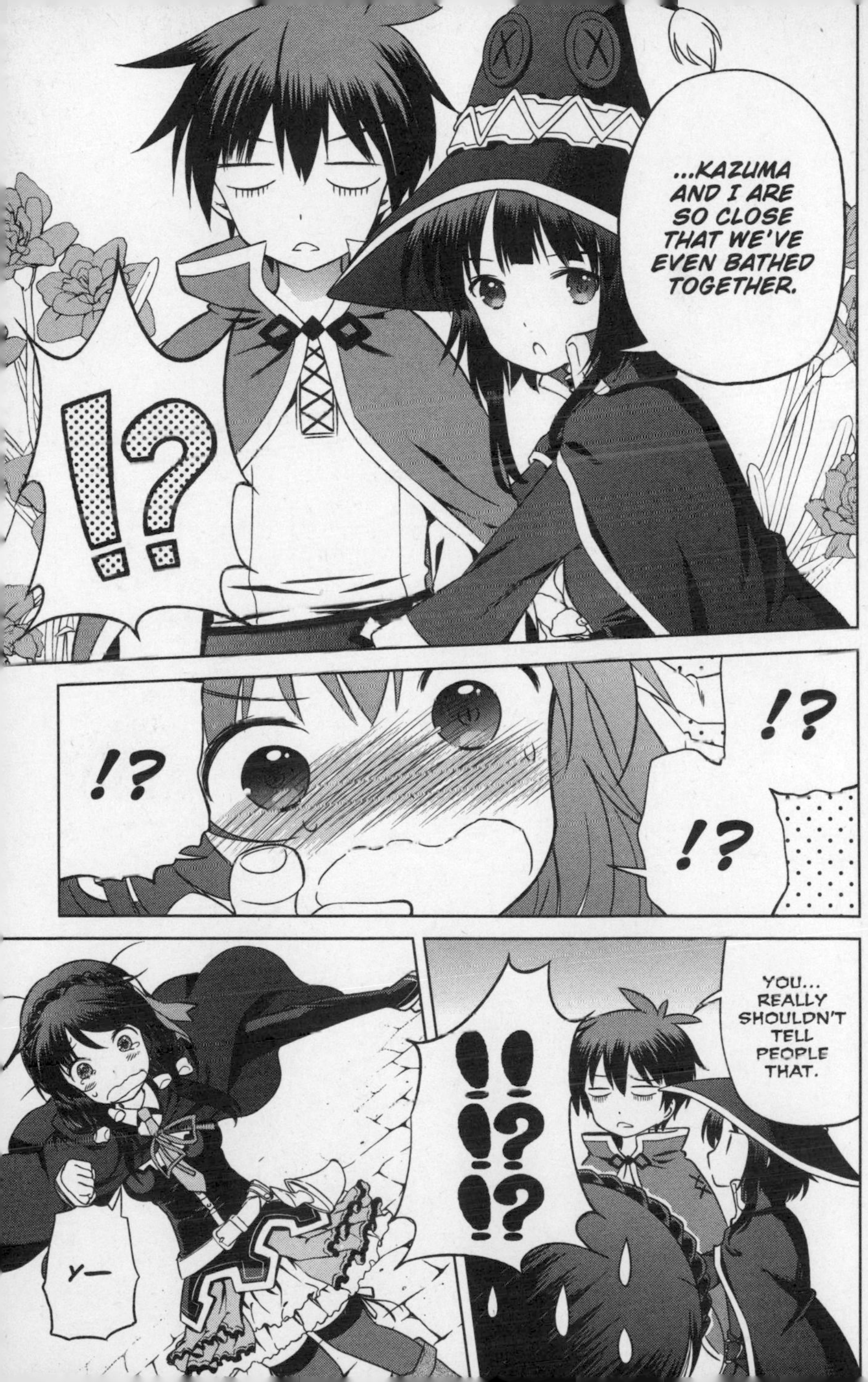
...KAZUMA AND I ARE SO CLOSE THAT WE'VE EVEN BATHED TOGETHER.
!?
!?
!?
!?
YOU... REALLY SHOULDN'T TELL PEOPLE THAT.
!!?!?
Y—

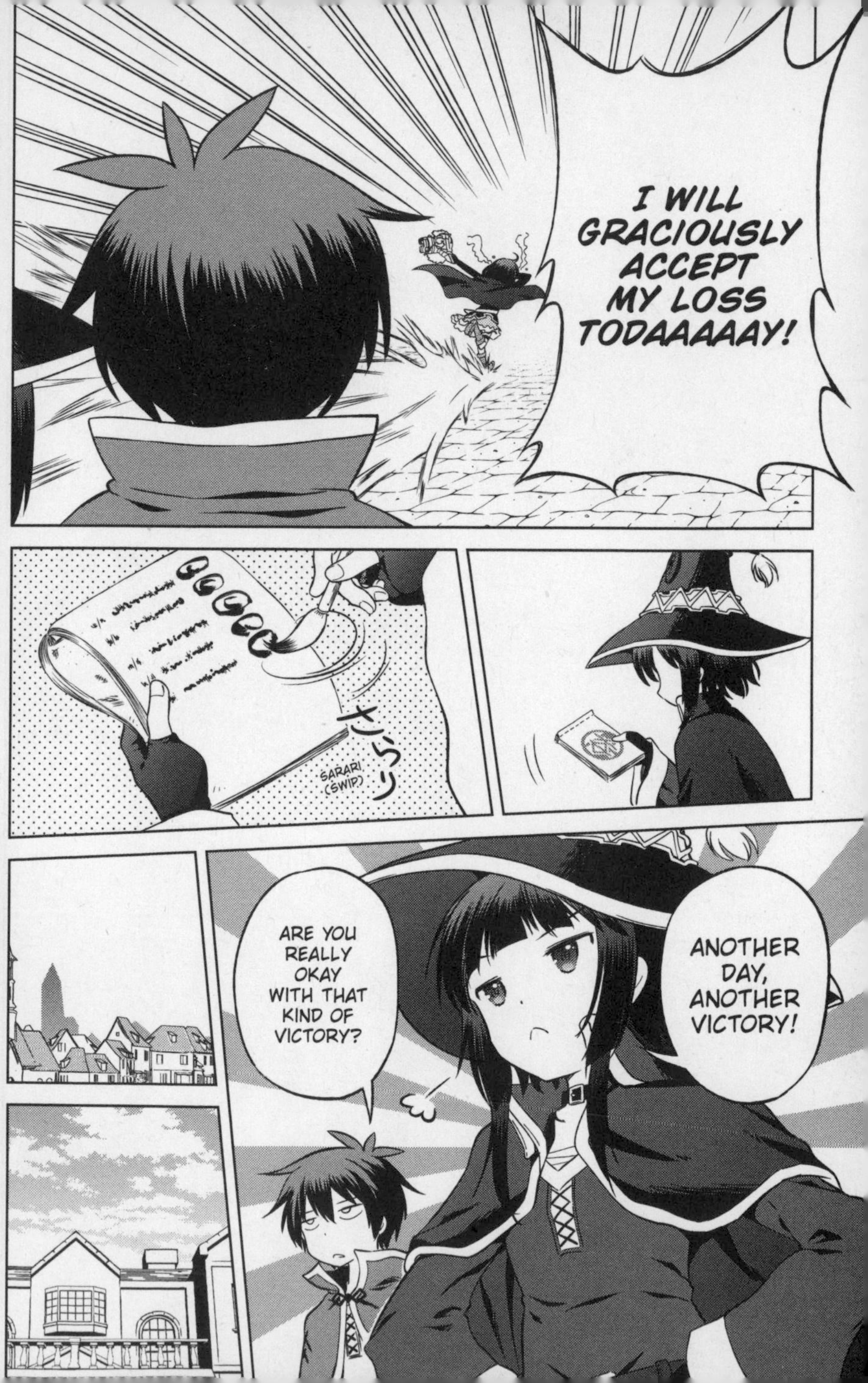
I WILL GRACIOUSLY ACCEPT MY LOSS TODAAAAAY!
さらり
SARARI (SWIP)
ANOTHER DAY, ANOTHER VICTORY!
ARE YOU REALLY OKAY WITH THAT KIND OF VICTORY?

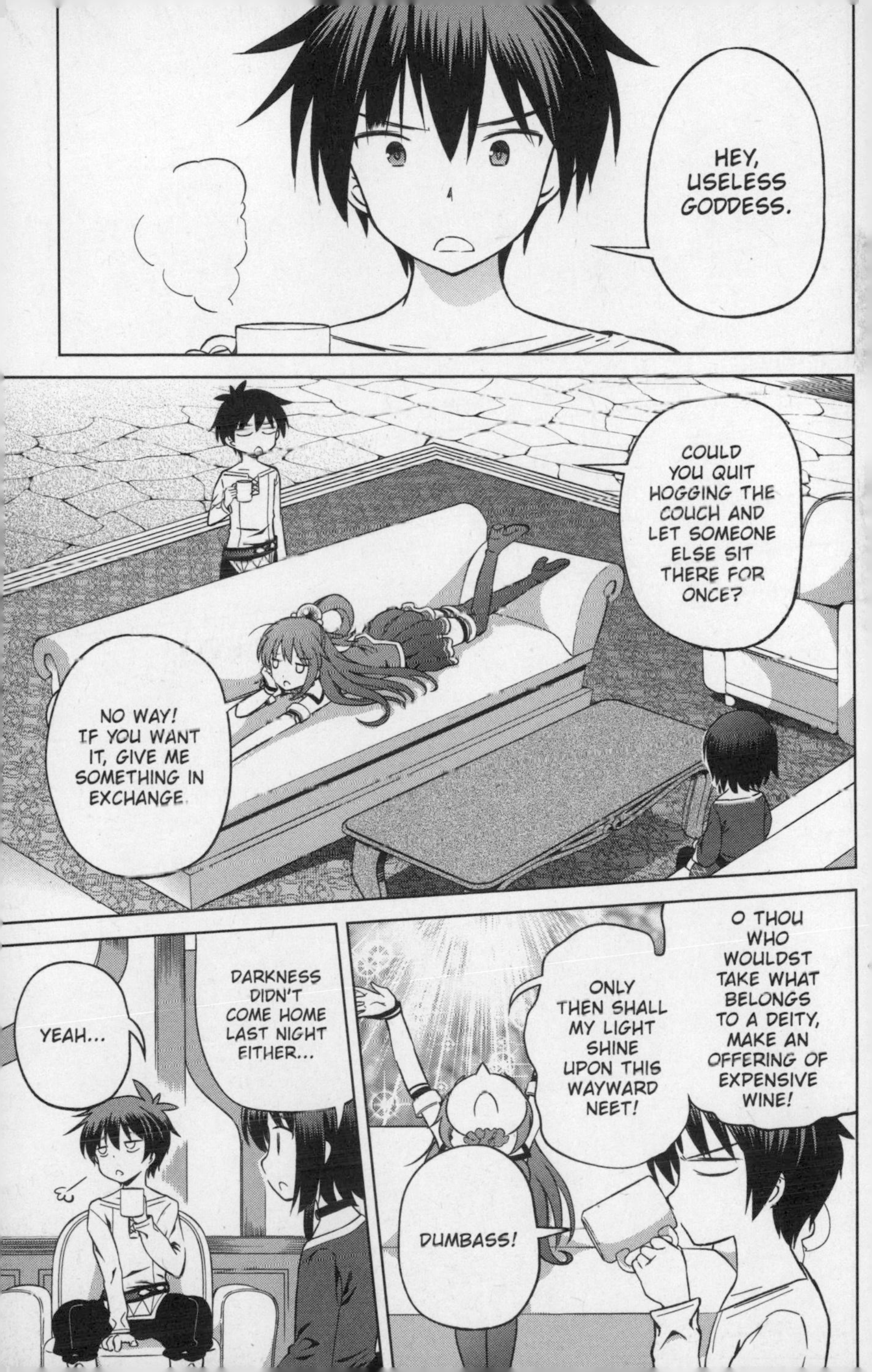
HEY, USELESS GODDESS.
COULD YOU QUIT HOGGING THE COUCH AND LET SOMEONE ELSE SIT THERE FOR ONCE?
NO WAY! IF YOU WANT IT, GIVE ME SOMETHING IN EXCHANGE.
O THOU WHO WOULDST TAKE WHAT BELONGS TO A DEITY, MAKE AN OFFERING OF EXPENSIVE WINE!
ONLY THEN SHALL MY LIGHT SHINE UPON THIS WAYWARD NEET!
DUMBASS!
DARKNESS DIDN'T COME HOME LAST NIGHT EITHER...
YEAH...

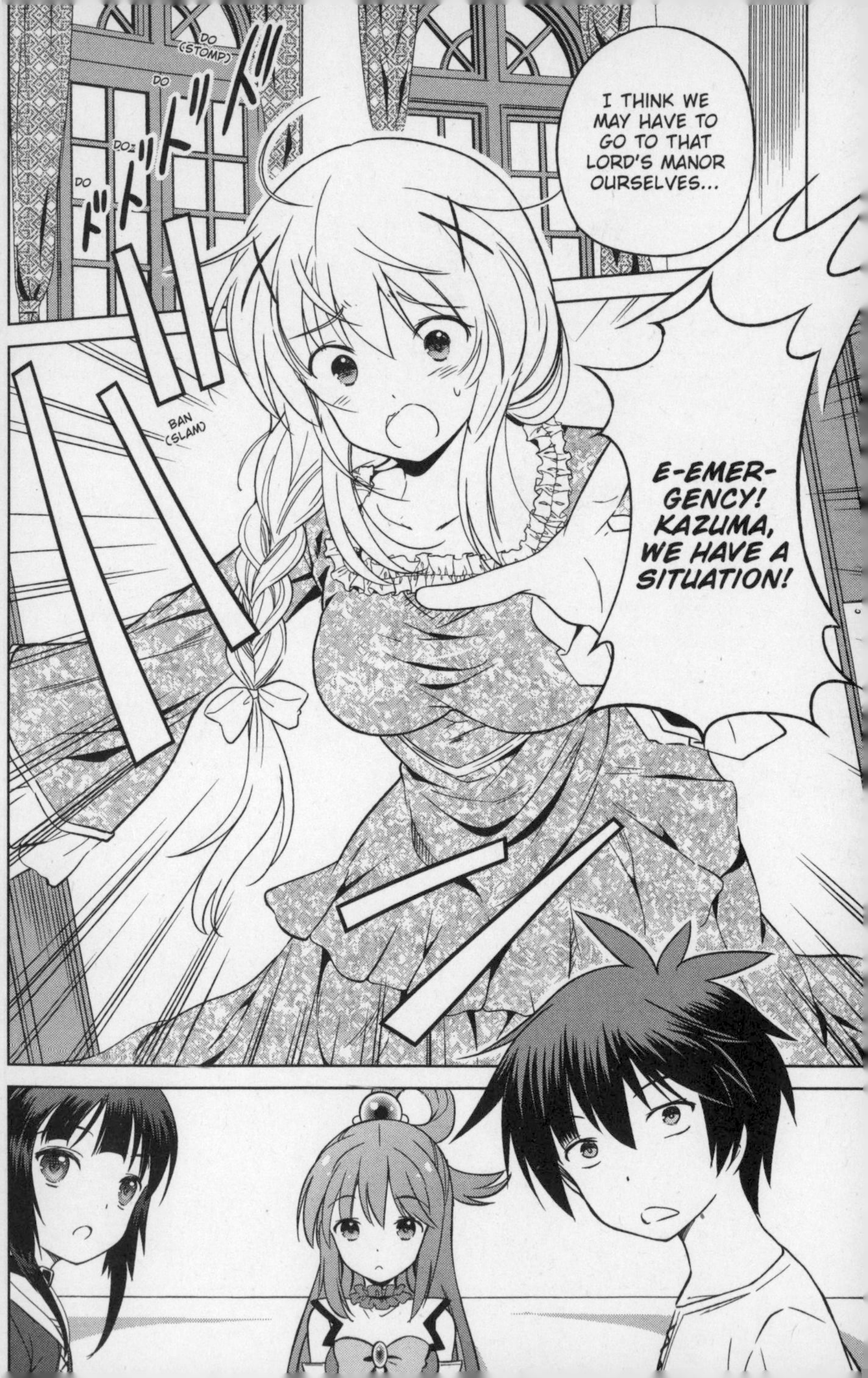

I THINK WE MAY HAVE TO GO TO THAT LORD'S MANOR OURSELVES...
DO (STOMP)
DO
DO
DO
BAN (SLAM)
E-EMER-GENCY! KAZUMA, WE HAVE A SITUATION!

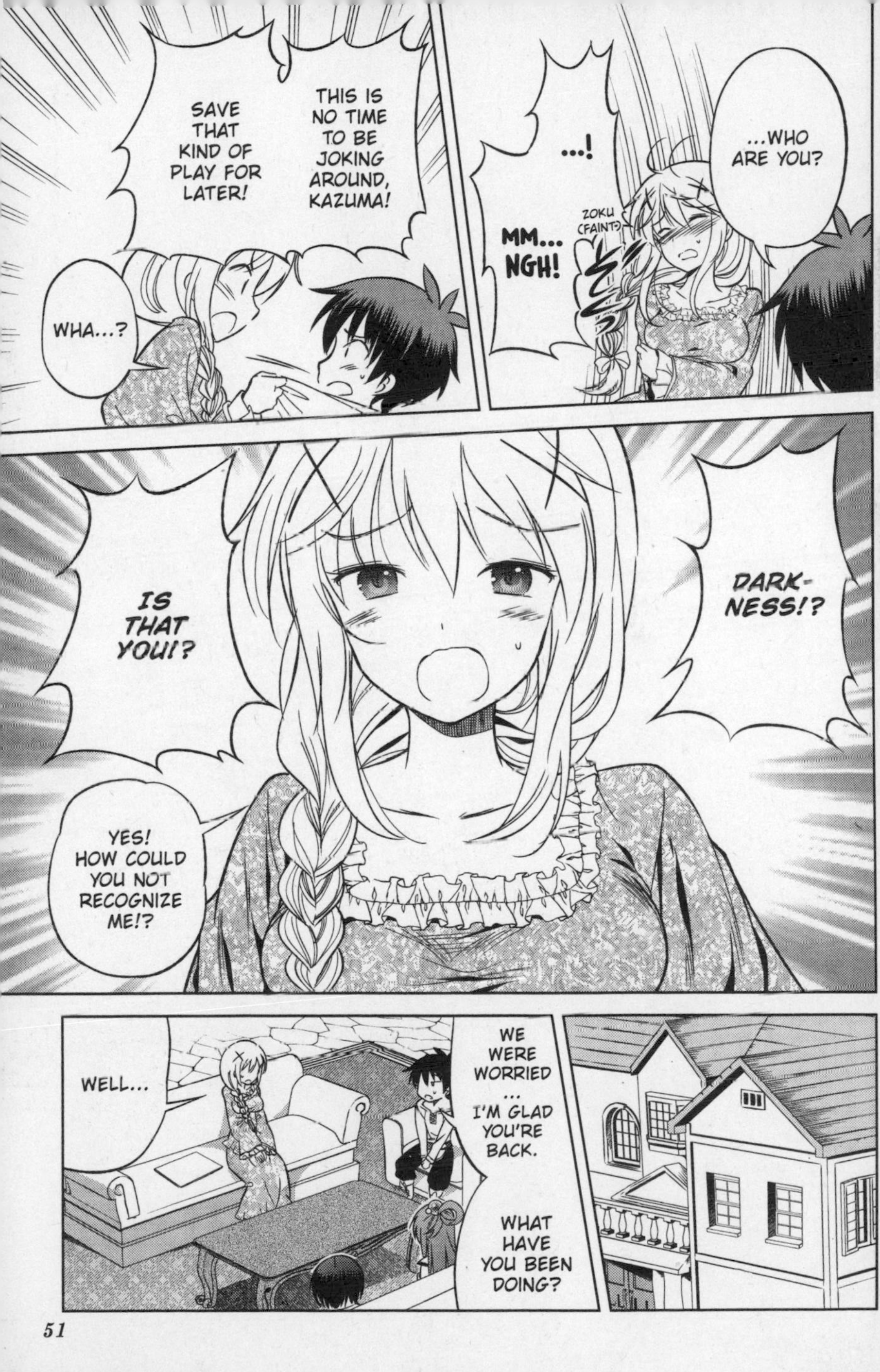
...WHO ARE YOU?
...!
ZOKU (FAINT)
MM... NGH!
THIS IS NO TIME TO BE JOKING AROUND, KAZUMA!
SAVE THAT KIND OF PLAY FOR LATER!
WHA...?
DARKNESS!?
IS THAT YOU!?
YES! HOW COULD YOU NOT RECOGNIZE ME!?
WE WERE WORRIED ... I'M GLAD YOU'RE BACK.
WHAT HAVE YOU BEEN DOING?
WELL...

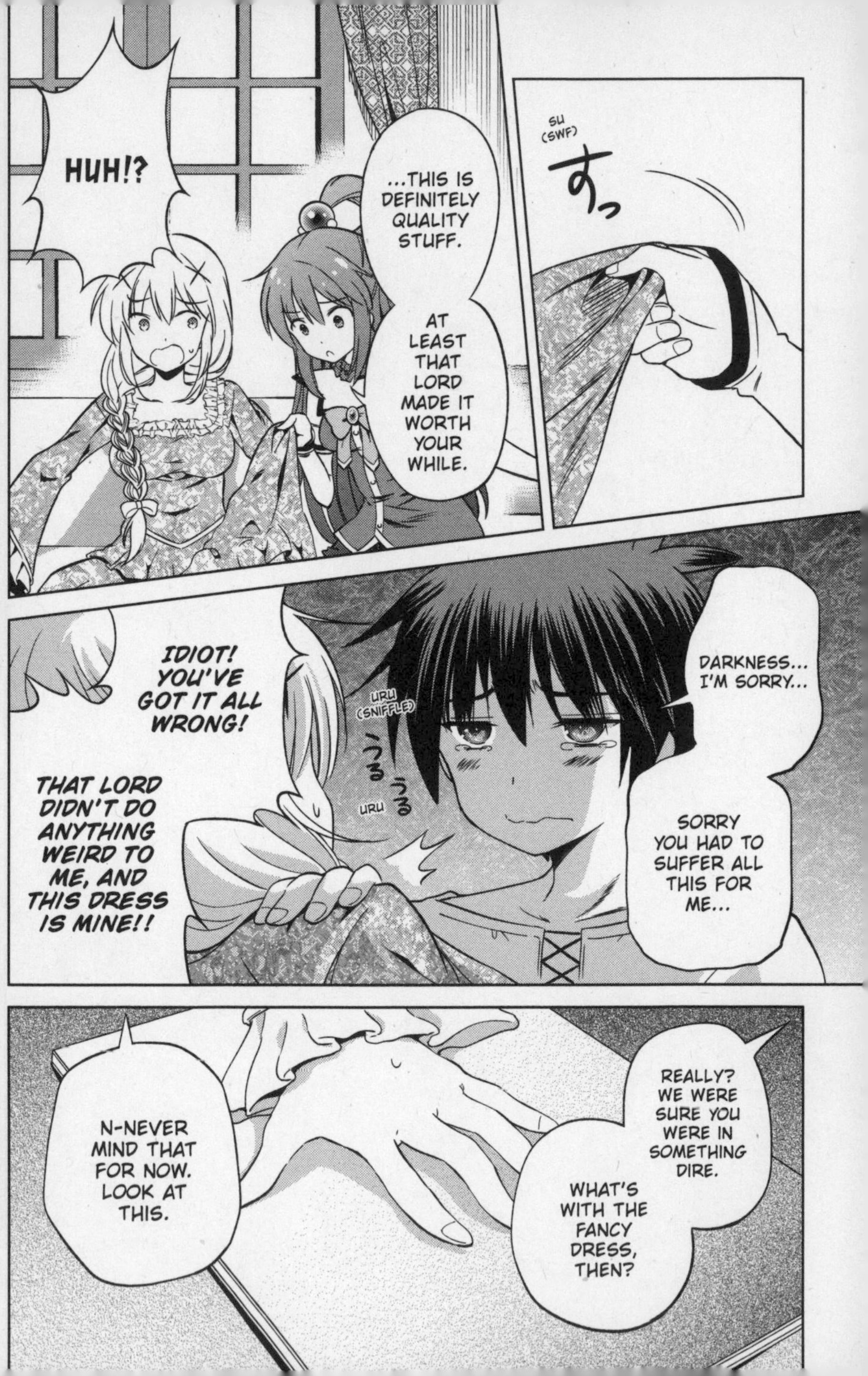
SU (SWF)
すっ
...THIS IS DEFINITELY QUALITY STUFF.
AT LEAST THAT LORD MADE IT WORTH YOUR WHILE.
HUH!?
DARKNESS... I'M SORRY...
SORRY YOU HAD TO SUFFER ALL THIS FOR ME...
URU (SNIFFLE)
うる
うる
URU
IDIOT! YOU'VE GOT IT ALL WRONG!
THAT LORD DIDN'T DO ANYTHING WEIRD TO ME, AND THIS DRESS IS MINE!!
REALLY? WE WERE SURE YOU WERE IN SOMETHING DIRE.
WHAT'S WITH THE FANCY DRESS, THEN?
N-NEVER MIND THAT FOR NOW. LOOK AT THIS.

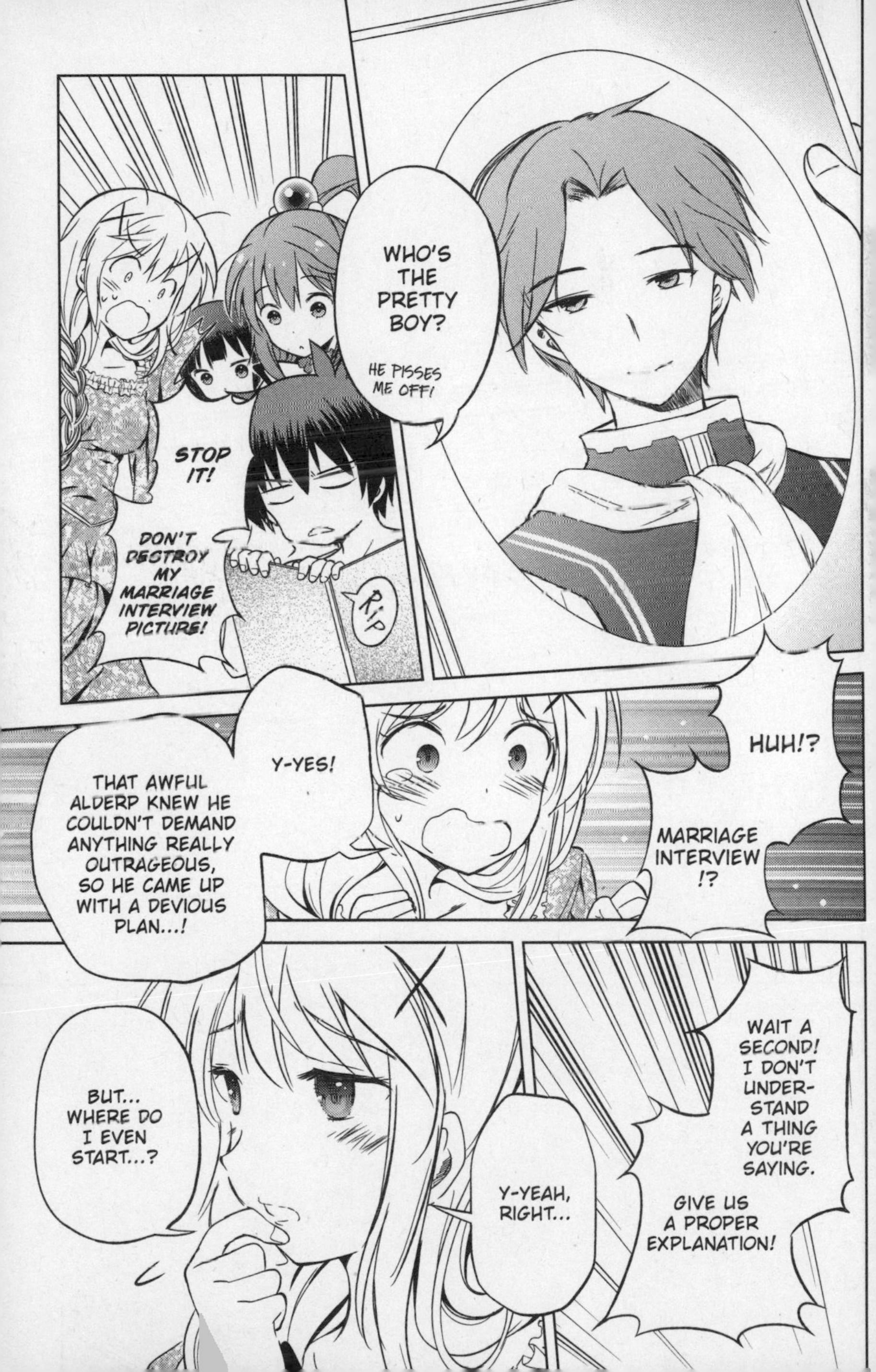
WHO'S THE PRETTY BOY?
HE PISSES ME OFF!
RIP
STOP IT!
DON'T DESTROY MY MARRIAGE INTERVIEW PICTURE!
HUH!?
MARRIAGE INTERVIEW!?
Y-YES!
THAT AWFUL ALDERP KNEW HE COULDN'T DEMAND ANYTHING REALLY OUTRAGEOUS, SO HE CAME UP WITH A DEVIOUS PLAN...!
WAIT A SECOND! I DON'T UNDER-STAND A THING YOU'RE SAYING.
GIVE US A PROPER EXPLANATION!
Y-YEAH, RIGHT...
BUT... WHERE DO I EVEN START...?

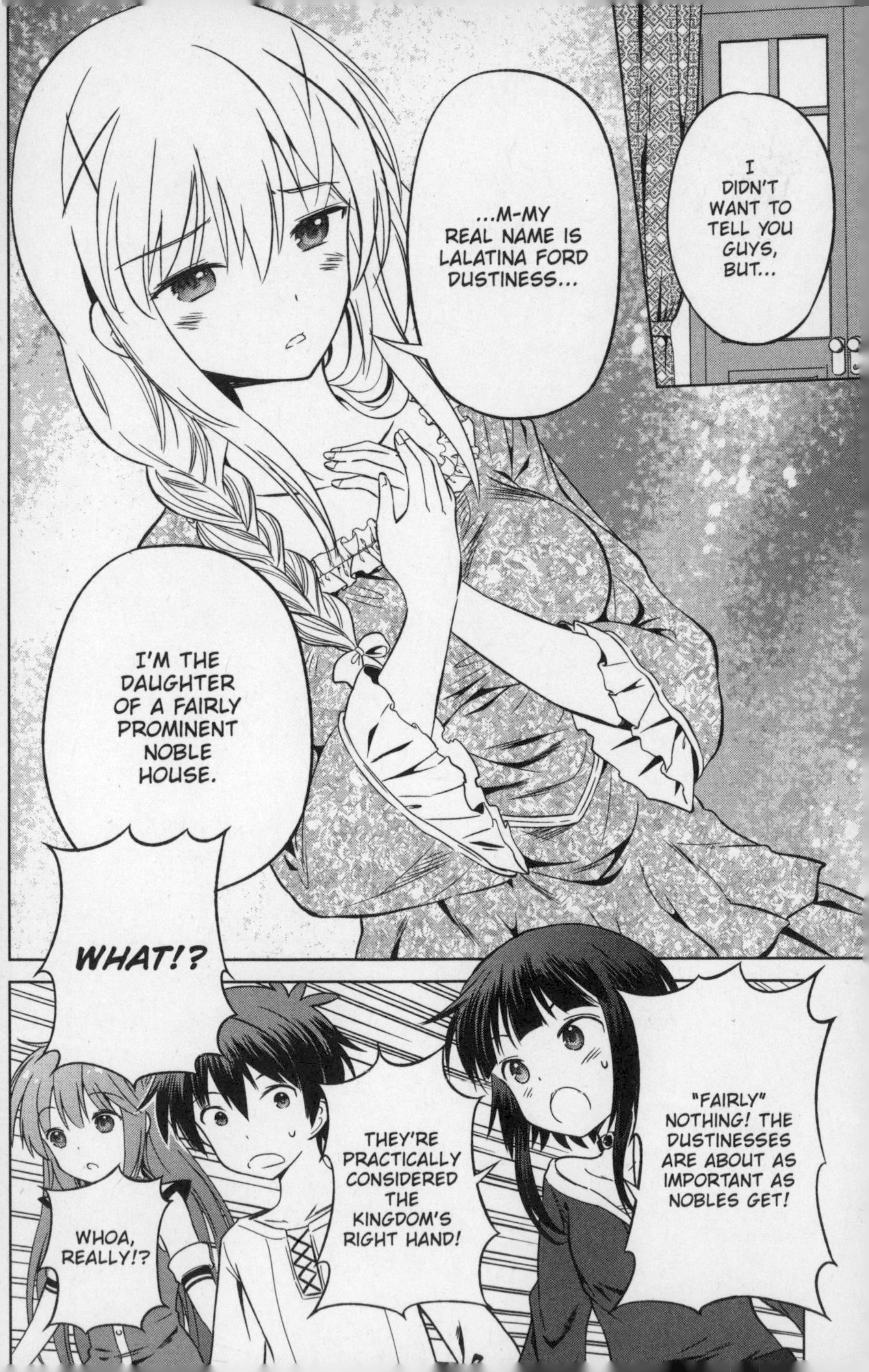
I DIDN'T WANT TO TELL YOU GUYS, BUT...
...M-MY REAL NAME IS LALATINA FORD DUSTINESS...
I'M THE DAUGHTER OF A FAIRLY PROMINENT NOBLE HOUSE.
WHAT!?
"FAIRLY" NOTHING! THE DUSTINESSES ARE ABOUT AS IMPORTANT AS NOBLES GET!
THEY'RE PRACTICALLY CONSIDERED THE KINGDOM'S RIGHT HAND!
WHOA, REALLY!?

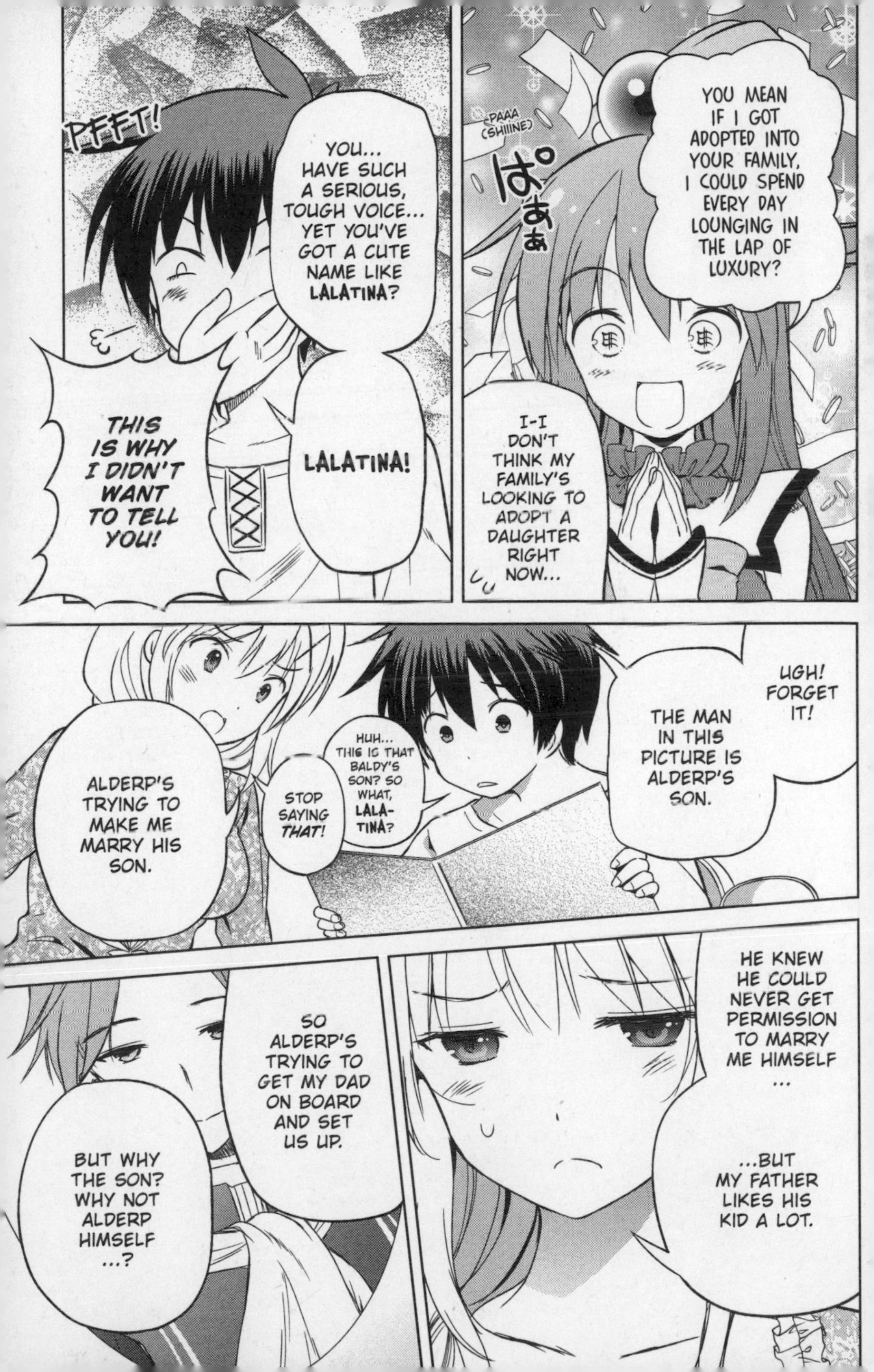

PAAA (SHIIINE)
ぱあぁ
YOU MEAN IF I GOT ADOPTED INTO YOUR FAMILY, I COULD SPEND EVERY DAY LOUNGING IN THE LAP OF LUXURY?
I-I DON'T THINK MY FAMILY'S LOOKING TO ADOPT A DAUGHTER RIGHT NOW...
PFFFT!
YOU... HAVE SUCH A SERIOUS, TOUGH VOICE... YET YOU'VE GOT A CUTE NAME LIKE LALATINA?
LALATINA!
THIS IS WHY I DIDN'T WANT TO TELL YOU!
UGH! FORGET IT!
THE MAN IN THIS PICTURE IS ALDERP'S SON.
HUH... THIS IS THAT BALDY'S SON? SO WHAT, LALA-TINA?
STOP SAYING THAT!
ALDERP'S TRYING TO MAKE ME MARRY HIS SON.
HE KNEW HE COULD NEVER GET PERMISSION TO MARRY ME HIMSELF...
...BUT MY FATHER LIKES HIS KID A LOT.
SO ALDERP'S TRYING TO GET MY DAD ON BOARD AND SET US UP.
BUT WHY THE SON? WHY NOT ALDERP HIMSELF...?

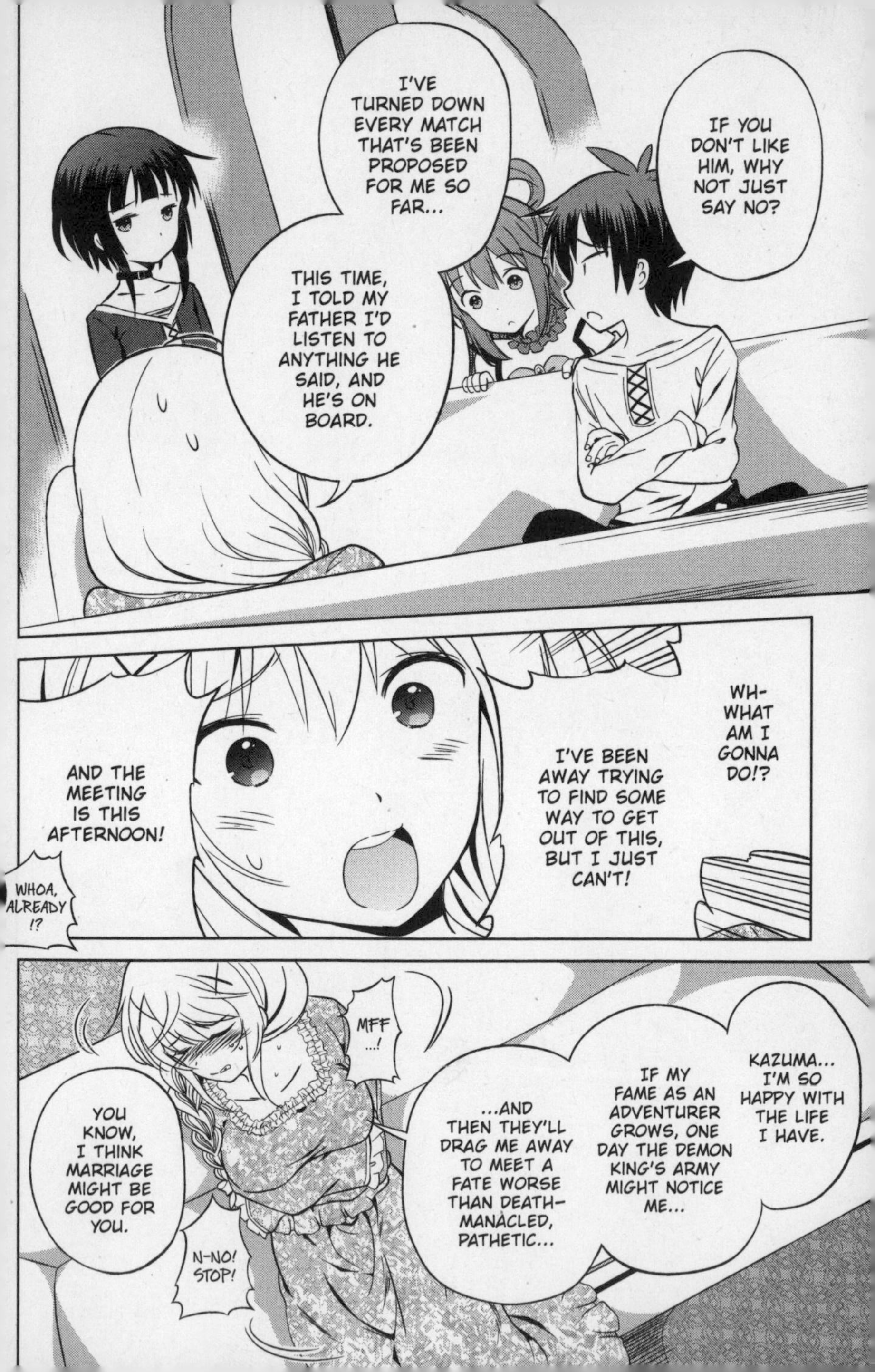
IF YOU DON'T LIKE HIM, WHY NOT JUST SAY NO?
I'VE TURNED DOWN EVERY MATCH THAT'S BEEN PROPOSED FOR ME SO FAR...
THIS TIME, I TOLD MY FATHER I'D LISTEN TO ANYTHING HE SAID, AND HE'S ON BOARD.
WH-WHAT AM I GONNA DO!?
I'VE BEEN AWAY TRYING TO FIND SOME WAY TO GET OUT OF THIS, BUT I JUST CAN'T!
AND THE MEETING IS THIS AFTERNOON!
WHOA, ALREADY!?
KAZUMA... I'M SO HAPPY WITH THE LIFE I HAVE.
IF MY FAME AS AN ADVENTURER GROWS, ONE DAY THE DEMON KING'S ARMY MIGHT NOTICE ME...
...AND THEN THEY'LL DRAG ME AWAY TO MEET A FATE WORSE THAN DEATH—MANACLED, PATHETIC...
MFF...!
YOU KNOW, I THINK MARRIAGE MIGHT BE GOOD FOR YOU.
N-NO! STOP!

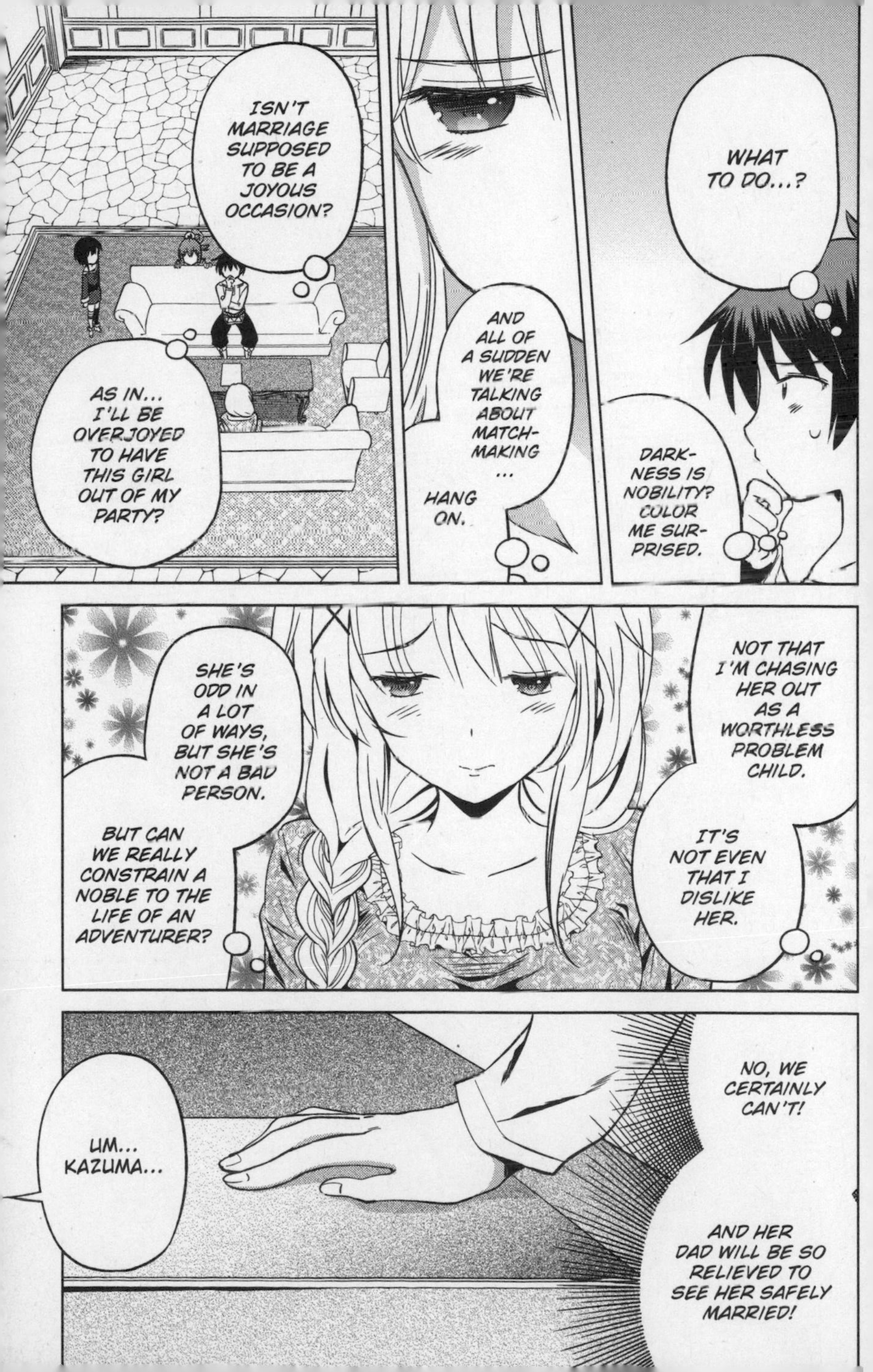
WHAT TO DO...?
DARKNESS IS NOBILITY? COLOR ME SURPRISED.
AND ALL OF A SUDDEN WE'RE TALKING ABOUT MATCHMAKING...
HANG ON.
ISN'T MARRIAGE SUPPOSED TO BE A JOYOUS OCCASION?
AS IN... I'LL BE OVERJOYED TO HAVE THIS GIRL OUT OF MY PARTY?
NOT THAT I'M CHASING HER OUT AS A WORTHLESS PROBLEM CHILD.
IT'S NOT EVEN THAT I DISLIKE HER.
SHE'S ODD IN A LOT OF WAYS, BUT SHE'S NOT A BAD PERSON.
BUT CAN WE REALLY CONSTRAIN A NOBLE TO THE LIFE OF AN ADVENTURER?
NO, WE CERTAINLY CAN'T!
AND HER DAD WILL BE SO RELIEVED TO SEE HER SAFELY MARRIED!
UM... KAZUMA...

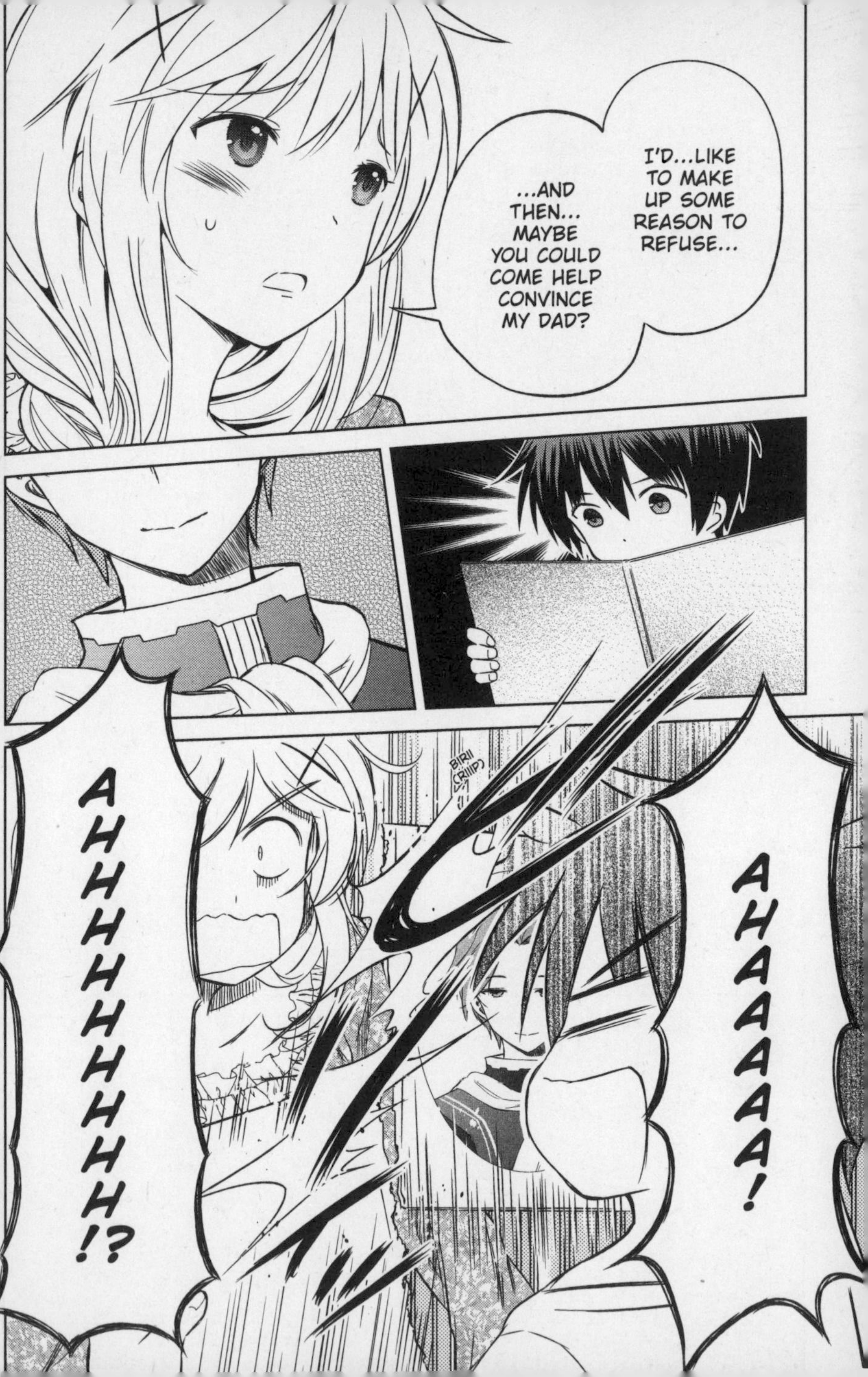
I'D...LIKE TO MAKE UP SOME REASON TO REFUSE...
...AND THEN... MAYBE YOU COULD COME HELP CONVINCE MY DAD?
AHAAAAAA!
BIRII (RIIIP)
AHHHHHHHHHH!?

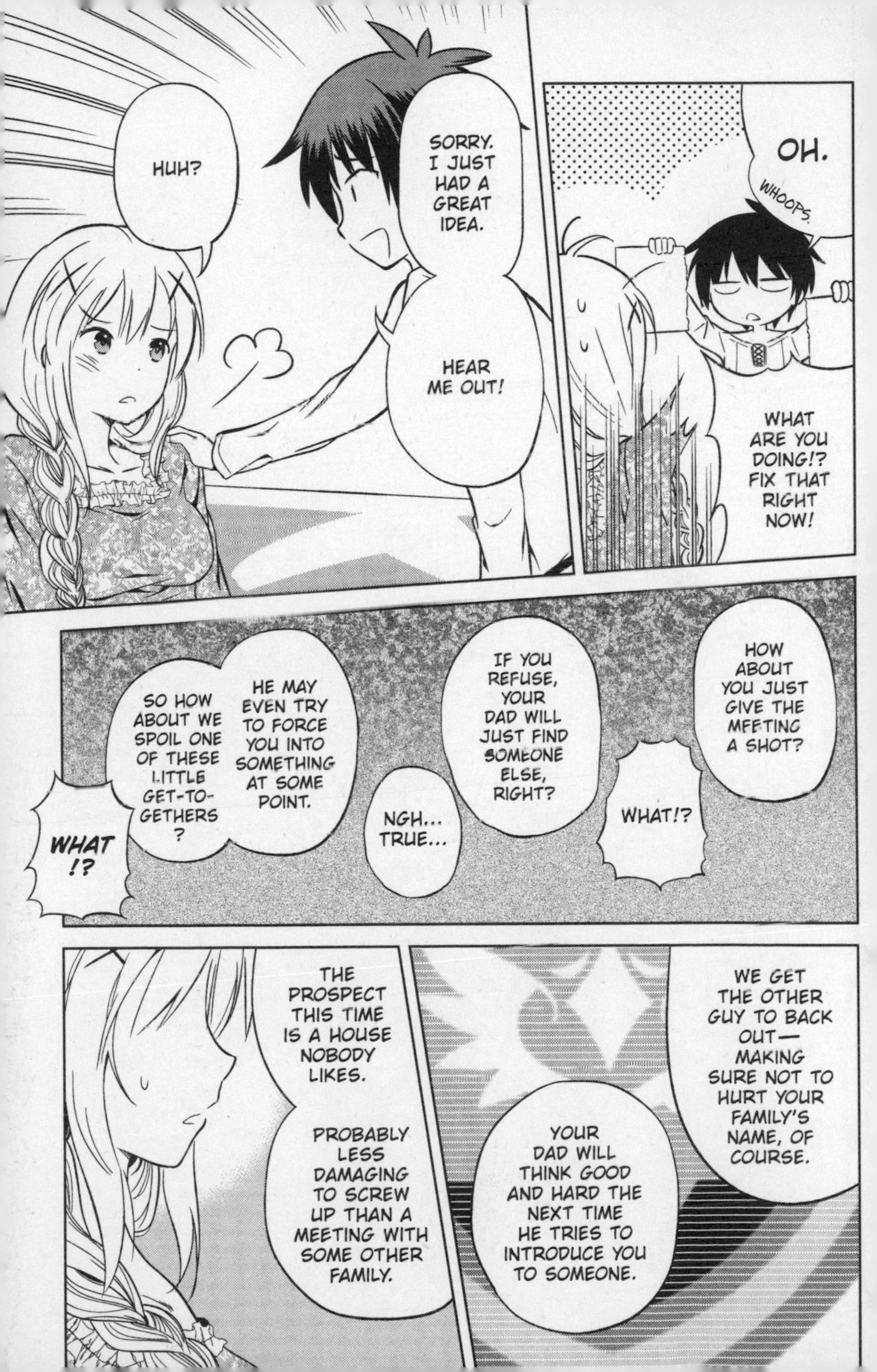
OH.
WHOOPS.
WHAT ARE YOU DOING!? FIX THAT RIGHT NOW!
SORRY. I JUST HAD A GREAT IDEA.
HUH?
HEAR ME OUT!
HOW ABOUT YOU JUST GIVE THE MEETING A SHOT?
WHAT!?
IF YOU REFUSE, YOUR DAD WILL JUST FIND SOMEONE ELSE, RIGHT?
NGH... TRUE...
HE MAY EVEN TRY TO FORCE YOU INTO SOMETHING AT SOME POINT.
SO HOW ABOUT WE SPOIL ONE OF THESE LITTLE GET-TO-GETHERS?
WHAT!?
WE GET THE OTHER GUY TO BACK OUT— MAKING SURE NOT TO HURT YOUR FAMILY'S NAME, OF COURSE.
YOUR DAD WILL THINK GOOD AND HARD THE NEXT TIME HE TRIES TO INTRODUCE YOU TO SOMEONE.
THE PROSPECT THIS TIME IS A HOUSE NOBODY LIKES.
PROBABLY LESS DAMAGING TO SCREW UP THAN A MEETING WITH SOME OTHER FAMILY.

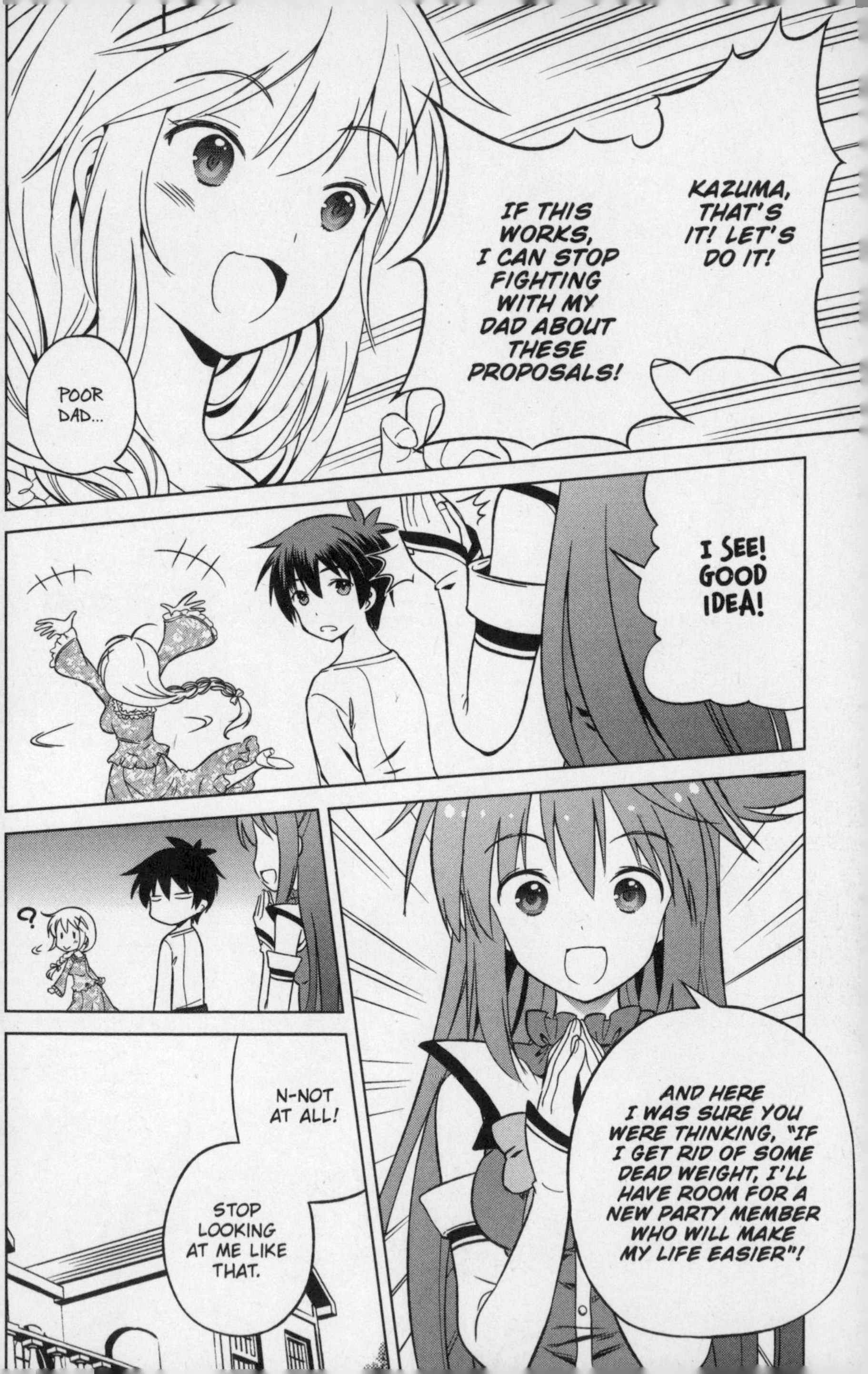
KAZUMA, THAT'S IT! LET'S DO IT!
IF THIS WORKS, I CAN STOP FIGHTING WITH MY DAD ABOUT THESE PROPOSALS!
POOR DAD...
I SEE! GOOD IDEA!
AND HERE I WAS SURE YOU WERE THINKING, "IF I GET RID OF SOME DEAD WEIGHT, I'LL HAVE ROOM FOR A NEW PARTY MEMBER WHO WILL MAKE MY LIFE EASIER"!
N-NOT AT ALL!
STOP LOOKING AT ME LIKE THAT.

CHAPTER 27 MAY THERE BE A GOOD MATCH FOR THIS NOBLE DAUGHTER! ①

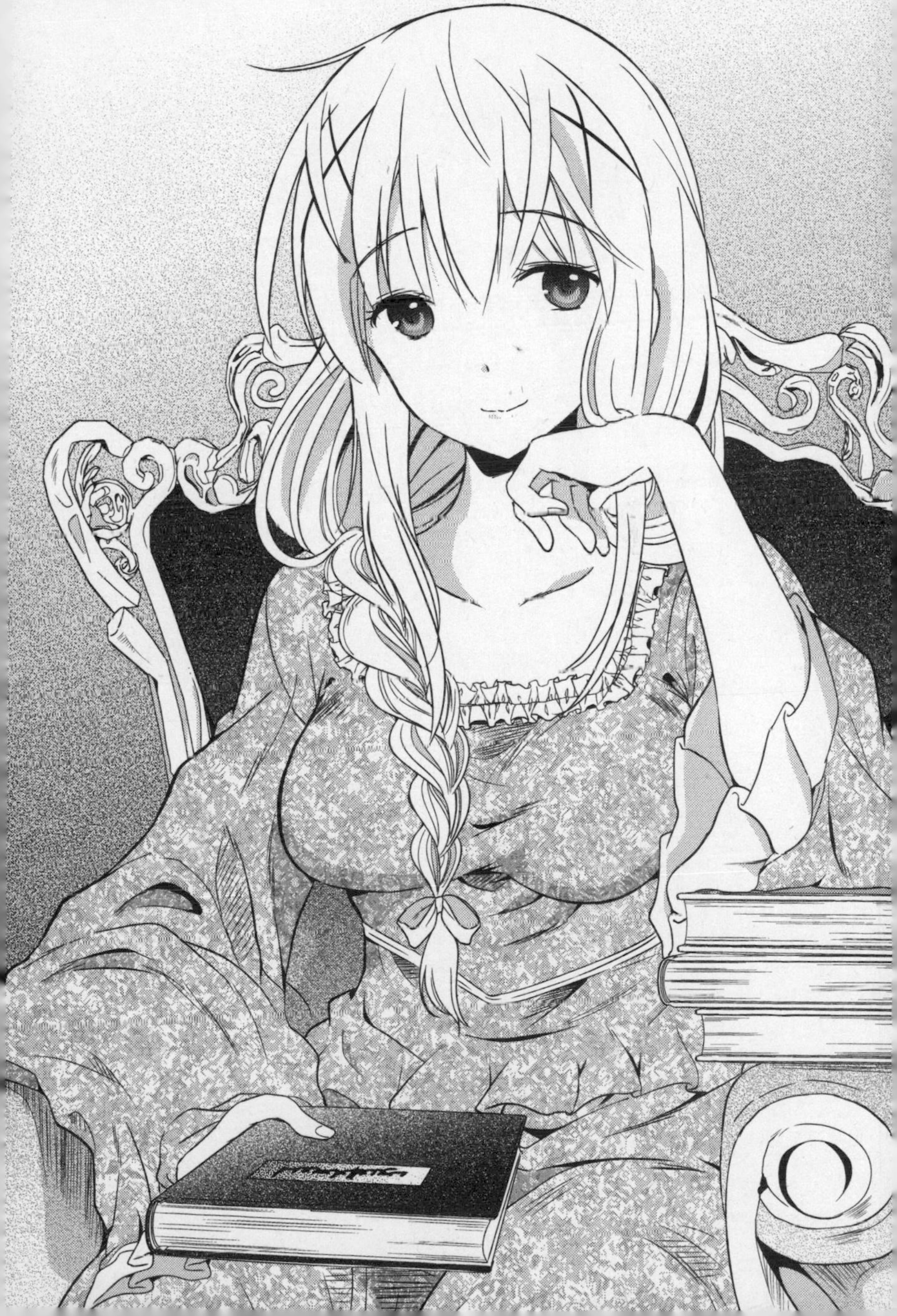

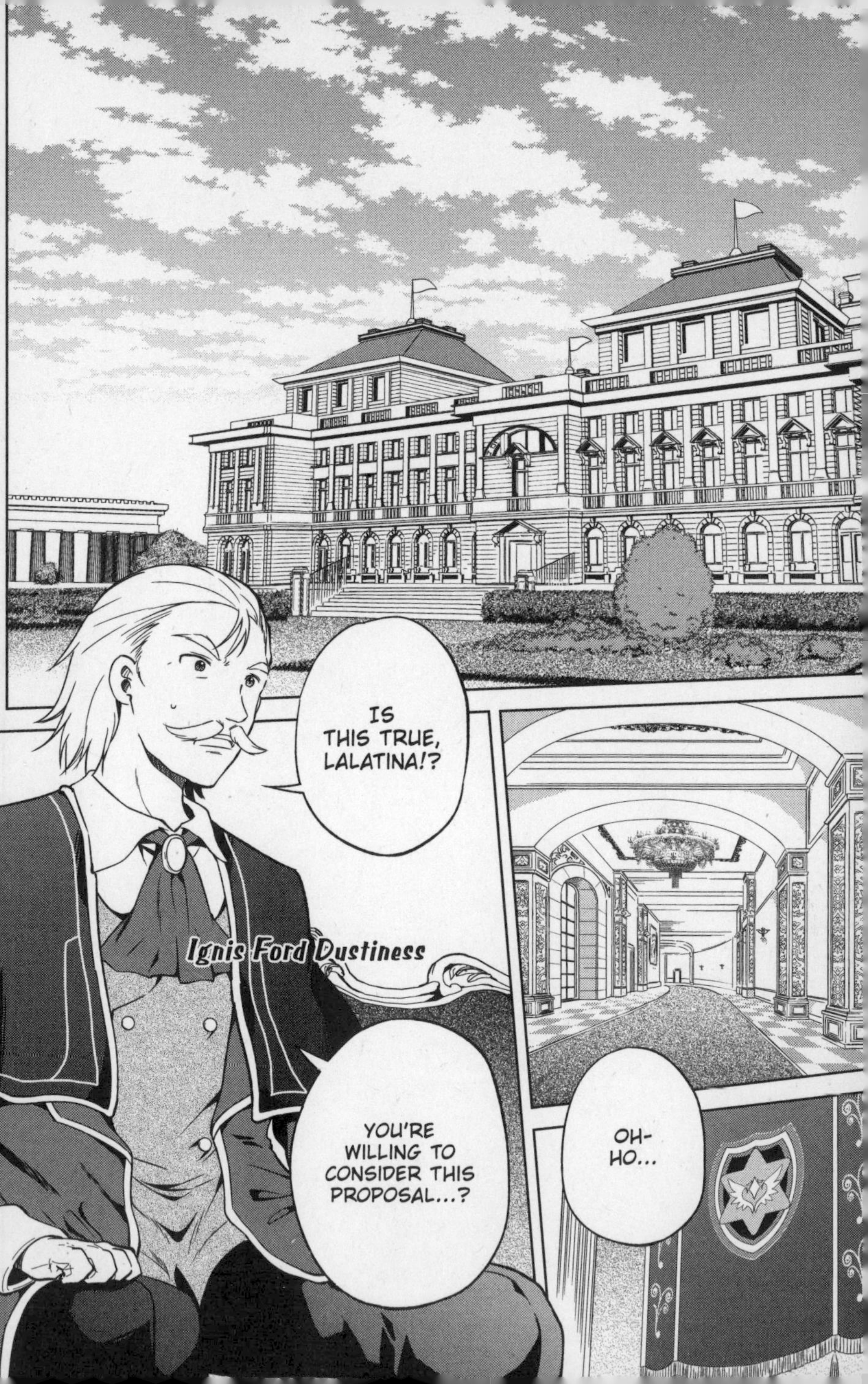
OH-HO...
IS THIS TRUE, LALATINA!?
Ignis Ford Dustiness
YOU'RE WILLING TO CONSIDER THIS PROPOSAL...?

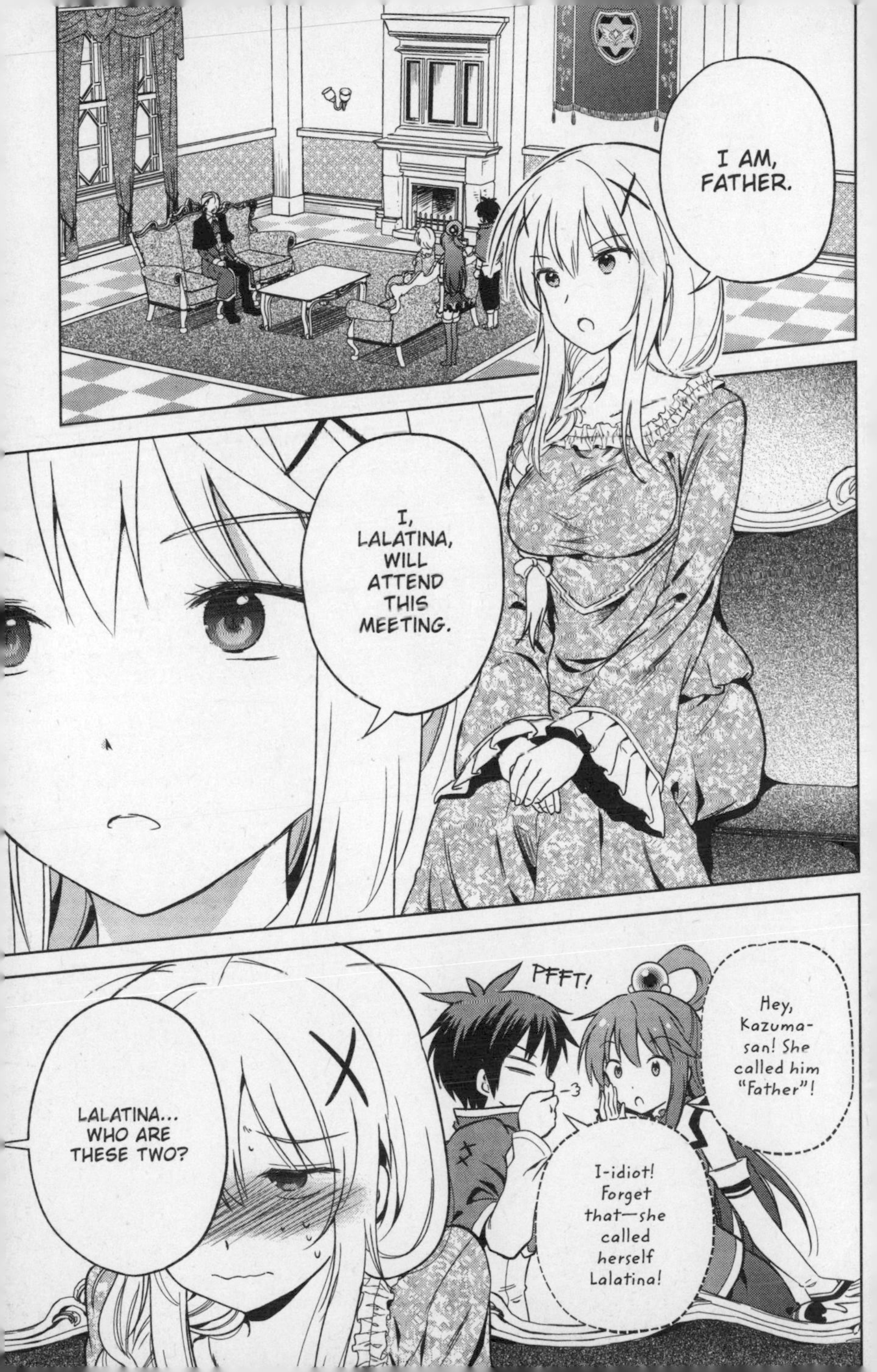
I AM, FATHER.
I, LALATINA, WILL ATTEND THIS MEETING.
Hey, Kazuma-san! She called him "Father"!
PFFT!
I-idiot! Forget that—she called herself Lalatina!
LALATINA... WHO ARE THESE TWO?

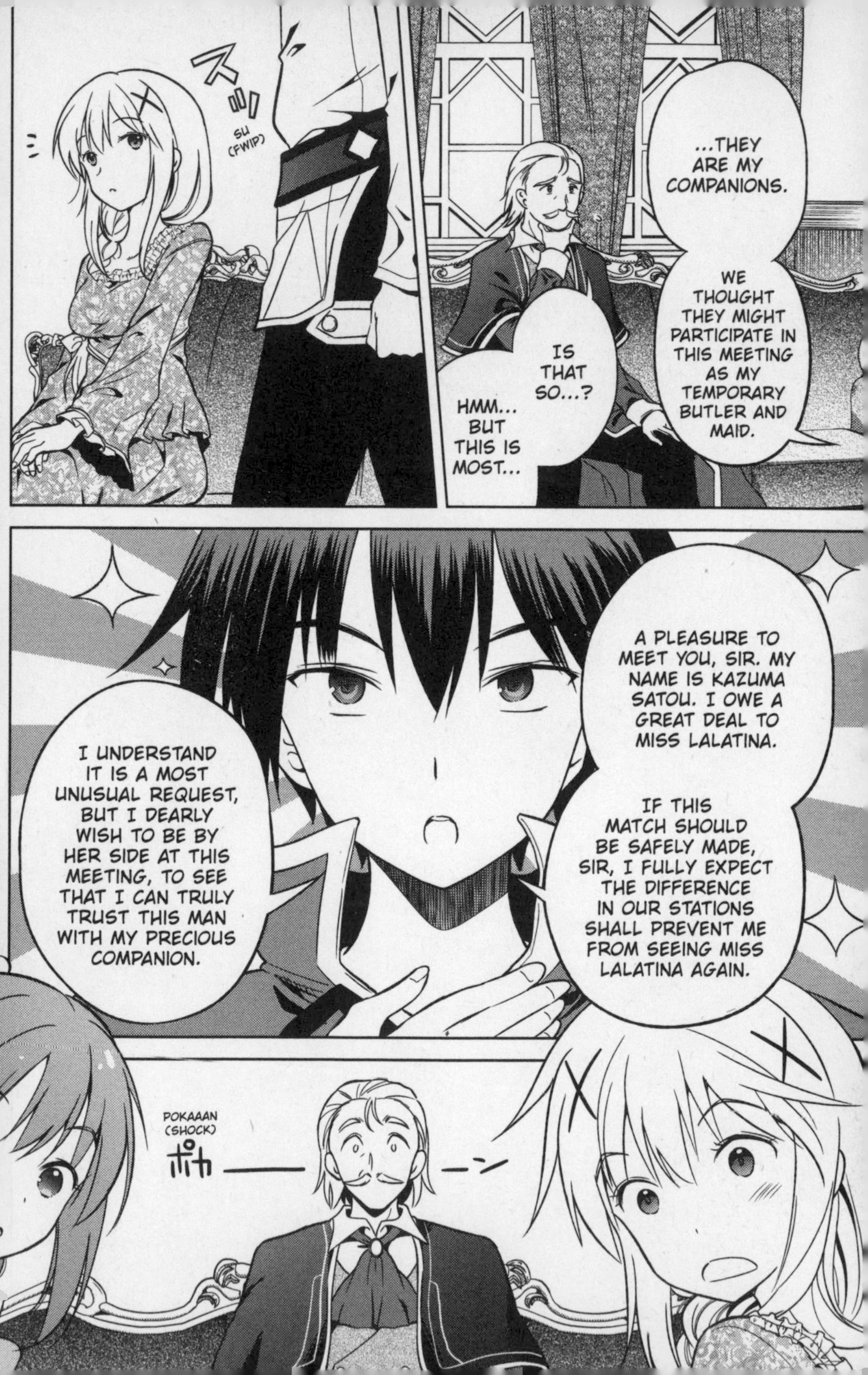
...THEY ARE MY COMPANIONS.
WE THOUGHT THEY MIGHT PARTICIPATE IN THIS MEETING AS MY TEMPORARY BUTLER AND MAID.
IS THAT SO...?
HMM... BUT THIS IS MOST...
SU (FWIP)
A PLEASURE TO MEET YOU, SIR. MY NAME IS KAZUMA SATOU. I OWE A GREAT DEAL TO MISS LALATINA.
IF THIS MATCH SHOULD BE SAFELY MADE, SIR, I FULLY EXPECT THE DIFFERENCE IN OUR STATIONS SHALL PREVENT ME FROM SEEING MISS LALATINA AGAIN.
I UNDERSTAND IT IS A MOST UNUSUAL REQUEST, BUT I DEARLY WISH TO BE BY HER SIDE AT THIS MEETING, TO SEE THAT I CAN TRULY TRUST THIS MAN WITH MY PRECIOUS COMPANION.
POKAAAN (SHOCK)
ポカ———ン

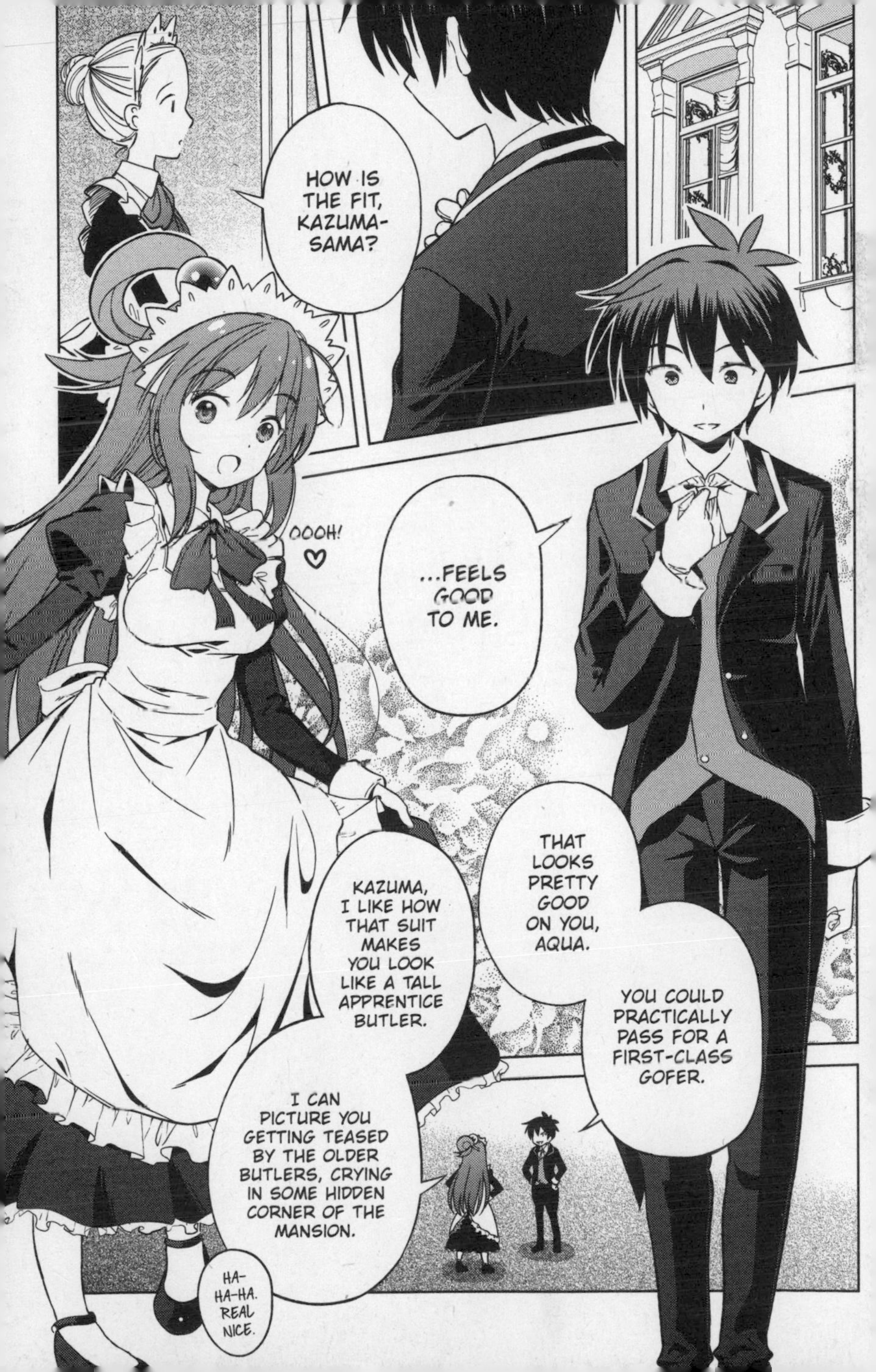
HOW IS THE FIT, KAZUMA-SAMA?
...FEELS GOOD TO ME.
OOOH! ♡
THAT LOOKS PRETTY GOOD ON YOU, AQUA.
KAZUMA, I LIKE HOW THAT SUIT MAKES YOU LOOK LIKE A TALL APPRENTICE BUTLER.
YOU COULD PRACTICALLY PASS FOR A FIRST-CLASS GOFER.
I CAN PICTURE YOU GETTING TEASED BY THE OLDER BUTLERS, CRYING IN SOME HIDDEN CORNER OF THE MANSION.
HA-HA-HA. REAL NICE.

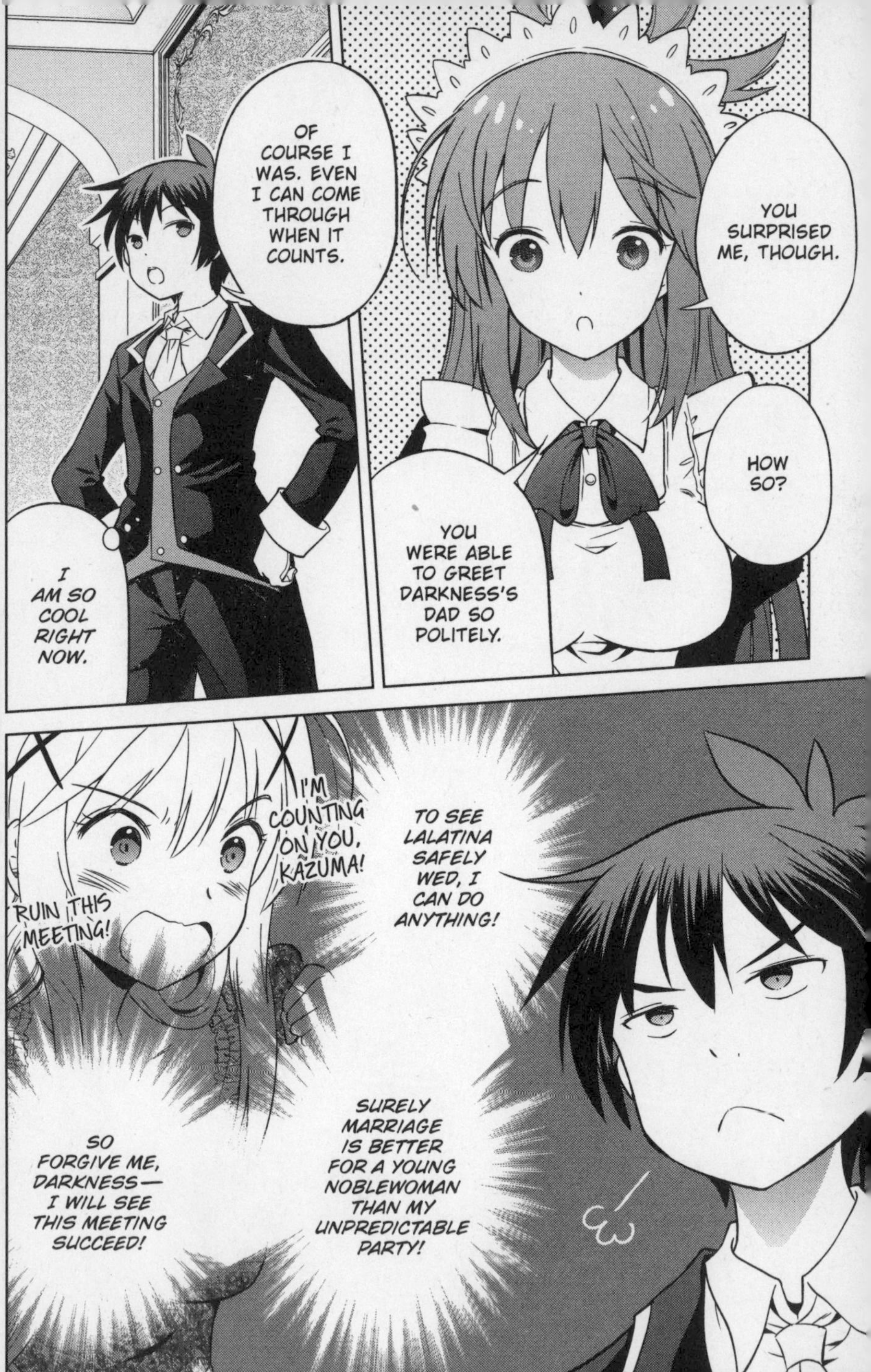
YOU SURPRISED ME, THOUGH.
HOW SO?
YOU WERE ABLE TO GREET DARKNESS'S DAD SO POLITELY.
OF COURSE I WAS. EVEN I CAN COME THROUGH WHEN IT COUNTS.
I AM SO COOL RIGHT NOW.
TO SEE LALATINA SAFELY WED, I CAN DO ANYTHING!
I'M COUNTING ON YOU, KAZUMA!
RUIN THIS MEETING!
SURELY MARRIAGE IS BETTER FOR A YOUNG NOBLEWOMAN THAN MY UNPREDICTABLE PARTY!
SO FORGIVE ME, DARKNESS— I WILL SEE THIS MEETING SUCCEED!

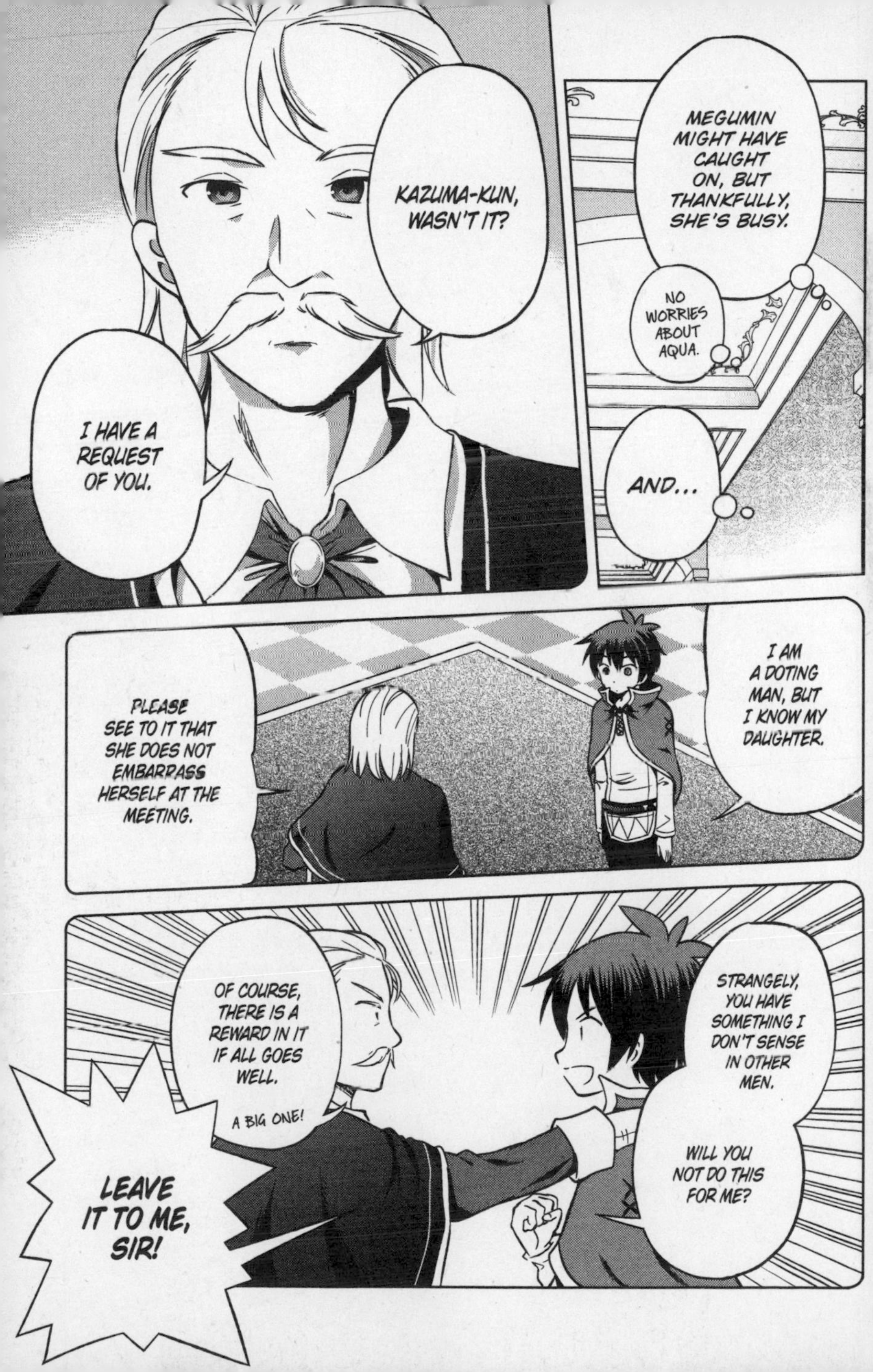
MEGUMIN MIGHT HAVE CAUGHT ON, BUT THANKFULLY, SHE'S BUSY.
NO WORRIES ABOUT AQUA.
AND...
KAZUMA-KUN, WASN'T IT?
I HAVE A REQUEST OF YOU.
I AM A DOTING MAN, BUT I KNOW MY DAUGHTER.
PLEASE SEE TO IT THAT SHE DOES NOT EMBARRASS HERSELF AT THE MEETING.
STRANGELY, YOU HAVE SOMETHING I DON'T SENSE IN OTHER MEN.
WILL YOU NOT DO THIS FOR ME?
OF COURSE, THERE IS A REWARD IN IT IF ALL GOES WELL.
A BIG ONE!
LEAVE IT TO ME, SIR!

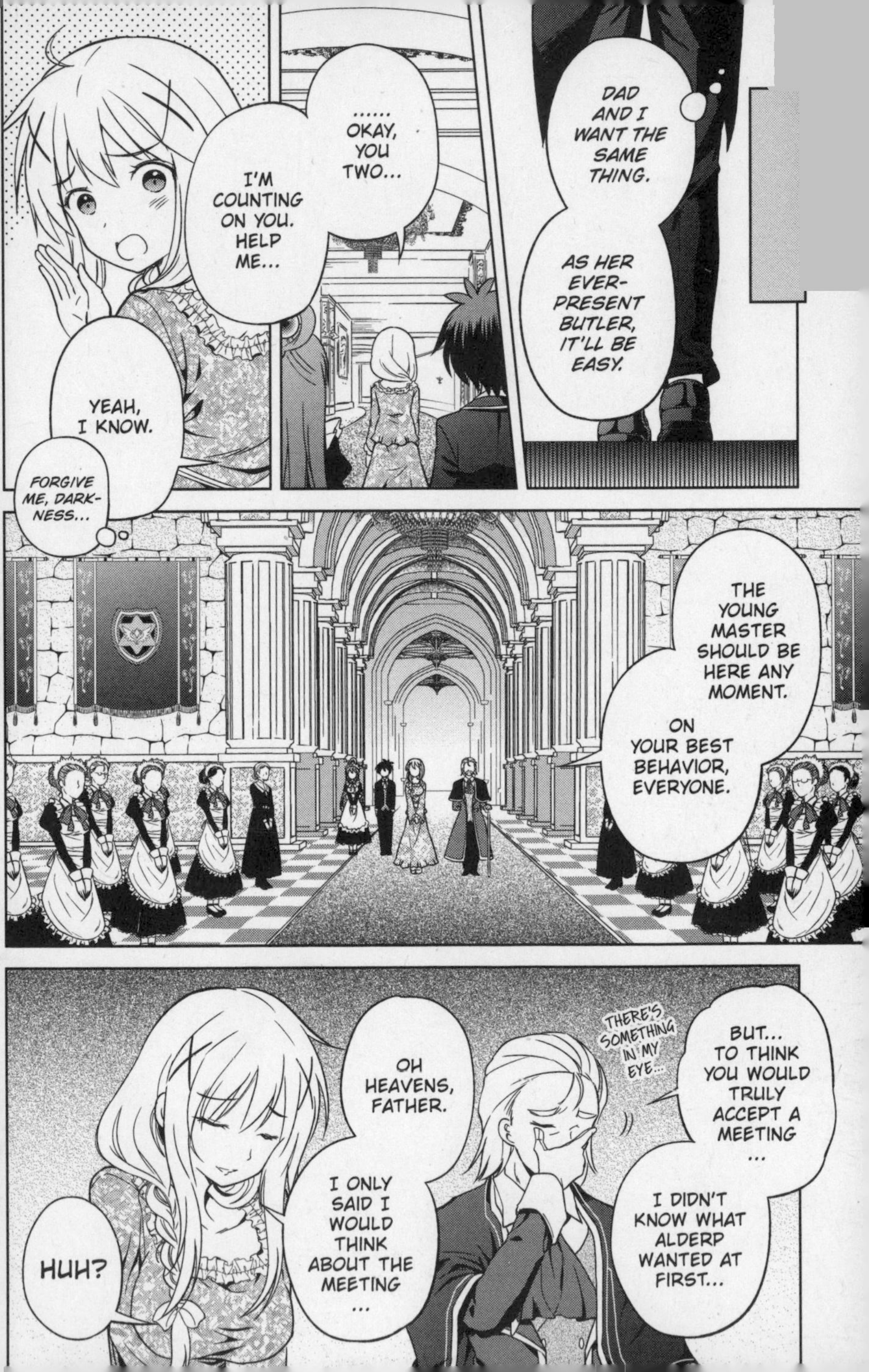
DAD AND I WANT THE SAME THING.
AS HER EVER-PRESENT BUTLER, IT'LL BE EASY.
...... OKAY, YOU TWO...
I'M COUNTING ON YOU. HELP ME...
YEAH, I KNOW.
FORGIVE ME, DARKNESS...
THE YOUNG MASTER SHOULD BE HERE ANY MOMENT.
ON YOUR BEST BEHAVIOR, EVERYONE.
BUT... TO THINK YOU WOULD TRULY ACCEPT A MEETING ...
THERE'S SOMETHING IN MY EYE...
I DIDN'T KNOW WHAT ALDERP WANTED AT FIRST...
OH HEAVENS, FATHER.
I ONLY SAID I WOULD THINK ABOUT THE MEETING ...
HUH?

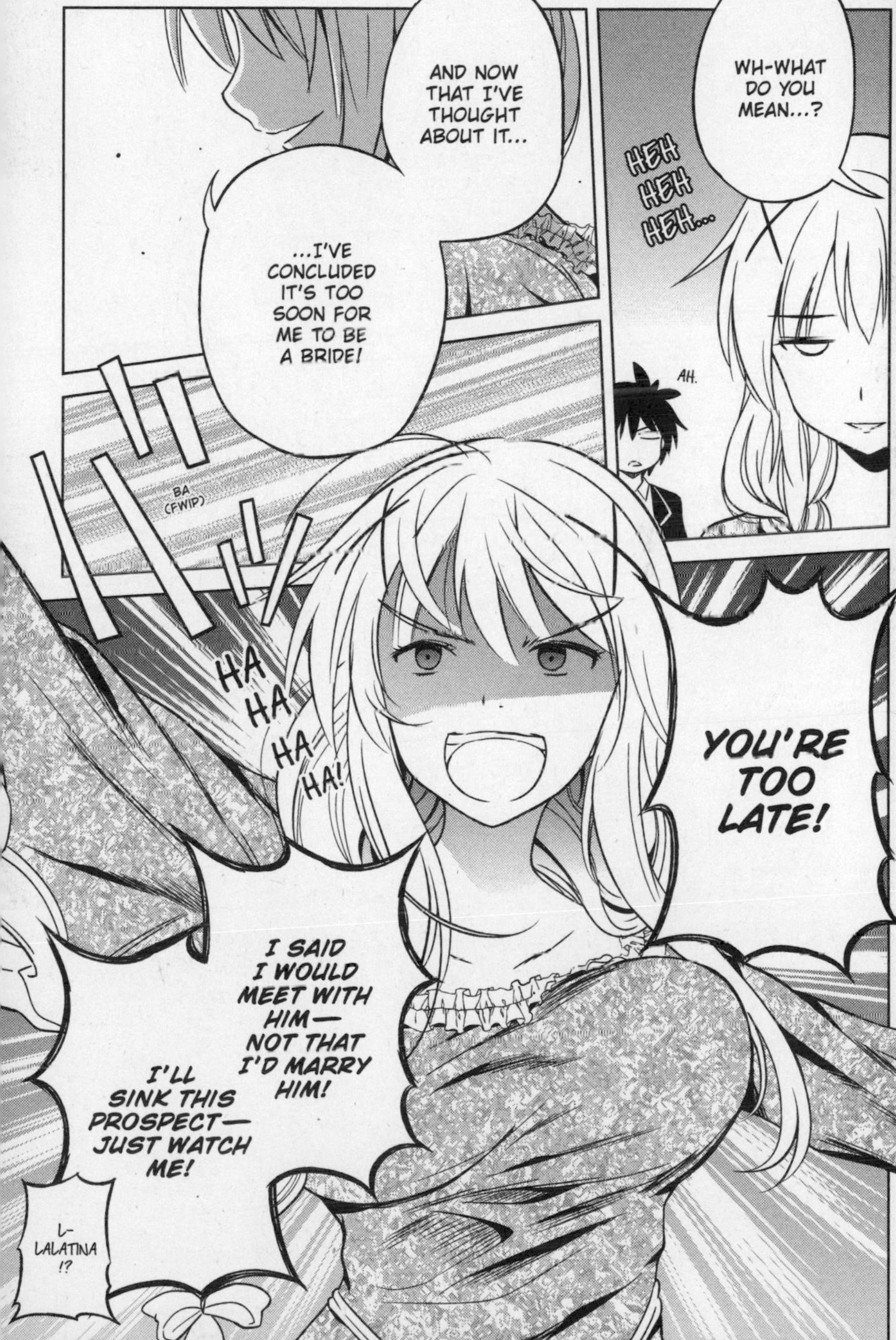
WH-WHAT DO YOU MEAN...?
HEH HEH HEH...
AH.
AND NOW THAT I'VE THOUGHT ABOUT IT...
...I'VE CONCLUDED IT'S TOO SOON FOR ME TO BE A BRIDE!
BA (FWIP)
YOU'RE TOO LATE!
HA HA HA HA!
I SAID I WOULD MEET WITH HIM—NOT THAT I'D MARRY HIM!
I'LL SINK THIS PROSPECT—JUST WATCH ME!
L-LALATINA!?

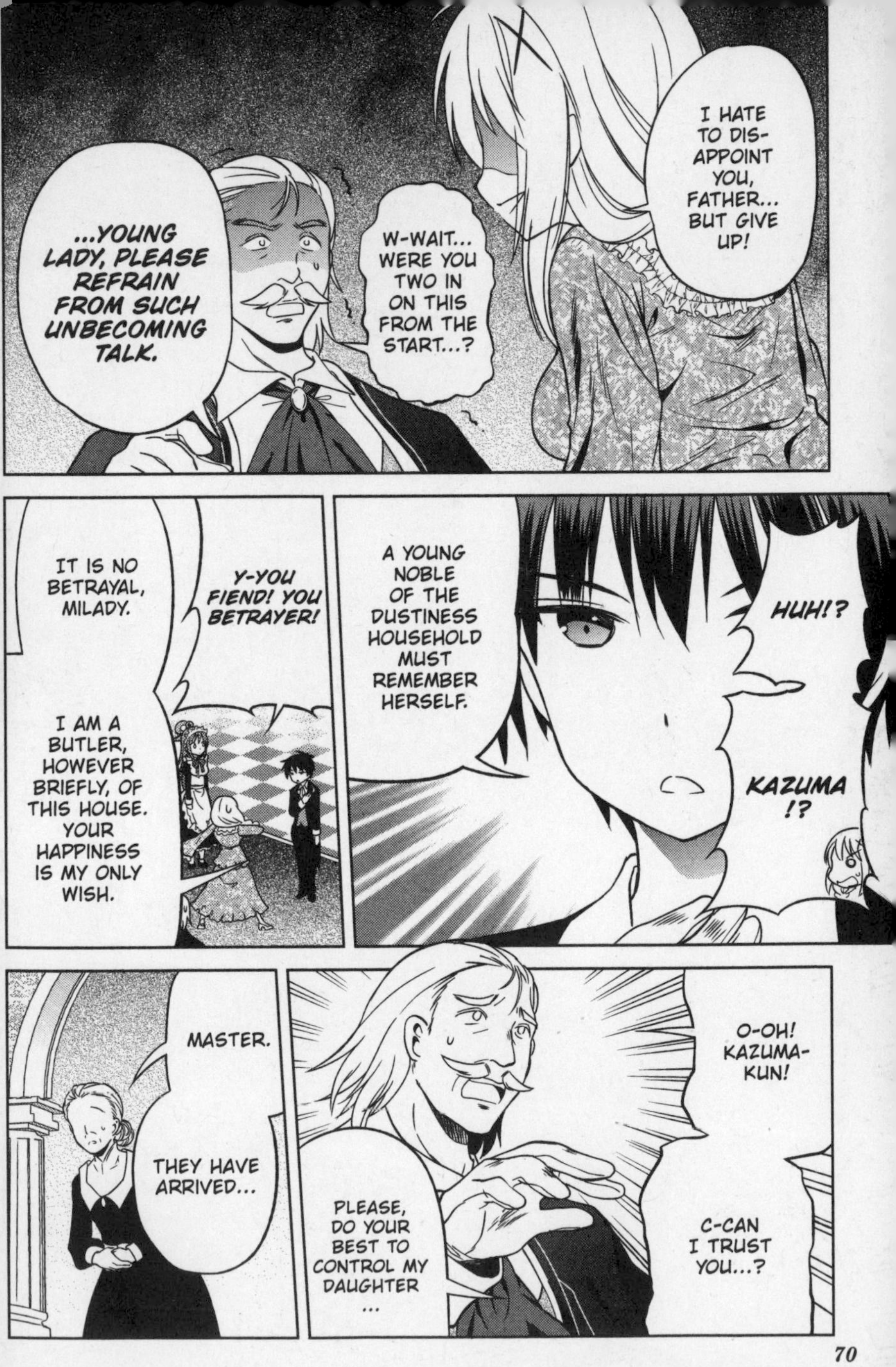
I HATE TO DIS-APPOINT YOU, FATHER... BUT GIVE UP!
W-WAIT... WERE YOU TWO IN ON THIS FROM THE START...?
...YOUNG LADY, PLEASE REFRAIN FROM SUCH UNBECOMING TALK.
HUH!?
A YOUNG NOBLE OF THE DUSTINESS HOUSEHOLD MUST REMEMBER HERSELF.
KAZUMA!?
Y-YOU FIEND! YOU BETRAYER!
IT IS NO BETRAYAL, MILADY.
I AM A BUTLER, HOWEVER BRIEFLY, OF THIS HOUSE. YOUR HAPPINESS IS MY ONLY WISH.
O-OH! KAZUMA-KUN!
C-CAN I TRUST YOU...?
PLEASE, DO YOUR BEST TO CONTROL MY DAUGHTER ...
MASTER.
THEY HAVE ARRIVED...

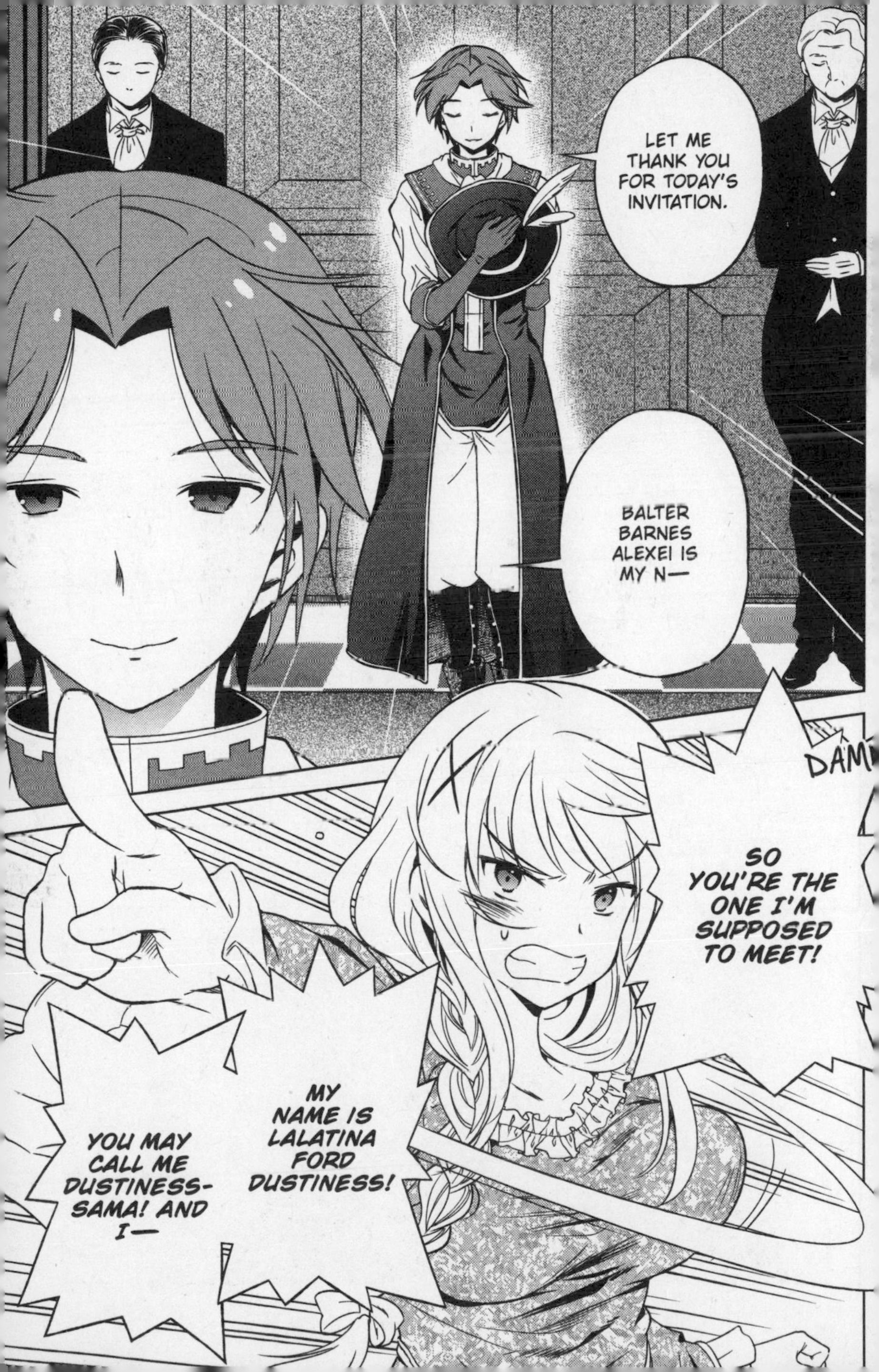
LET ME THANK YOU FOR TODAY'S INVITATION.
BALTER BARNES ALEXEI IS MY N—
DAM
SO YOU'RE THE ONE I'M SUPPOSED TO MEET!
MY NAME IS LALATINA FORD DUSTINESS!
YOU MAY CALL ME DUSTINESS-SAMA! AND I—

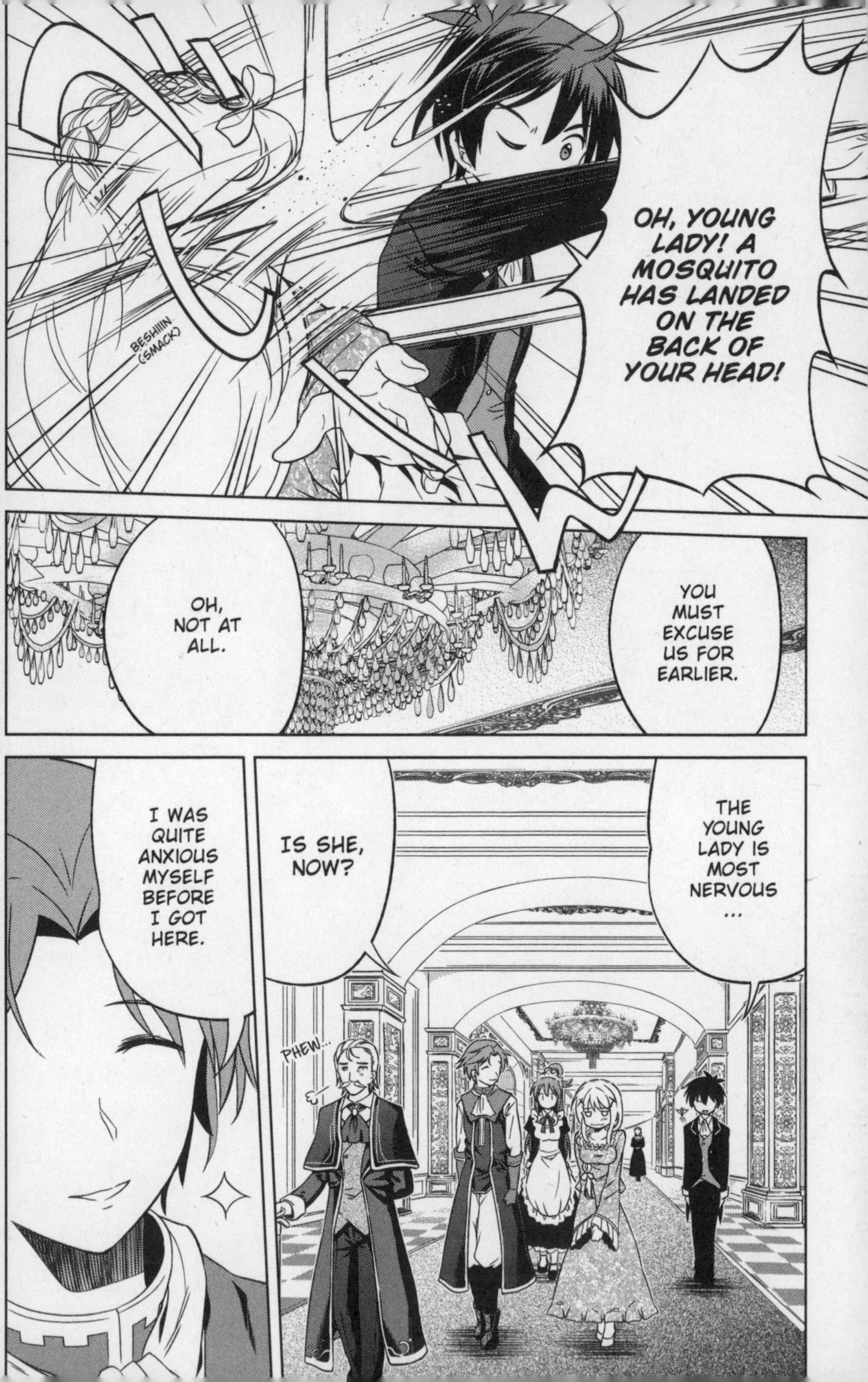
OH, YOUNG LADY! A MOSQUITO HAS LANDED ON THE BACK OF YOUR HEAD!
BESHIIN (SMACK)
YOU MUST EXCUSE US FOR EARLIER.
OH, NOT AT ALL.
THE YOUNG LADY IS MOST NERVOUS ...
IS SHE, NOW?
PHEW...
I WAS QUITE ANXIOUS MYSELF BEFORE I GOT HERE.

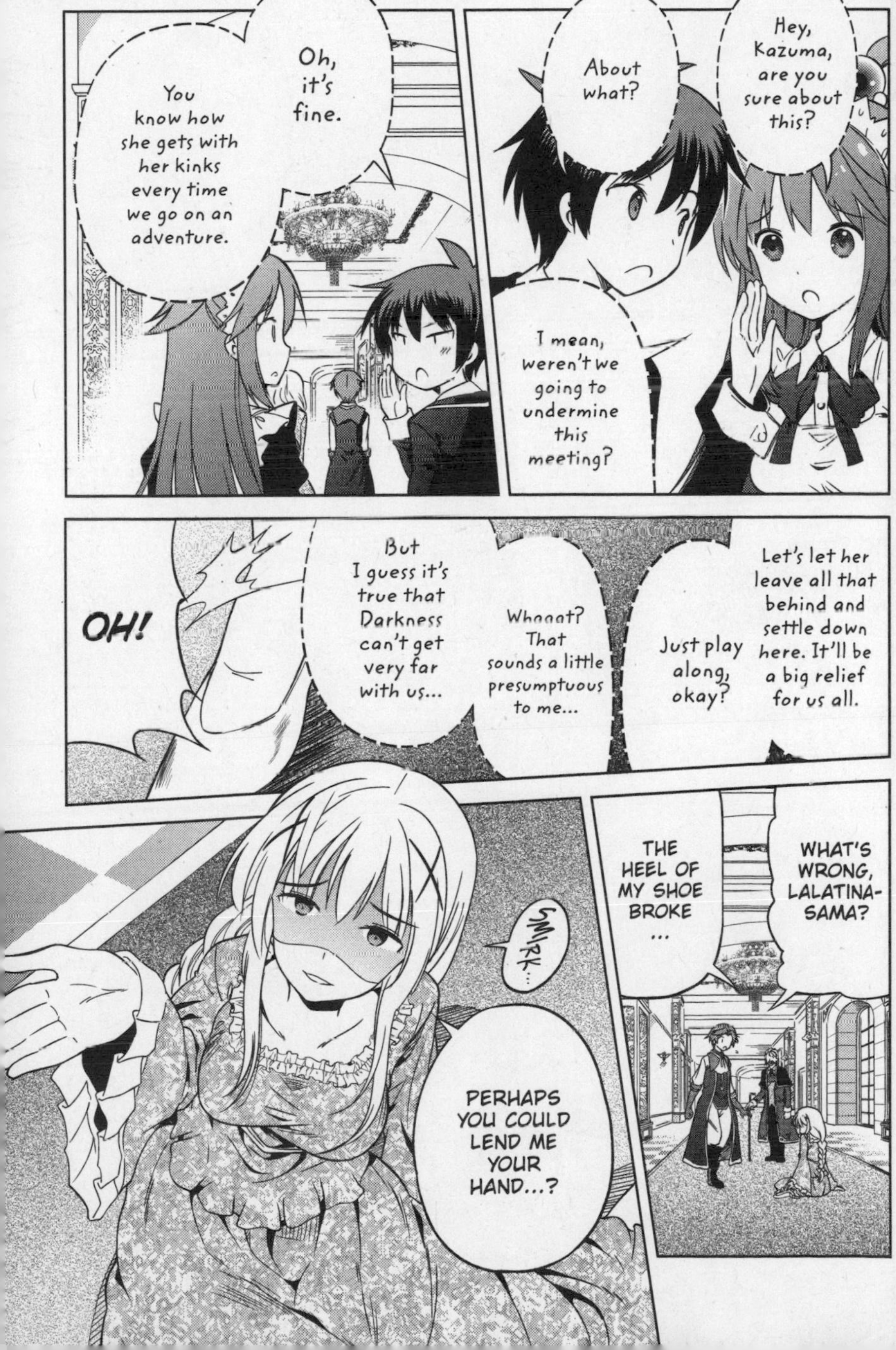
Hey, Kazuma, are you sure about this?
About what?
I mean, weren't we going to undermine this meeting?
Oh, it's fine.
You know how she gets with her kinks every time we go on an adventure.
Let's let her leave all that behind and settle down here. It'll be a big relief for us all.
Just play along, okay?
Whaaat? That sounds a little presumptuous to me...
But I guess it's true that Darkness can't get very far with us...
OH!
WHAT'S WRONG, LALATINA-SAMA?
THE HEEL OF MY SHOE BROKE ...
SMIRK...
PERHAPS YOU COULD LEND ME YOUR HAND...?

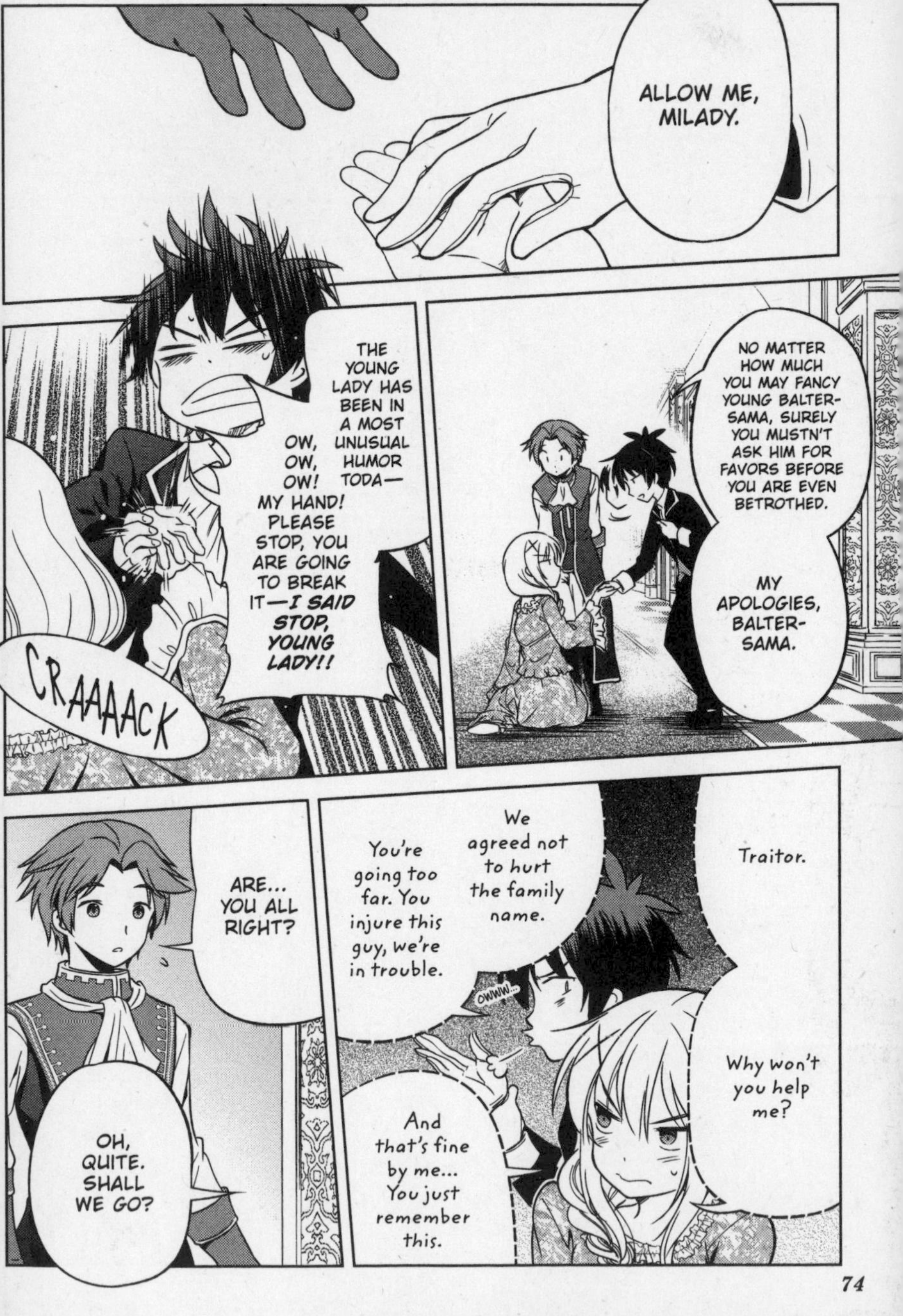
ALLOW ME, MILADY.
NO MATTER HOW MUCH YOU MAY FANCY YOUNG BALTER-SAMA, SURELY YOU MUSTN'T ASK HIM FOR FAVORS BEFORE YOU ARE EVEN BETROTHED.
MY APOLOGIES, BALTER-SAMA.
THE YOUNG LADY HAS BEEN IN A MOST UNUSUAL HUMOR TODA—
OW, OW, OW! MY HAND! PLEASE STOP, YOU ARE GOING TO BREAK IT—*I SAID STOP, YOUNG LADY!!*
CRAAAACK
Traitor.
We agreed not to hurt the family name.
You're going too far. You injure this guy, we're in trouble.
Why won't you help me?
OWWW...
And that's fine by me... You just remember this.
ARE... YOU ALL RIGHT?
OH, QUITE. SHALL WE GO?

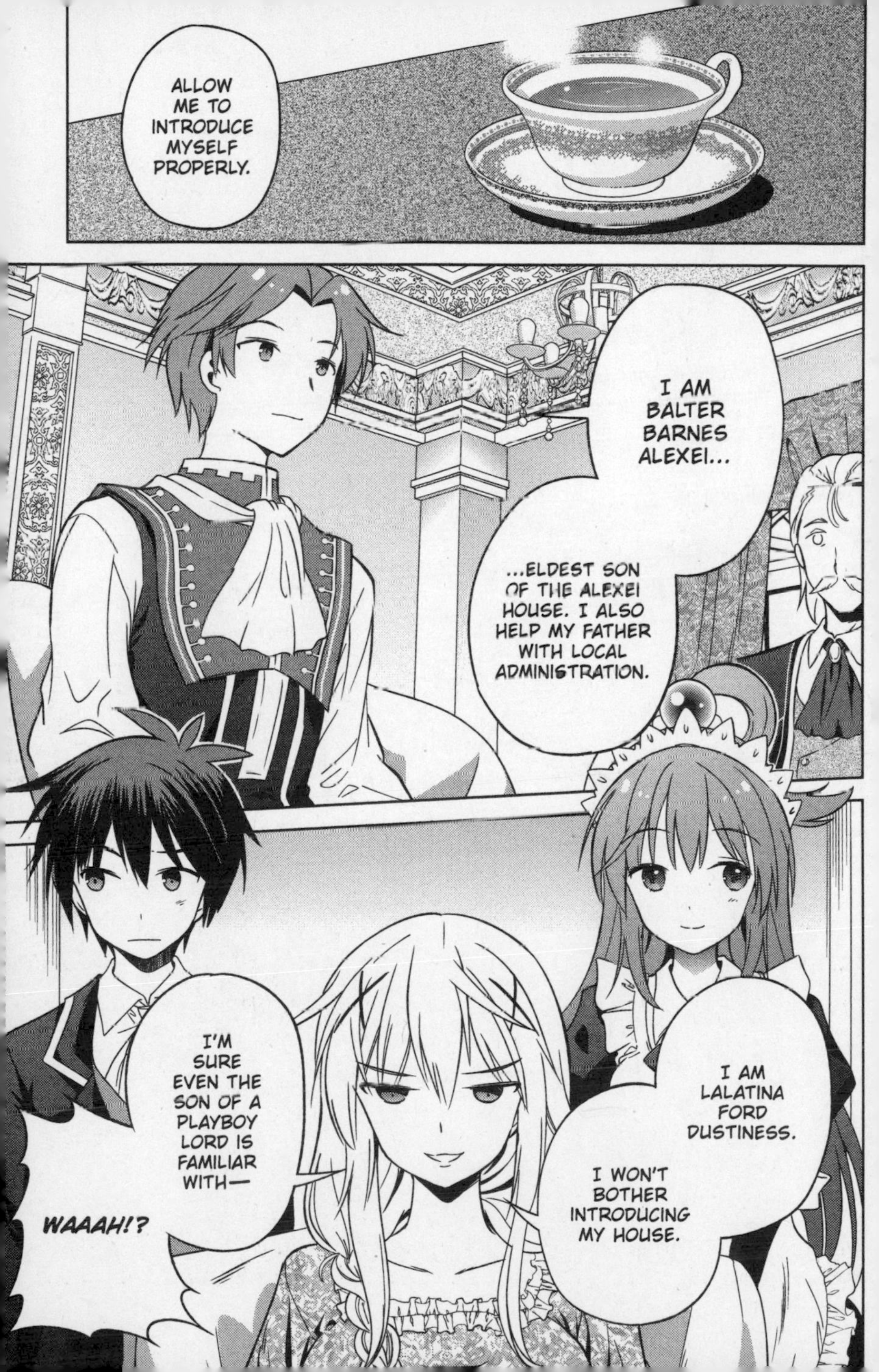
ALLOW ME TO INTRODUCE MYSELF PROPERLY.
I AM BALTER BARNES ALEXEI...
...ELDEST SON OF THE ALEXEI HOUSE. I ALSO HELP MY FATHER WITH LOCAL ADMINISTRATION.
I AM LALATINA FORD DUSTINESS.
I WON'T BOTHER INTRODUCING MY HOUSE.
I'M SURE EVEN THE SON OF A PLAYBOY LORD IS FAMILIAR WITH—
WAAAH!?

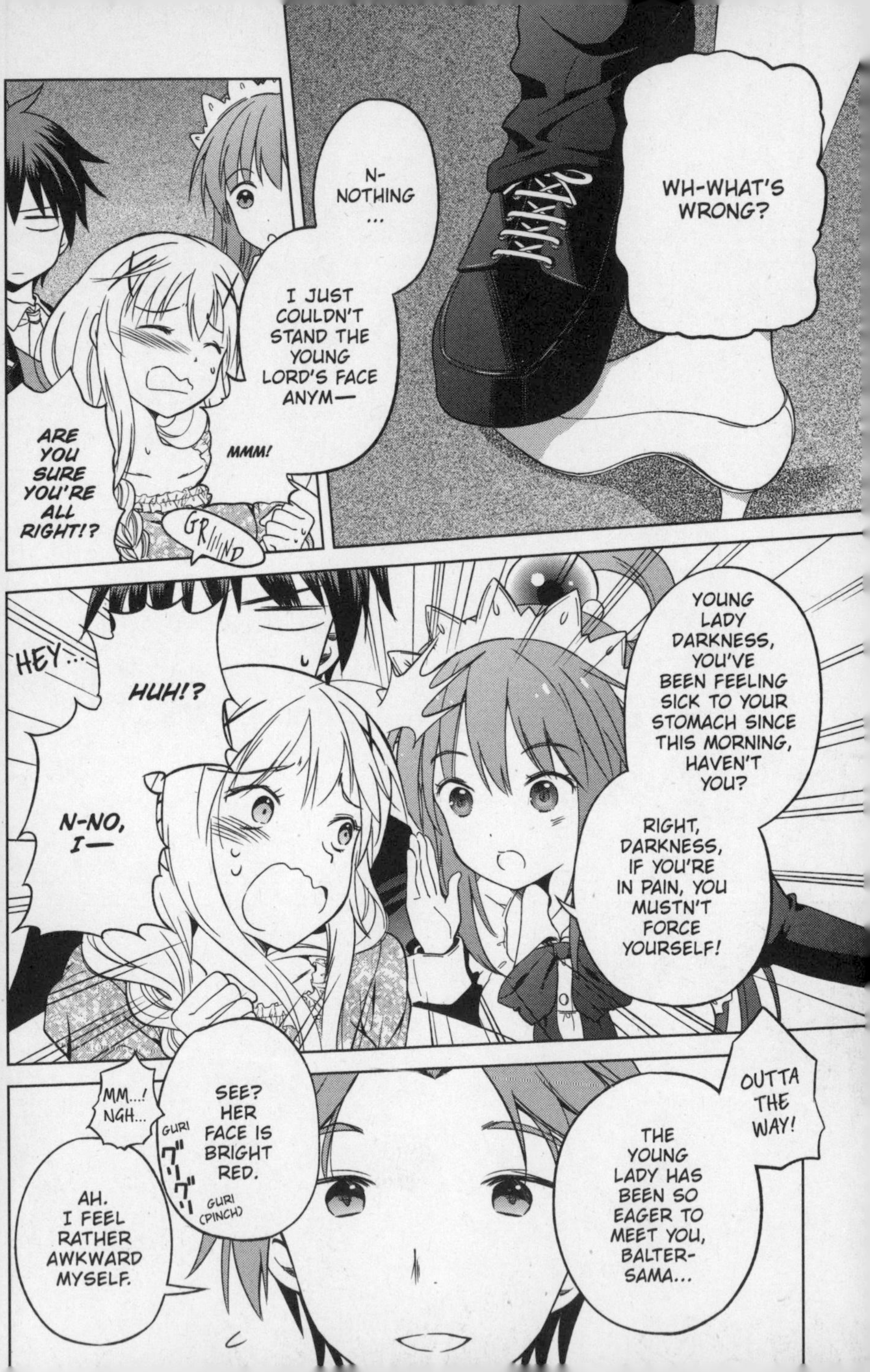
WH-WHAT'S WRONG?
N-NOTHING...
I JUST COULDN'T STAND THE YOUNG LORD'S FACE ANYM—
MMM!
GRIIIND
ARE YOU SURE YOU'RE ALL RIGHT!?
YOUNG LADY DARKNESS, YOU'VE BEEN FEELING SICK TO YOUR STOMACH SINCE THIS MORNING, HAVEN'T YOU?
RIGHT, DARKNESS, IF YOU'RE IN PAIN, YOU MUSTN'T FORCE YOURSELF!
HUH!?
HEY...
N-NO, I—
OUTTA THE WAY!
THE YOUNG LADY HAS BEEN SO EAGER TO MEET YOU, BALTER-SAMA...
SEE? HER FACE IS BRIGHT RED.
GURI
グリグリ
GURI (PINCH)
MM...! NGH...
AH. I FEEL RATHER AWKWARD MYSELF.

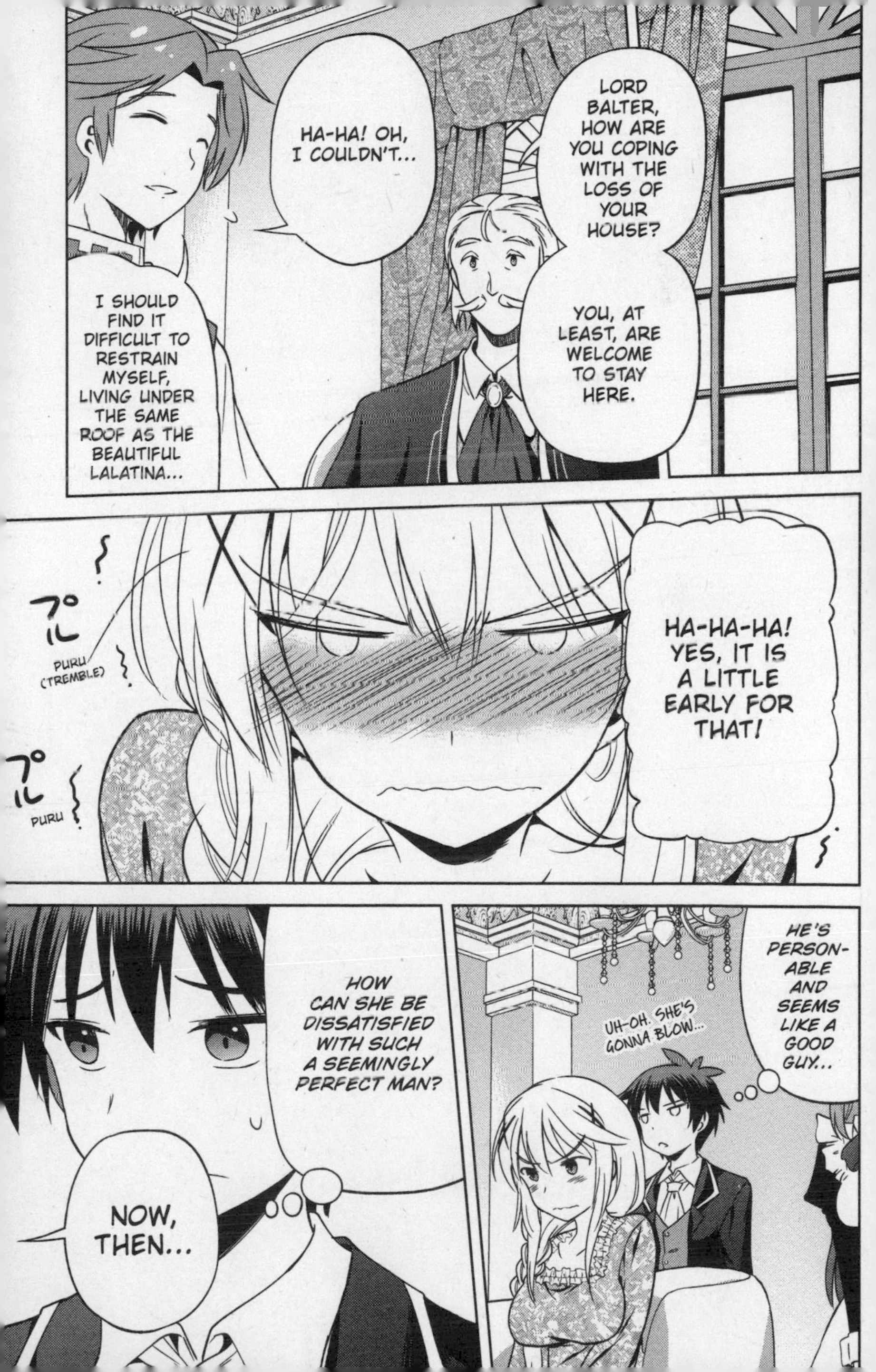
LORD BALTER, HOW ARE YOU COPING WITH THE LOSS OF YOUR HOUSE?
YOU, AT LEAST, ARE WELCOME TO STAY HERE.
HA-HA! OH, I COULDN'T...
I SHOULD FIND IT DIFFICULT TO RESTRAIN MYSELF, LIVING UNDER THE SAME ROOF AS THE BEAUTIFUL LALATINA...
HA-HA-HA! YES, IT IS A LITTLE EARLY FOR THAT!
プル
PURU (TREMBLE)
プル
PURU
HE'S PERSONABLE AND SEEMS LIKE A GOOD GUY...
UH-OH. SHE'S GONNA BLOW...
HOW CAN SHE BE DISSATISFIED WITH SUCH A SEEMINGLY PERFECT MAN?
NOW, THEN...

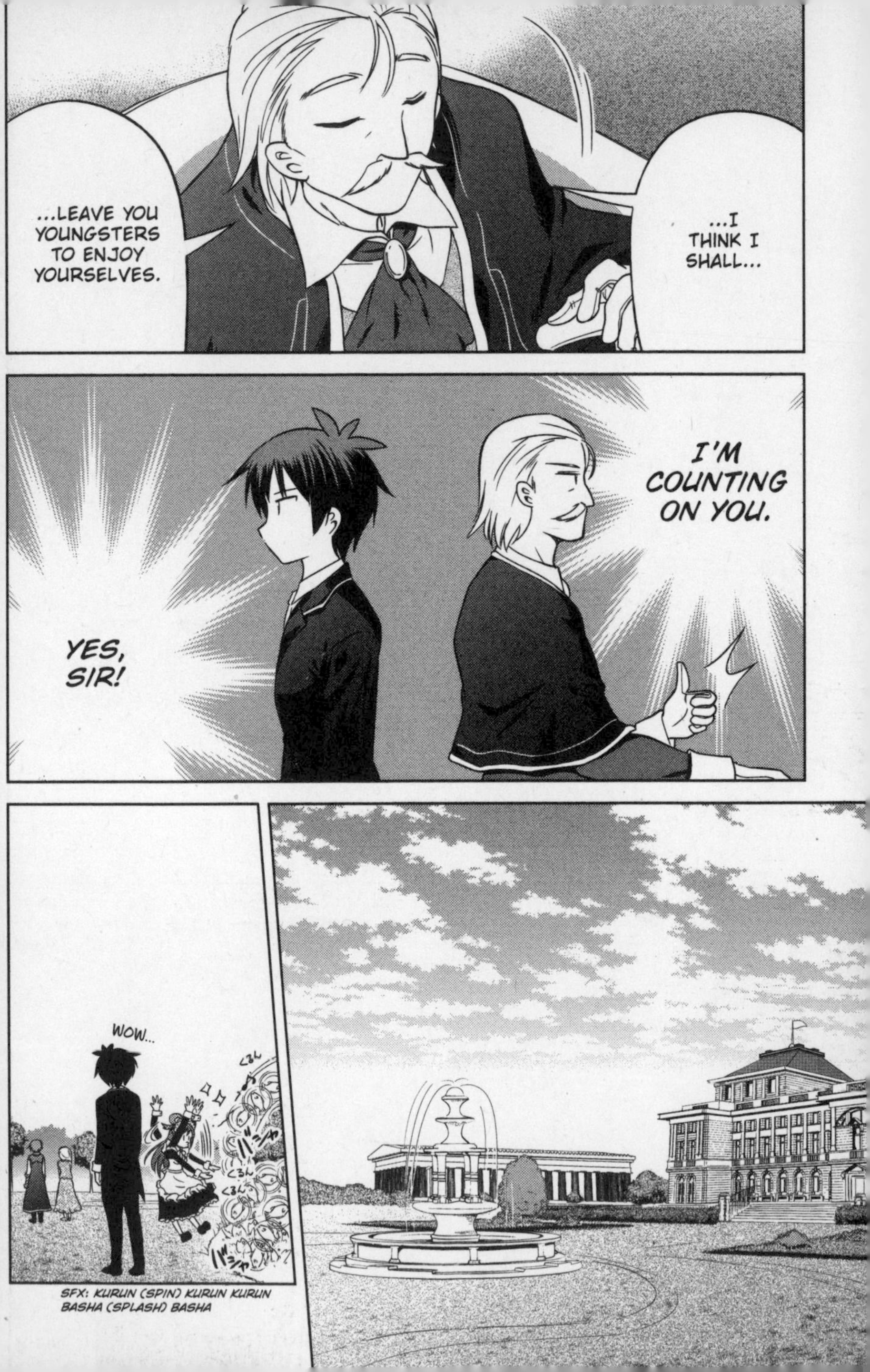
...I THINK I SHALL...
...LEAVE YOU YOUNGSTERS TO ENJOY YOURSELVES.
I'M COUNTING ON YOU.
YES, SIR!
WOW...
SFX: KURUN (SPIN) KURUN KURUN BASHA (SPLASH) BASHA

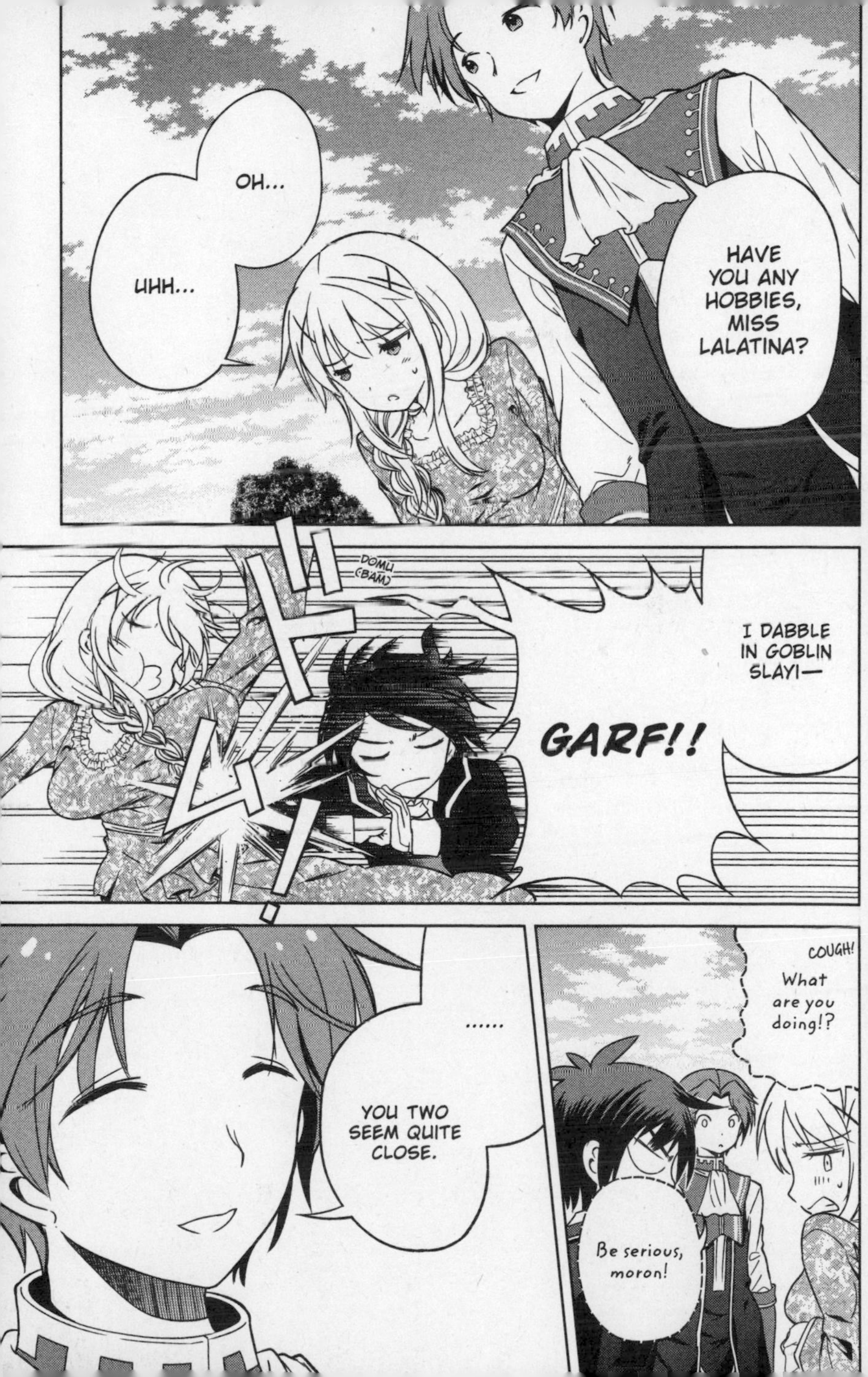
HAVE YOU ANY HOBBIES, MISS LALATINA?
OH...
UHH...
I DABBLE IN GOBLIN SLAYI—
GARF!!
DOMU (BAM)
COUGH!
What are you doing!?
Be serious, moron!
......
YOU TWO SEEM QUITE CLOSE.

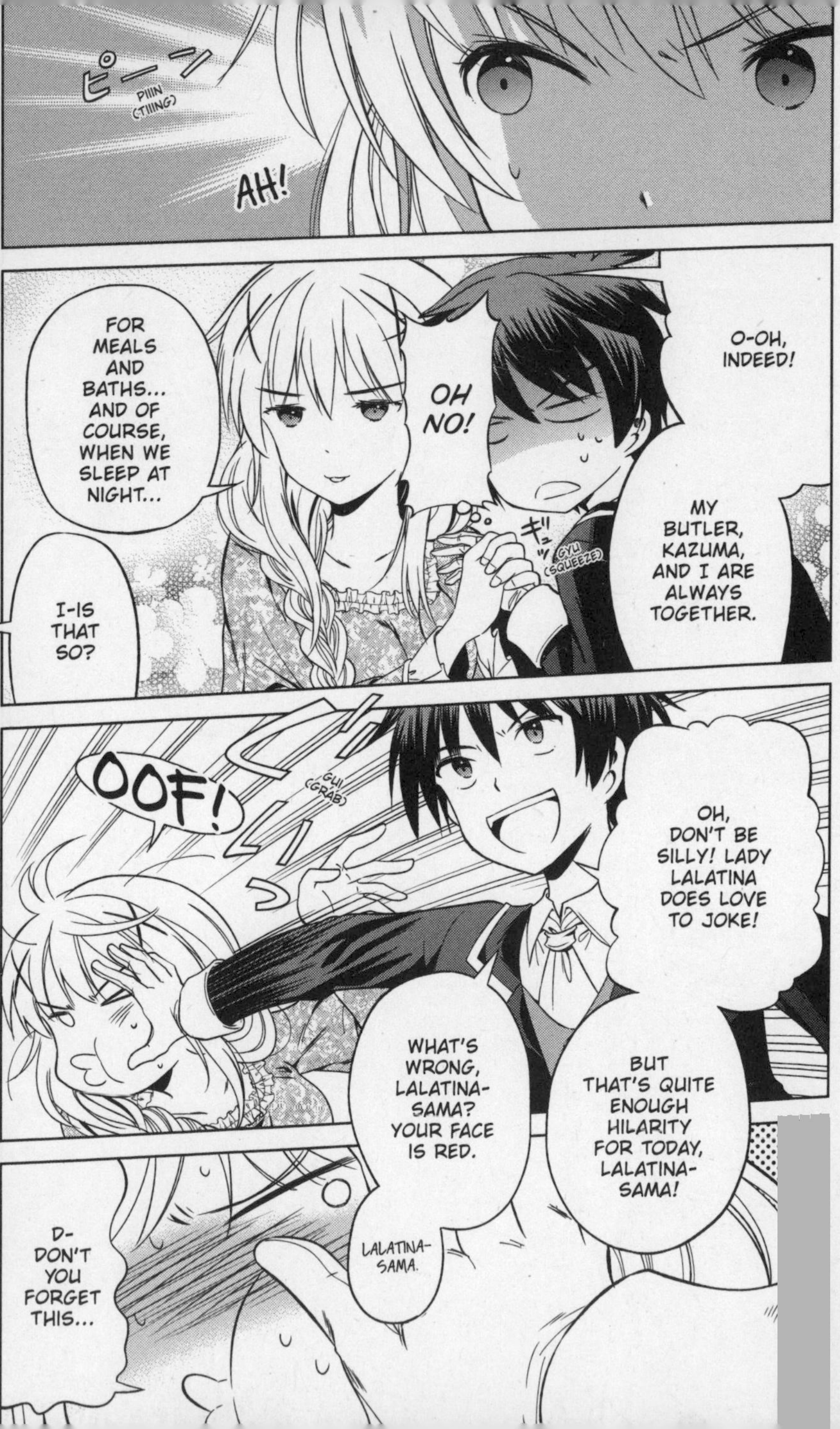
ピーン
PIIIN (TIIING)
AH!
O-OH, INDEED!
MY BUTLER, KAZUMA, AND I ARE ALWAYS TOGETHER.
OH NO!
ギュ
GYU (SQUEEZE)
FOR MEALS AND BATHS... AND OF COURSE, WHEN WE SLEEP AT NIGHT...
I-IS THAT SO?
OH, DON'T BE SILLY! LADY LALATINA DOES LOVE TO JOKE!
GUI (GRAB)
OOF!
BUT THAT'S QUITE ENOUGH HILARITY FOR TODAY, LALATINA-SAMA!
WHAT'S WRONG, LALATINA-SAMA? YOUR FACE IS RED.
LALATINA-SAMA.
D-DON'T YOU FORGET THIS...

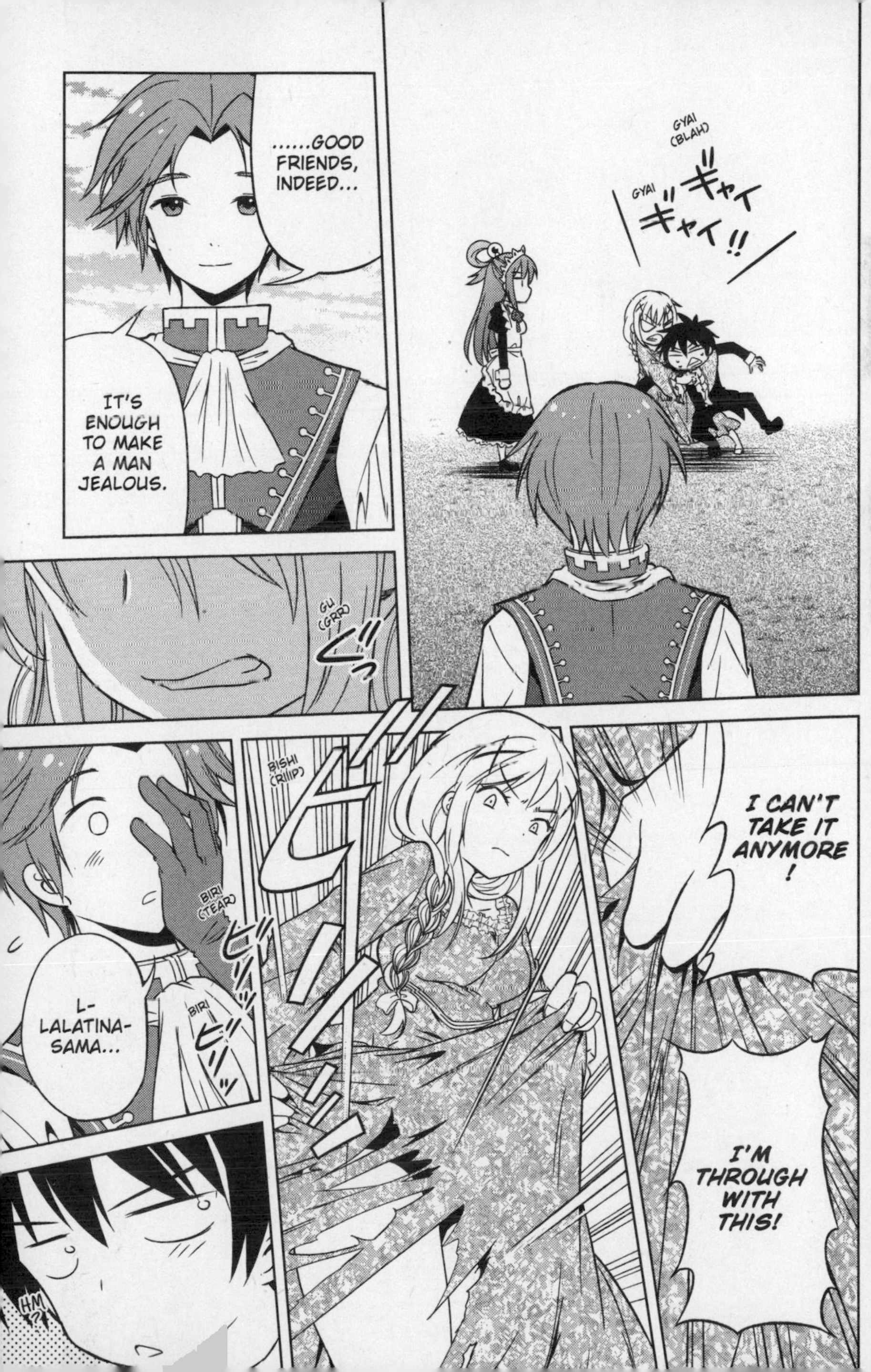
GYAI (BLAH)
ギャイ
GYAI
ギャイ!!
......GOOD FRIENDS, INDEED...
IT'S ENOUGH TO MAKE A MAN JEALOUS.
GU (GRR)
ぐっ
I CAN'T TAKE IT ANYMORE!
I'M THROUGH WITH THIS!
BISHI (RIIIP)
BIRI (TEAR)
ビッ
BIRI
ビッ
L-LALATINA-SAMA...
HM?

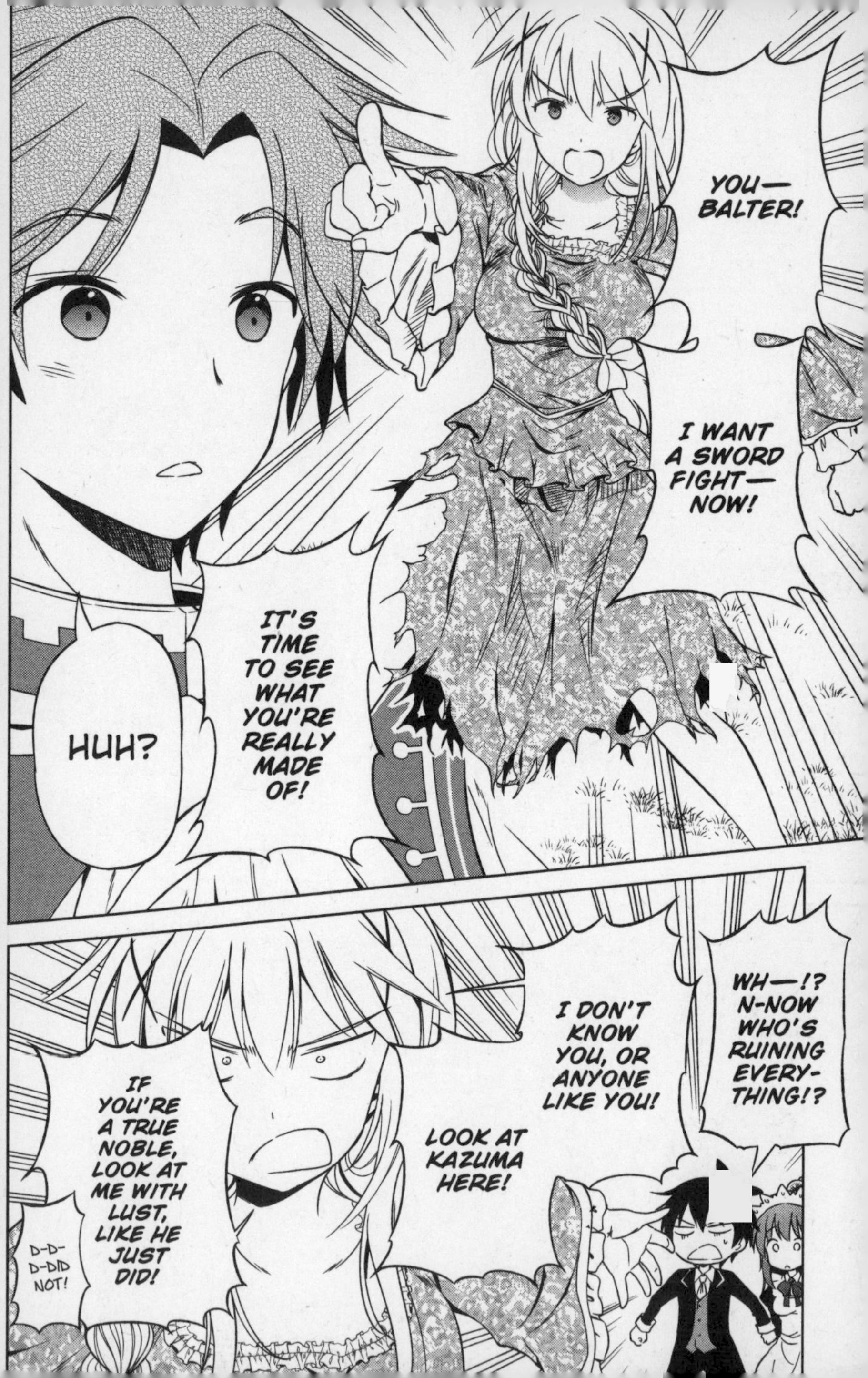
YOU—BALTER!
I WANT A SWORD FIGHT—NOW!
IT'S TIME TO SEE WHAT YOU'RE REALLY MADE OF!
HUH?
WH—!? N-NOW WHO'S RUINING EVERY-THING!?
I DON'T KNOW YOU, OR ANYONE LIKE YOU!
LOOK AT KAZUMA HERE!
IF YOU'RE A TRUE NOBLE, LOOK AT ME WITH LUST, LIKE HE JUST DID!
D-D-D-DID NOT!

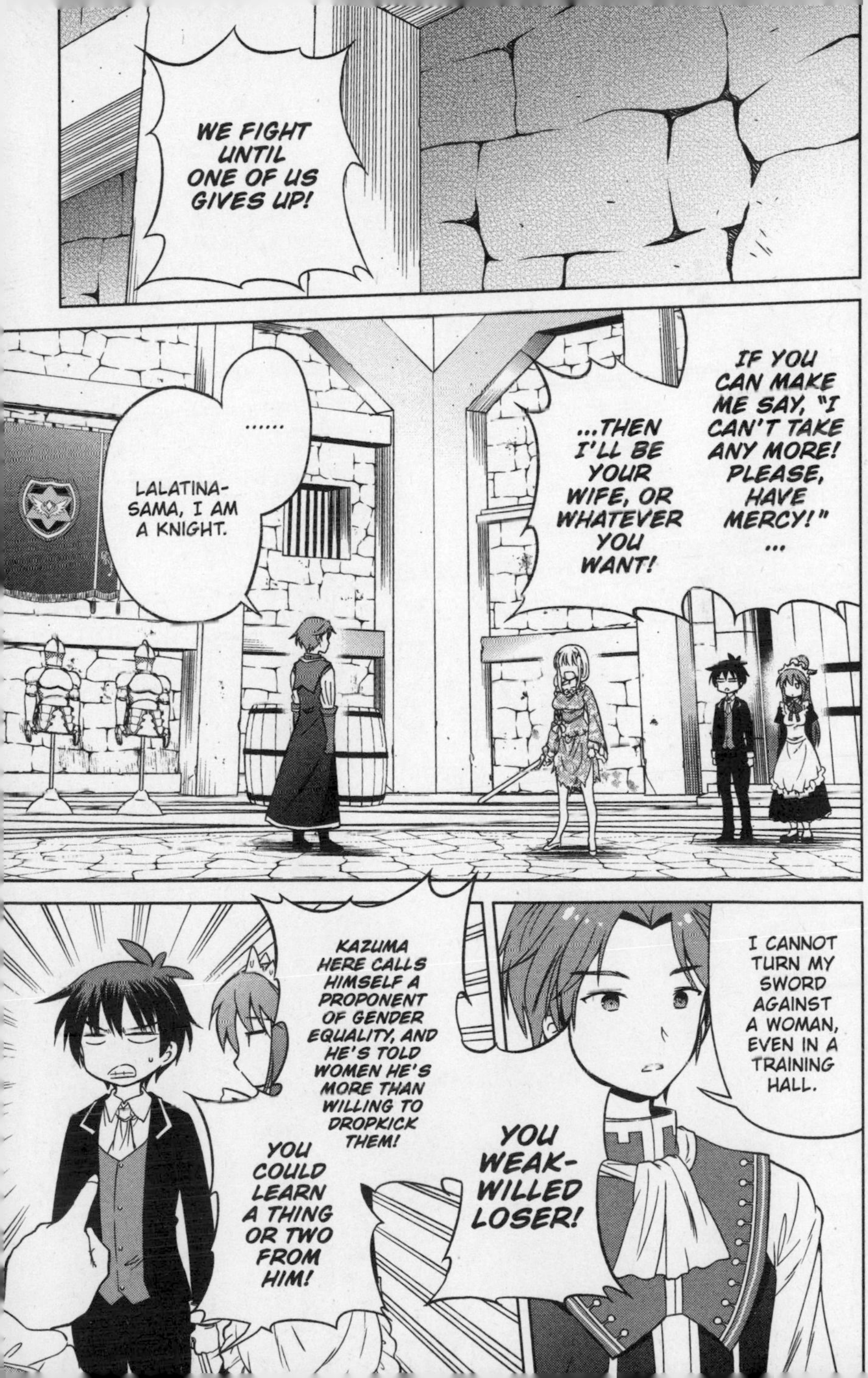
WE FIGHT UNTIL ONE OF US GIVES UP!
IF YOU CAN MAKE ME SAY, "I CAN'T TAKE ANY MORE! PLEASE, HAVE MERCY!" ...
...THEN I'LL BE YOUR WIFE, OR WHATEVER YOU WANT!
......
LALATINA-SAMA, I AM A KNIGHT.
I CANNOT TURN MY SWORD AGAINST A WOMAN, EVEN IN A TRAINING HALL.
YOU WEAK-WILLED LOSER!
KAZUMA HERE CALLS HIMSELF A PROPONENT OF GENDER EQUALITY, AND HE'S TOLD WOMEN HE'S MORE THAN WILLING TO DROPKICK THEM!
YOU COULD LEARN A THING OR TWO FROM HIM!

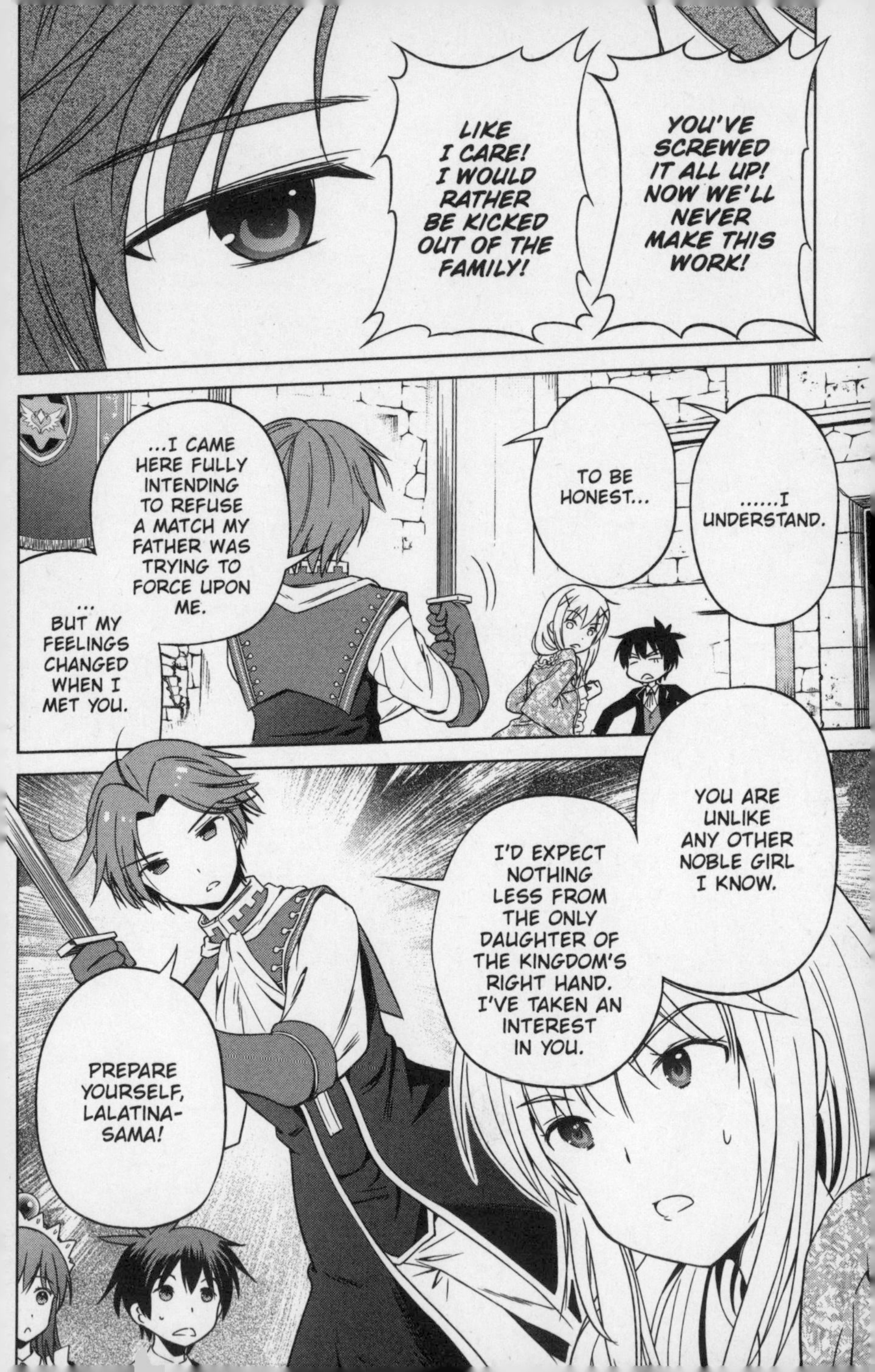
YOU'VE SCREWED IT ALL UP! NOW WE'LL NEVER MAKE THIS WORK!
LIKE I CARE! I WOULD RATHER BE KICKED OUT OF THE FAMILY!
......I UNDERSTAND.
TO BE HONEST...
...I CAME HERE FULLY INTENDING TO REFUSE A MATCH MY FATHER WAS TRYING TO FORCE UPON ME.
... BUT MY FEELINGS CHANGED WHEN I MET YOU.
YOU ARE UNLIKE ANY OTHER NOBLE GIRL I KNOW.
I'D EXPECT NOTHING LESS FROM THE ONLY DAUGHTER OF THE KINGDOM'S RIGHT HAND. I'VE TAKEN AN INTEREST IN YOU.
PREPARE YOURSELF, LALATINA-SAMA!

KA
(FWAH)

CLATTER

LOOKS
LIKE...

...I
WIN.

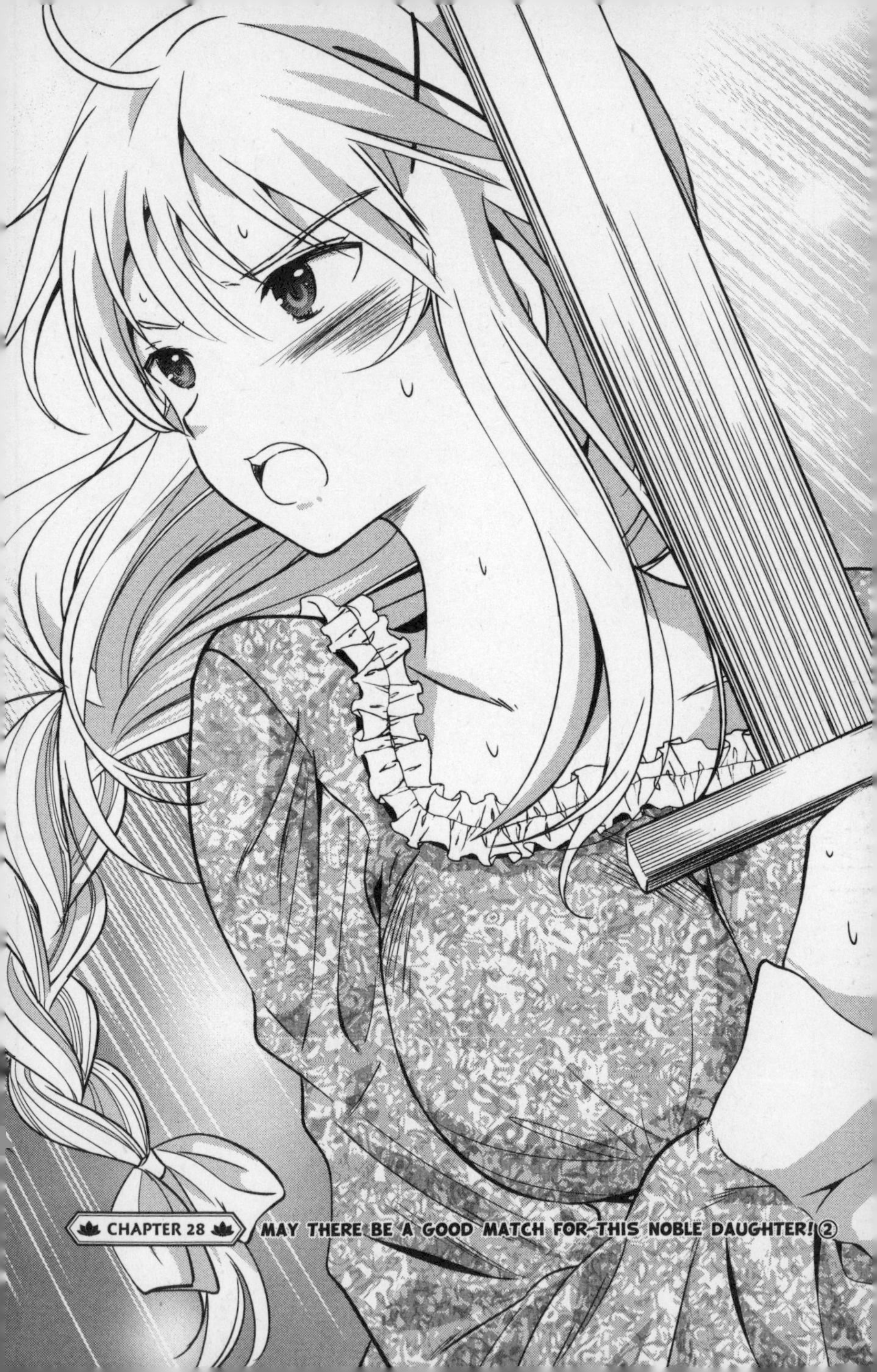
CHAPTER 28
MAY THERE BE A GOOD MATCH FOR THIS NOBLE DAUGHTER! ②

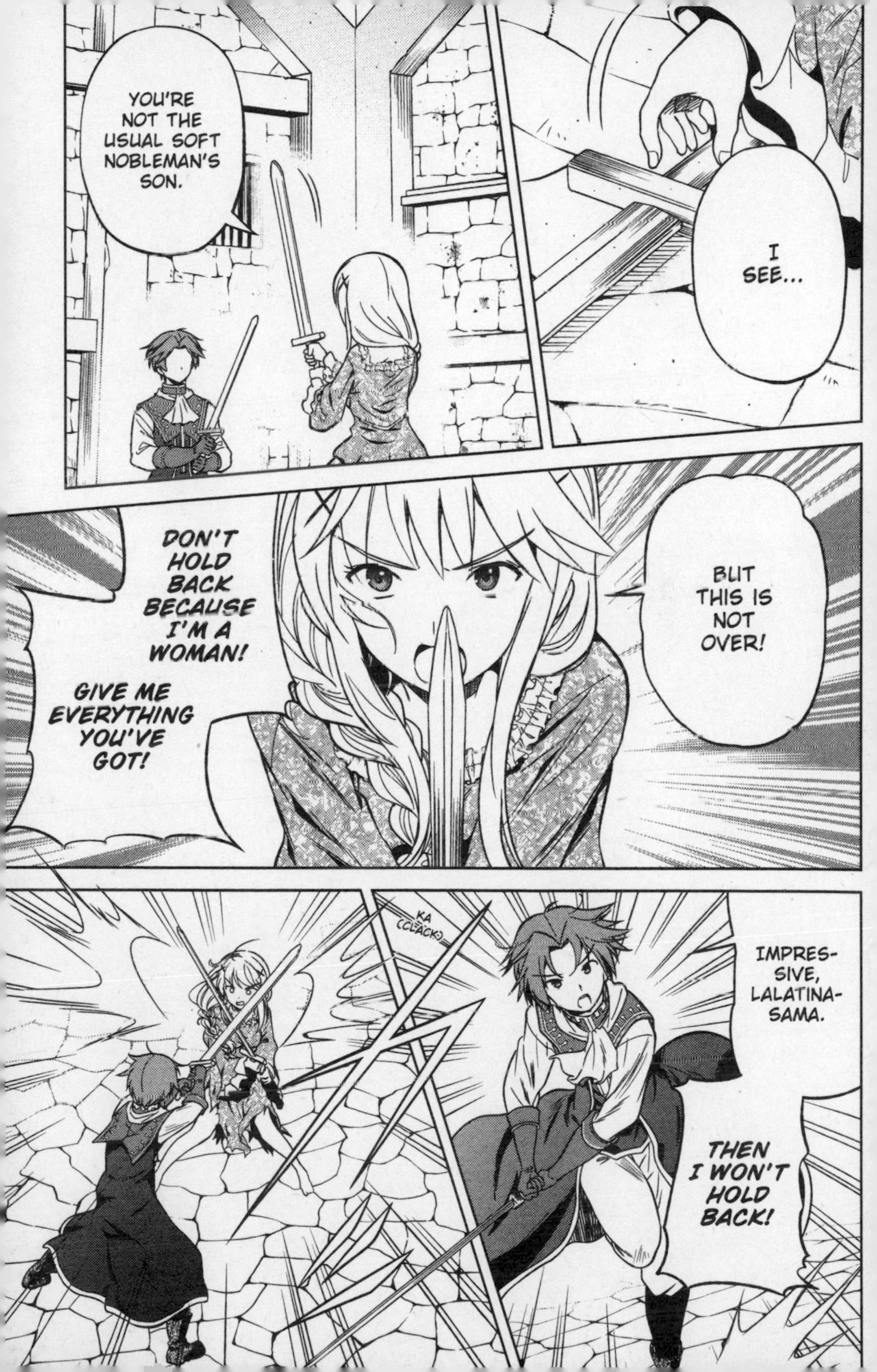
I SEE...
YOU'RE NOT THE USUAL SOFT NOBLEMAN'S SON.
BUT THIS IS NOT OVER!
DON'T HOLD BACK BECAUSE I'M A WOMAN!
GIVE ME EVERYTHING YOU'VE GOT!
IMPRES-SIVE, LALATINA-SAMA.
KA (CLACK)
THEN I WON'T HOLD BACK!

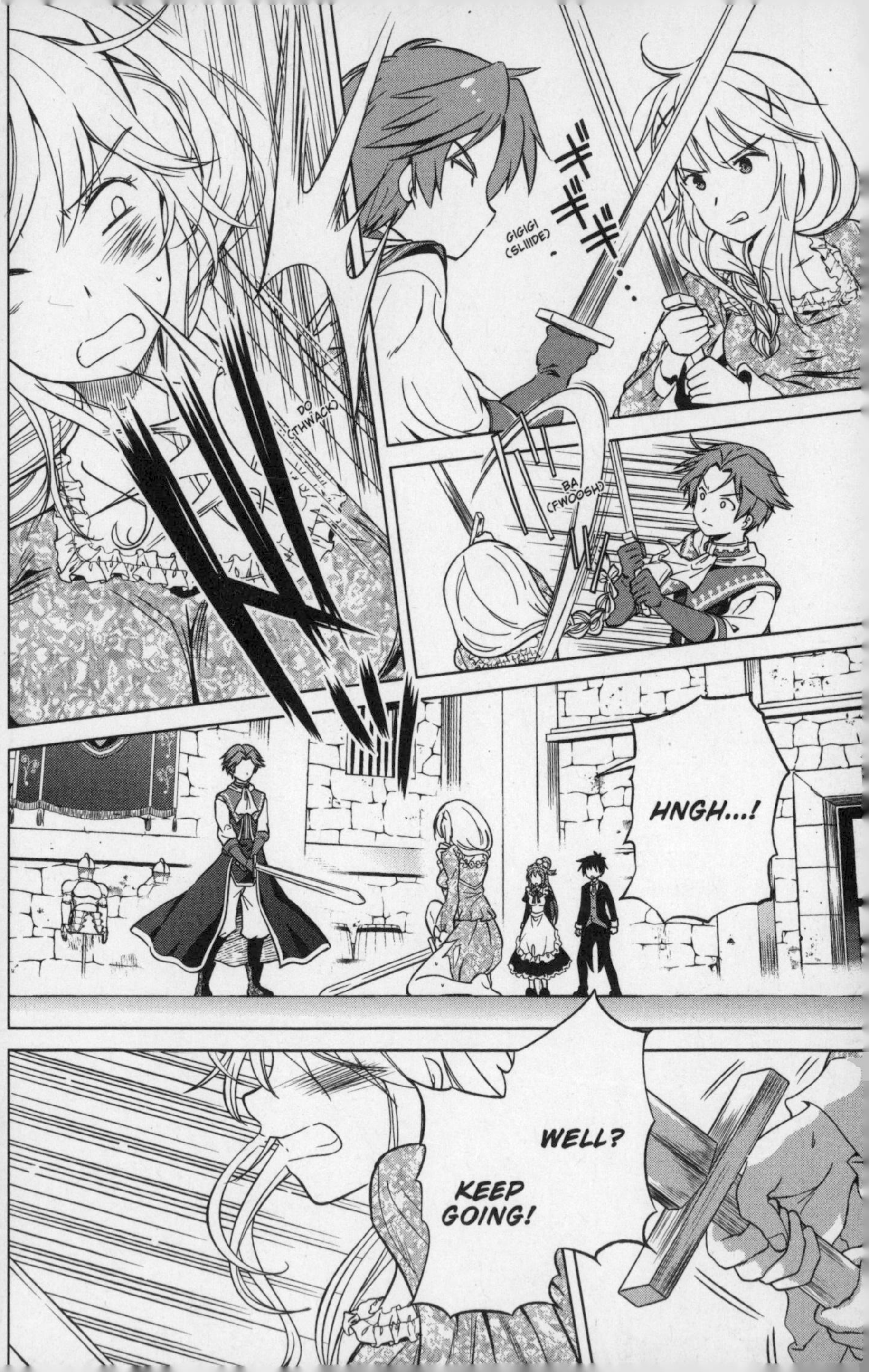
GIGIGI (SLIIIDE)
BA (FWOOSH)
DO (THWACK)
HNGH...!
WELL?
KEEP GOING!

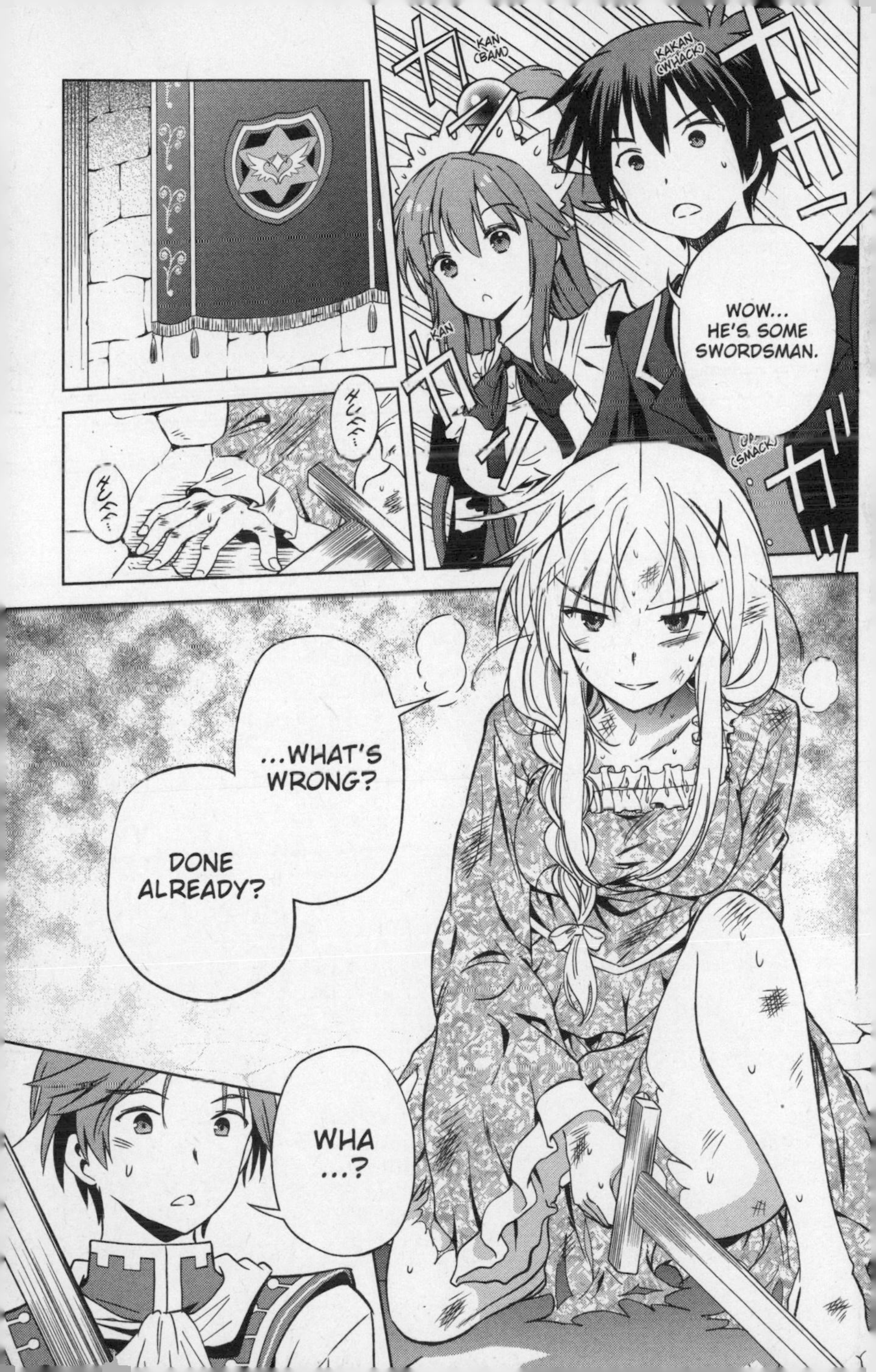
KAKAN (WHACK)
KAN (BAM)
WOW... HE'S SOME SWORDSMAN.
KAN
(SMACK)
...WHAT'S WRONG?
DONE ALREADY?
WHA ...?

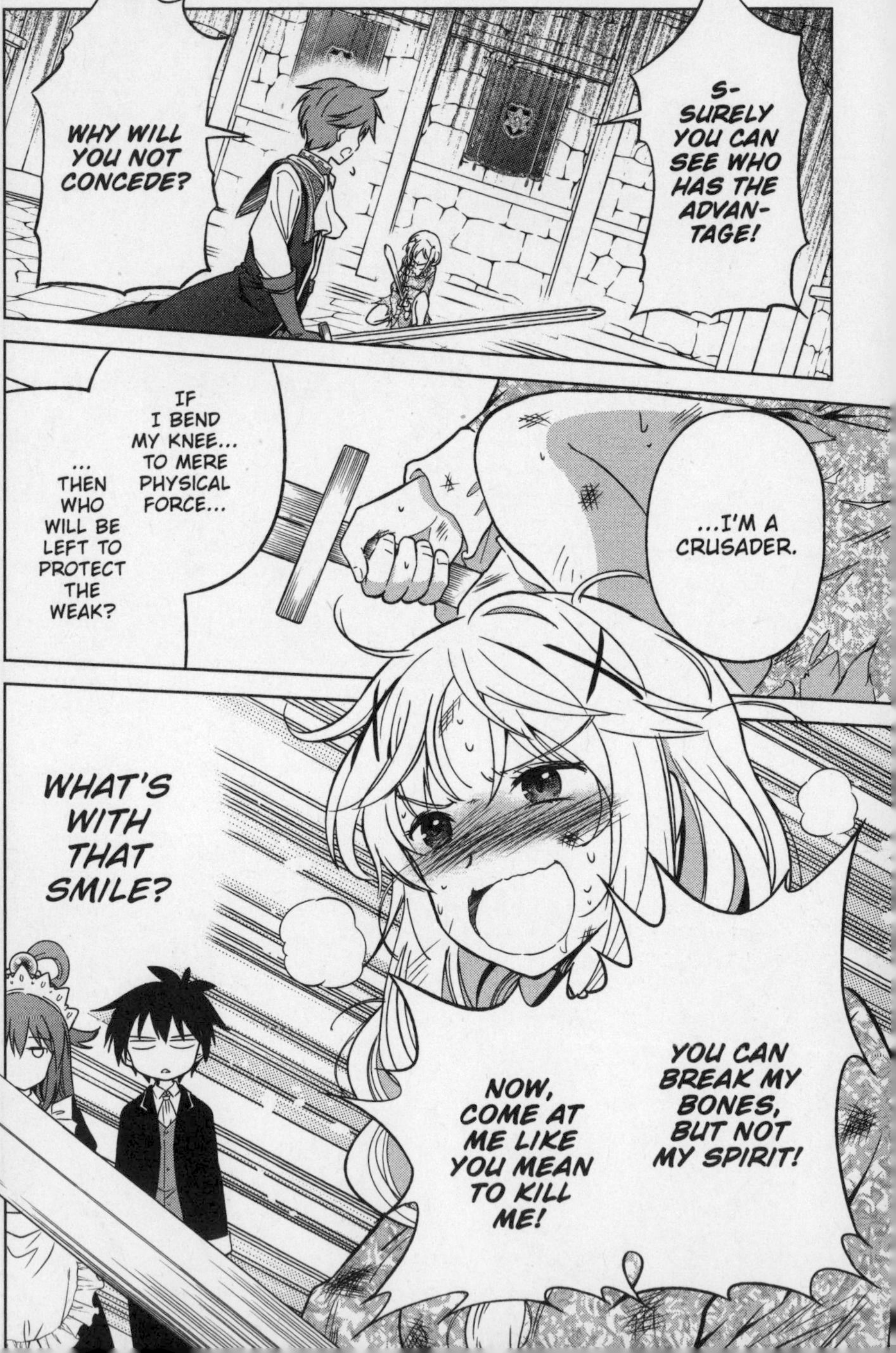
S-SURELY YOU CAN SEE WHO HAS THE ADVANTAGE!
WHY WILL YOU NOT CONCEDE?
...I'M A CRUSADER.
IF I BEND MY KNEE... TO MERE PHYSICAL FORCE...
... THEN WHO WILL BE LEFT TO PROTECT THE WEAK?
YOU CAN BREAK MY BONES, BUT NOT MY SPIRIT!
NOW, COME AT ME LIKE YOU MEAN TO KILL ME!
WHAT'S WITH THAT SMILE?

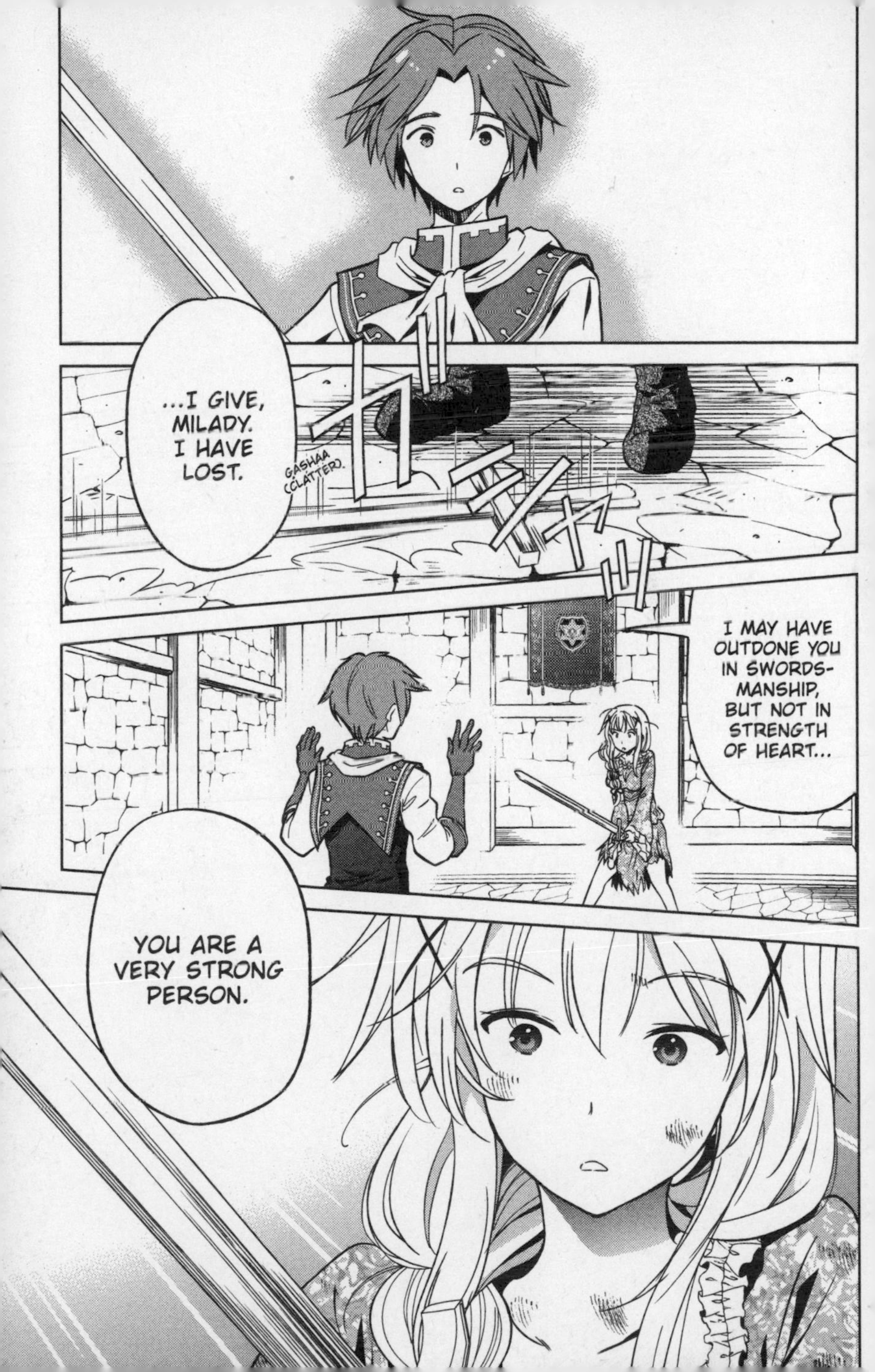
...I GIVE, MILADY. I HAVE LOST.
GASHAA (CLATTER)
I MAY HAVE OUTDONE YOU IN SWORDS-MANSHIP, BUT NOT IN STRENGTH OF HEART...
YOU ARE A VERY STRONG PERSON.

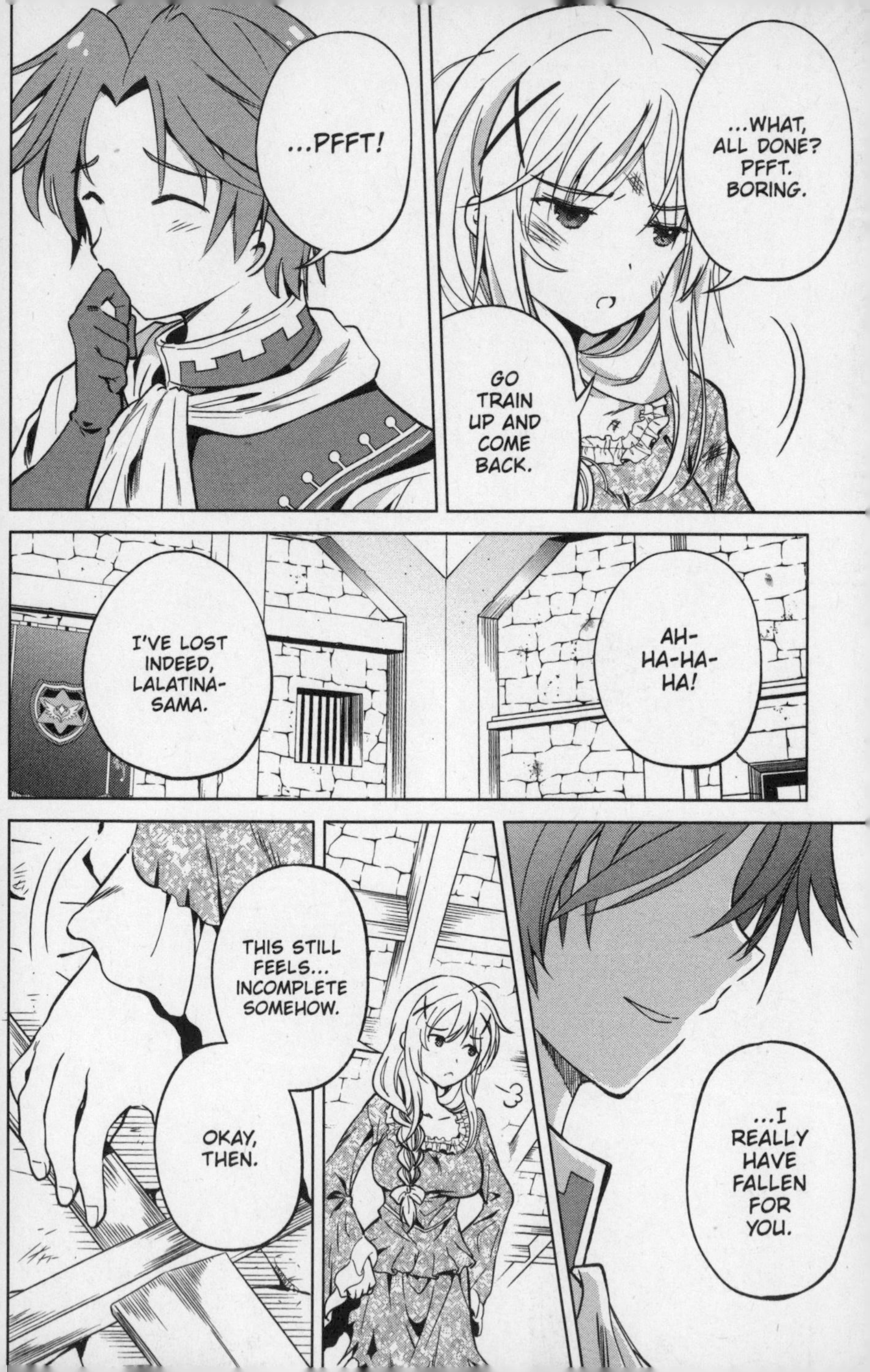
...WHAT, ALL DONE? PFFT. BORING.
GO TRAIN UP AND COME BACK.
...PFFT!
AH-HA-HA-HA!
I'VE LOST INDEED, LALATINA-SAMA.
...I REALLY HAVE FALLEN FOR YOU.
THIS STILL FEELS... INCOMPLETE SOMEHOW.
OKAY, THEN.

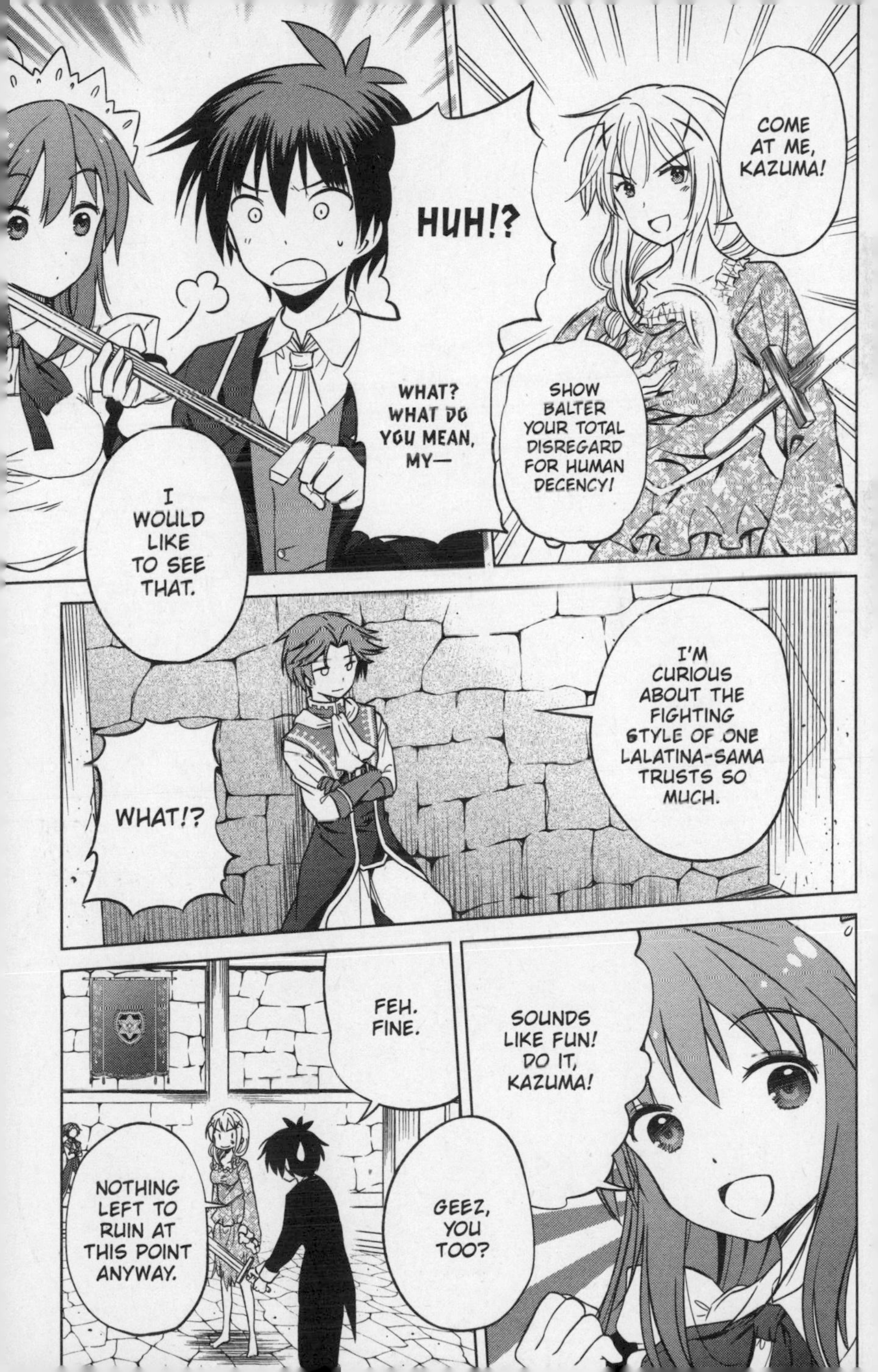
COME AT ME, KAZUMA!
HUH!?
SHOW BALTER YOUR TOTAL DISREGARD FOR HUMAN DECENCY!
WHAT? WHAT DO YOU MEAN, MY—
I WOULD LIKE TO SEE THAT.
I'M CURIOUS ABOUT THE FIGHTING STYLE OF ONE LALATINA-SAMA TRUSTS SO MUCH.
WHAT!?
SOUNDS LIKE FUN! DO IT, KAZUMA!
GEEZ, YOU TOO?
FEH. FINE.
NOTHING LEFT TO RUIN AT THIS POINT ANYWAY.

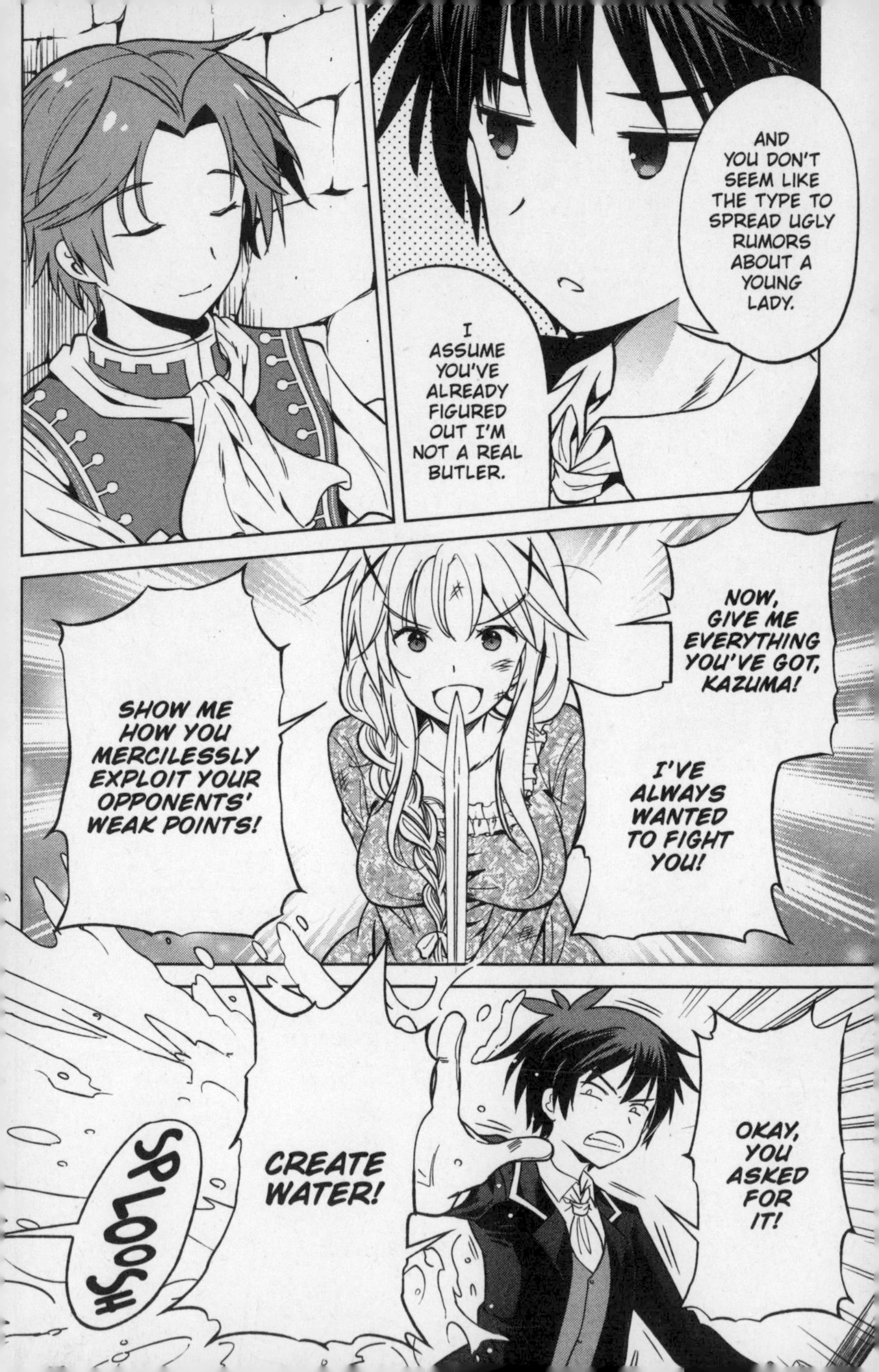
I ASSUME YOU'VE ALREADY FIGURED OUT I'M NOT A REAL BUTLER.
AND YOU DON'T SEEM LIKE THE TYPE TO SPREAD UGLY RUMORS ABOUT A YOUNG LADY.
NOW, GIVE ME EVERYTHING YOU'VE GOT, KAZUMA!
I'VE ALWAYS WANTED TO FIGHT YOU!
SHOW ME HOW YOU MERCILESSLY EXPLOIT YOUR OPPONENTS' WEAK POINTS!
OKAY, YOU ASKED FOR IT!
CREATE WATER!
SPLOOSH

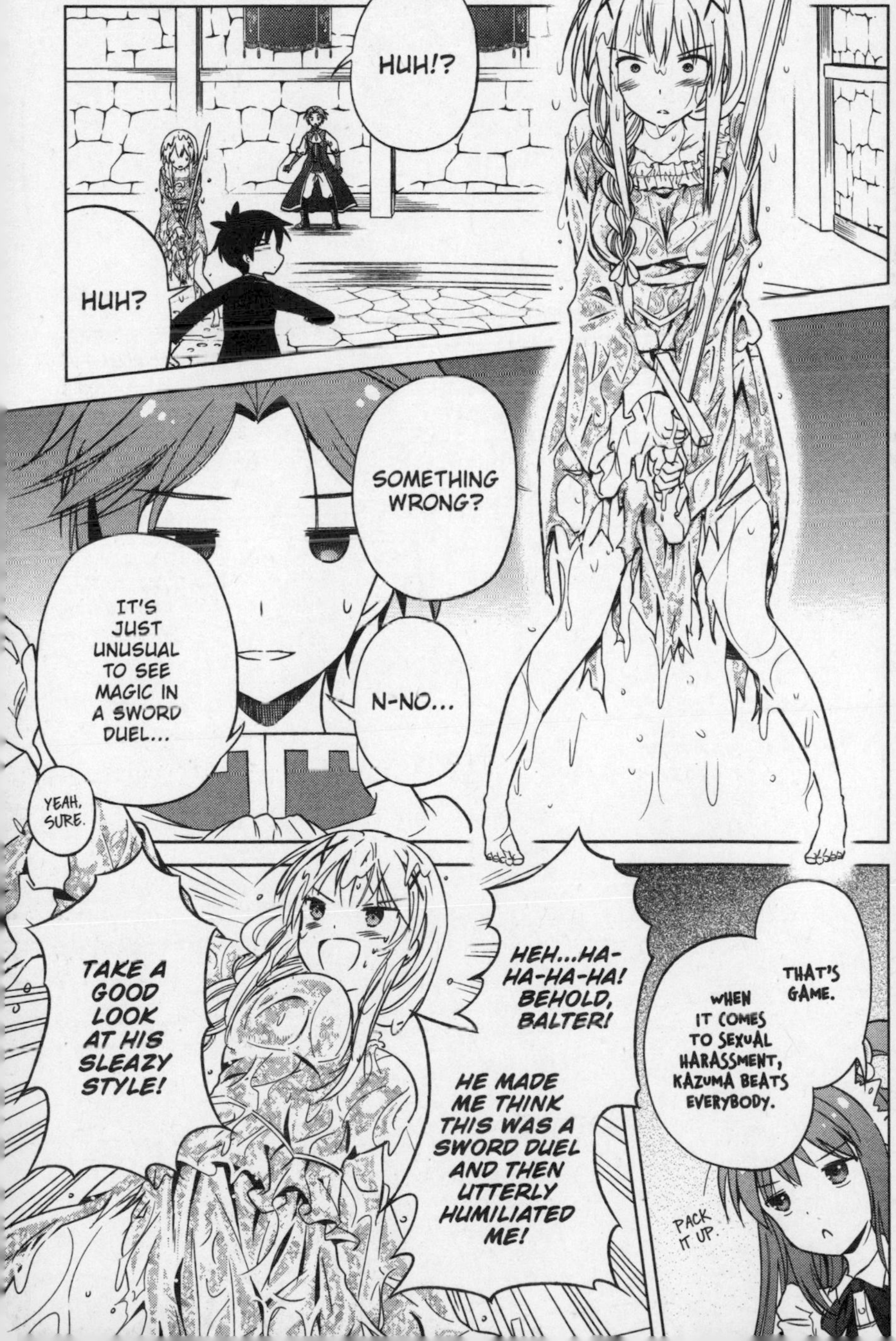
HUH!?
HUH?
SOMETHING WRONG?
N-NO...
IT'S JUST UNUSUAL TO SEE MAGIC IN A SWORD DUEL...
YEAH, SURE.
THAT'S GAME.
WHEN IT COMES TO SEXUAL HARASSMENT, KAZUMA BEATS EVERYBODY.
PACK IT UP.
HEH...HA-HA-HA-HA! BEHOLD, BALTER!
TAKE A GOOD LOOK AT HIS SLEAZY STYLE!
HE MADE ME THINK THIS WAS A SWORD DUEL AND THEN UTTERLY HUMILIATED ME!

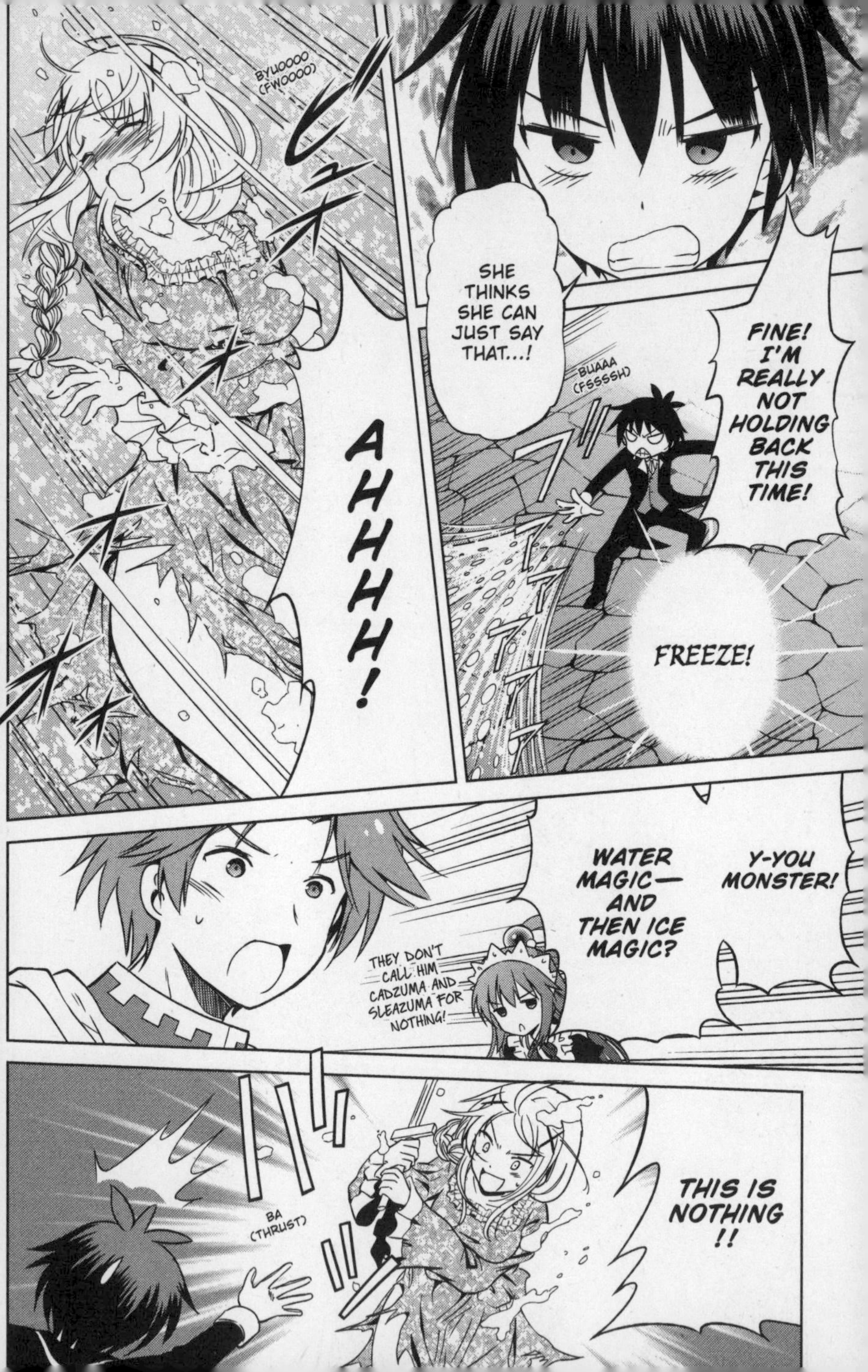
SHE THINKS SHE CAN JUST SAY THAT...!
FINE! I'M REALLY NOT HOLDING BACK THIS TIME!
BUAAA (FSSSSH)
FREEZE!
BYUOOOO (FWOOOO)
AHHHHH!
Y-YOU MONSTER!
WATER MAGIC— AND THEN ICE MAGIC?
THEY DON'T CALL HIM CADZUMA AND SLEAZUMA FOR NOTHING!
THIS IS NOTHING!!
BA (THRUST)

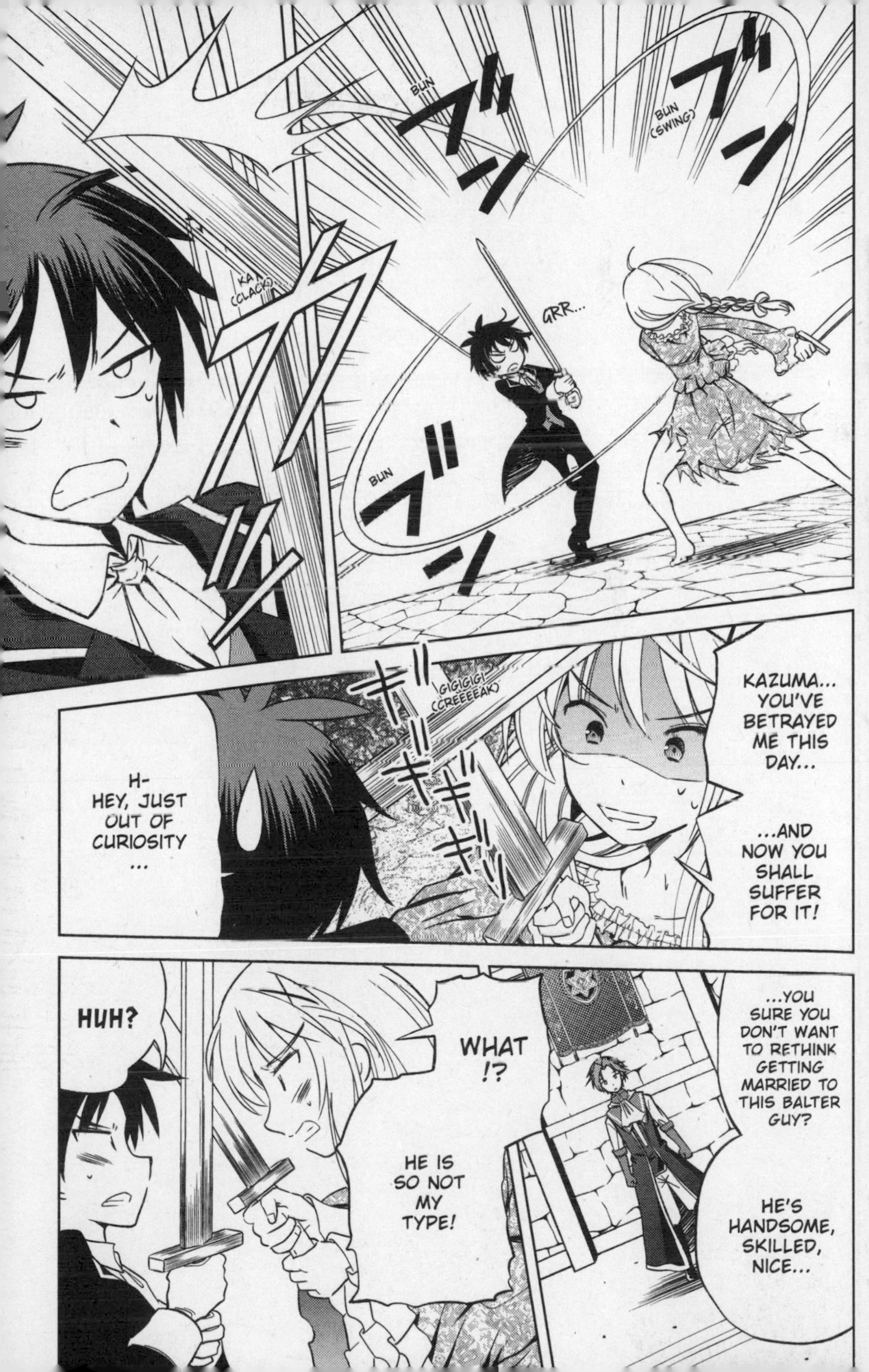
BUN (SWING)
BUN
GRR...
BUN
KA (CLACK)...
KAZUMA... YOU'VE BETRAYED ME THIS DAY...
...AND NOW YOU SHALL SUFFER FOR IT!
GIGIGIGI (CREEEEAK)
H- HEY, JUST OUT OF CURIOSITY ...
...YOU SURE YOU DON'T WANT TO RETHINK GETTING MARRIED TO THIS BALTER GUY?
HE'S HANDSOME, SKILLED, NICE...
WHAT !?
HE IS SO NOT MY TYPE!
HUH?

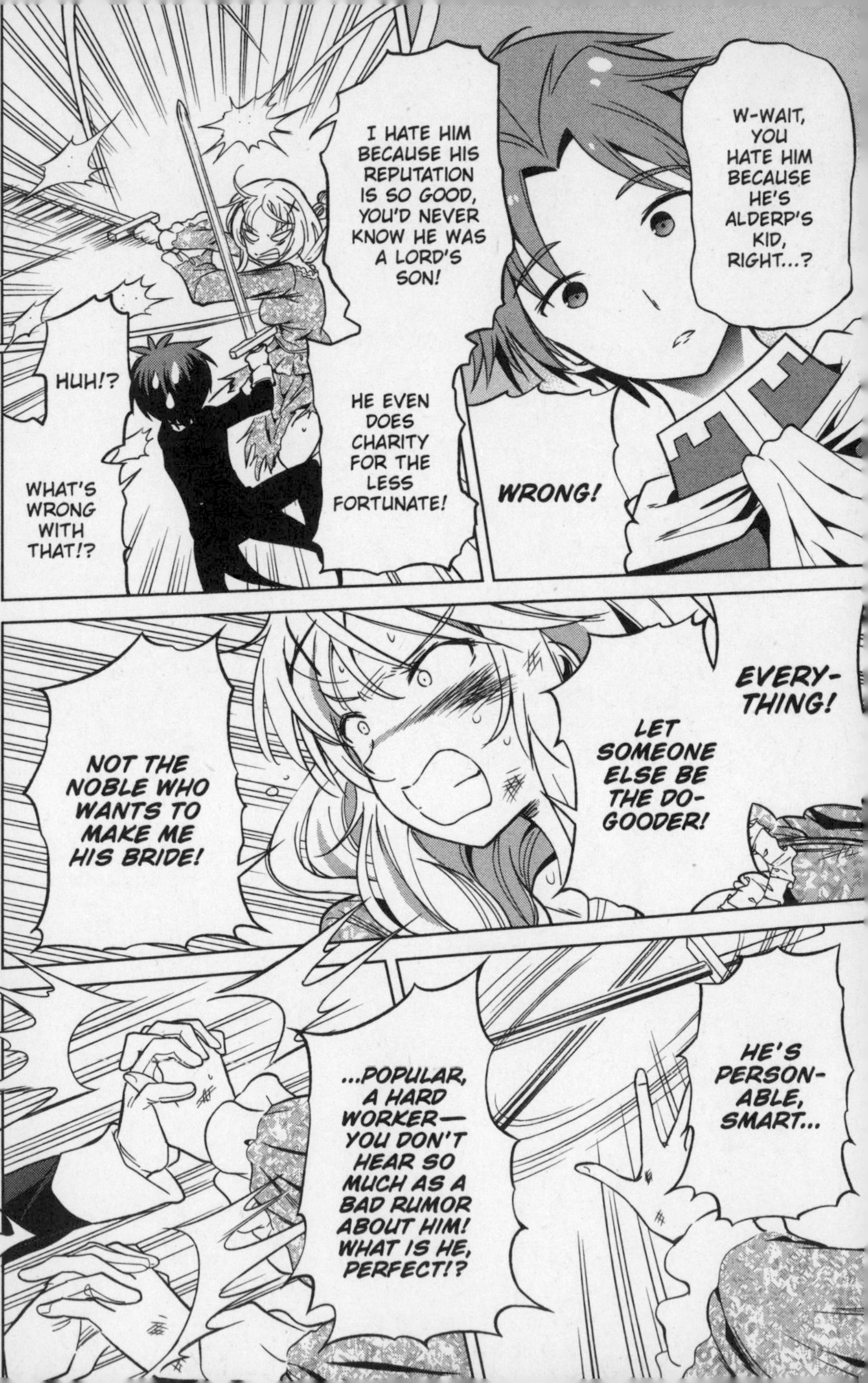
W-WAIT, YOU HATE HIM BECAUSE HE'S ALDERP'S KID, RIGHT...?
WRONG!
I HATE HIM BECAUSE HIS REPUTATION IS SO GOOD, YOU'D NEVER KNOW HE WAS A LORD'S SON!
HE EVEN DOES CHARITY FOR THE LESS FORTUNATE!
HUH!?
WHAT'S WRONG WITH THAT!?
EVERY-THING!
LET SOMEONE ELSE BE THE DO-GOODER!
NOT THE NOBLE WHO WANTS TO MAKE ME HIS BRIDE!
HE'S PERSON-ABLE, SMART...
...POPULAR, A HARD WORKER—YOU DON'T HEAR SO MUCH AS A BAD RUMOR ABOUT HIM! WHAT IS HE, PERFECT!?

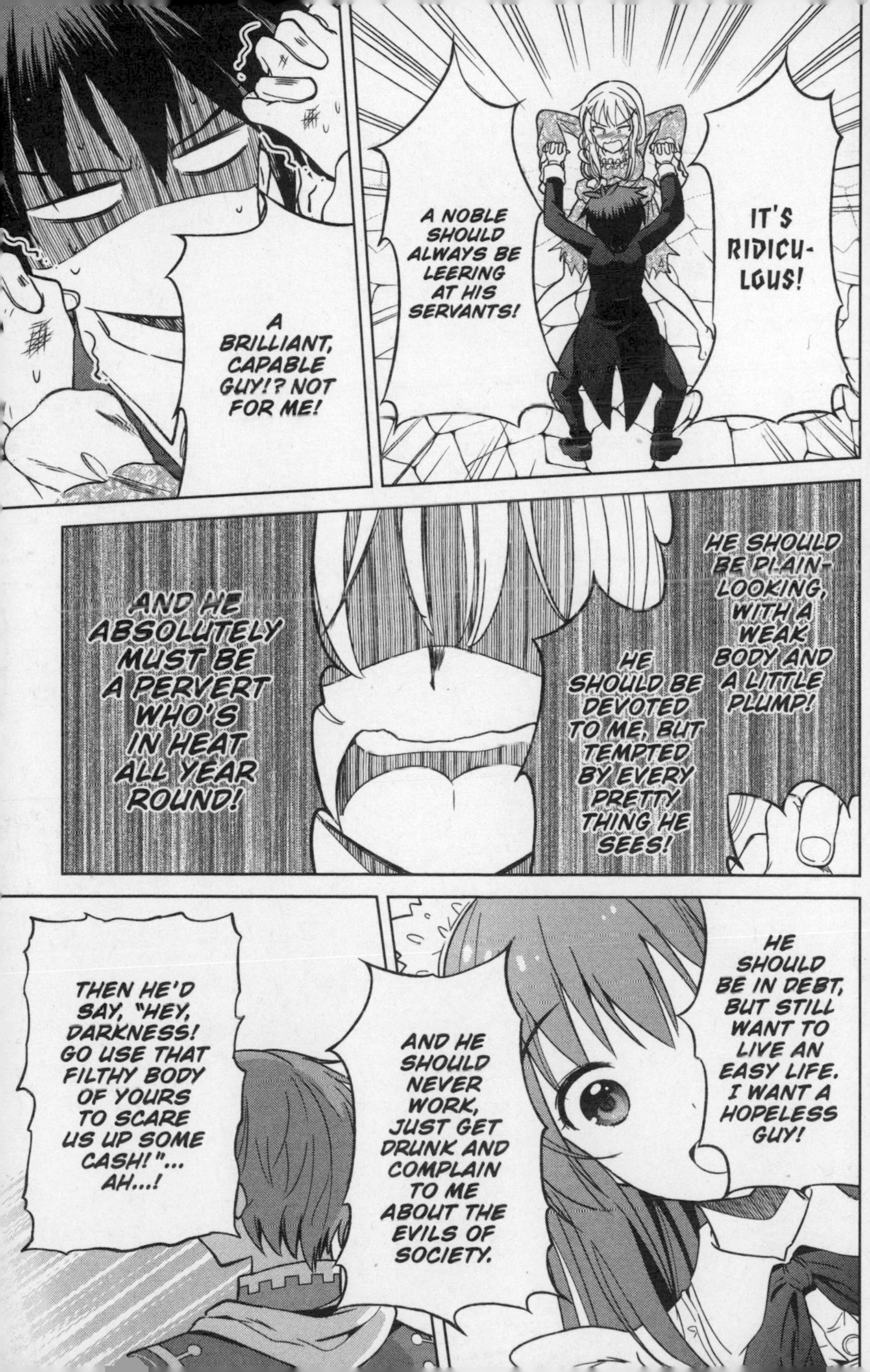
IT'S RIDICU-LOUS!
A NOBLE SHOULD ALWAYS BE LEERING AT HIS SERVANTS!
A BRILLIANT, CAPABLE GUY!? NOT FOR ME!
HE SHOULD BE PLAIN-LOOKING, WITH A WEAK BODY AND A LITTLE PLUMP!
HE SHOULD BE DEVOTED TO ME, BUT TEMPTED BY EVERY PRETTY THING HE SEES!
AND HE ABSOLUTELY MUST BE A PERVERT WHO'S IN HEAT ALL YEAR ROUND!
HE SHOULD BE IN DEBT, BUT STILL WANT TO LIVE AN EASY LIFE. I WANT A HOPELESS GUY!
AND HE SHOULD NEVER WORK, JUST GET DRUNK AND COMPLAIN TO ME ABOUT THE EVILS OF SOCIETY.
THEN HE'D SAY, "HEY, DARKNESS! GO USE THAT FILTHY BODY OF YOURS TO SCARE US UP SOME CASH!"... AH...!

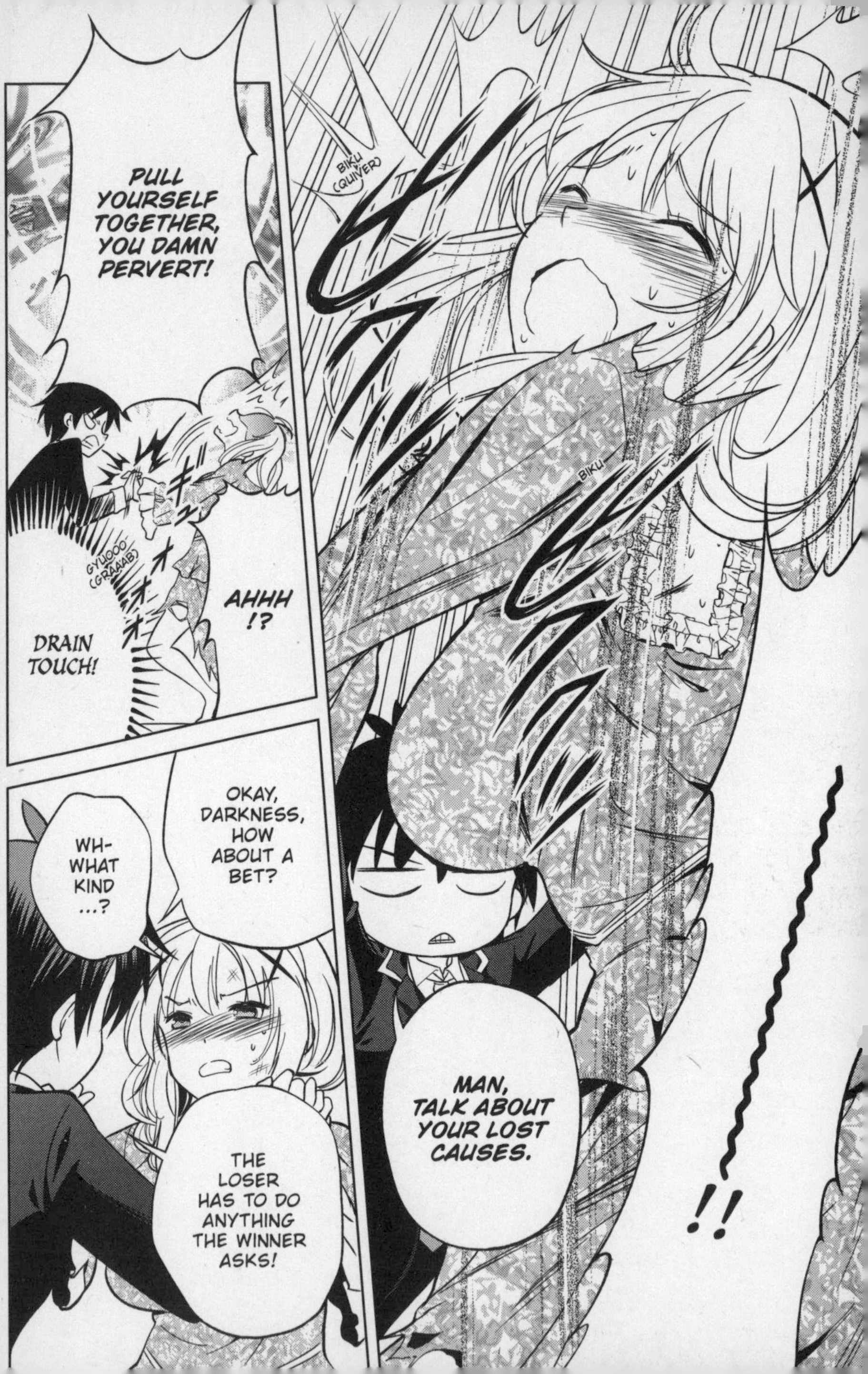
BIKU (QUIVER)
BIKU
MAN, TALK ABOUT YOUR LOST CAUSES.
——!!
PULL YOURSELF TOGETHER, YOU DAMN PERVERT!
AHHH!?
GYUOOO (GRAAAB)
DRAIN TOUCH!
OKAY, DARKNESS, HOW ABOUT A BET?
WH-WHAT KIND...?
THE LOSER HAS TO DO ANYTHING THE WINNER ASKS!

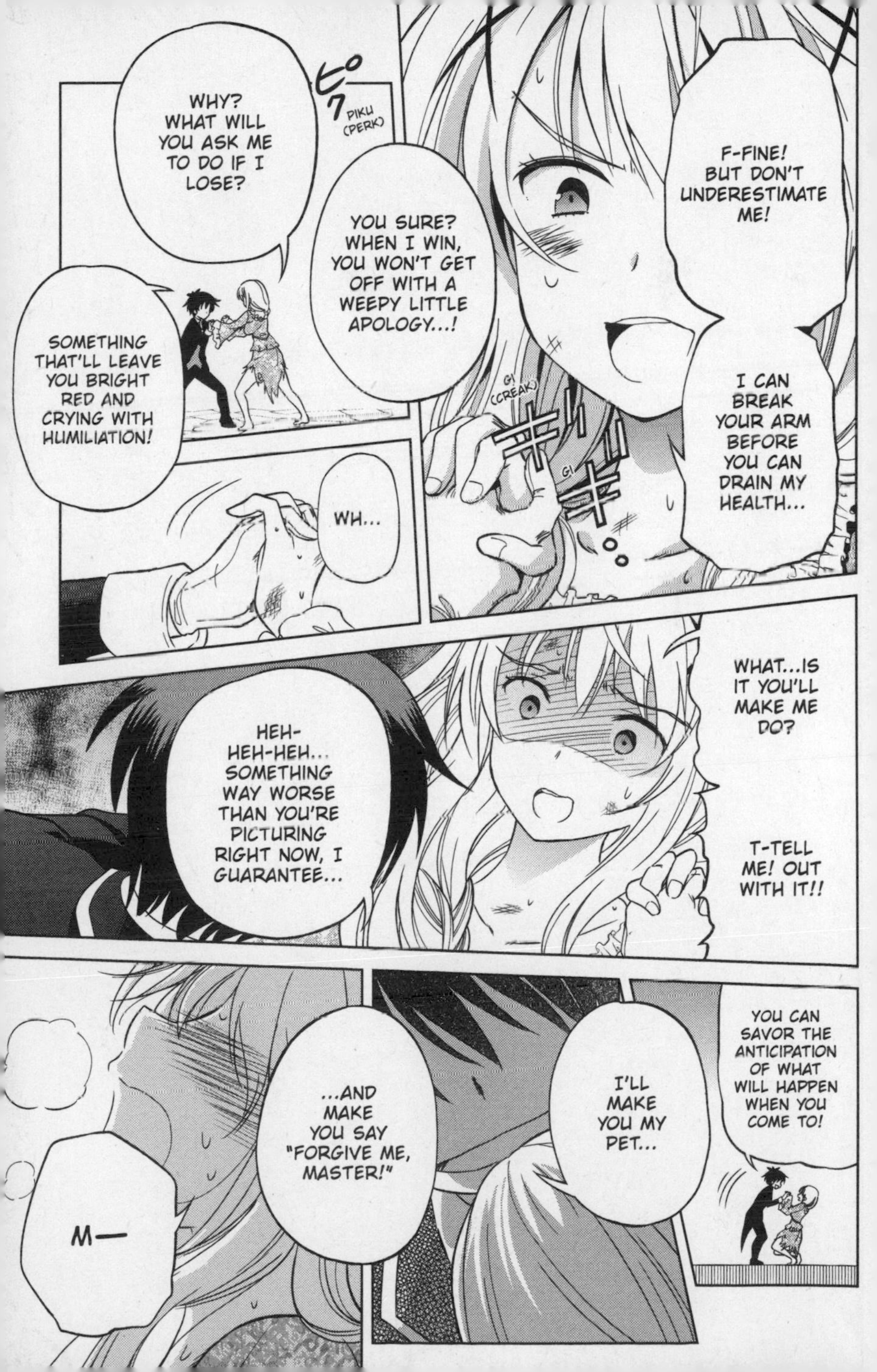
F-FINE! BUT DON'T UNDERESTIMATE ME!
I CAN BREAK YOUR ARM BEFORE YOU CAN DRAIN MY HEALTH...
GI (CREAK)
GI
YOU SURE? WHEN I WIN, YOU WON'T GET OFF WITH A WEEPY LITTLE APOLOGY...!
ピク
PIKU (PERK)
WHY? WHAT WILL YOU ASK ME TO DO IF I LOSE?
SOMETHING THAT'LL LEAVE YOU BRIGHT RED AND CRYING WITH HUMILIATION!
WH...
WHAT...IS IT YOU'LL MAKE ME DO?
T-TELL ME! OUT WITH IT!!
HEH-HEH-HEH... SOMETHING WAY WORSE THAN YOU'RE PICTURING RIGHT NOW, I GUARANTEE...
YOU CAN SAVOR THE ANTICIPATION OF WHAT WILL HAPPEN WHEN YOU COME TO!
I'LL MAKE YOU MY PET...
...AND MAKE YOU SAY "FORGIVE ME, MASTER!"
M—

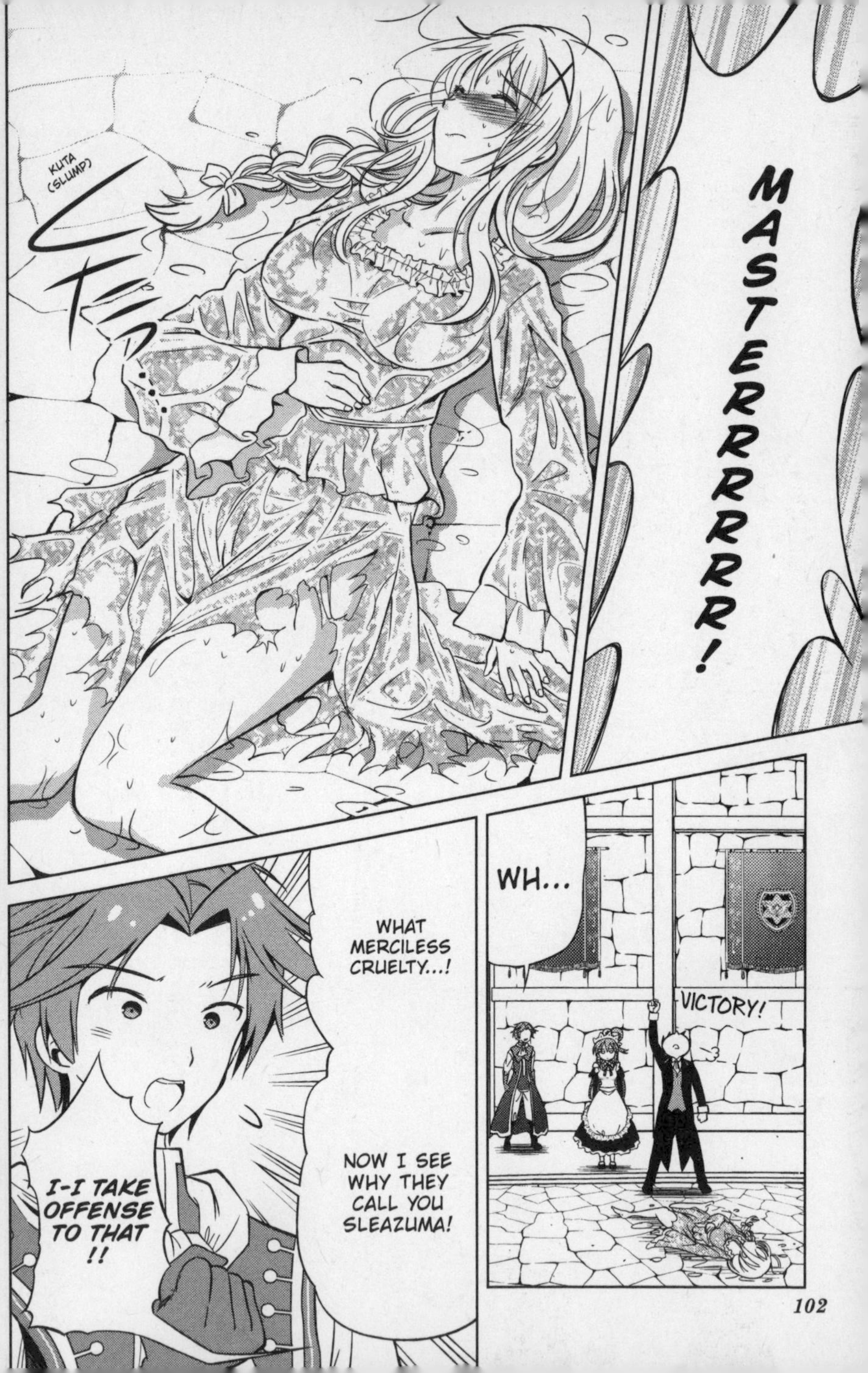
MASTERRRRRRR!
KUTA (SLUMP)
WH...
VICTORY!
WHAT MERCILESS CRUELTY...!
NOW I SEE WHY THEY CALL YOU SLEAZUMA!
I-I TAKE OFFENSE TO THAT !!

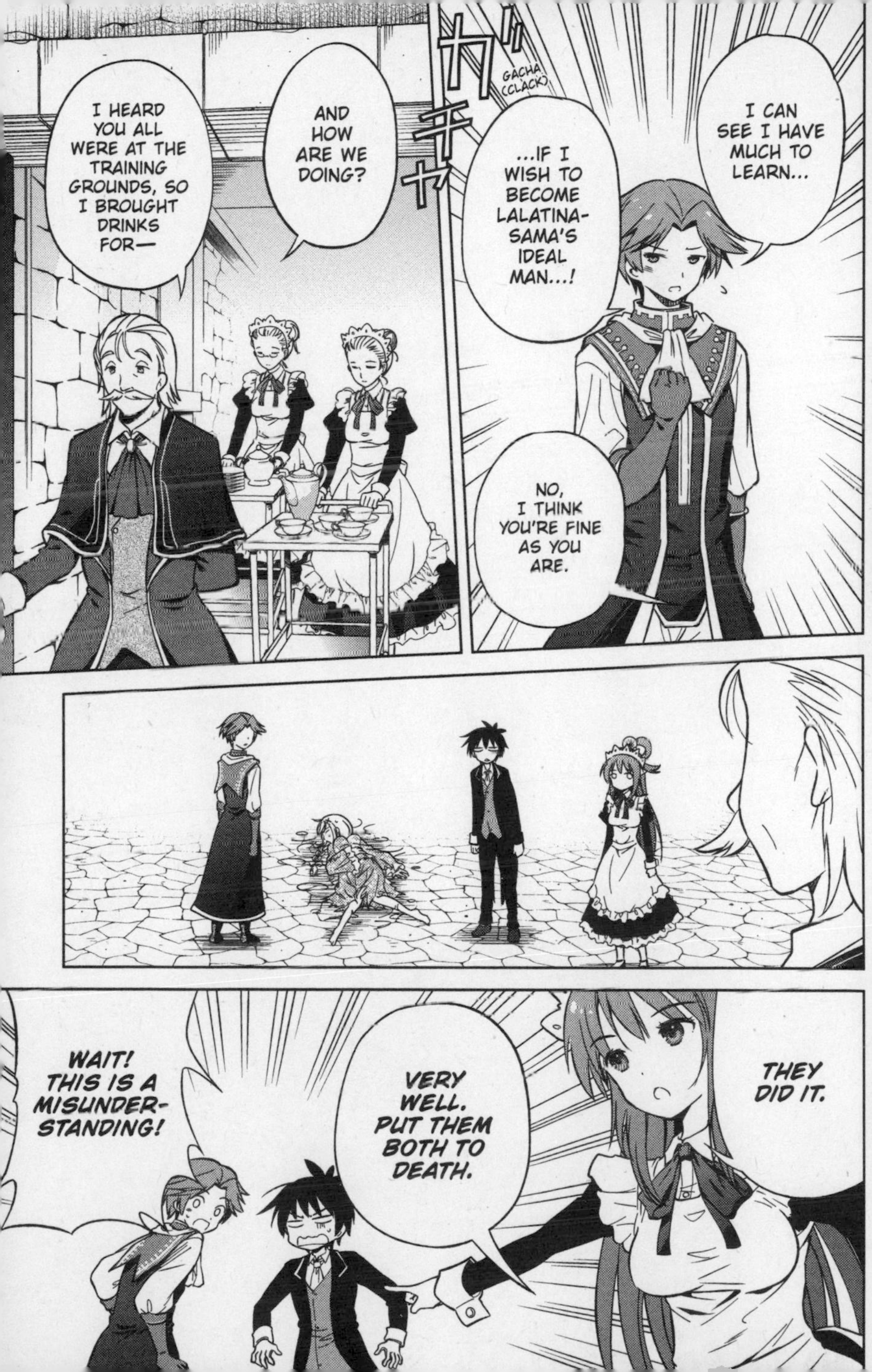
I CAN SEE I HAVE MUCH TO LEARN...
...IF I WISH TO BECOME LALATINA-SAMA'S IDEAL MAN...!
NO, I THINK YOU'RE FINE AS YOU ARE.
GACHA (CLACK)
AND HOW ARE WE DOING?
I HEARD YOU ALL WERE AT THE TRAINING GROUNDS, SO I BROUGHT DRINKS FOR—
THEY DID IT.
VERY WELL. PUT THEM BOTH TO DEATH.
WAIT! THIS IS A MISUNDER-STANDING!

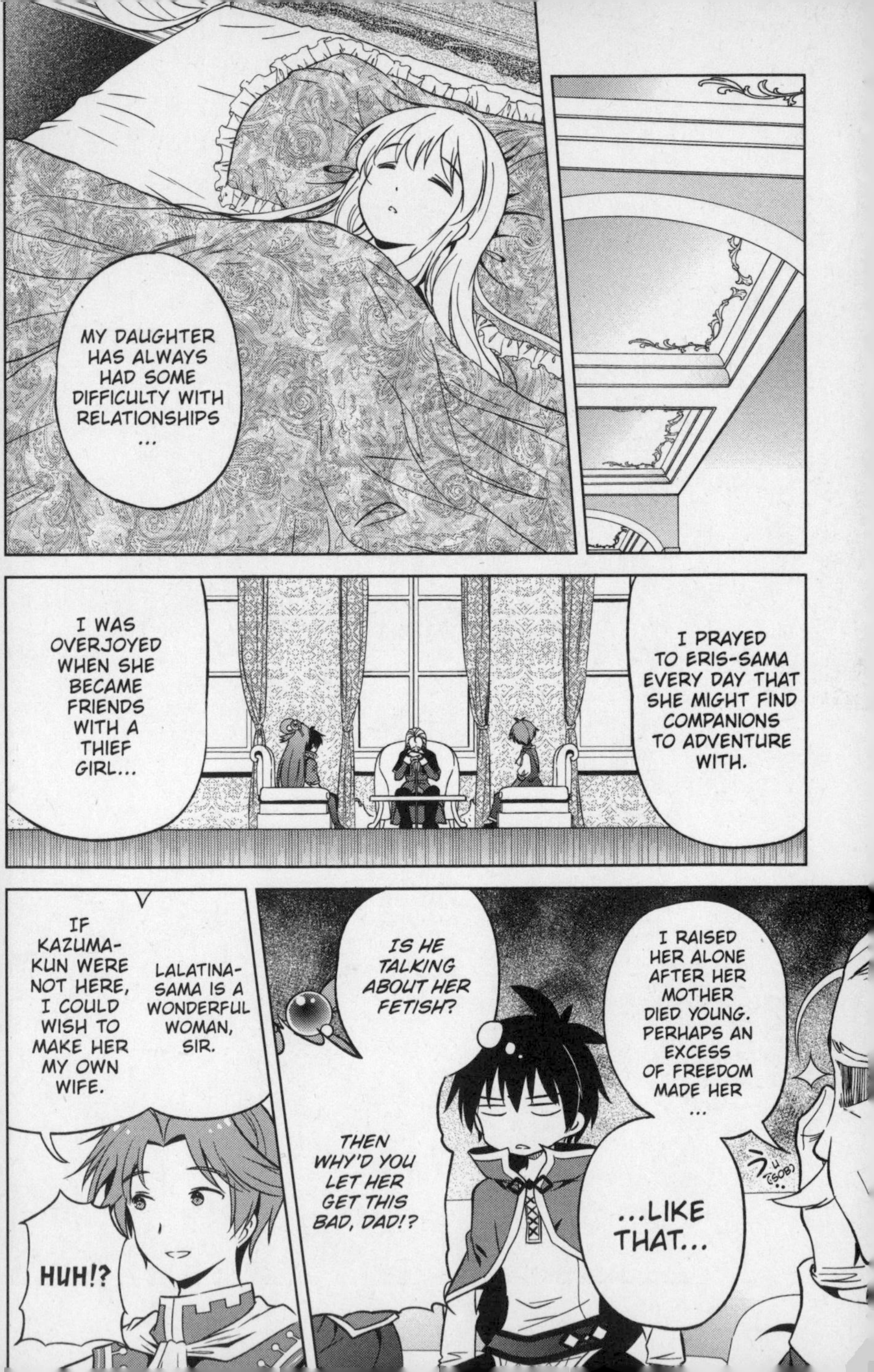
MY DAUGHTER HAS ALWAYS HAD SOME DIFFICULTY WITH RELATIONSHIPS ...
I PRAYED TO ERIS-SAMA EVERY DAY THAT SHE MIGHT FIND COMPANIONS TO ADVENTURE WITH.
I WAS OVERJOYED WHEN SHE BECAME FRIENDS WITH A THIEF GIRL...
I RAISED HER ALONE AFTER HER MOTHER DIED YOUNG. PERHAPS AN EXCESS OF FREEDOM MADE HER ...
(SOB)
...LIKE THAT...
IS HE TALKING ABOUT HER FETISH?
THEN WHY'D YOU LET HER GET THIS BAD, DAD!?
LALATINA-SAMA IS A WONDERFUL WOMAN, SIR.
IF KAZUMA-KUN WERE NOT HERE, I COULD WISH TO MAKE HER MY OWN WIFE.
HUH!?

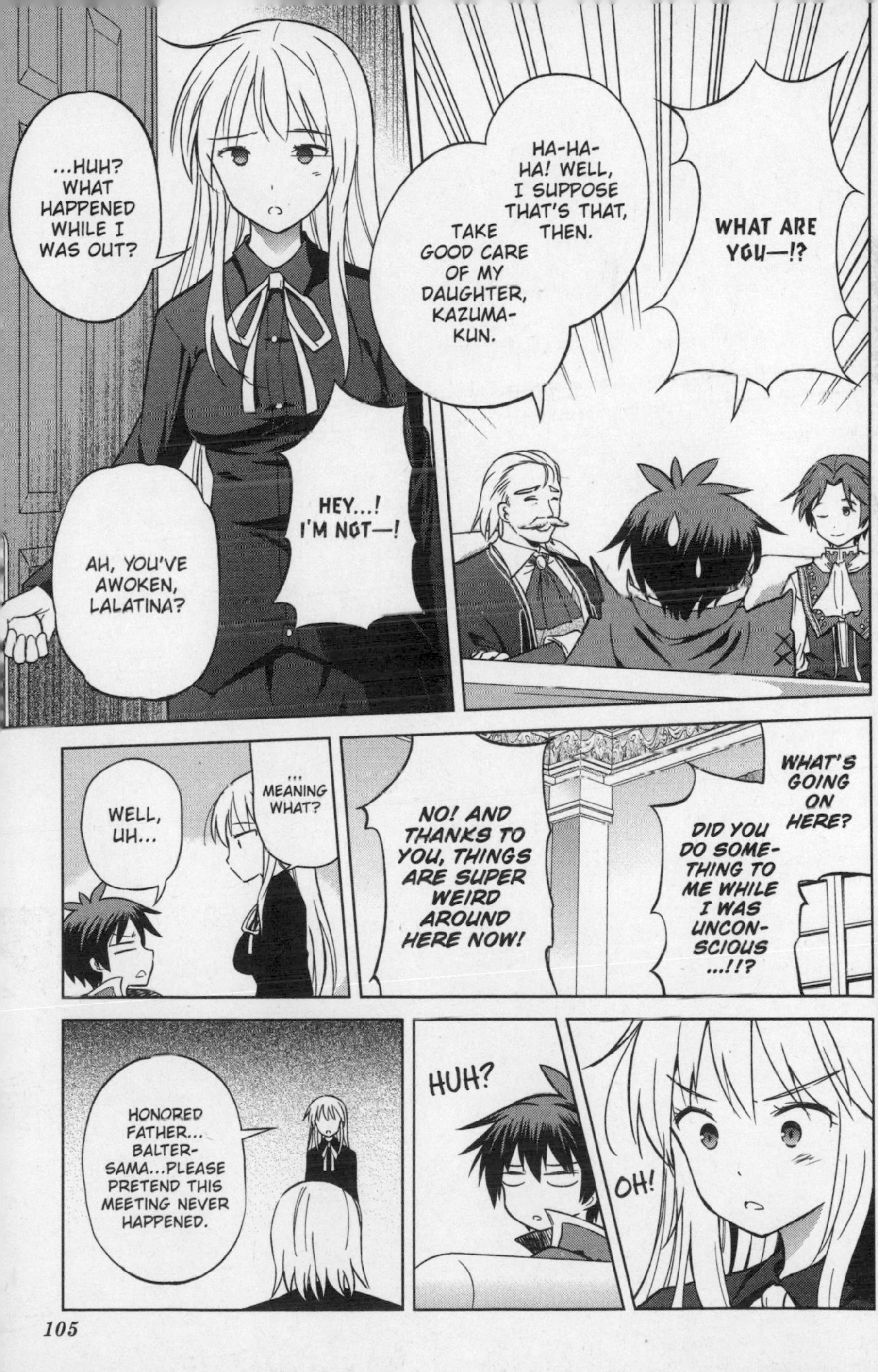
WHAT ARE YOU—!?
HA-HA-HA! WELL, I SUPPOSE THAT'S THAT, THEN.
TAKE GOOD CARE OF MY DAUGHTER, KAZUMA-KUN.
HEY...! I'M NOT—!
AH, YOU'VE AWOKEN, LALATINA?
...HUH? WHAT HAPPENED WHILE I WAS OUT?
WHAT'S GOING ON HERE?
DID YOU DO SOMETHING TO ME WHILE I WAS UNCONSCIOUS ...!!?
NO! AND THANKS TO YOU, THINGS ARE SUPER WEIRD AROUND HERE NOW!
...MEANING WHAT?
WELL, UH...
OH!
HUH?
HONORED FATHER... BALTER-SAMA...PLEASE PRETEND THIS MEETING NEVER HAPPENED.

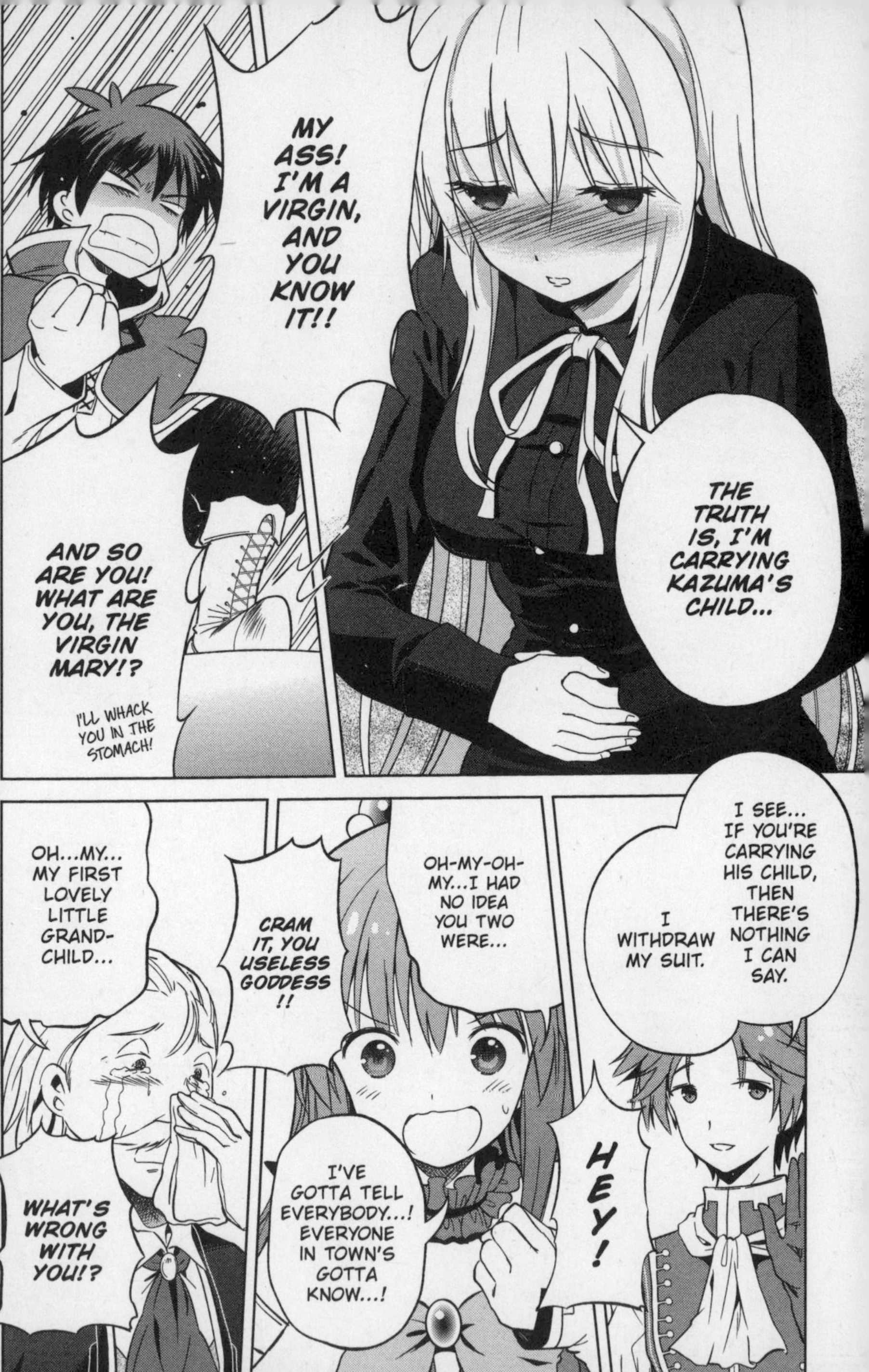

THE TRUTH IS, I'M CARRYING KAZUMA'S CHILD...
MY ASS! I'M A VIRGIN, AND YOU KNOW IT!!
AND SO ARE YOU! WHAT ARE YOU, THE VIRGIN MARY!?
I'LL WHACK YOU IN THE STOMACH!
I SEE... IF YOU'RE CARRYING HIS CHILD, THEN THERE'S NOTHING I CAN SAY.
I WITHDRAW MY SUIT.
HEY!
OH-MY-OH-MY...I HAD NO IDEA YOU TWO WERE...
CRAM IT, YOU USELESS GODDESS!!
I'VE GOTTA TELL EVERYBODY...! EVERYONE IN TOWN'S GOTTA KNOW...!
OH...MY... MY FIRST LOVELY LITTLE GRAND-CHILD...
WHAT'S WRONG WITH YOU!?

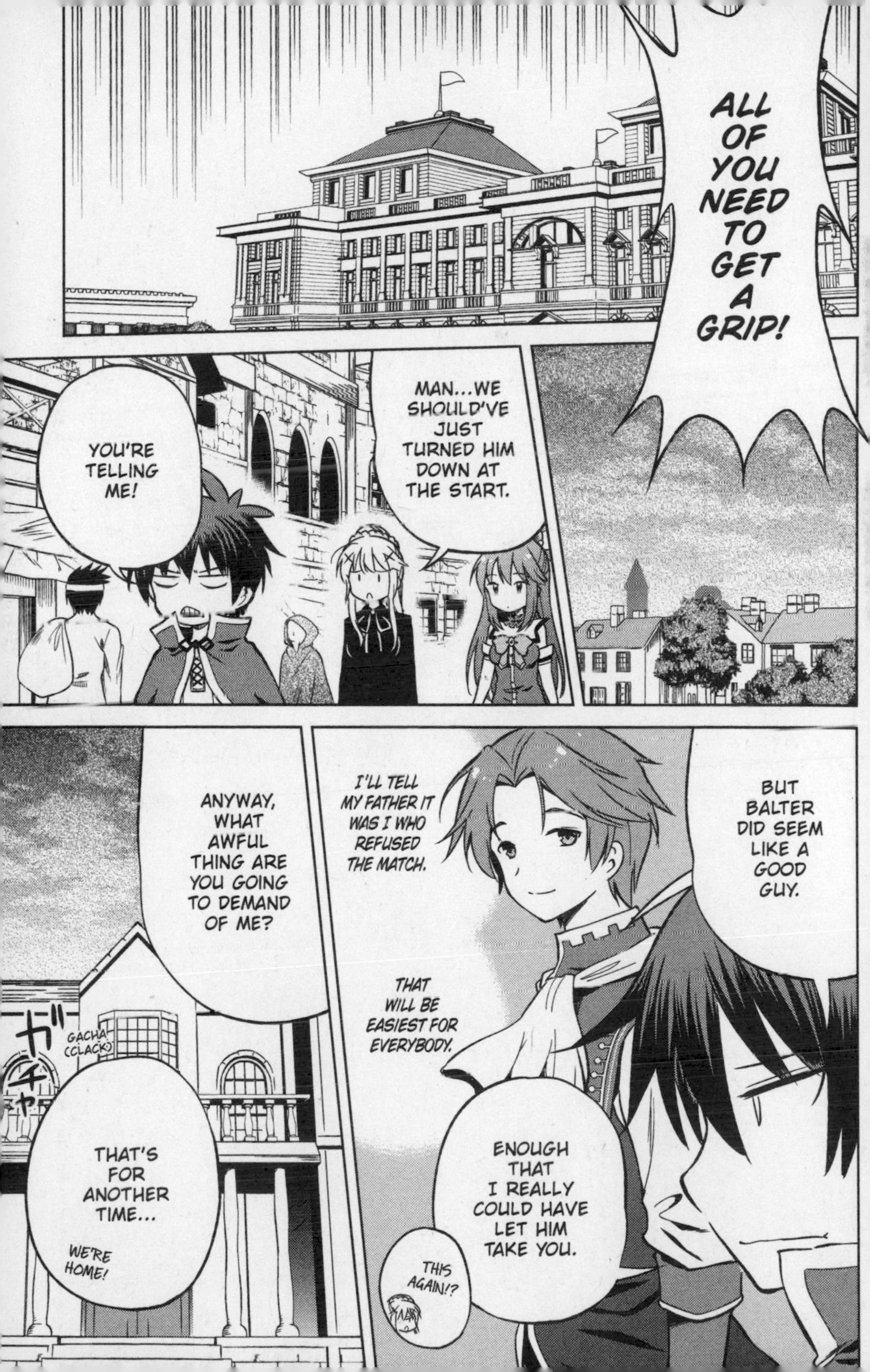
ALL OF YOU NEED TO GET A GRIP!
MAN...WE SHOULD'VE JUST TURNED HIM DOWN AT THE START.
YOU'RE TELLING ME!
BUT BALTER DID SEEM LIKE A GOOD GUY.
I'LL TELL MY FATHER IT WAS I WHO REFUSED THE MATCH.
THAT WILL BE EASIEST FOR EVERYBODY.
ENOUGH THAT I REALLY COULD HAVE LET HIM TAKE YOU.
THIS AGAIN!?
ANYWAY, WHAT AWFUL THING ARE YOU GOING TO DEMAND OF ME?
ガチャ
GACHA (CLACK)
THAT'S FOR ANOTHER TIME...
WE'RE HOME!

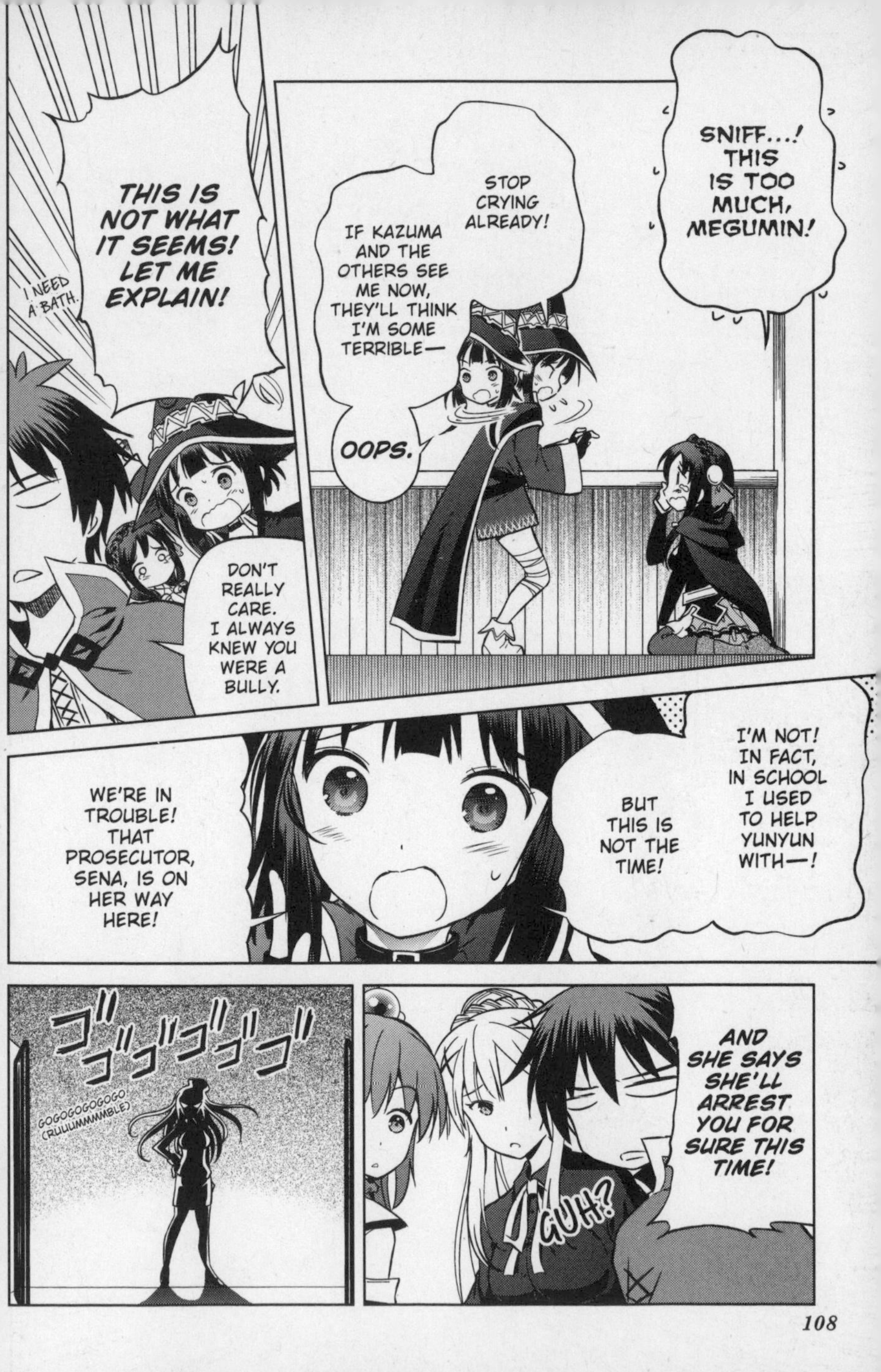
SNIFF...! THIS IS TOO MUCH, MEGUMIN!
STOP CRYING ALREADY!
IF KAZUMA AND THE OTHERS SEE ME NOW, THEY'LL THINK I'M SOME TERRIBLE—
OOPS.
THIS IS NOT WHAT IT SEEMS! LET ME EXPLAIN!
I NEED A BATH.
DON'T REALLY CARE. I ALWAYS KNEW YOU WERE A BULLY.
I'M NOT! IN FACT, IN SCHOOL I USED TO HELP YUNYUN WITH—!
BUT THIS IS NOT THE TIME!
WE'RE IN TROUBLE! THAT PROSECUTOR, SENA, IS ON HER WAY HERE!
AND SHE SAYS SHE'LL ARREST YOU FOR SURE THIS TIME!
GUH?
ゴゴゴゴゴゴ
GOGOGOGOGOGO (RUUUMMMMBLE)

CHAPTER 29 MAY THIS MASKED KNIGHT SUBMIT! ①

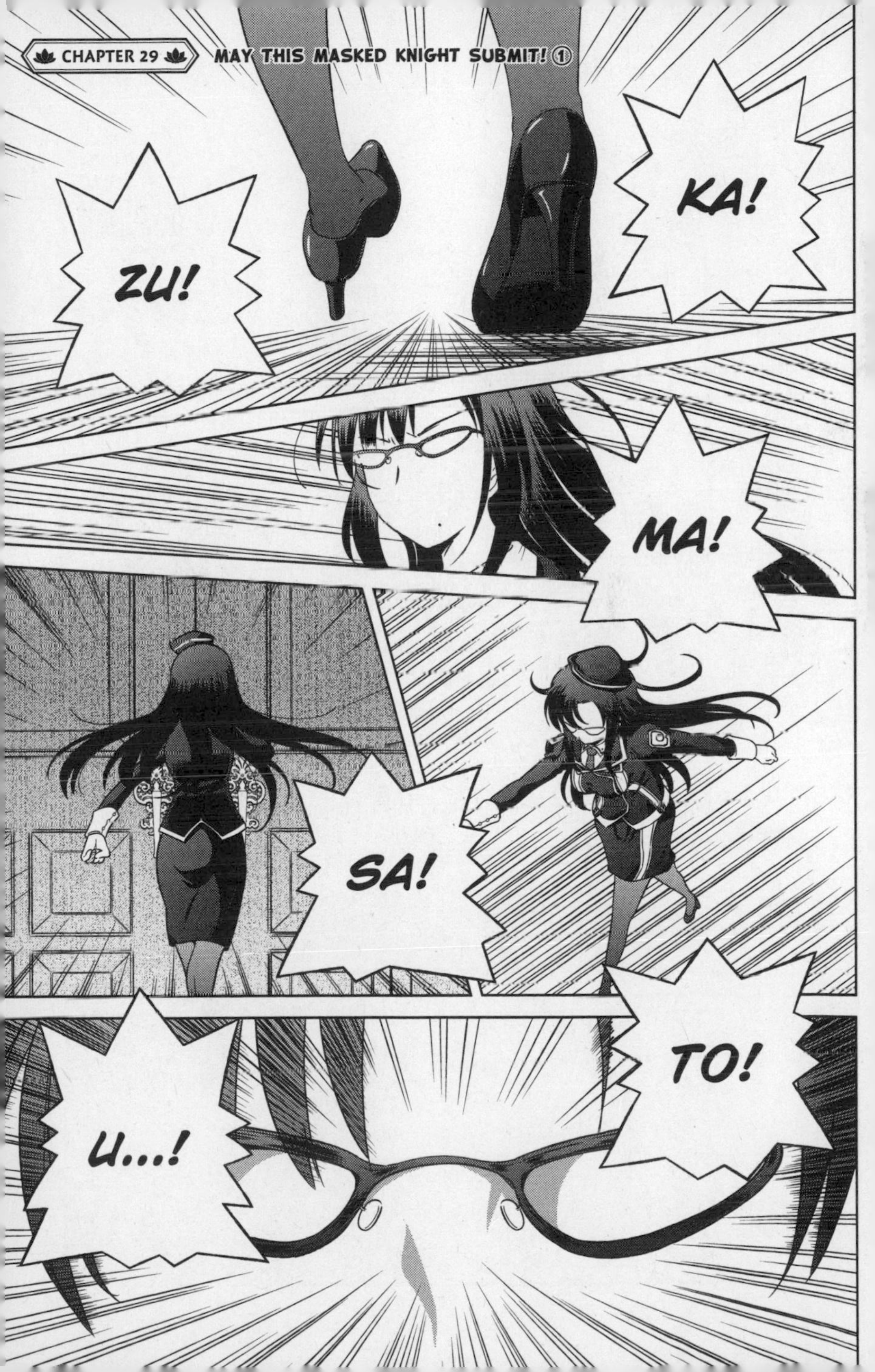
KA!
ZU!
MA!
SA!
TO!
U...!

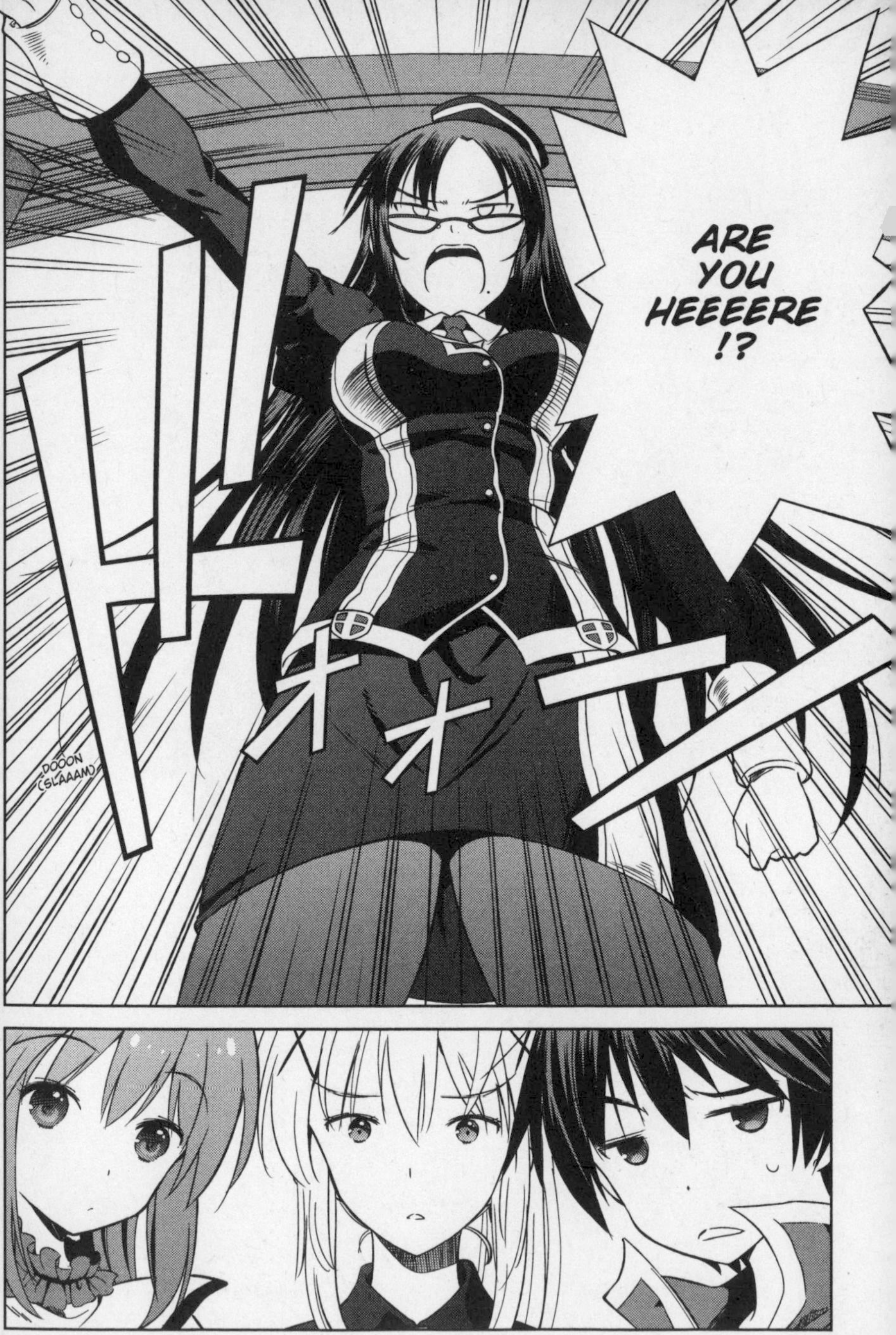
ARE YOU HEEEERE !?
DOOON (SLAAAM)

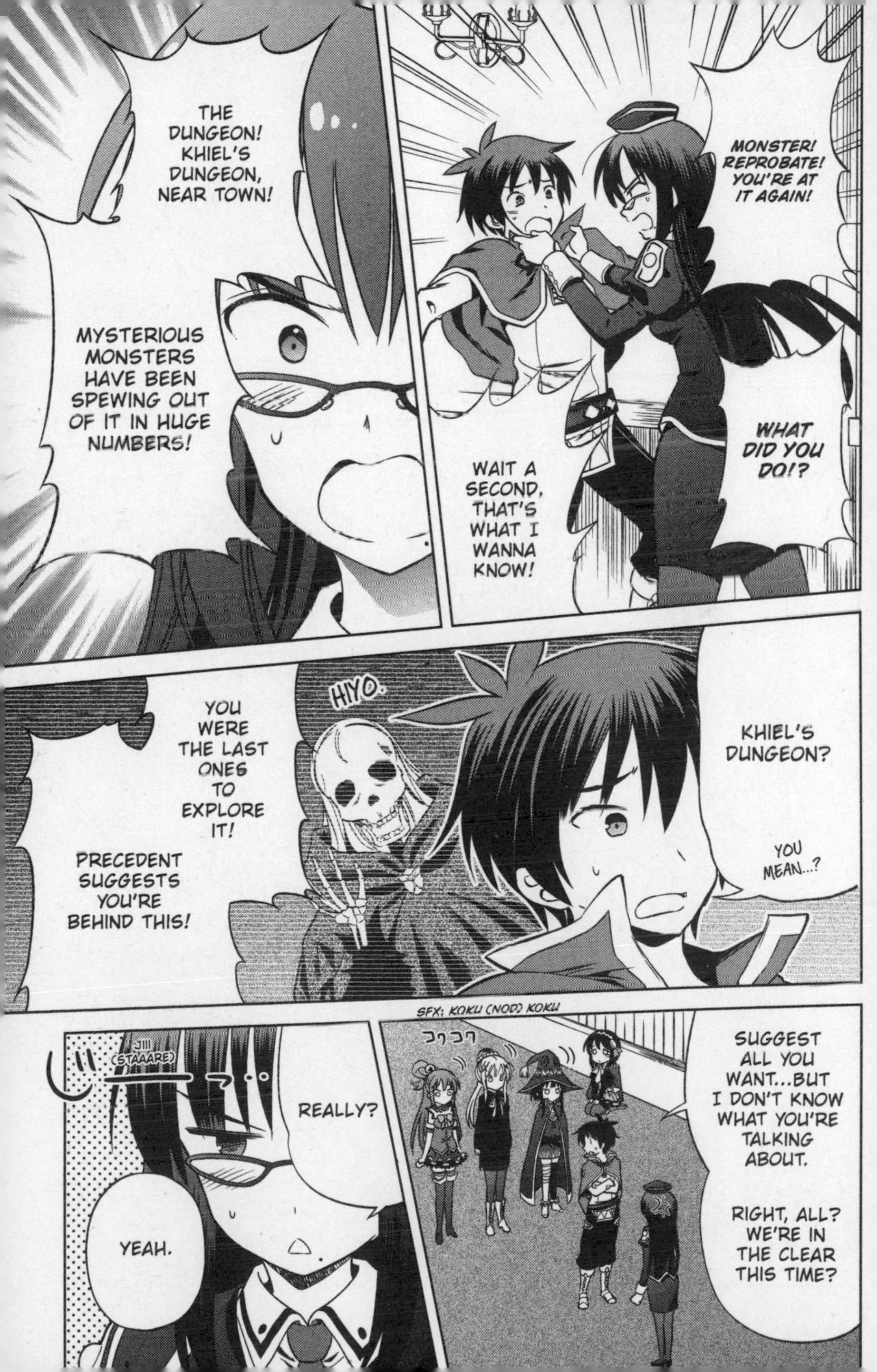
MONSTER! REPROBATE! YOU'RE AT IT AGAIN!
WHAT DID YOU DO!?
WAIT A SECOND, THAT'S WHAT I WANNA KNOW!
THE DUNGEON! KHIEL'S DUNGEON, NEAR TOWN!
MYSTERIOUS MONSTERS HAVE BEEN SPEWING OUT OF IT IN HUGE NUMBERS!
KHIEL'S DUNGEON?
YOU MEAN...?
HIYO.
YOU WERE THE LAST ONES TO EXPLORE IT!
PRECEDENT SUGGESTS YOU'RE BEHIND THIS!
SFX: KOKU (NOD) KOKU
SUGGEST ALL YOU WANT...BUT I DON'T KNOW WHAT YOU'RE TALKING ABOUT.
RIGHT, ALL? WE'RE IN THE CLEAR THIS TIME?
コクコク
JIII (STAAARE)
REALLY?
YEAH.

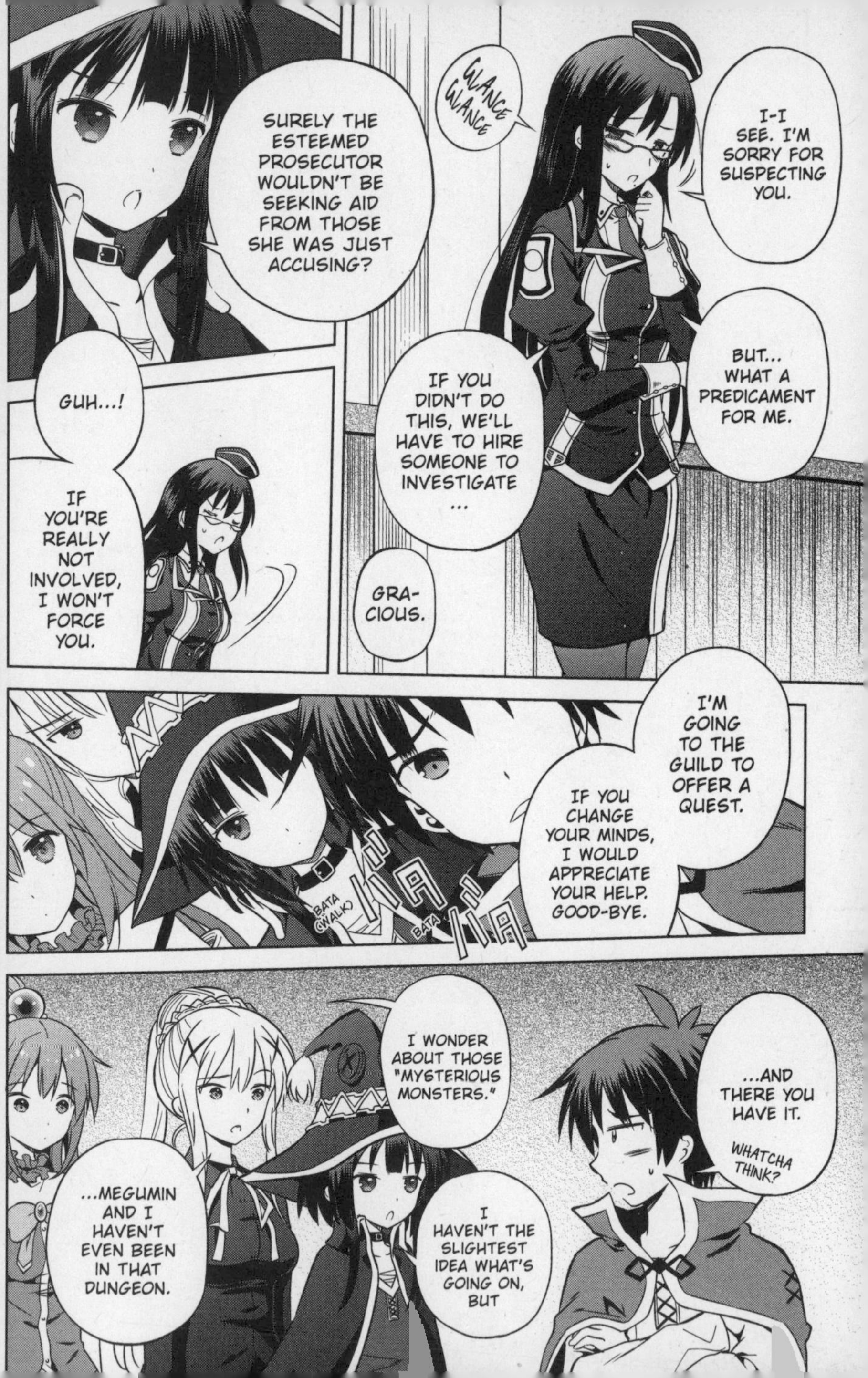
I-I SEE. I'M SORRY FOR SUSPECTING YOU.
GLANCE GLANCE
BUT... WHAT A PREDICAMENT FOR ME.
IF YOU DIDN'T DO THIS, WE'LL HAVE TO HIRE SOMEONE TO INVESTIGATE...
GRACIOUS.
SURELY THE ESTEEMED PROSECUTOR WOULDN'T BE SEEKING AID FROM THOSE SHE WAS JUST ACCUSING?
GUH...!
IF YOU'RE REALLY NOT INVOLVED, I WON'T FORCE YOU.
I'M GOING TO THE GUILD TO OFFER A QUEST.
IF YOU CHANGE YOUR MINDS, I WOULD APPRECIATE YOUR HELP. GOOD-BYE.
BATA (WALK)
BATA
...AND THERE YOU HAVE IT.
WHATCHA THINK?
I WONDER ABOUT THOSE "MYSTERIOUS MONSTERS."
I HAVEN'T THE SLIGHTEST IDEA WHAT'S GOING ON, BUT
...MEGUMIN AND I HAVEN'T EVEN BEEN IN THAT DUNGEON.

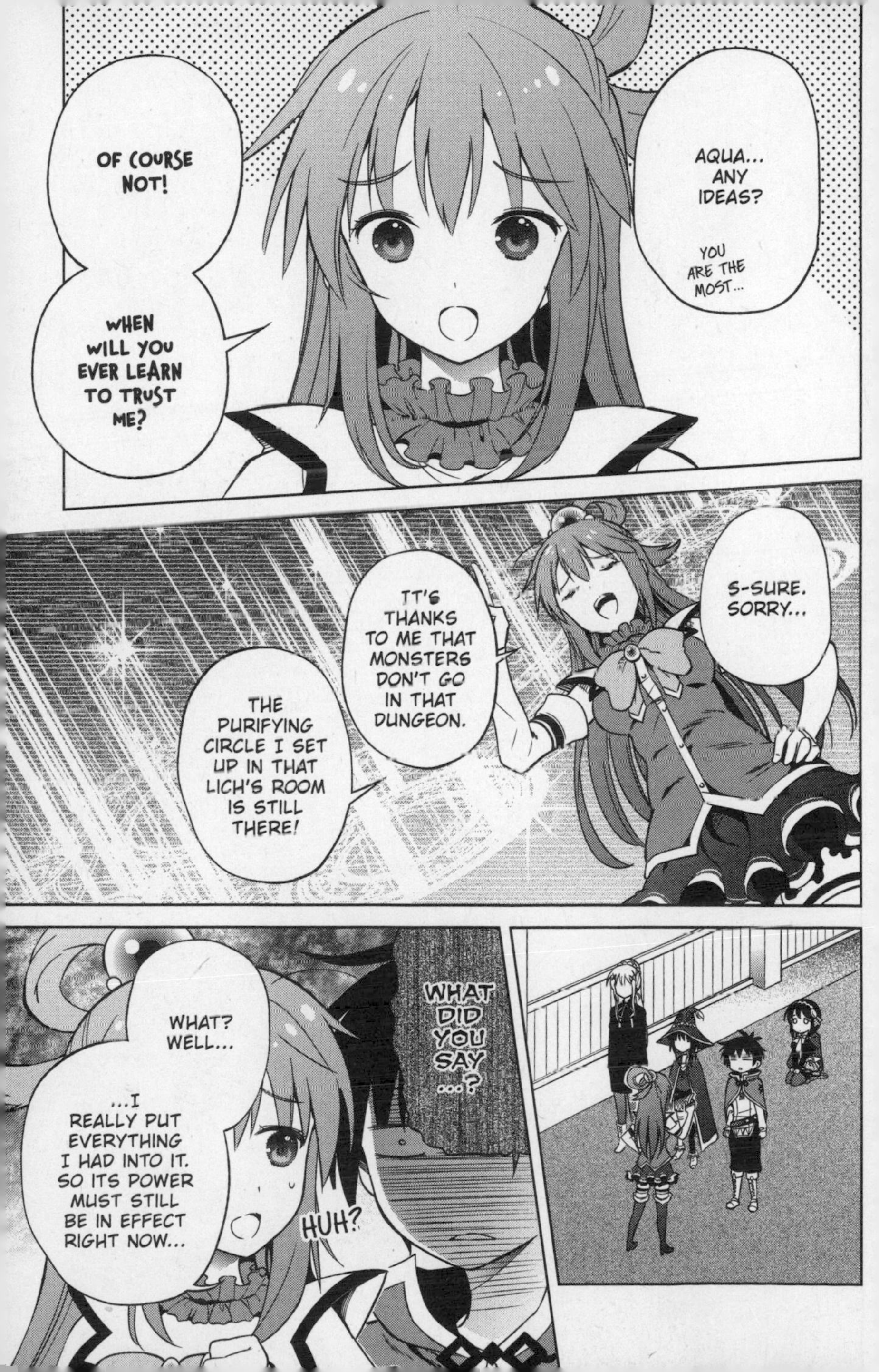
AQUA... ANY IDEAS?
YOU ARE THE MOST...
OF COURSE NOT!
WHEN WILL YOU EVER LEARN TO TRUST ME?
S-SURE. SORRY...
IT'S THANKS TO ME THAT MONSTERS DON'T GO IN THAT DUNGEON.
THE PURIFYING CIRCLE I SET UP IN THAT LICH'S ROOM IS STILL THERE!
WHAT DID YOU SAY...?
WHAT? WELL...
...I REALLY PUT EVERYTHING I HAD INTO IT. SO ITS POWER MUST STILL BE IN EFFECT RIGHT NOW...
HUH?

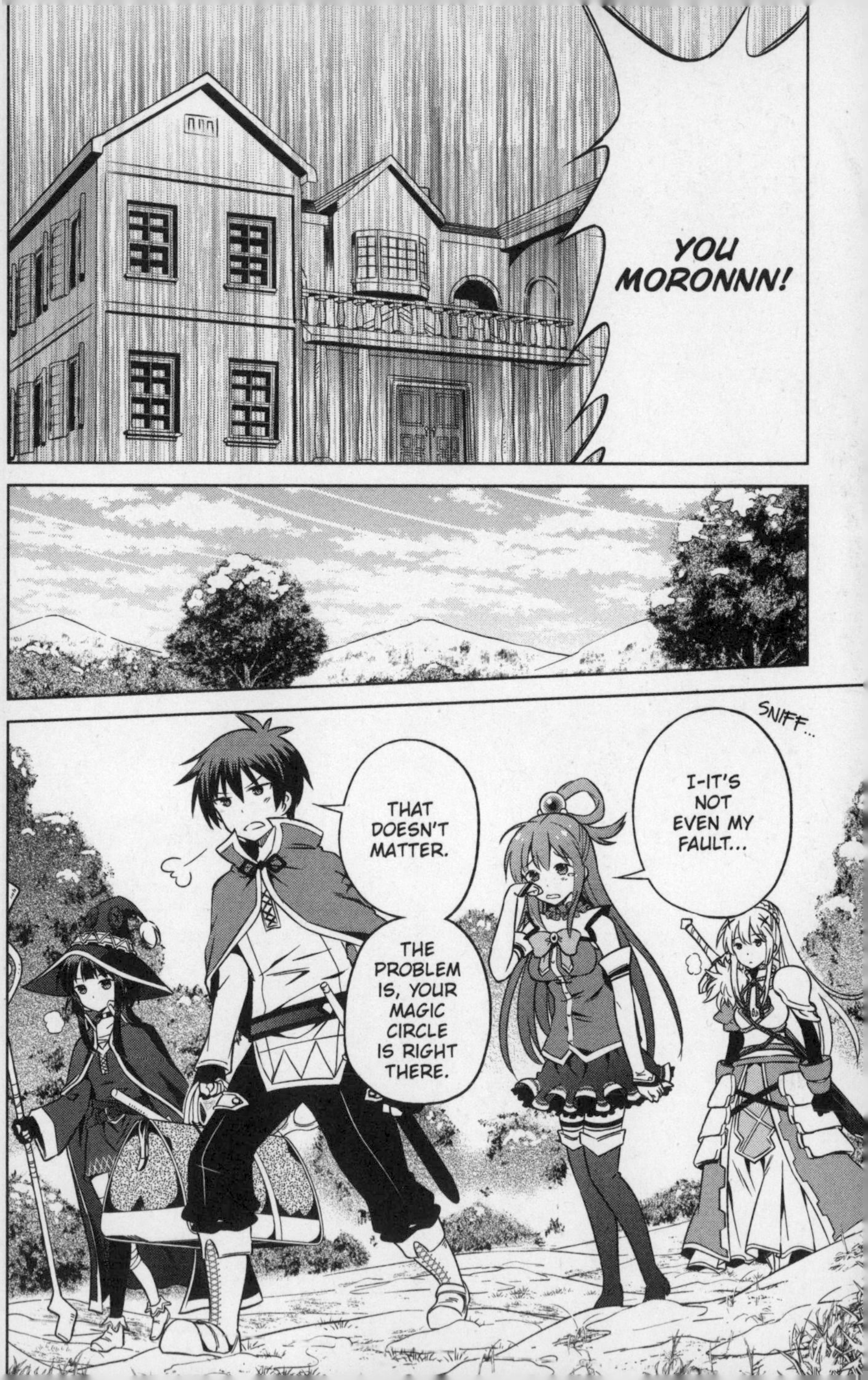
YOU MORONNN!
SNIFF...
I-IT'S NOT EVEN MY FAULT...
THAT DOESN'T MATTER.
THE PROBLEM IS, YOUR MAGIC CIRCLE IS RIGHT THERE.

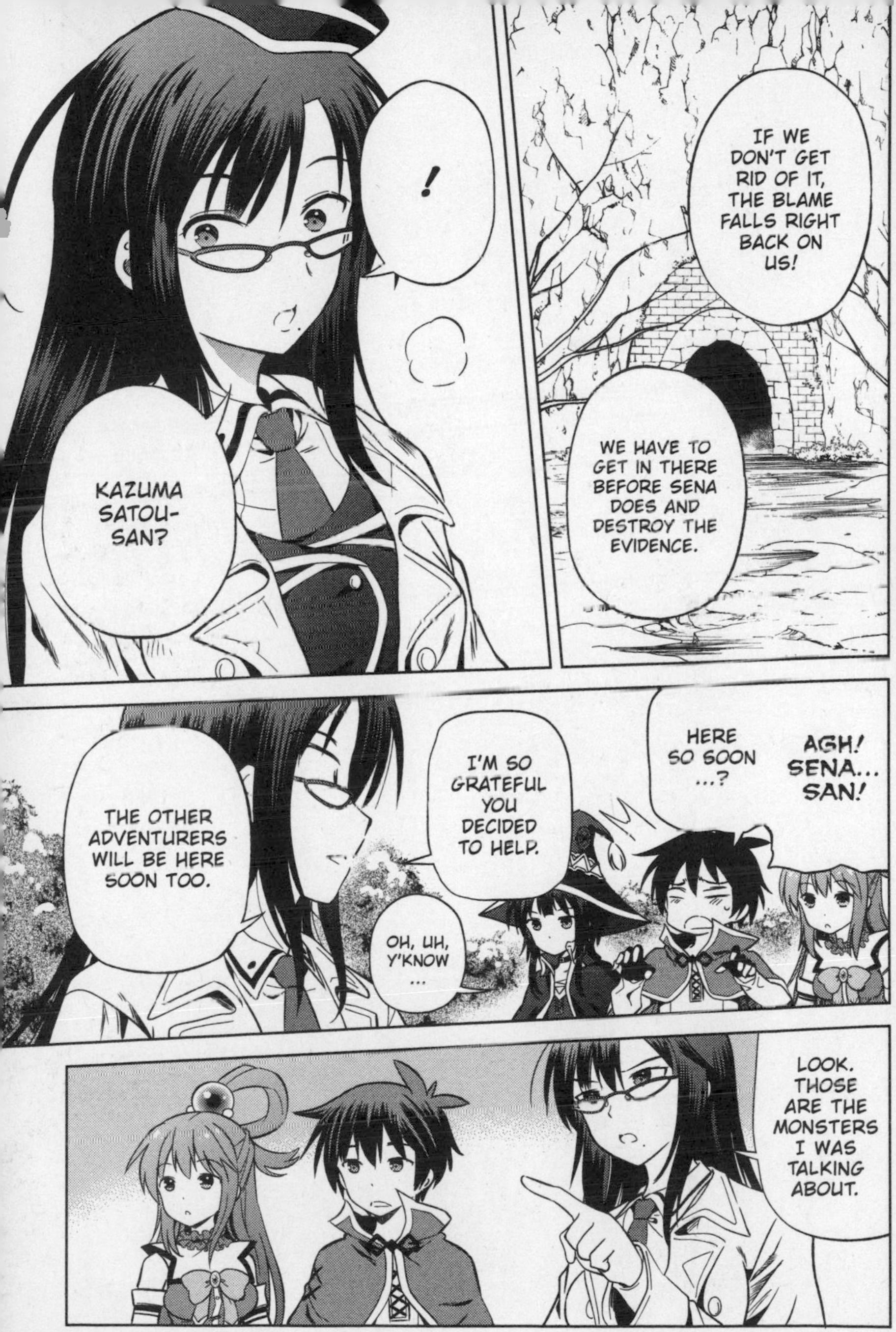
IF WE DON'T GET RID OF IT, THE BLAME FALLS RIGHT BACK ON US!
WE HAVE TO GET IN THERE BEFORE SENA DOES AND DESTROY THE EVIDENCE.
!
KAZUMA SATOU-SAN?
AGH! SENA... SAN!
HERE SO SOON ...?
I'M SO GRATEFUL YOU DECIDED TO HELP.
OH, UH, Y'KNOW ...
THE OTHER ADVENTURERS WILL BE HERE SOON TOO.
LOOK. THOSE ARE THE MONSTERS I WAS TALKING ABOUT.

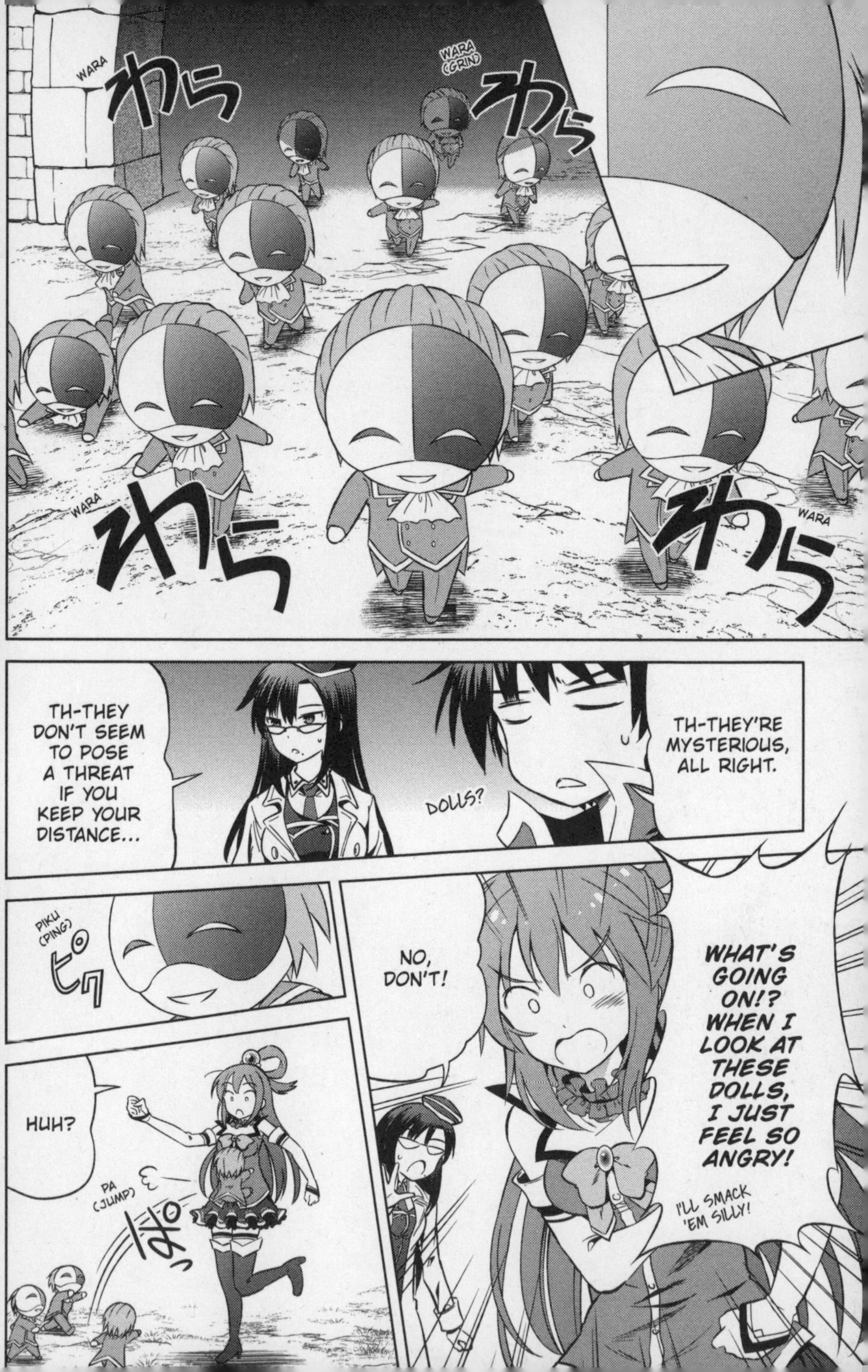

WARA (GRIN)
わら
WARA
わら
WARA
わら
WARA
わら
TH-THEY'RE MYSTERIOUS, ALL RIGHT.
DOLLS?
TH-THEY DON'T SEEM TO POSE A THREAT IF YOU KEEP YOUR DISTANCE...
WHAT'S GOING ON!? WHEN I LOOK AT THESE DOLLS, I JUST FEEL SO ANGRY!
I'LL SMACK 'EM SILLY!
NO, DON'T!
PIKU (PING)
ピク
HUH?
PA (JUMP)
ぱっ

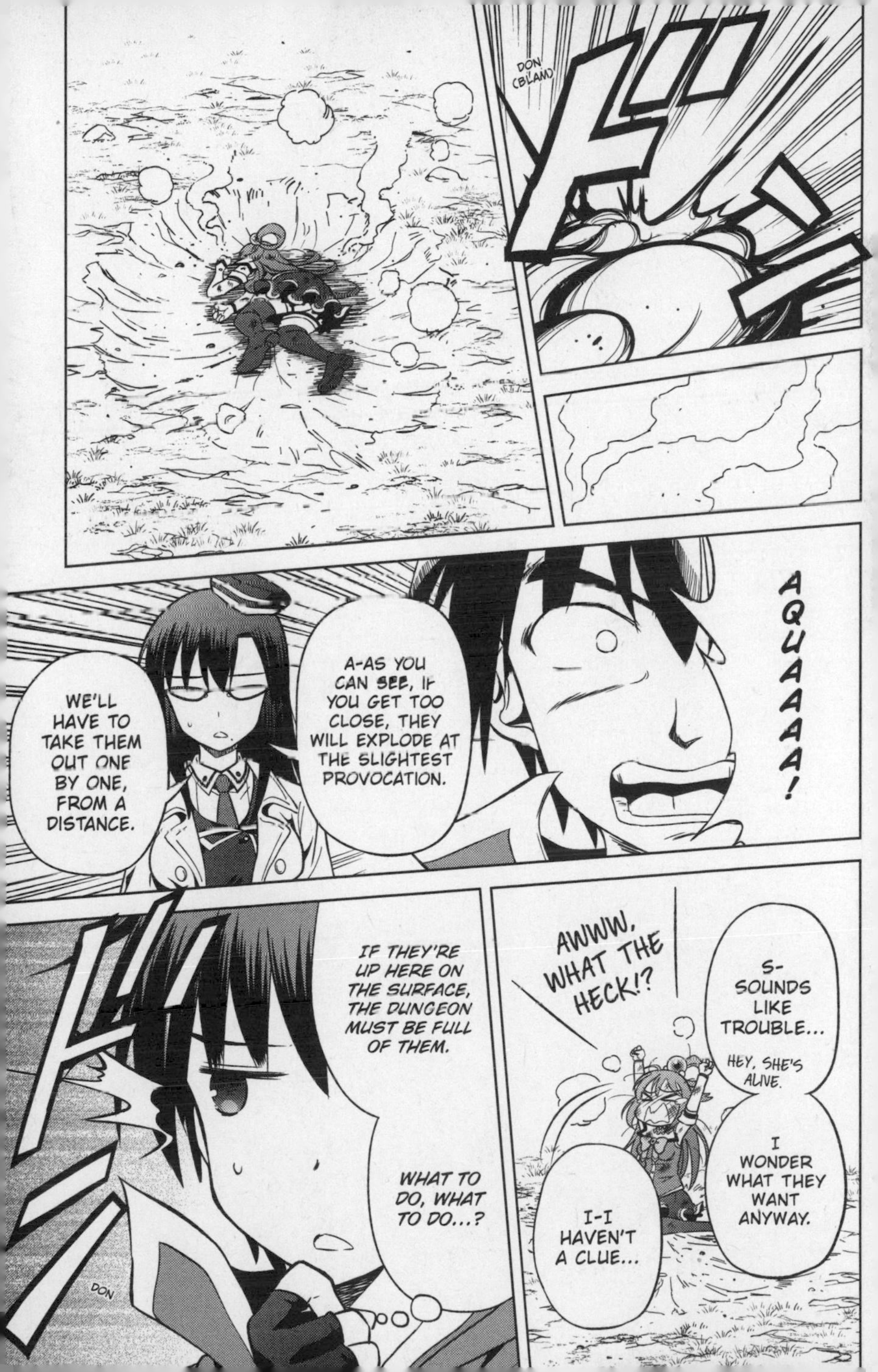
DON (BLAM)
AQUAAAAA!
A-AS YOU CAN SEE, IF YOU GET TOO CLOSE, THEY WILL EXPLODE AT THE SLIGHTEST PROVOCATION.
WE'LL HAVE TO TAKE THEM OUT ONE BY ONE, FROM A DISTANCE.
S-SOUNDS LIKE TROUBLE...
AWWW, WHAT THE HECK!?
HEY, SHE'S ALIVE.
I WONDER WHAT THEY WANT ANYWAY.
I-I HAVEN'T A CLUE...
IF THEY'RE UP HERE ON THE SURFACE, THE DUNGEON MUST BE FULL OF THEM.
WHAT TO DO, WHAT TO DO...?
DON

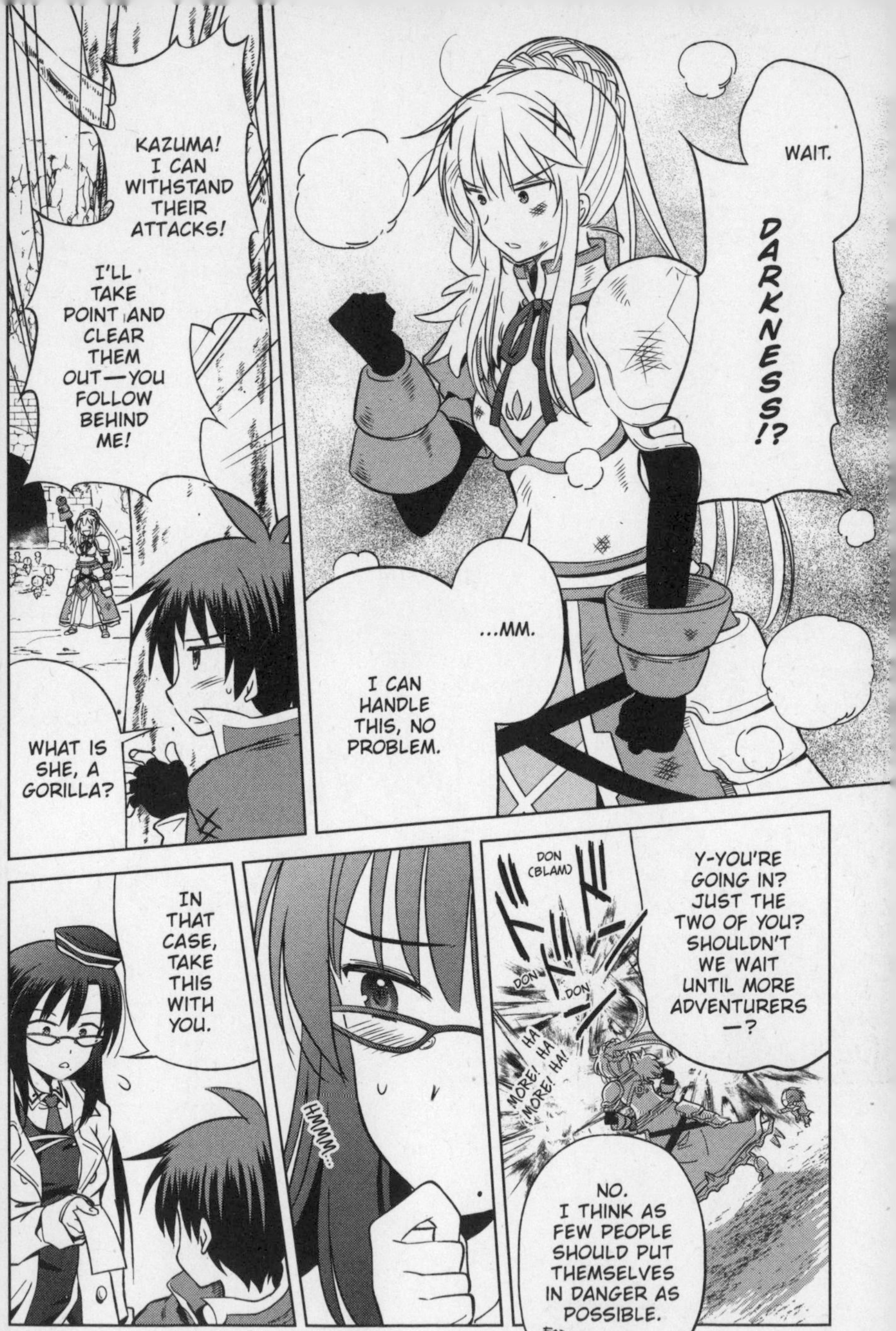
WAIT.
DARKNESS!?
...MM.
I CAN HANDLE THIS, NO PROBLEM.
KAZUMA! I CAN WITHSTAND THEIR ATTACKS!
I'LL TAKE POINT AND CLEAR THEM OUT—YOU FOLLOW BEHIND ME!
WHAT IS SHE, A GORILLA?
Y-YOU'RE GOING IN? JUST THE TWO OF YOU? SHOULDN'T WE WAIT UNTIL MORE ADVENTURERS—?
DON (BLAM)
DON
DON
HA HA HA!
MORE! MORE!
NO. I THINK AS FEW PEOPLE SHOULD PUT THEMSELVES IN DANGER AS POSSIBLE.
FOR VARIOUS REASONS.
HMMM...
IN THAT CASE, TAKE THIS WITH YOU.

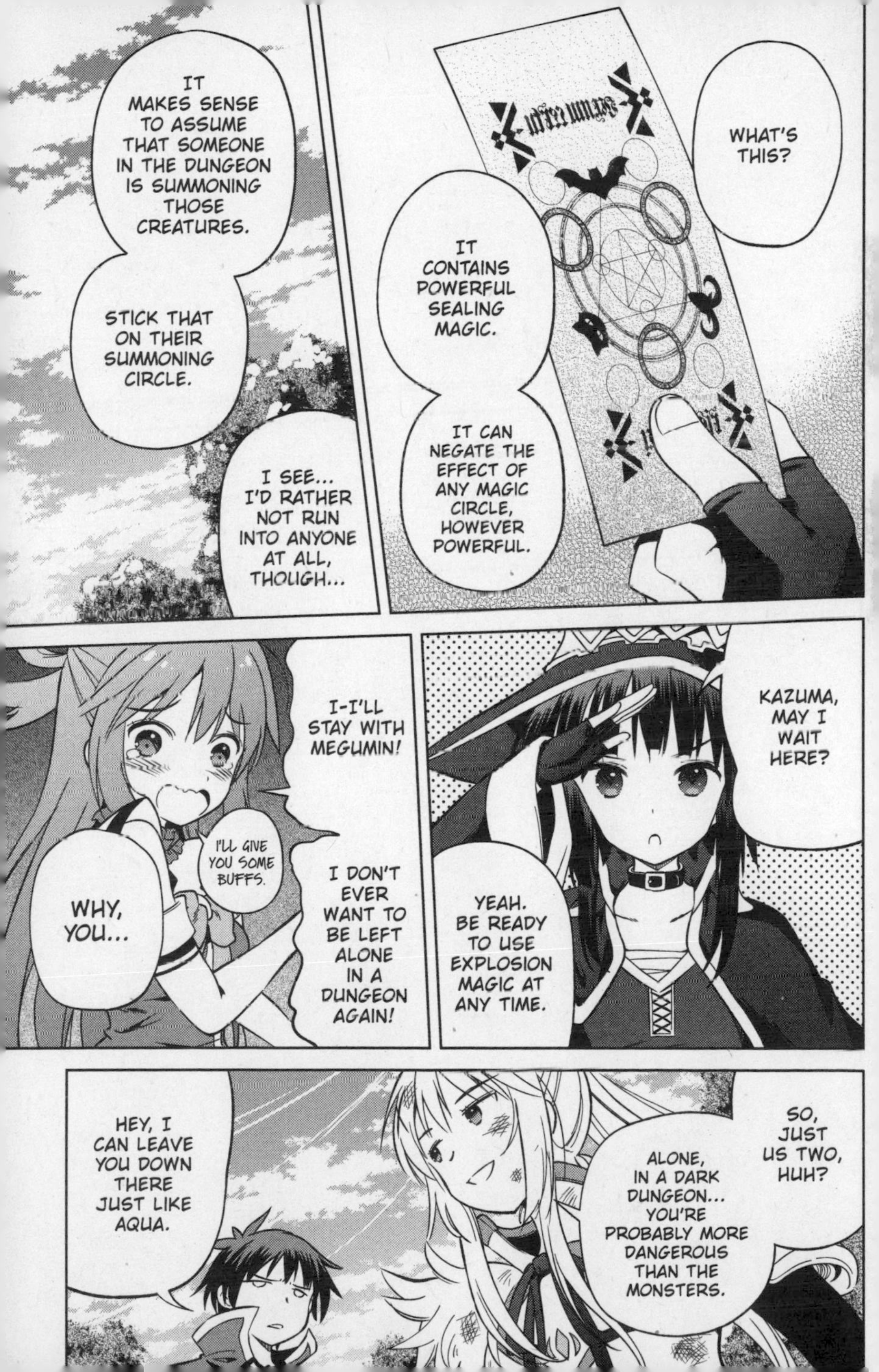
WHAT'S THIS?
IT CONTAINS POWERFUL SEALING MAGIC.
IT CAN NEGATE THE EFFECT OF ANY MAGIC CIRCLE, HOWEVER POWERFUL.
IT MAKES SENSE TO ASSUME THAT SOMEONE IN THE DUNGEON IS SUMMONING THOSE CREATURES.
STICK THAT ON THEIR SUMMONING CIRCLE.
I SEE... I'D RATHER NOT RUN INTO ANYONE AT ALL, THOUGH...
KAZUMA, MAY I WAIT HERE?
YEAH. BE READY TO USE EXPLOSION MAGIC AT ANY TIME.
I-I'LL STAY WITH MEGUMIN!
I DON'T EVER WANT TO BE LEFT ALONE IN A DUNGEON AGAIN!
I'LL GIVE YOU SOME BUFFS.
WHY, YOU...
SO, JUST US TWO, HUH?
ALONE, IN A DARK DUNGEON... YOU'RE PROBABLY MORE DANGEROUS THAN THE MONSTERS.
HEY, I CAN LEAVE YOU DOWN THERE JUST LIKE AQUA.

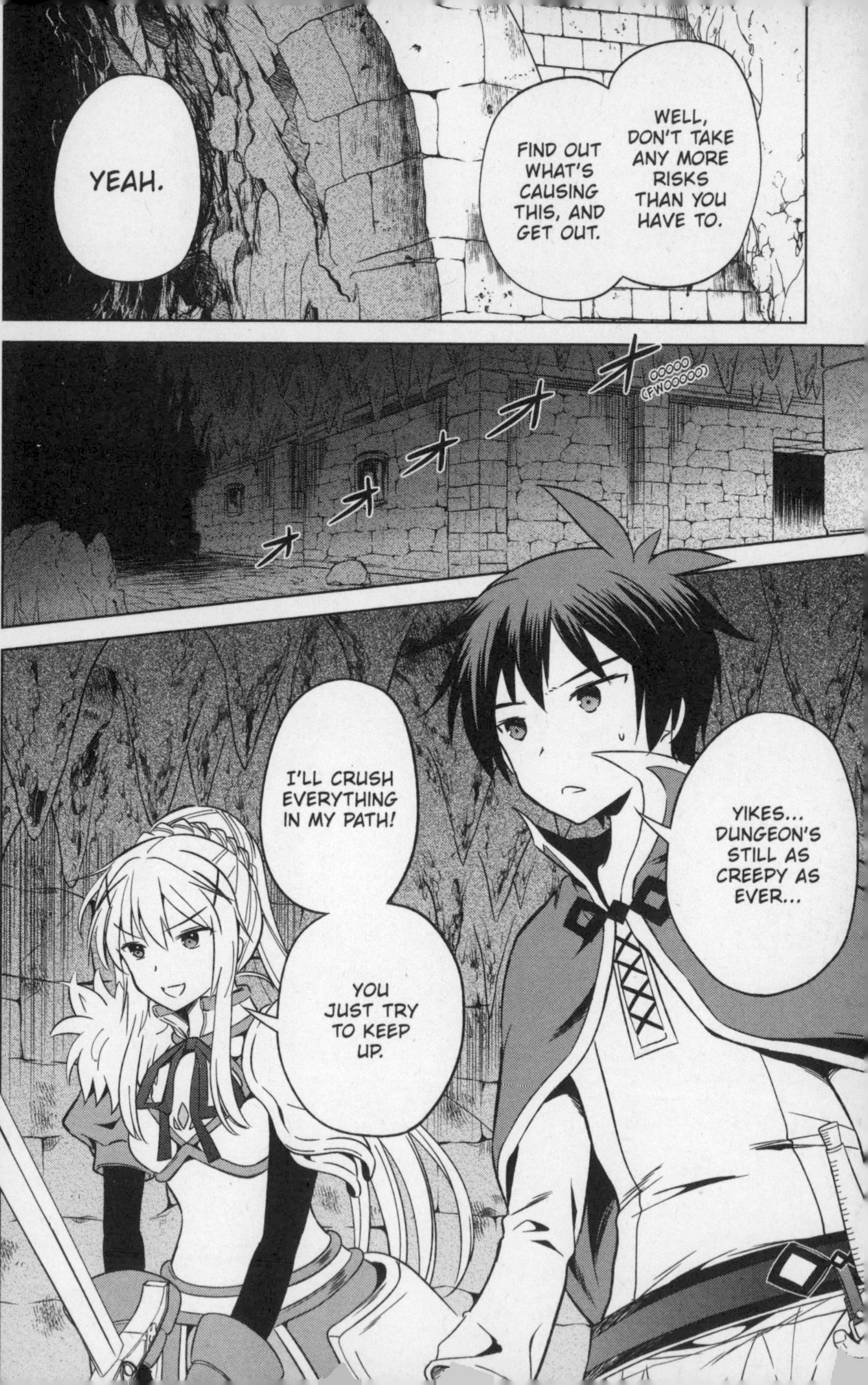
WELL, DON'T TAKE ANY MORE RISKS THAN YOU HAVE TO.
FIND OUT WHAT'S CAUSING THIS, AND GET OUT.
YEAH.
OOOOO (FWOOOOO)
YIKES... DUNGEON'S STILL AS CREEPY AS EVER...
I'LL CRUSH EVERYTHING IN MY PATH!
YOU JUST TRY TO KEEP UP.

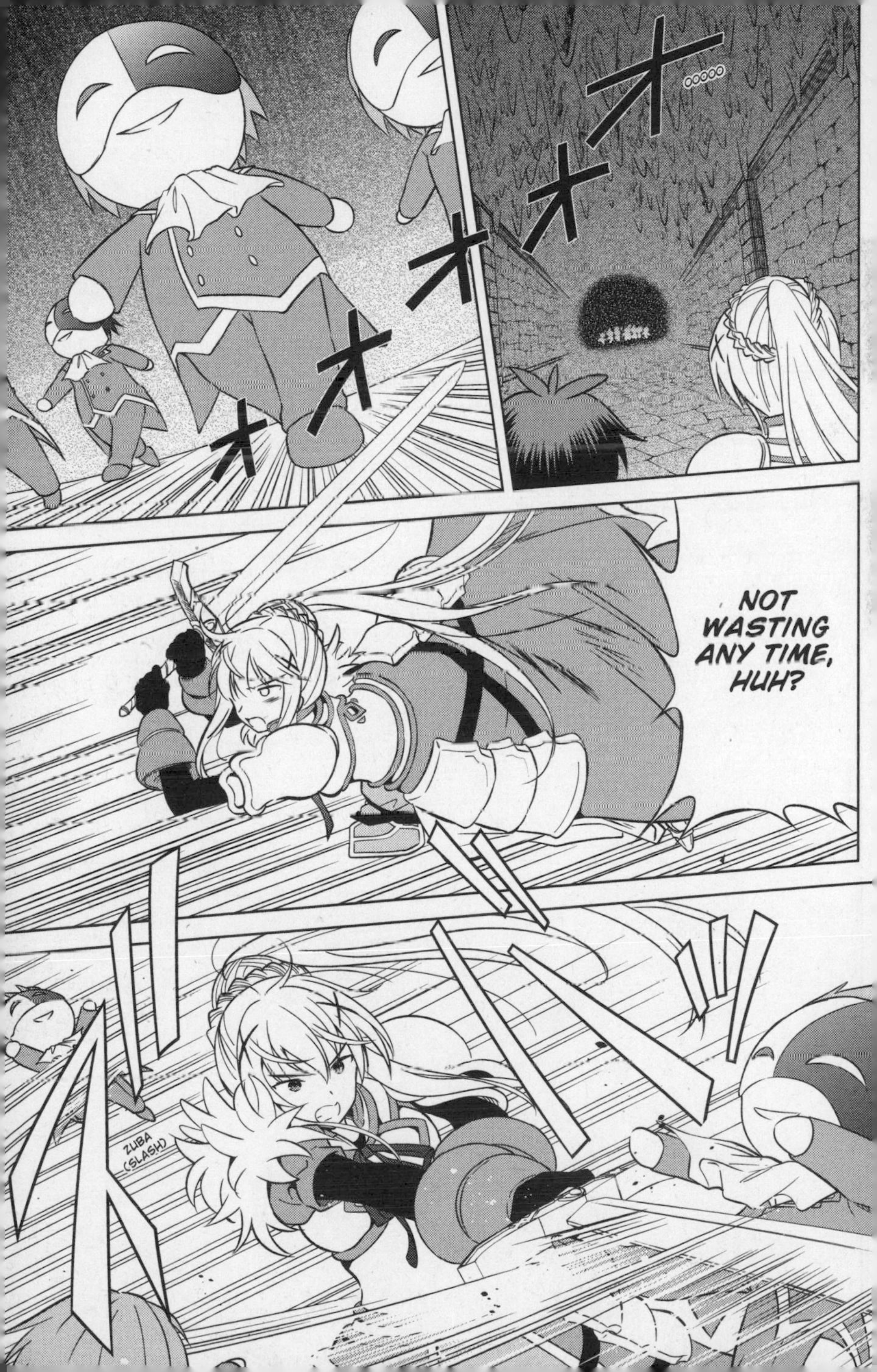
OOOOO
NOT WASTING ANY TIME, HUH?
ZUBA (SLASH)

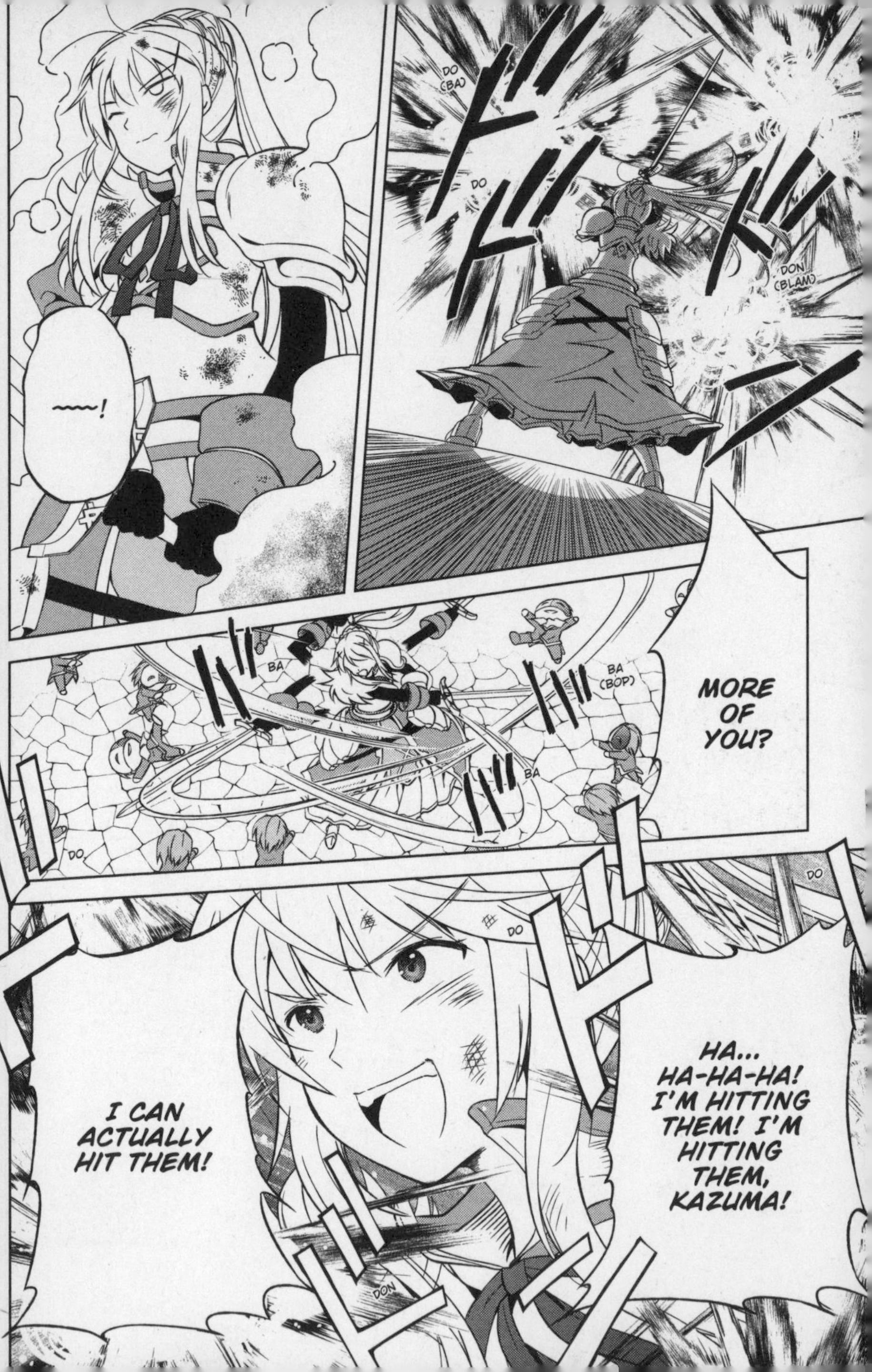
DO (BA)
DO
DON (BLAM)
~~~!
MORE OF YOU?
BA (BOP)
BA
BA
DO
DO
DO
HA... HA-HA-HA! I'M HITTING THEM! I'M HITTING THEM, KAZUMA!
I CAN ACTUALLY HIT THEM!
DON
~~~

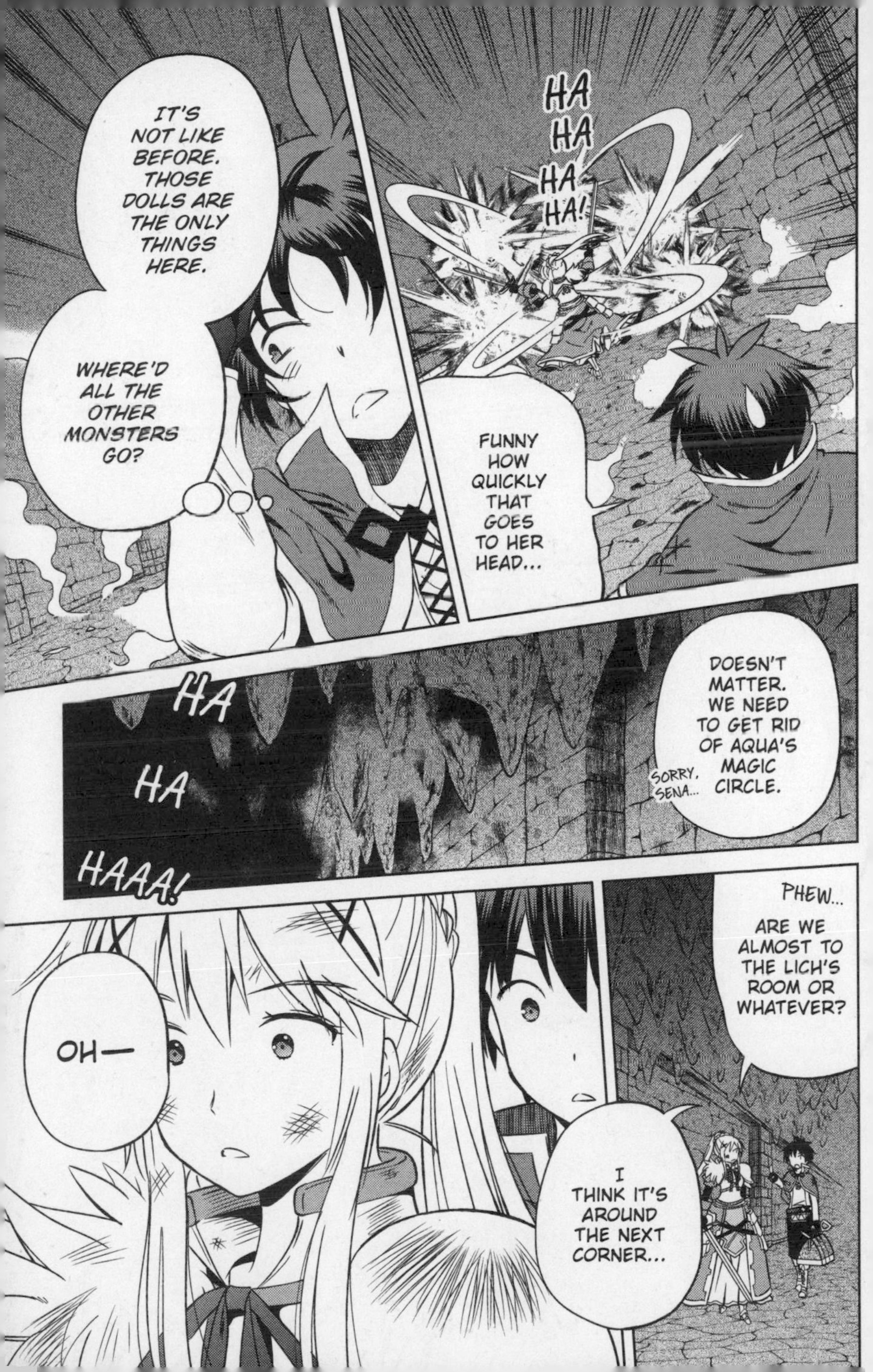
HA HA HA HA!
FUNNY HOW QUICKLY THAT GOES TO HER HEAD...
IT'S NOT LIKE BEFORE. THOSE DOLLS ARE THE ONLY THINGS HERE.
WHERE'D ALL THE OTHER MONSTERS GO?
DOESN'T MATTER. WE NEED TO GET RID OF AQUA'S MAGIC CIRCLE.
SORRY, SENA...
HA HA HAAA!
PHEW...
ARE WE ALMOST TO THE LICH'S ROOM OR WHATEVER?
I THINK IT'S AROUND THE NEXT CORNER...
OH—

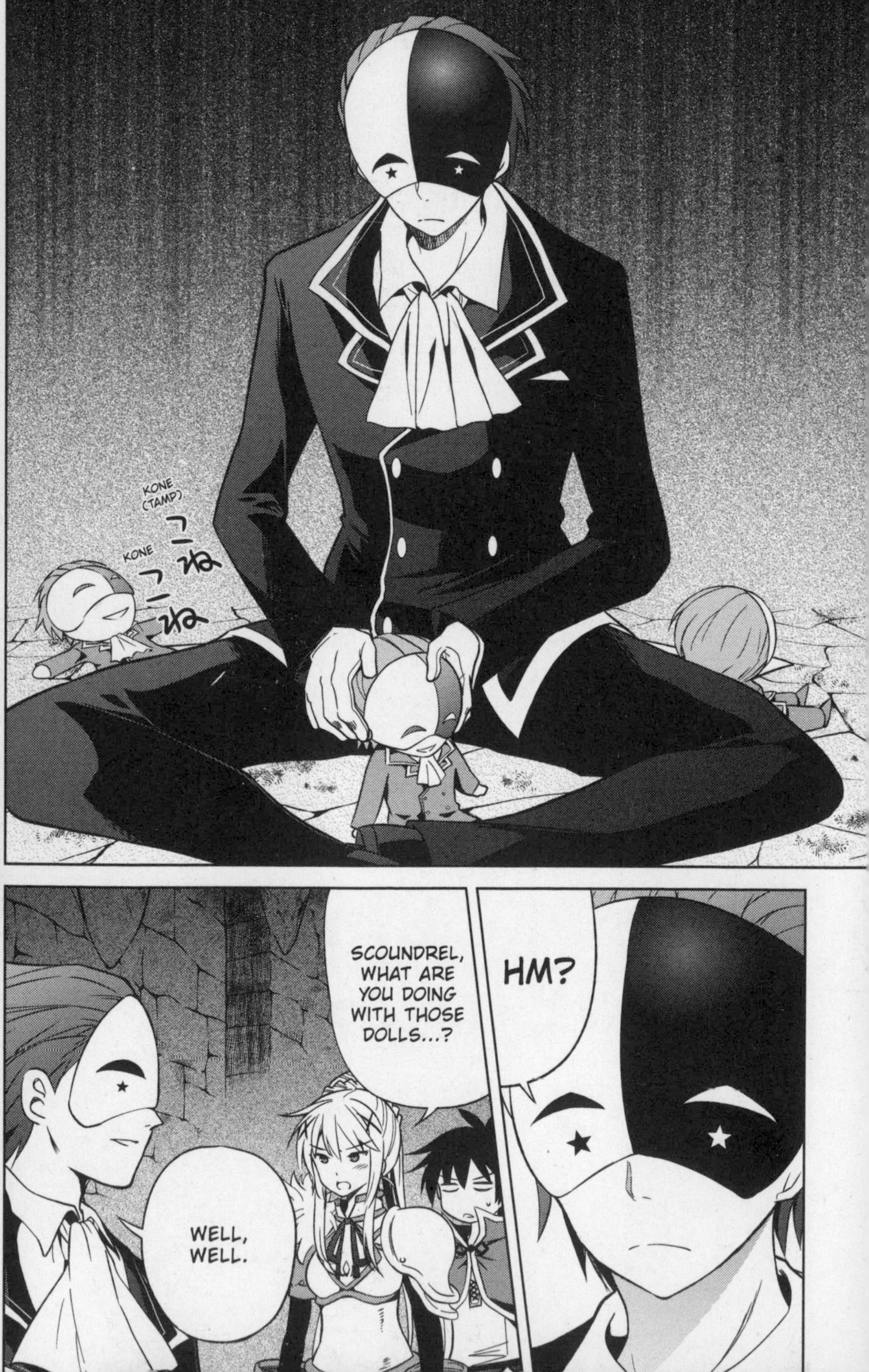
KONE (TAMP)
こね
KONE
こね
HM?
SCOUNDREL, WHAT ARE YOU DOING WITH THOSE DOLLS...?
WELL, WELL.

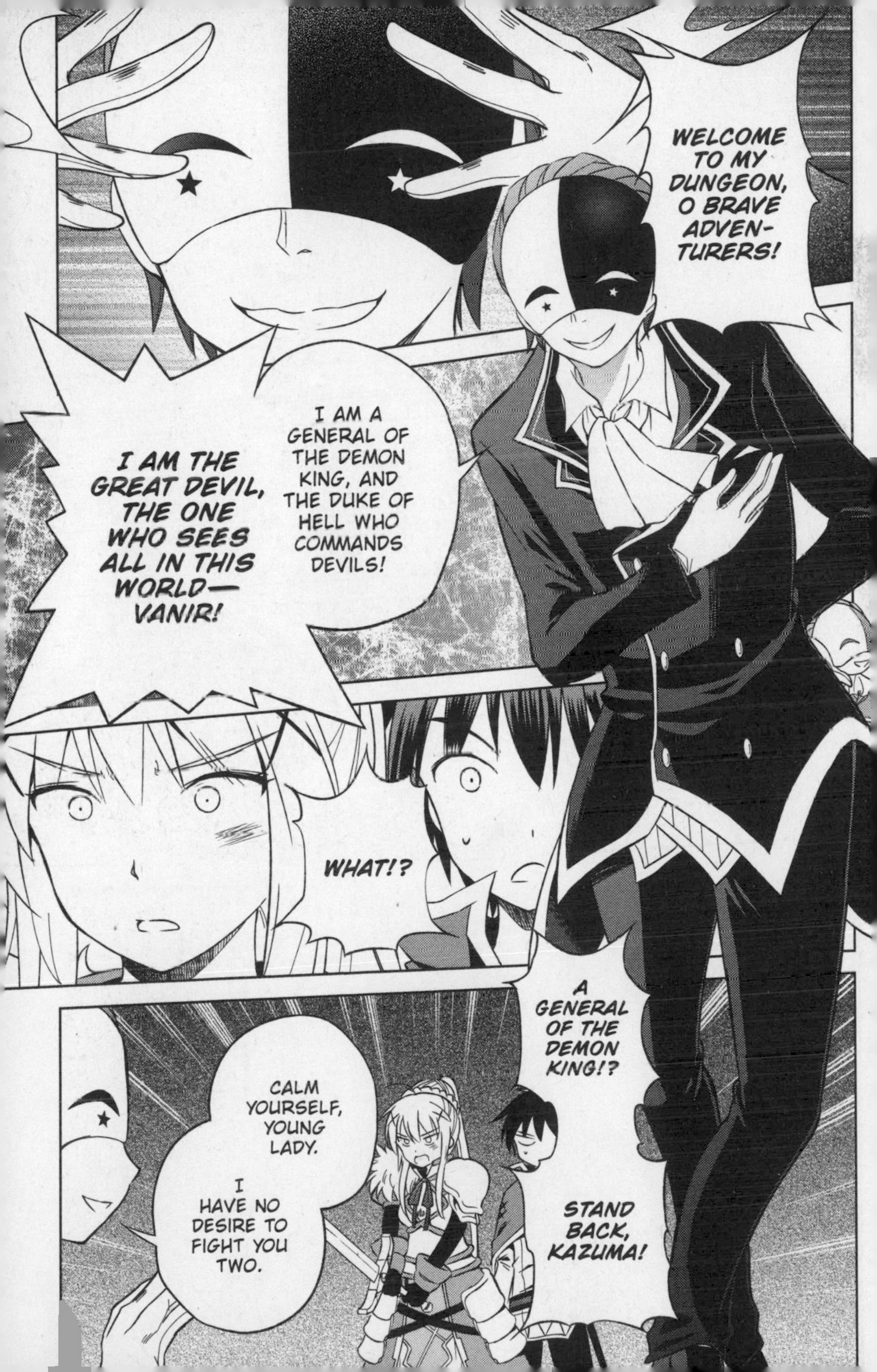

WELCOME TO MY DUNGEON, O BRAVE ADVENTURERS!
I AM A GENERAL OF THE DEMON KING, AND THE DUKE OF HELL WHO COMMANDS DEVILS!
I AM THE GREAT DEVIL, THE ONE WHO SEES ALL IN THIS WORLD—VANIR!
WHAT!?
A GENERAL OF THE DEMON KING!?
STAND BACK, KAZUMA!
CALM YOURSELF, YOUNG LADY.
I HAVE NO DESIRE TO FIGHT YOU TWO.

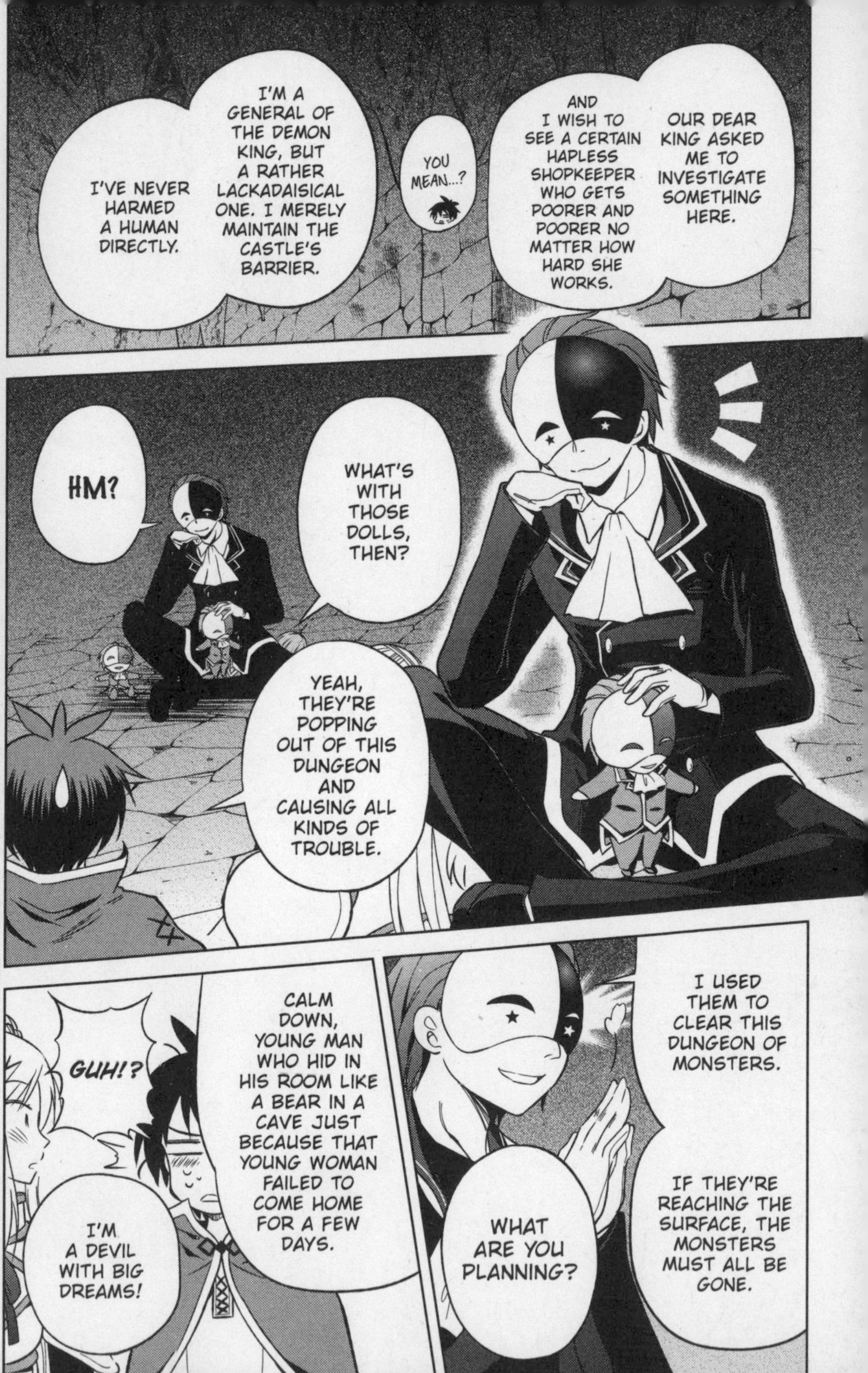
OUR DEAR KING ASKED ME TO INVESTIGATE SOMETHING HERE.
AND I WISH TO SEE A CERTAIN HAPLESS SHOPKEEPER WHO GETS POORER AND POORER NO MATTER HOW HARD SHE WORKS.
YOU MEAN...?
I'M A GENERAL OF THE DEMON KING, BUT A RATHER LACKADAISICAL ONE. I MERELY MAINTAIN THE CASTLE'S BARRIER.
I'VE NEVER HARMED A HUMAN DIRECTLY.
WHAT'S WITH THOSE DOLLS, THEN?
HM?
YEAH, THEY'RE POPPING OUT OF THIS DUNGEON AND CAUSING ALL KINDS OF TROUBLE.
I USED THEM TO CLEAR THIS DUNGEON OF MONSTERS.
IF THEY'RE REACHING THE SURFACE, THE MONSTERS MUST ALL BE GONE.
WHAT ARE YOU PLANNING?
CALM DOWN, YOUNG MAN WHO HID IN HIS ROOM LIKE A BEAR IN A CAVE JUST BECAUSE THAT YOUNG WOMAN FAILED TO COME HOME FOR A FEW DAYS.
GUH!?
I'M A DEVIL WITH BIG DREAMS!

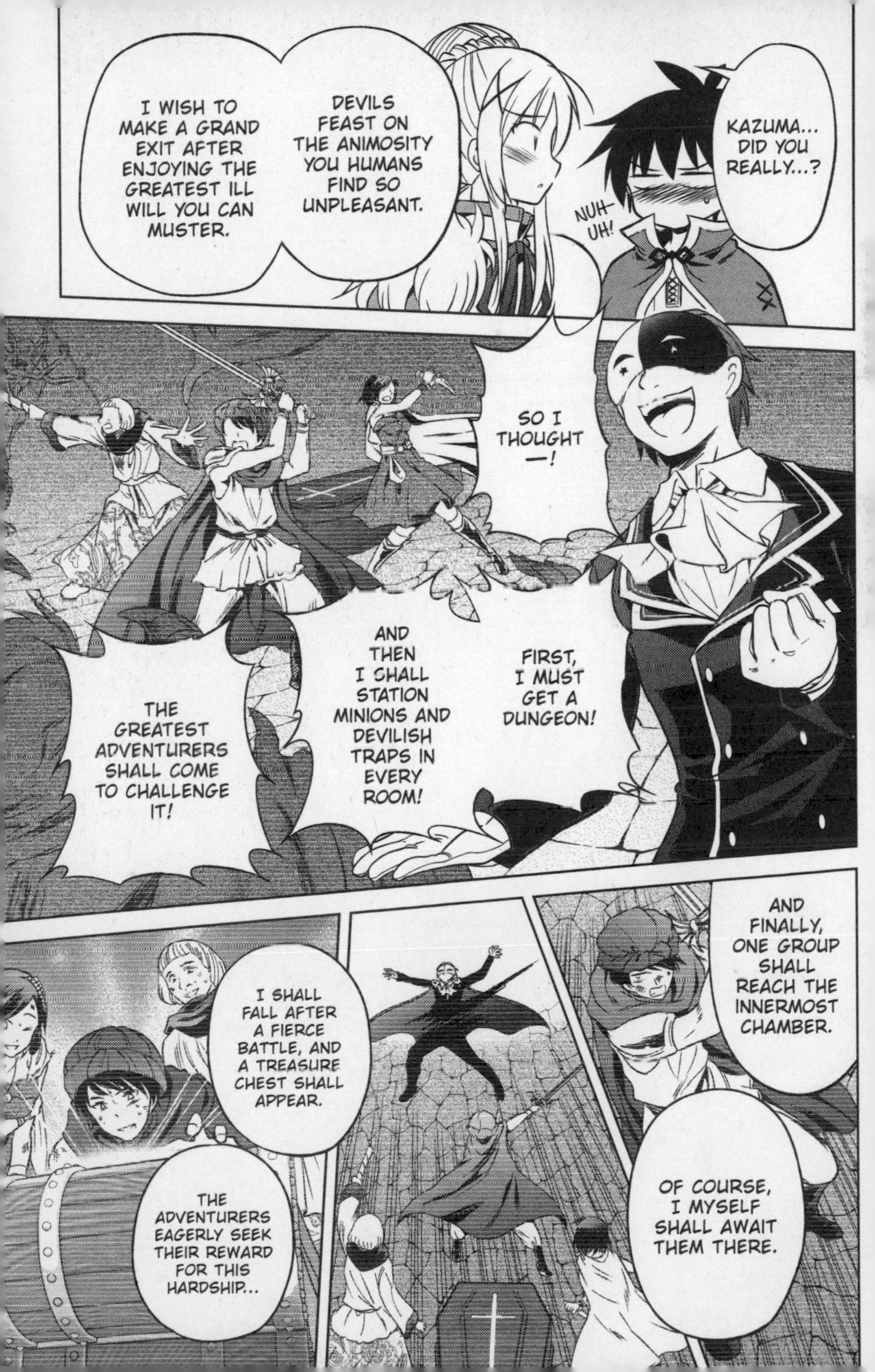
KAZUMA... DID YOU REALLY...?
NUH-UH!
DEVILS FEAST ON THE ANIMOSITY YOU HUMANS FIND SO UNPLEASANT.
I WISH TO MAKE A GRAND EXIT AFTER ENJOYING THE GREATEST ILL WILL YOU CAN MUSTER.
SO I THOUGHT—!
FIRST, I MUST GET A DUNGEON!
AND THEN I SHALL STATION MINIONS AND DEVILISH TRAPS IN EVERY ROOM!
THE GREATEST ADVENTURERS SHALL COME TO CHALLENGE IT!
AND FINALLY, ONE GROUP SHALL REACH THE INNERMOST CHAMBER.
OF COURSE, I MYSELF SHALL AWAIT THEM THERE.
I SHALL FALL AFTER A FIERCE BATTLE, AND A TREASURE CHEST SHALL APPEAR.
THE ADVENTURERS EAGERLY SEEK THEIR REWARD FOR THIS HARDSHIP...

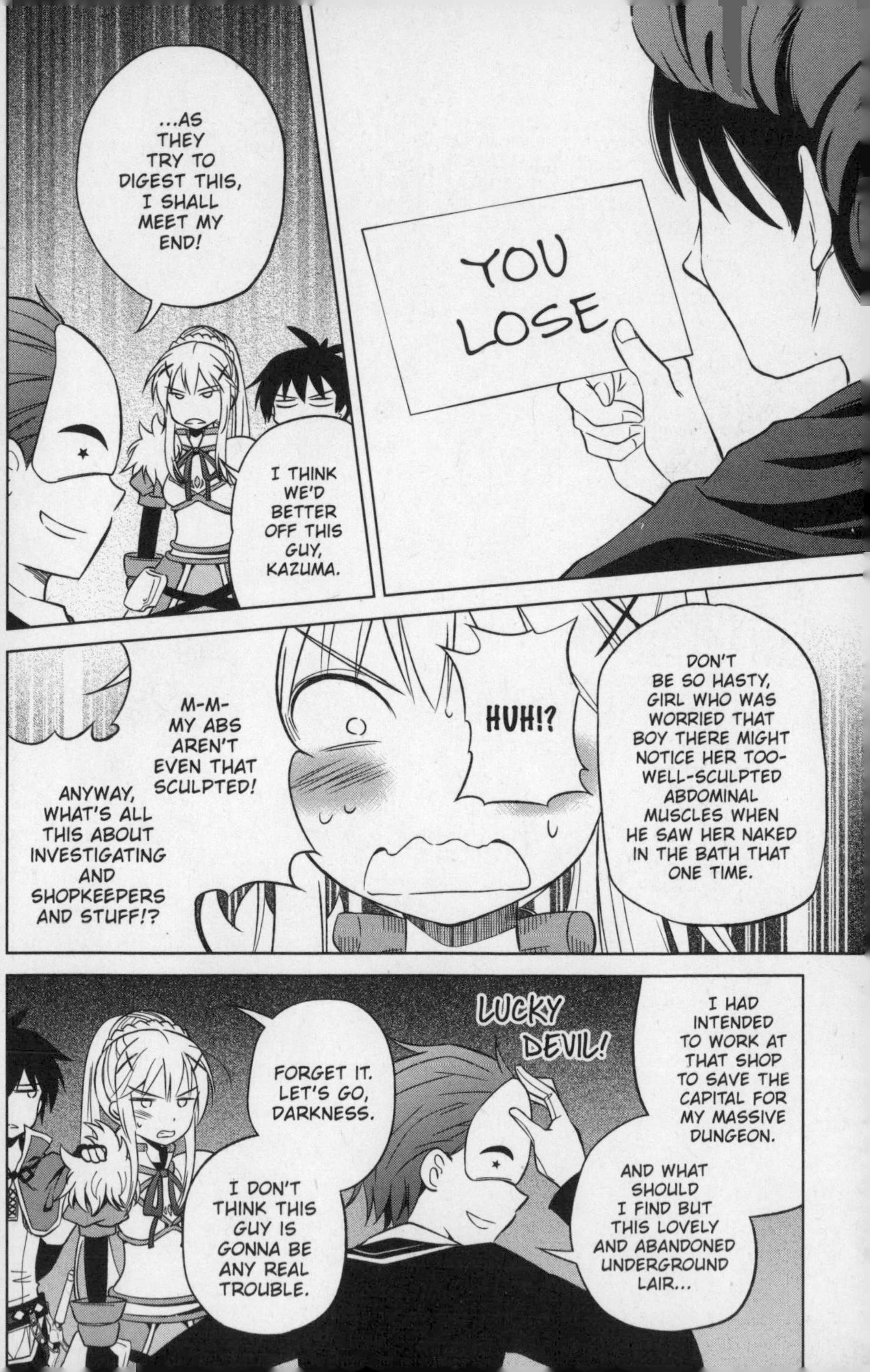
YOU LOSE
...AS THEY TRY TO DIGEST THIS, I SHALL MEET MY END!
I THINK WE'D BETTER OFF THIS GUY, KAZUMA.
DON'T BE SO HASTY, GIRL WHO WAS WORRIED THAT BOY THERE MIGHT NOTICE HER TOO-WELL-SCULPTED ABDOMINAL MUSCLES WHEN HE SAW HER NAKED IN THE BATH THAT ONE TIME.
HUH!?
M-M-MY ABS AREN'T EVEN THAT SCULPTED!
ANYWAY, WHAT'S ALL THIS ABOUT INVESTIGATING AND SHOPKEEPERS AND STUFF!?
I HAD INTENDED TO WORK AT THAT SHOP TO SAVE THE CAPITAL FOR MY MASSIVE DUNGEON.
LUCKY DEVIL!
AND WHAT SHOULD I FIND BUT THIS LOVELY AND ABANDONED UNDERGROUND LAIR...
FORGET IT. LET'S GO, DARKNESS.
I DON'T THINK THIS GUY IS GONNA BE ANY REAL TROUBLE.

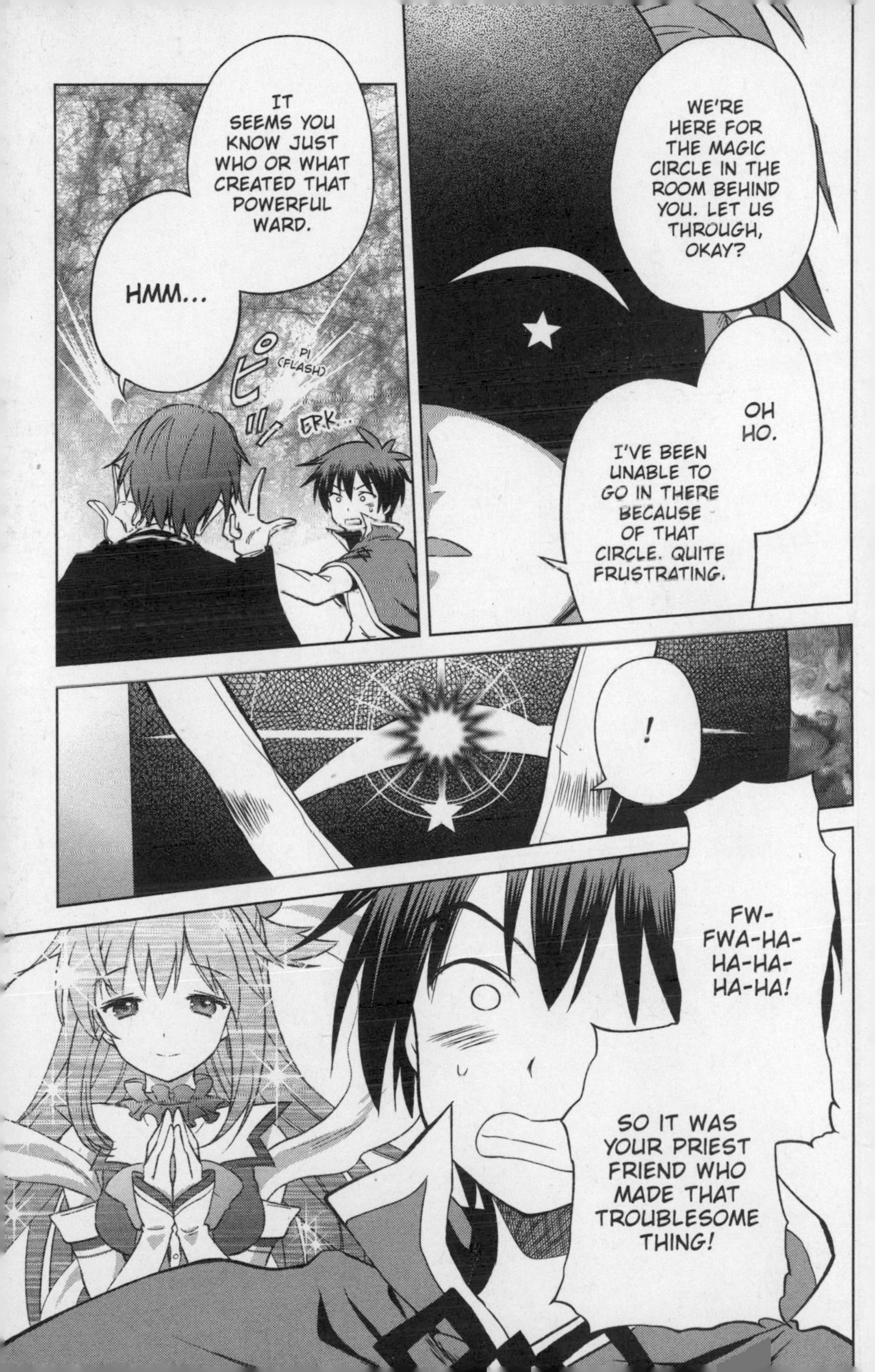
WE'RE HERE FOR THE MAGIC CIRCLE IN THE ROOM BEHIND YOU. LET US THROUGH, OKAY?
OH HO.
I'VE BEEN UNABLE TO GO IN THERE BECAUSE OF THAT CIRCLE. QUITE FRUSTRATING.
IT SEEMS YOU KNOW JUST WHO OR WHAT CREATED THAT POWERFUL WARD.
HMM...
PI (FLASH)
ERK...
!
FW- FWA-HA-HA-HA-HA-HA!
SO IT WAS YOUR PRIEST FRIEND WHO MADE THAT TROUBLESOME THING!

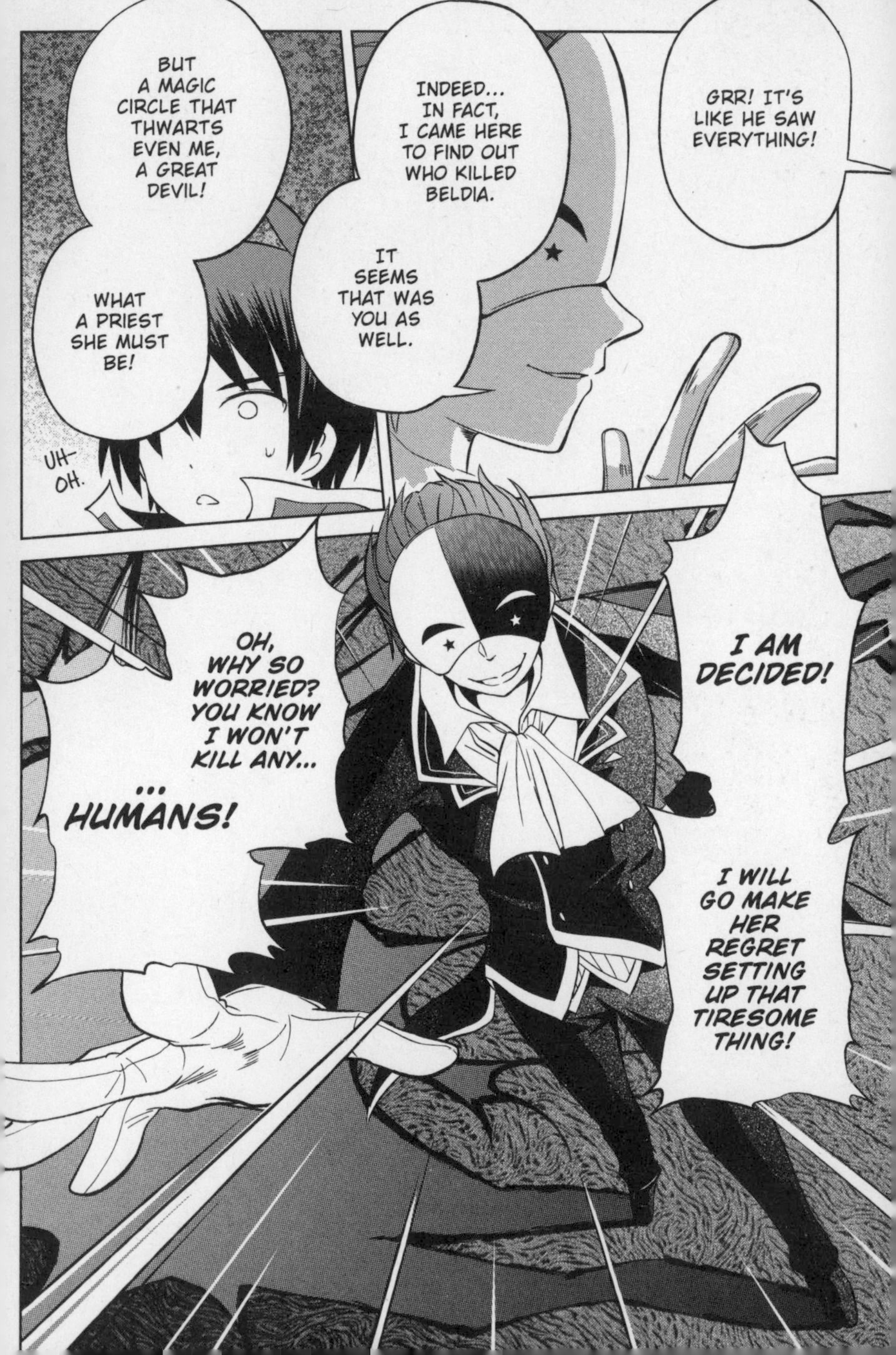
GRR! IT'S LIKE HE SAW EVERYTHING!
INDEED... IN FACT, I CAME HERE TO FIND OUT WHO KILLED BELDIA.
IT SEEMS THAT WAS YOU AS WELL.
BUT A MAGIC CIRCLE THAT THWARTS EVEN ME, A GREAT DEVIL!
WHAT A PRIEST SHE MUST BE!
UH-OH.
I AM DECIDED!
I WILL GO MAKE HER REGRET SETTING UP THAT TIRESOME THING!
OH, WHY SO WORRIED? YOU KNOW I WON'T KILL ANY...
...HUMANS!

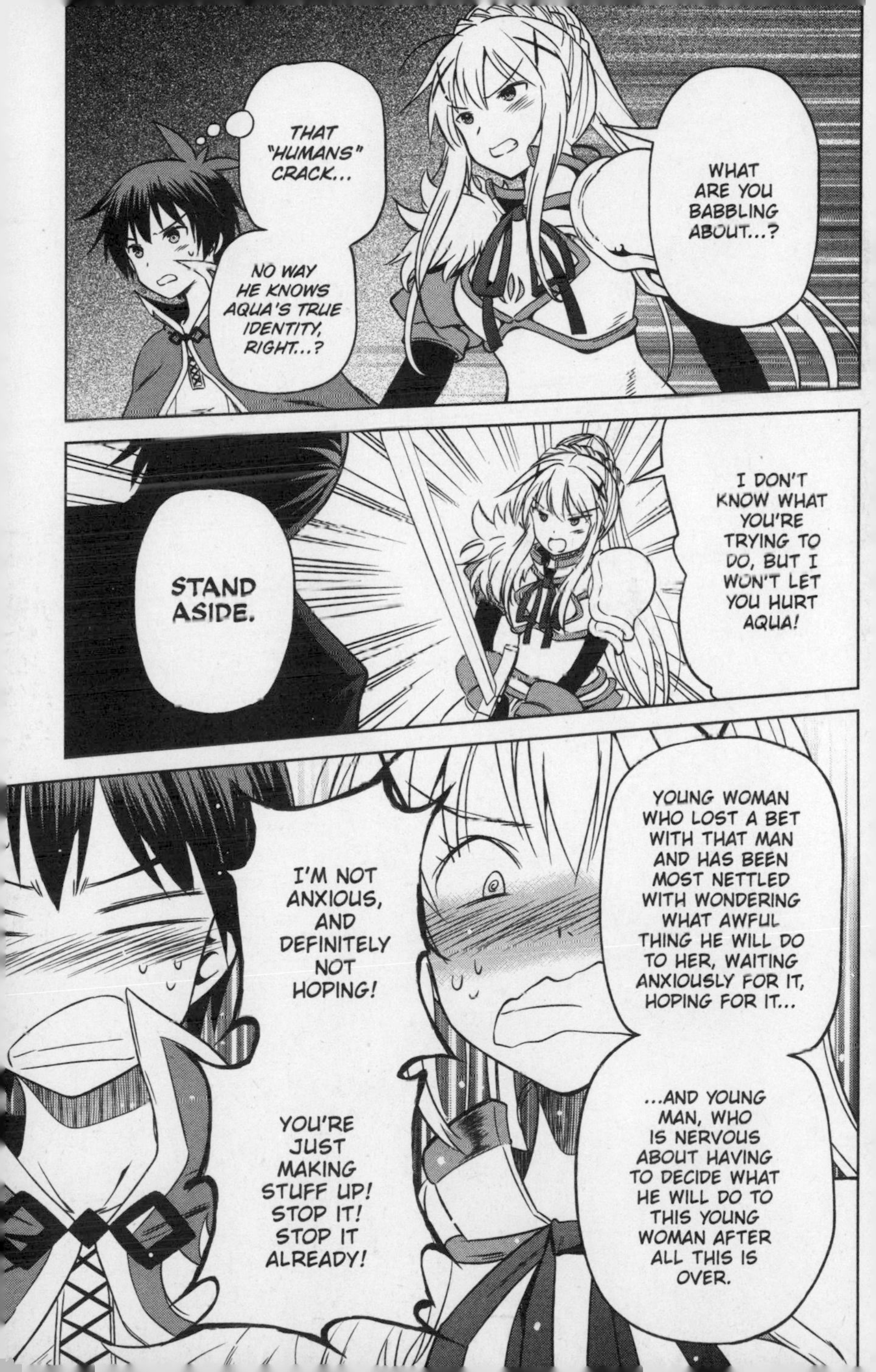
WHAT ARE YOU BABBLING ABOUT...?
THAT "HUMANS" CRACK...
NO WAY HE KNOWS AQUA'S TRUE IDENTITY, RIGHT...?
I DON'T KNOW WHAT YOU'RE TRYING TO DO, BUT I WON'T LET YOU HURT AQUA!
STAND ASIDE.
YOUNG WOMAN WHO LOST A BET WITH THAT MAN AND HAS BEEN MOST NETTLED WITH WONDERING WHAT AWFUL THING HE WILL DO TO HER, WAITING ANXIOUSLY FOR IT, HOPING FOR IT...
I'M NOT ANXIOUS, AND DEFINITELY NOT HOPING!
...AND YOUNG MAN, WHO IS NERVOUS ABOUT HAVING TO DECIDE WHAT HE WILL DO TO THIS YOUNG WOMAN AFTER ALL THIS IS OVER.
YOU'RE JUST MAKING STUFF UP! STOP IT! STOP IT ALREADY!

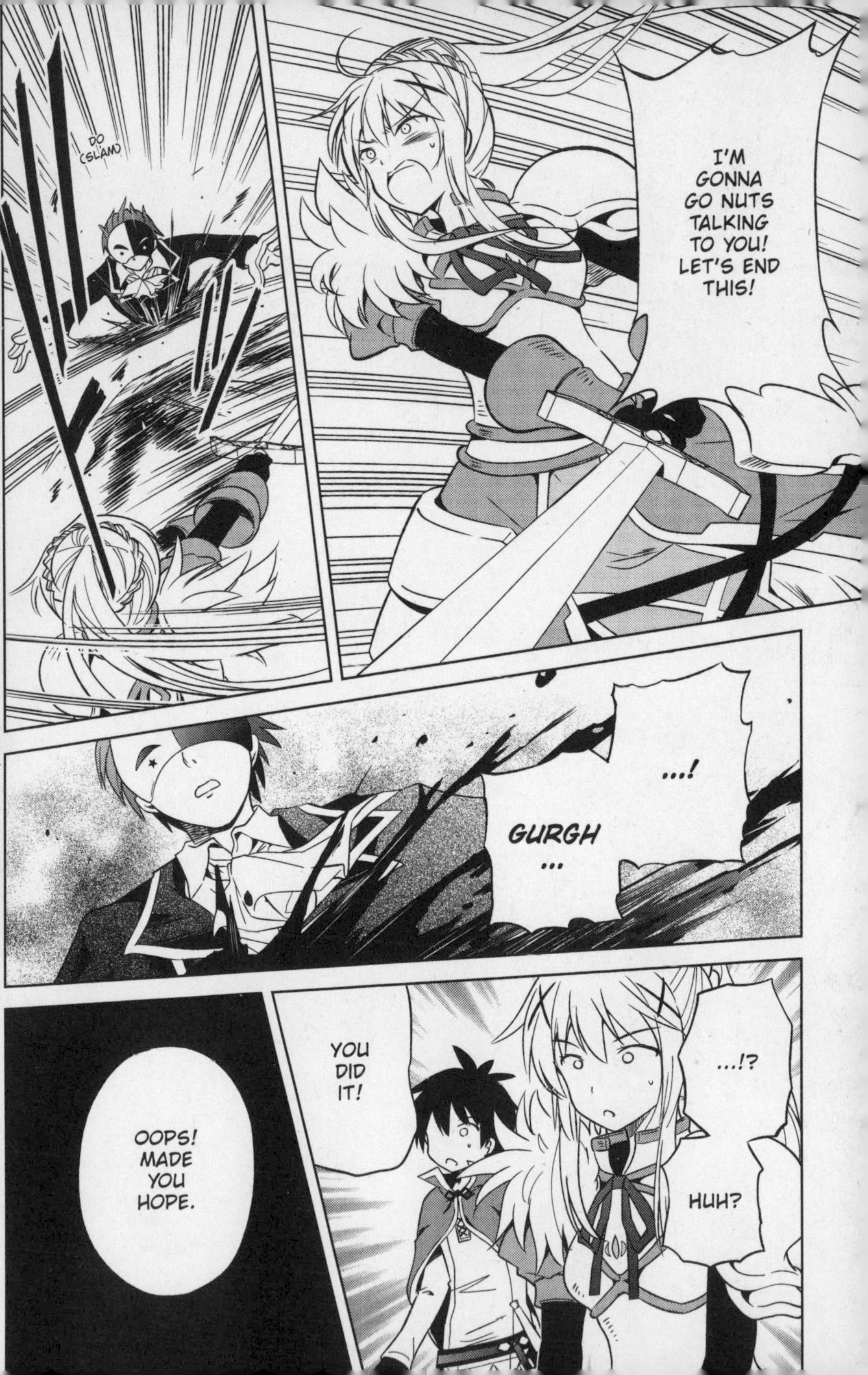
I'M GONNA GO NUTS TALKING TO YOU! LET'S END THIS!
DO (SLAM)
...!
GURGH ...
...!?
YOU DID IT!
HUH?
OOPS! MADE YOU HOPE.

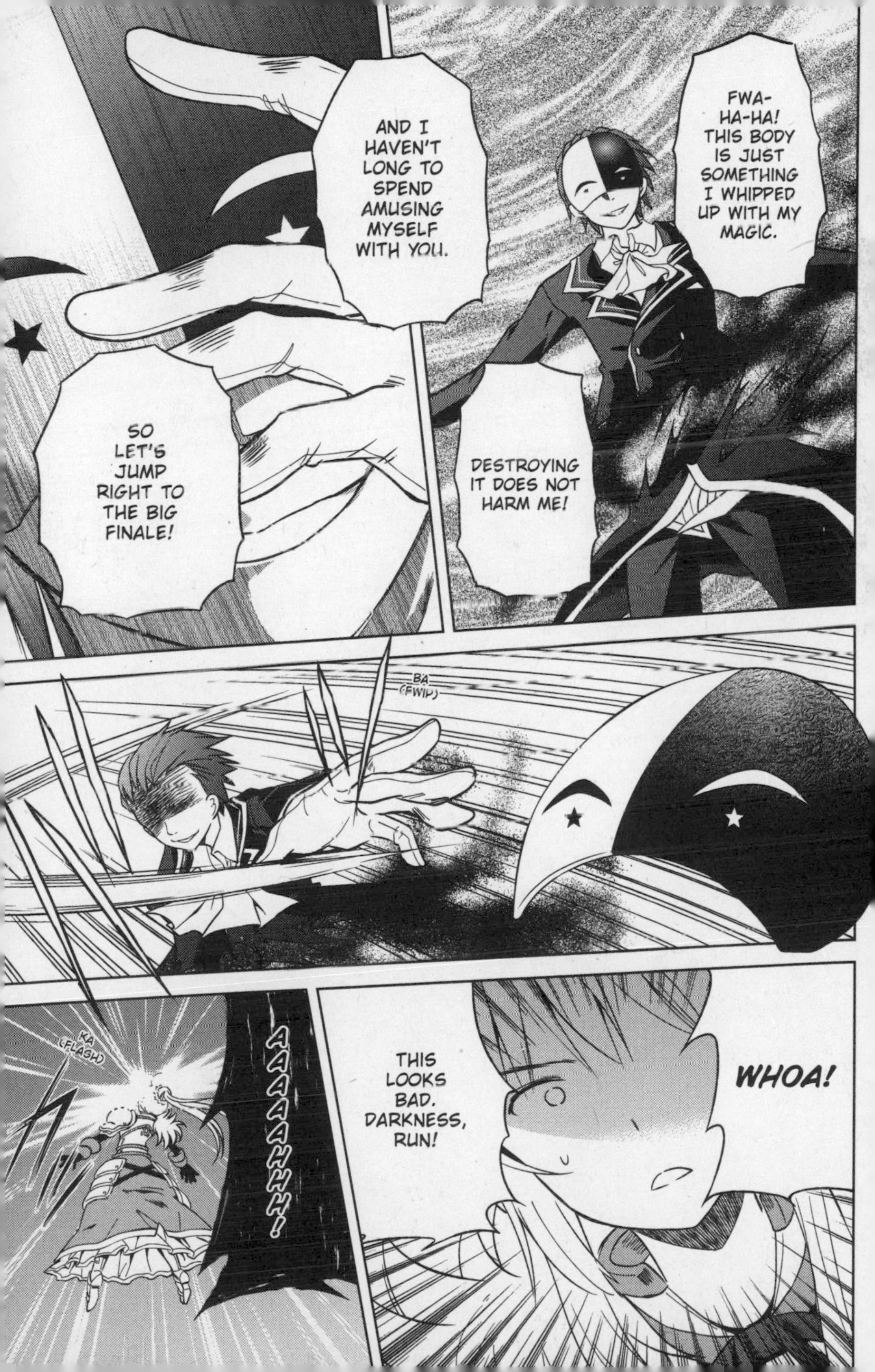
FWA-HA-HA! THIS BODY IS JUST SOMETHING I WHIPPED UP WITH MY MAGIC.
DESTROYING IT DOES NOT HARM ME!
AND I HAVEN'T LONG TO SPEND AMUSING MYSELF WITH YOU.
SO LET'S JUMP RIGHT TO THE BIG FINALE!
BA (FWIP)
WHOA!
THIS LOOKS BAD. DARKNESS, RUN!
AAAAAHHHH!
KA (FLASH)

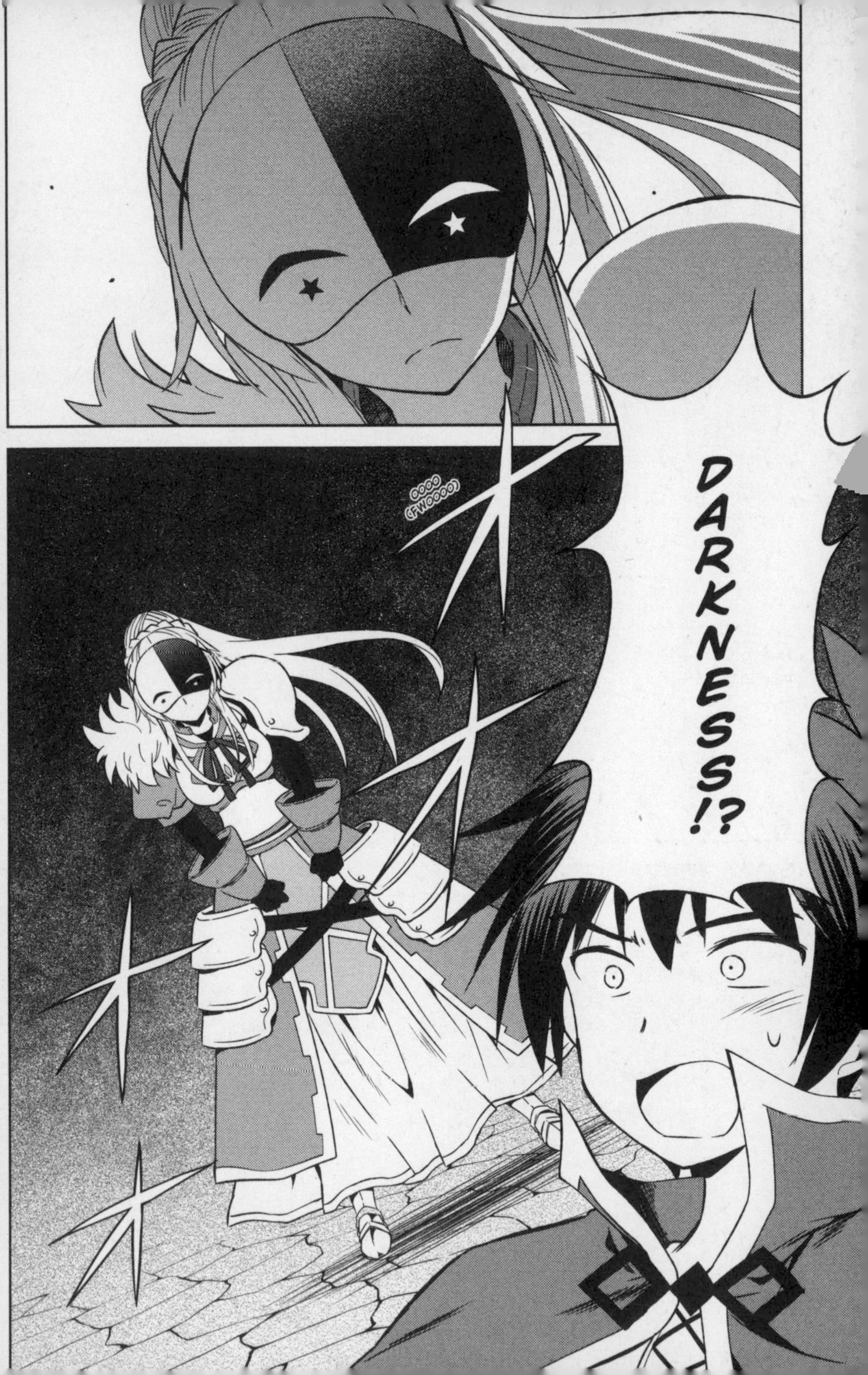
DARKNESS!?
OOOO
(FWOOOO)

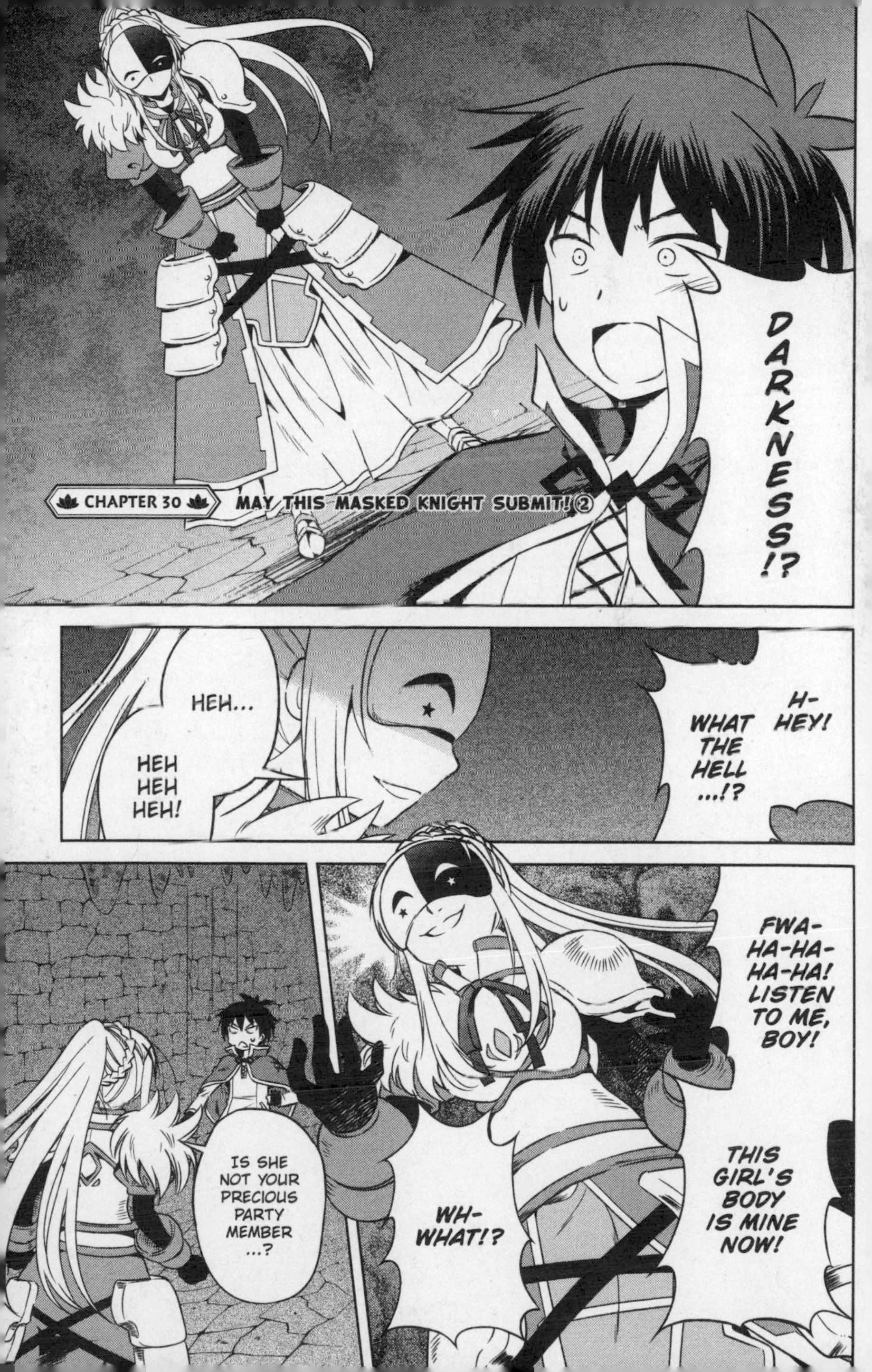
DARKNESS!?
CHAPTER 30 MAY THIS MASKED KNIGHT SUBMIT! ②
H- HEY!
WHAT THE HELL ...!?
HEH...
HEH HEH HEH!
FWA-HA-HA-HA-HA! LISTEN TO ME, BOY!
THIS GIRL'S BODY IS MINE NOW!
WH-WHAT!?
IS SHE NOT YOUR PRECIOUS PARTY MEMBER ...?

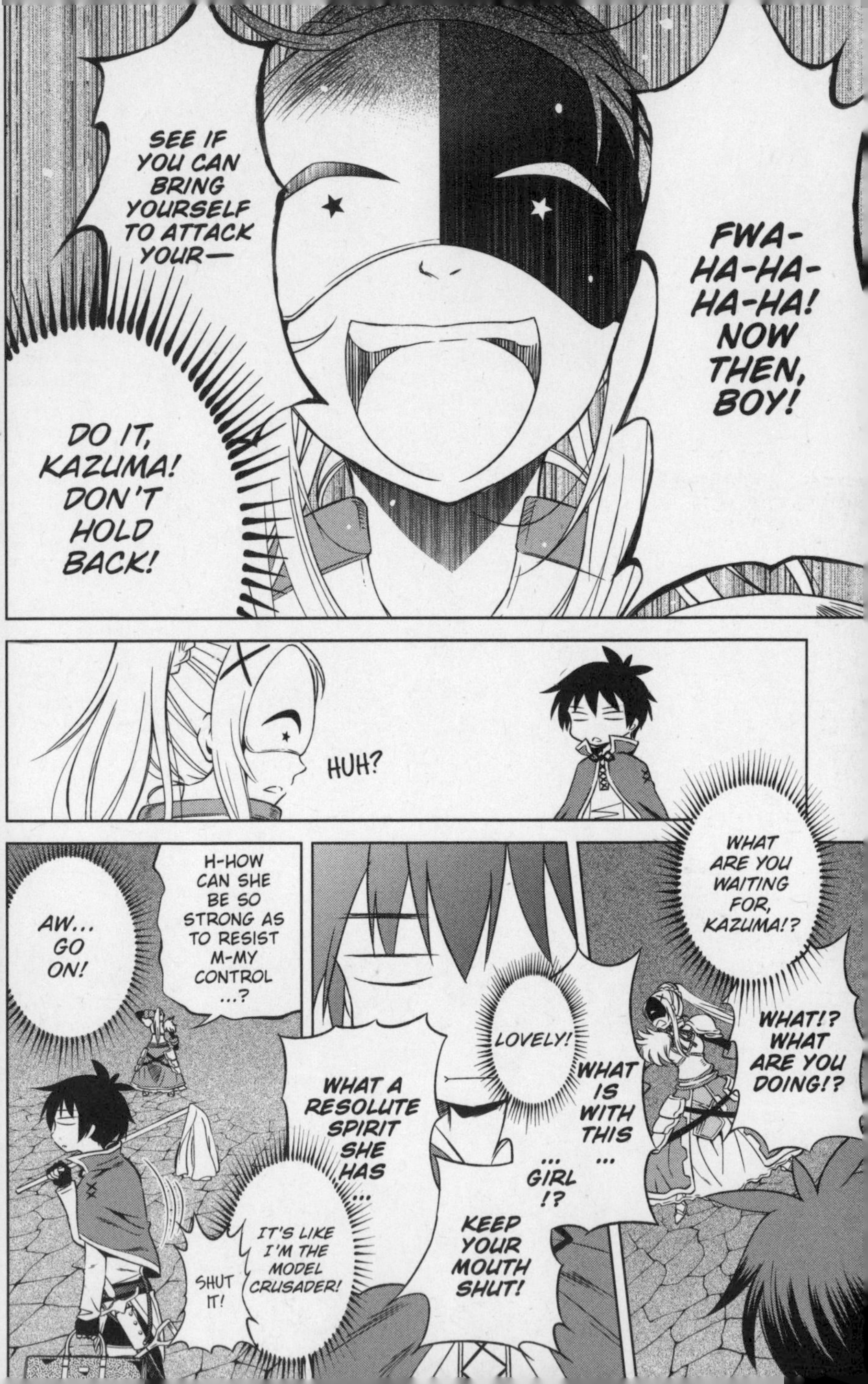
FWA-HA-HA-HA-HA! NOW THEN, BOY!
SEE IF YOU CAN BRING YOURSELF TO ATTACK YOUR—
DO IT, KAZUMA! DON'T HOLD BACK!
HUH?
WHAT ARE YOU WAITING FOR, KAZUMA!?
WHAT!? WHAT ARE YOU DOING!?
WHAT IS WITH THIS ... GIRL!?
LOVELY!
WHAT A RESOLUTE SPIRIT SHE HAS ...
KEEP YOUR MOUTH SHUT!
IT'S LIKE I'M THE MODEL CRUSADER!
SHUT IT!
H-HOW CAN SHE BE SO STRONG AS TO RESIST M-MY CONTROL ...?
AW... GO ON!

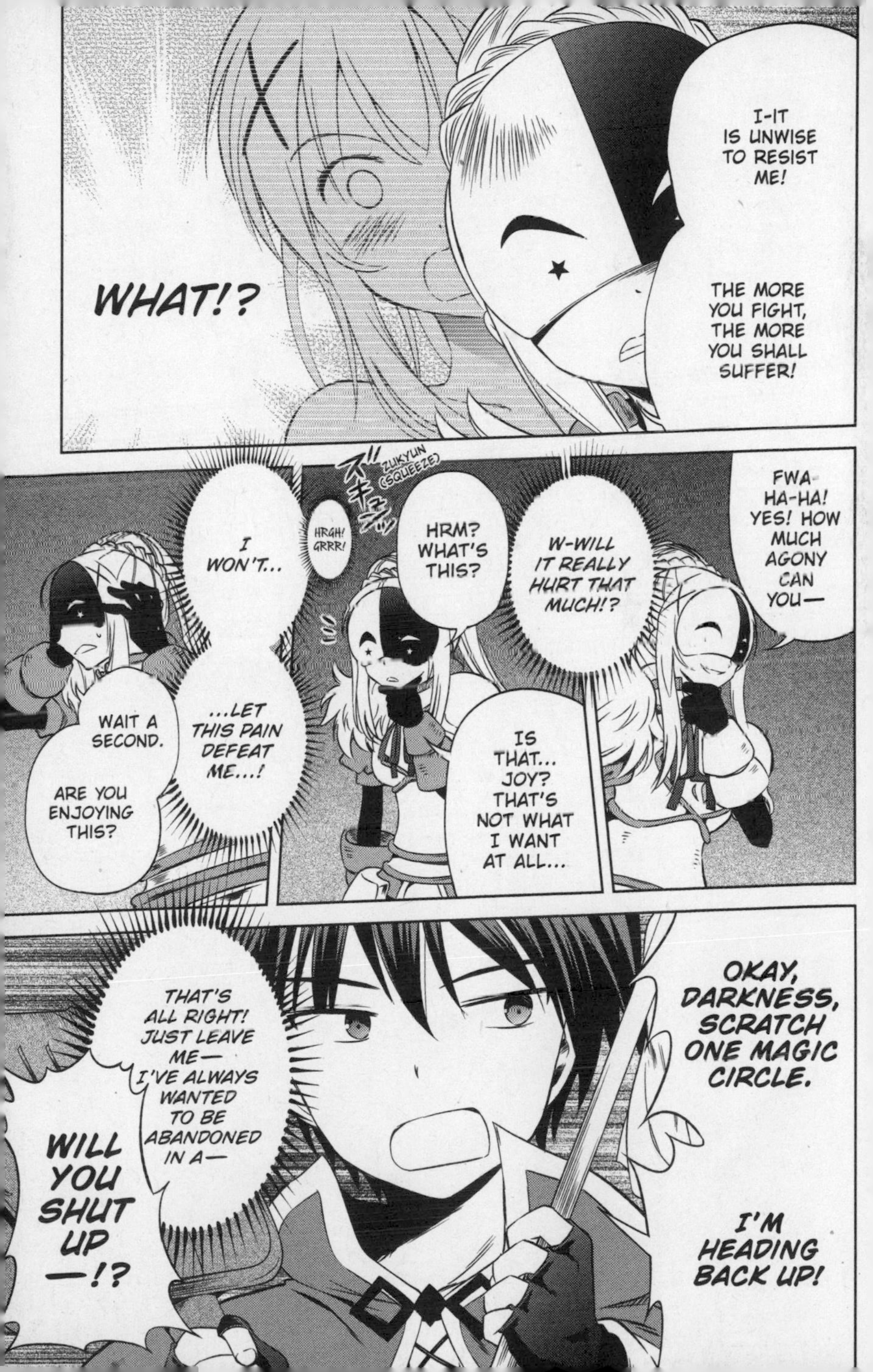
I-IT IS UNWISE TO RESIST ME!
THE MORE YOU FIGHT, THE MORE YOU SHALL SUFFER!
WHAT!?
FWA-HA-HA! YES! HOW MUCH AGONY CAN YOU—
IS THAT... JOY? THAT'S NOT WHAT I WANT AT ALL...
W-WILL IT REALLY HURT THAT MUCH!?
HRM? WHAT'S THIS?
ZUKYUN (SQUEEZE)
HRGH! GRRR!
I WON'T...
...LET THIS PAIN DEFEAT ME...!
WAIT A SECOND.
ARE YOU ENJOYING THIS?
OKAY, DARKNESS, SCRATCH ONE MAGIC CIRCLE.
I'M HEADING BACK UP!
THAT'S ALL RIGHT! JUST LEAVE ME— I'VE ALWAYS WANTED TO BE ABANDONED IN A—
WILL YOU SHUT UP—!?

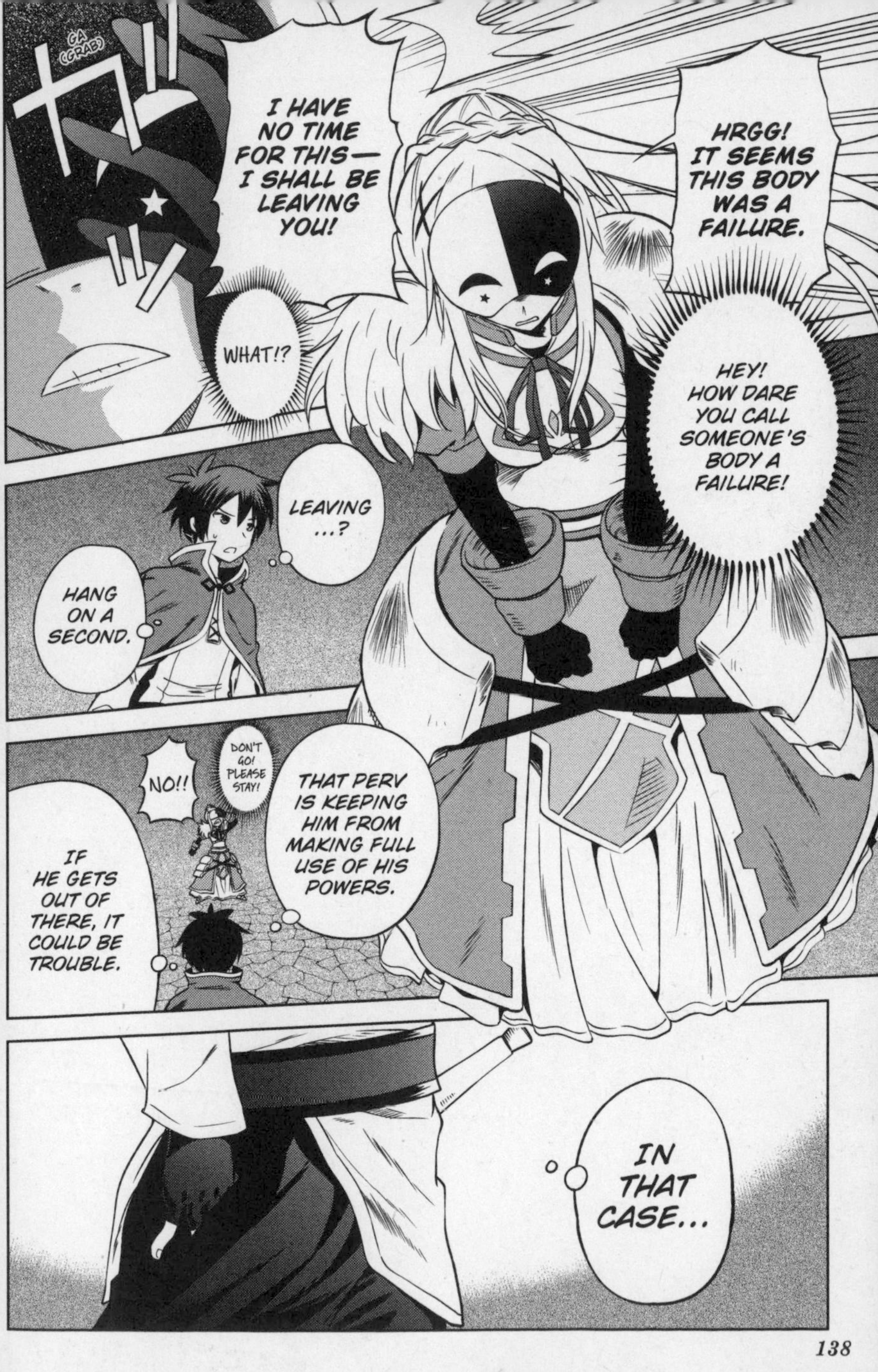
HRGG! IT SEEMS THIS BODY WAS A FAILURE.
I HAVE NO TIME FOR THIS— I SHALL BE LEAVING YOU!
GA (GRAB)
WHAT!?
HEY! HOW DARE YOU CALL SOMEONE'S BODY A FAILURE!
LEAVING ...?
HANG ON A SECOND.
THAT PERV IS KEEPING HIM FROM MAKING FULL USE OF HIS POWERS.
DON'T GO! PLEASE STAY!
NO!!
IF HE GETS OUT OF THERE, IT COULD BE TROUBLE.
IN THAT CASE...

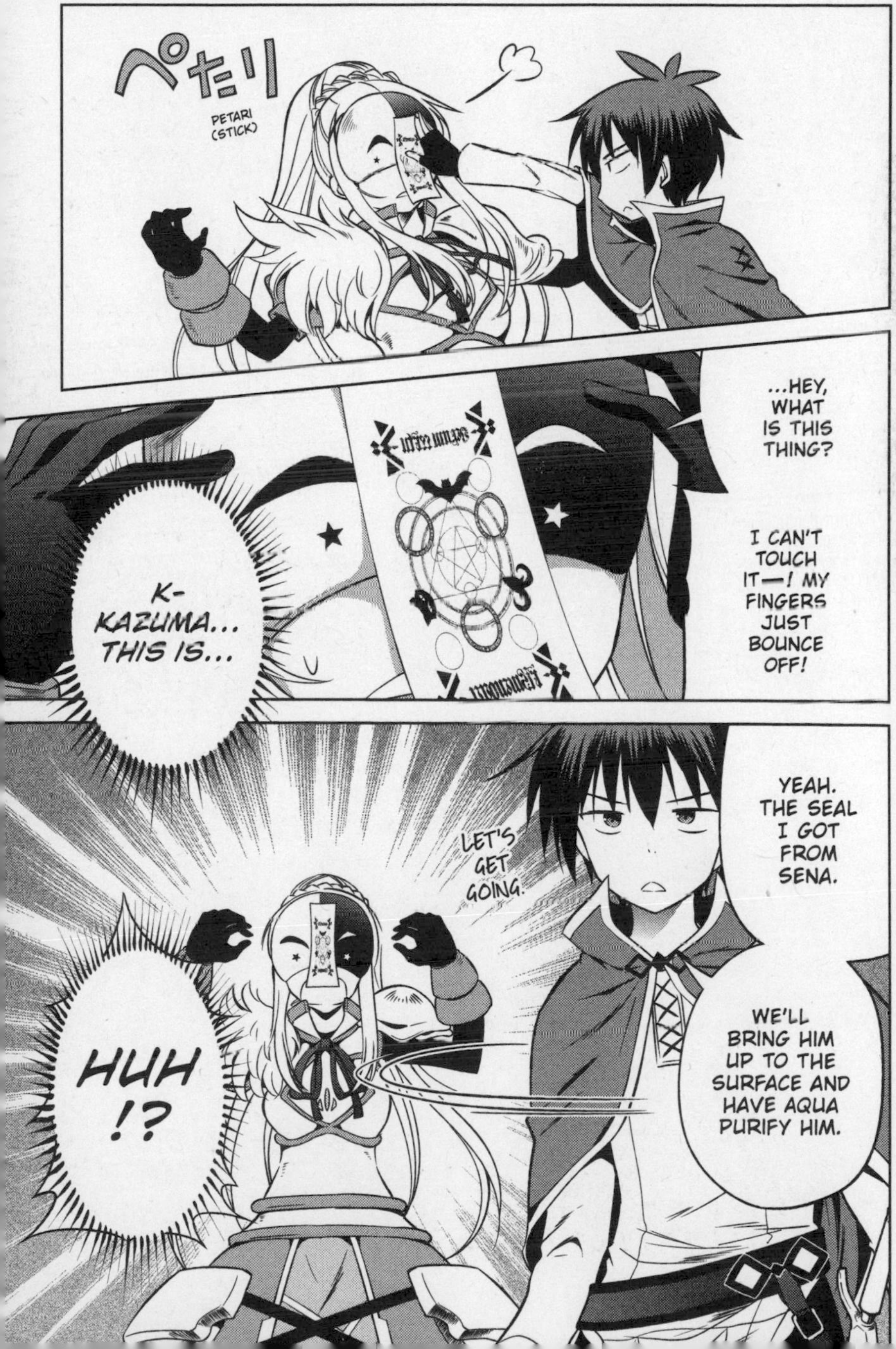
ぺたり
PETARI (STICK)
...HEY, WHAT IS THIS THING?
I CAN'T TOUCH IT—! MY FINGERS JUST BOUNCE OFF!
K-KAZUMA... THIS IS...
YEAH. THE SEAL I GOT FROM SENA.
WE'LL BRING HIM UP TO THE SURFACE AND HAVE AQUA PURIFY HIM.
LET'S GET GOING.
HUH!?

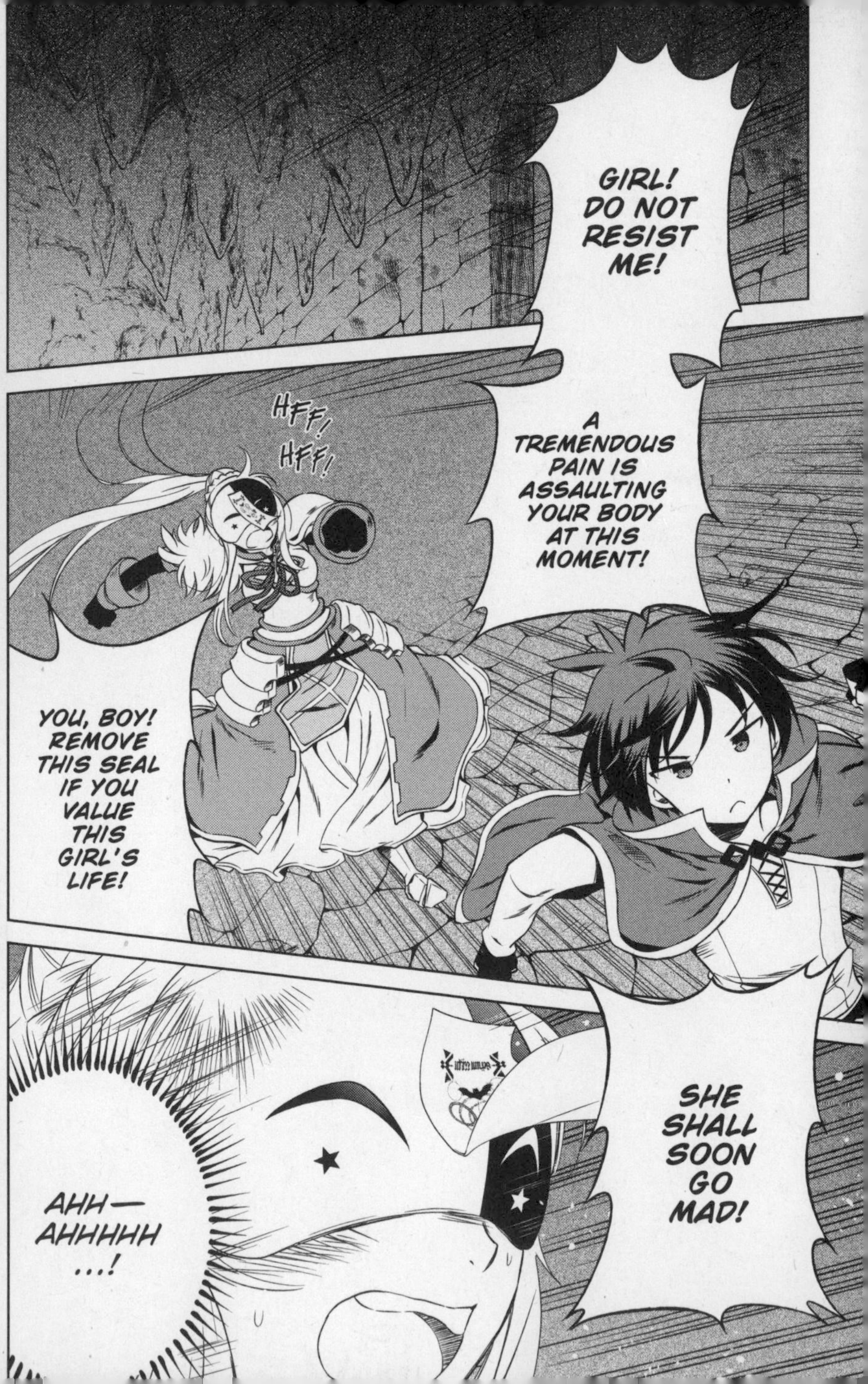
GIRL! DO NOT RESIST ME!
A TREMENDOUS PAIN IS ASSAULTING YOUR BODY AT THIS MOMENT!
HFF! HFF!
YOU, BOY! REMOVE THIS SEAL IF YOU VALUE THIS GIRL'S LIFE!
SHE SHALL SOON GO MAD!
AHH—AHHHHH ...!

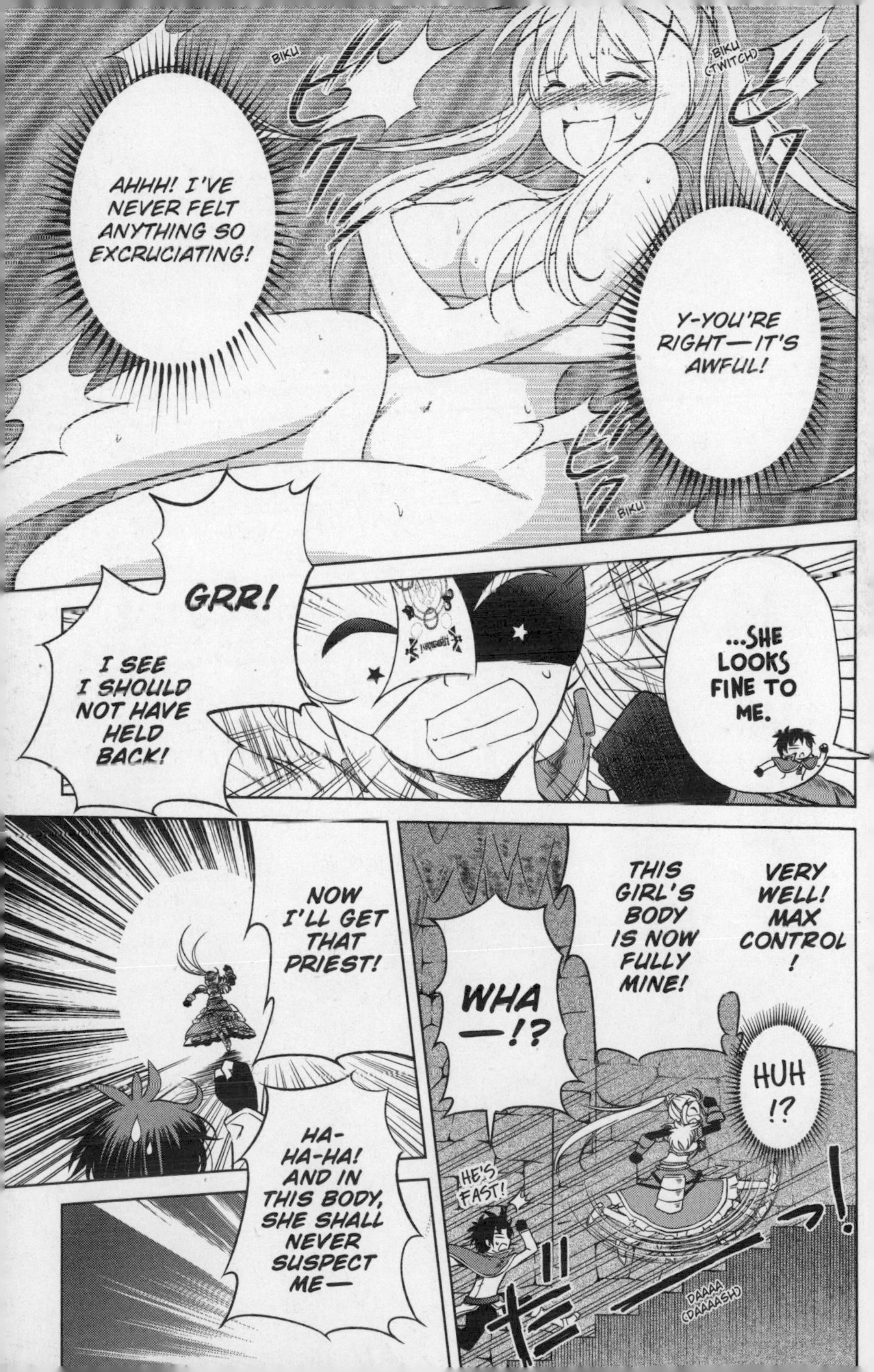
BIKU (TWITCH)
Y-YOU'RE RIGHT—IT'S AWFUL!
BIKU
AHHH! I'VE NEVER FELT ANYTHING SO EXCRUCIATING!
BIKU
...SHE LOOKS FINE TO ME.
GRR!
I SEE I SHOULD NOT HAVE HELD BACK!
VERY WELL! MAX CONTROL!
THIS GIRL'S BODY IS NOW FULLY MINE!
HUH!?
WHA—!?
HE'S FAST!
DAAAA (DAAAASH)
NOW I'LL GET THAT PRIEST!
HA-HA-HA! AND IN THIS BODY, SHE SHALL NEVER SUSPECT ME—

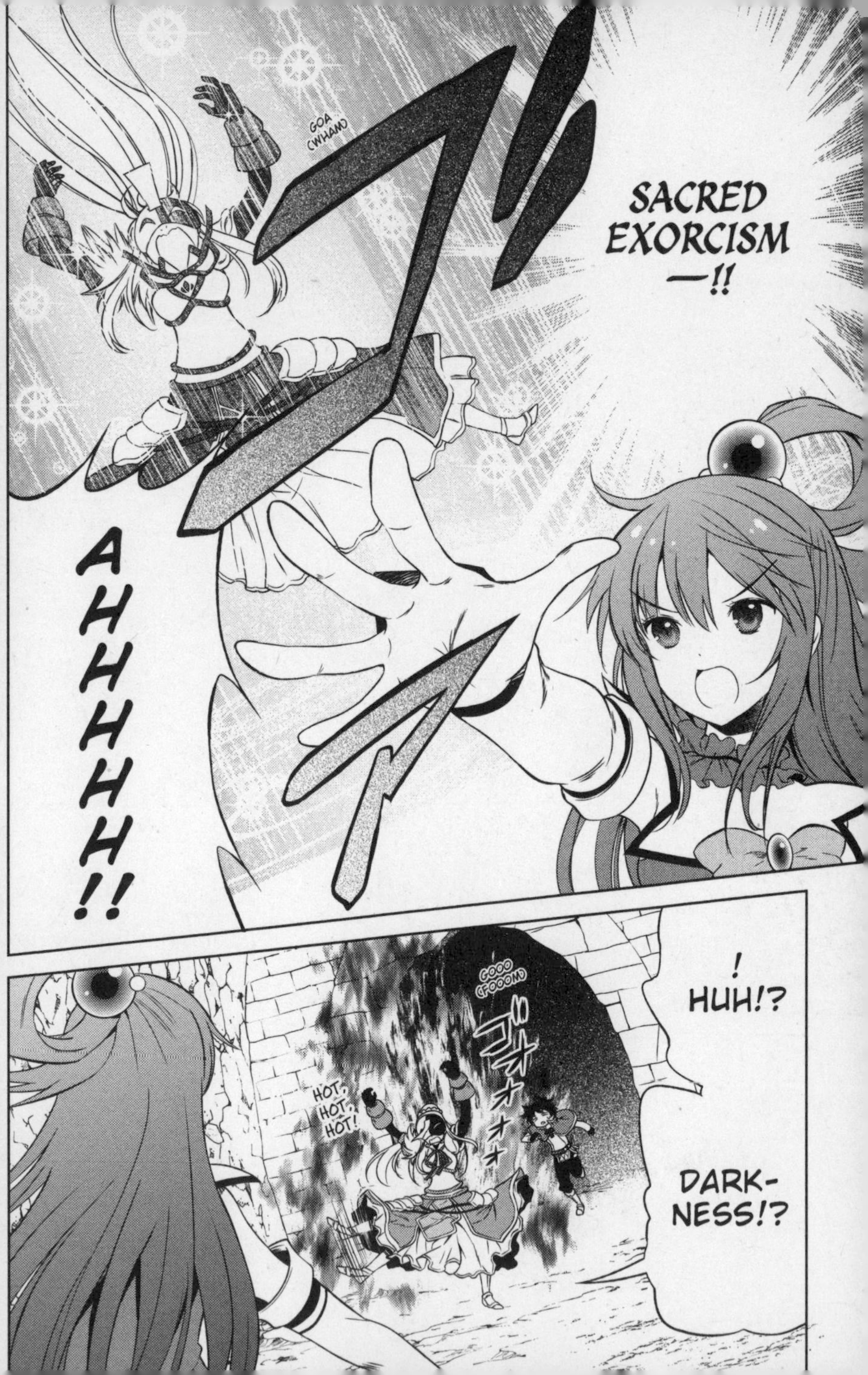
SACRED EXORCISM—!!
GOA (WHAM)
AHHHHH!!
! HUH!?
DARK-NESS!?
GOOO (FOOOM)
HOT, HOT, HOT!

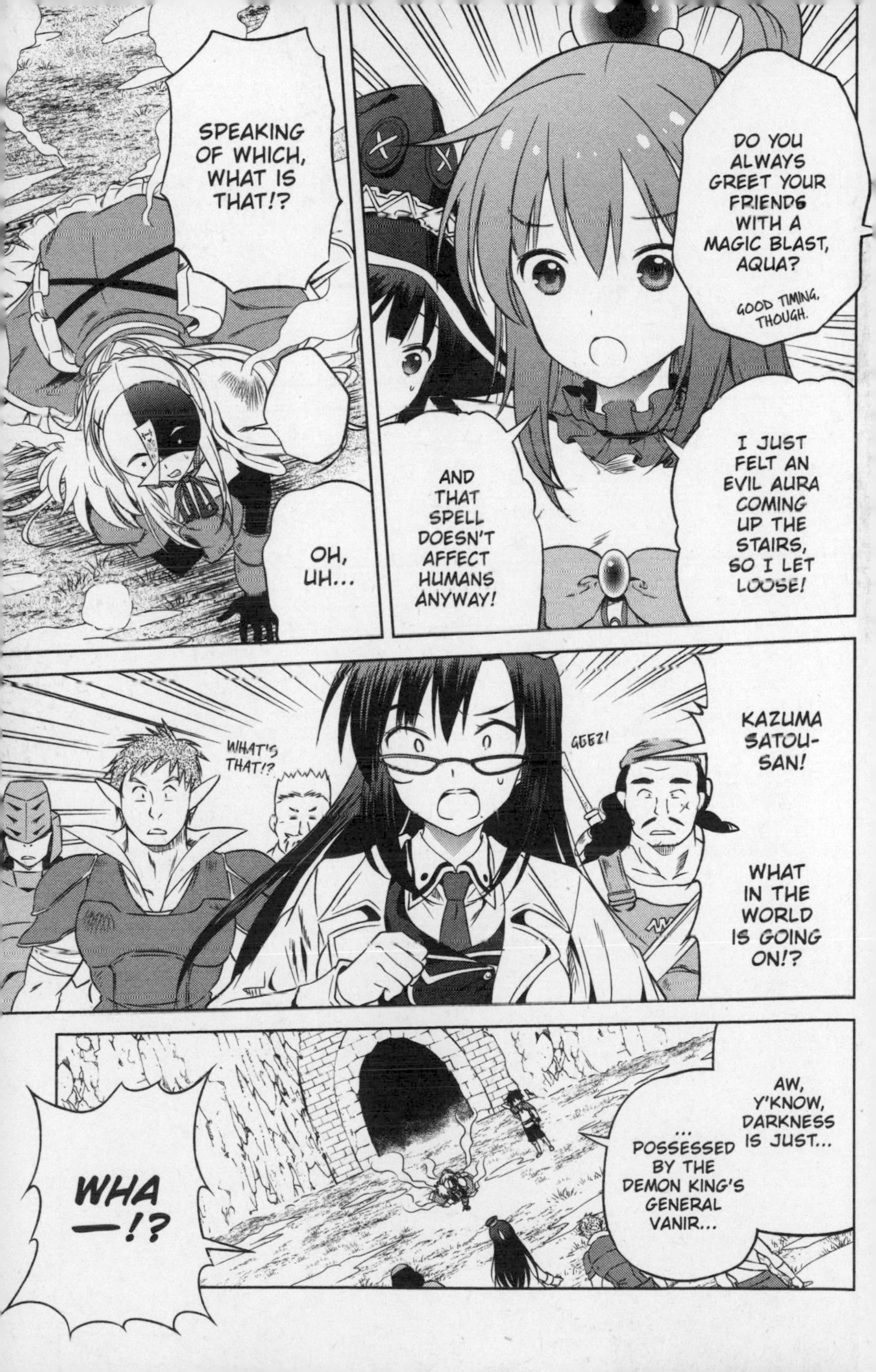
DO YOU ALWAYS GREET YOUR FRIENDS WITH A MAGIC BLAST, AQUA?
GOOD TIMING, THOUGH.
I JUST FELT AN EVIL AURA COMING UP THE STAIRS, SO I LET LOOSE!
AND THAT SPELL DOESN'T AFFECT HUMANS ANYWAY!
SPEAKING OF WHICH, WHAT IS THAT!?
OH, UH...
KAZUMA SATOU-SAN!
WHAT IN THE WORLD IS GOING ON!?
GEEZ!
WHAT'S THAT!?
AW, Y'KNOW, DARKNESS IS JUST...
...POSSESSED BY THE DEMON KING'S GENERAL VANIR...
WHA—!?

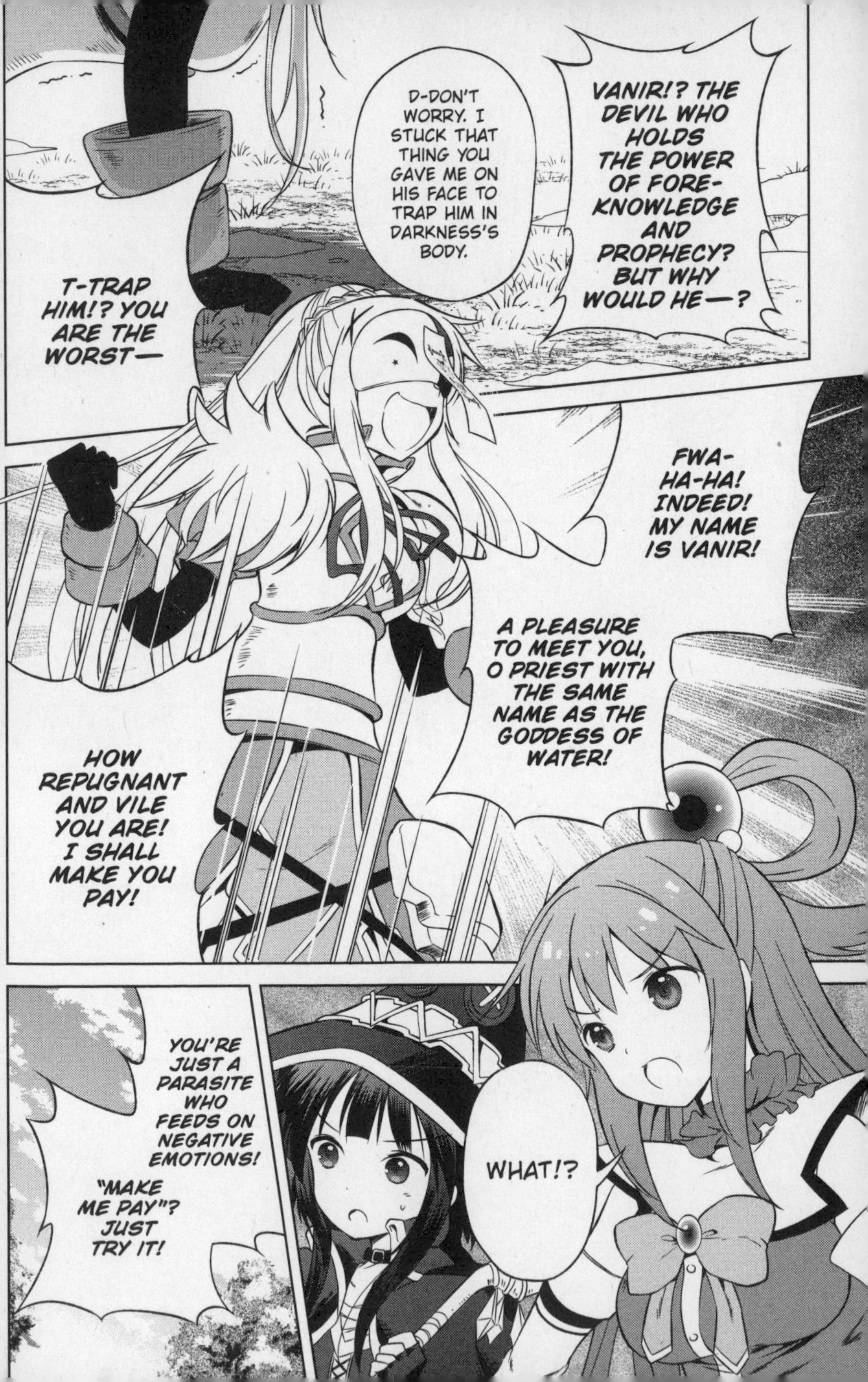
VANIR!? THE DEVIL WHO HOLDS THE POWER OF FORE-KNOWLEDGE AND PROPHECY? BUT WHY WOULD HE—?
D-DON'T WORRY. I STUCK THAT THING YOU GAVE ME ON HIS FACE TO TRAP HIM IN DARKNESS'S BODY.
T-TRAP HIM!? YOU ARE THE WORST—
FWA-HA-HA! INDEED! MY NAME IS VANIR!
A PLEASURE TO MEET YOU, O PRIEST WITH THE SAME NAME AS THE GODDESS OF WATER!
HOW REPUGNANT AND VILE YOU ARE! I SHALL MAKE YOU PAY!
WHAT!?
YOU'RE JUST A PARASITE WHO FEEDS ON NEGATIVE EMOTIONS!
"MAKE ME PAY"? JUST TRY IT!

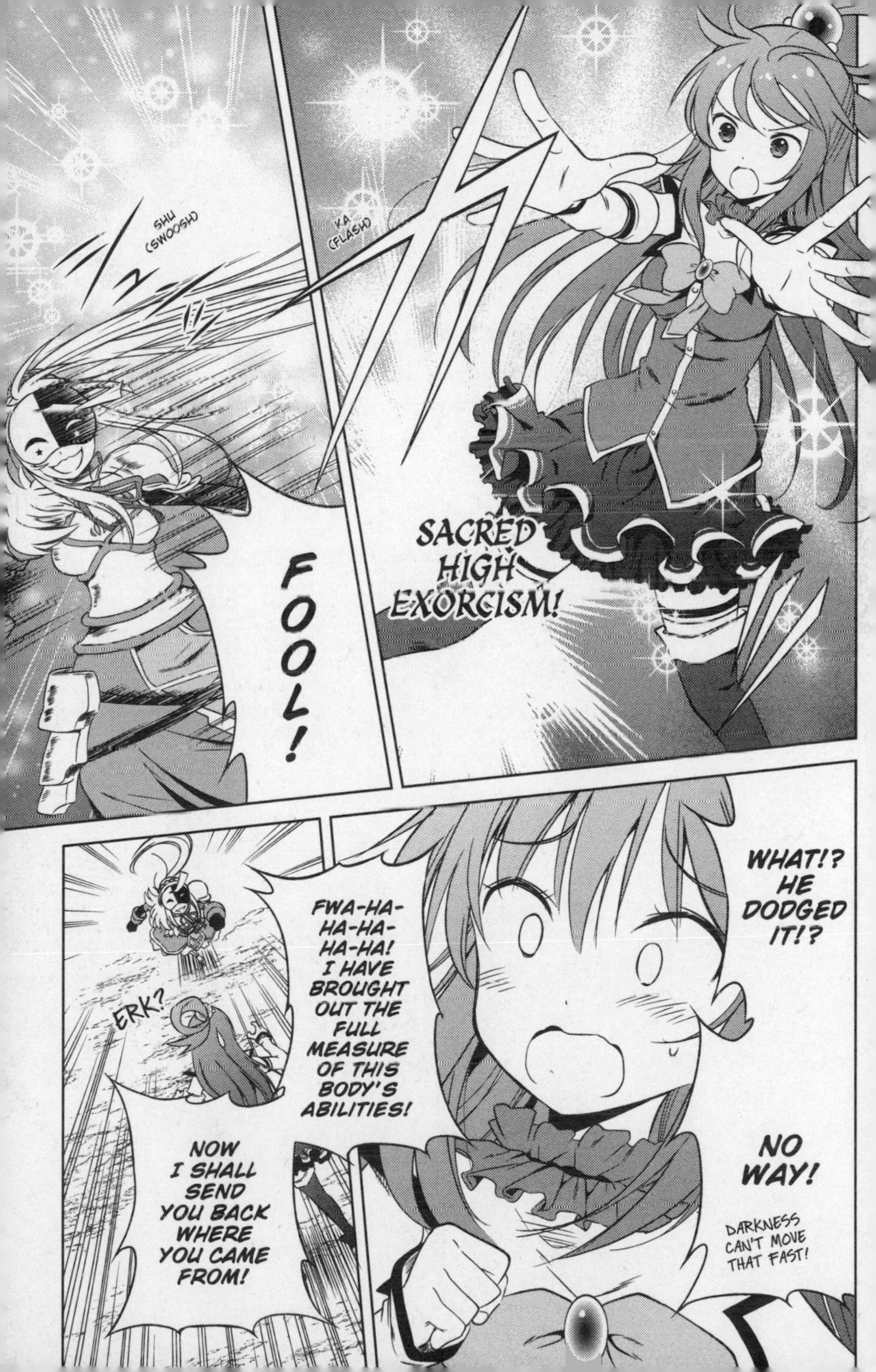
KA (FLASH)
SACRED HIGH EXORCISM!
SHU (SWOOSH)
FOOL!
WHAT!? HE DODGED IT!?
NO WAY!
DARKNESS CAN'T MOVE THAT FAST!
FWA-HA-HA-HA-HA-HA! I HAVE BROUGHT OUT THE FULL MEASURE OF THIS BODY'S ABILITIES!
ERK?
NOW I SHALL SEND YOU BACK WHERE YOU CAME FROM!

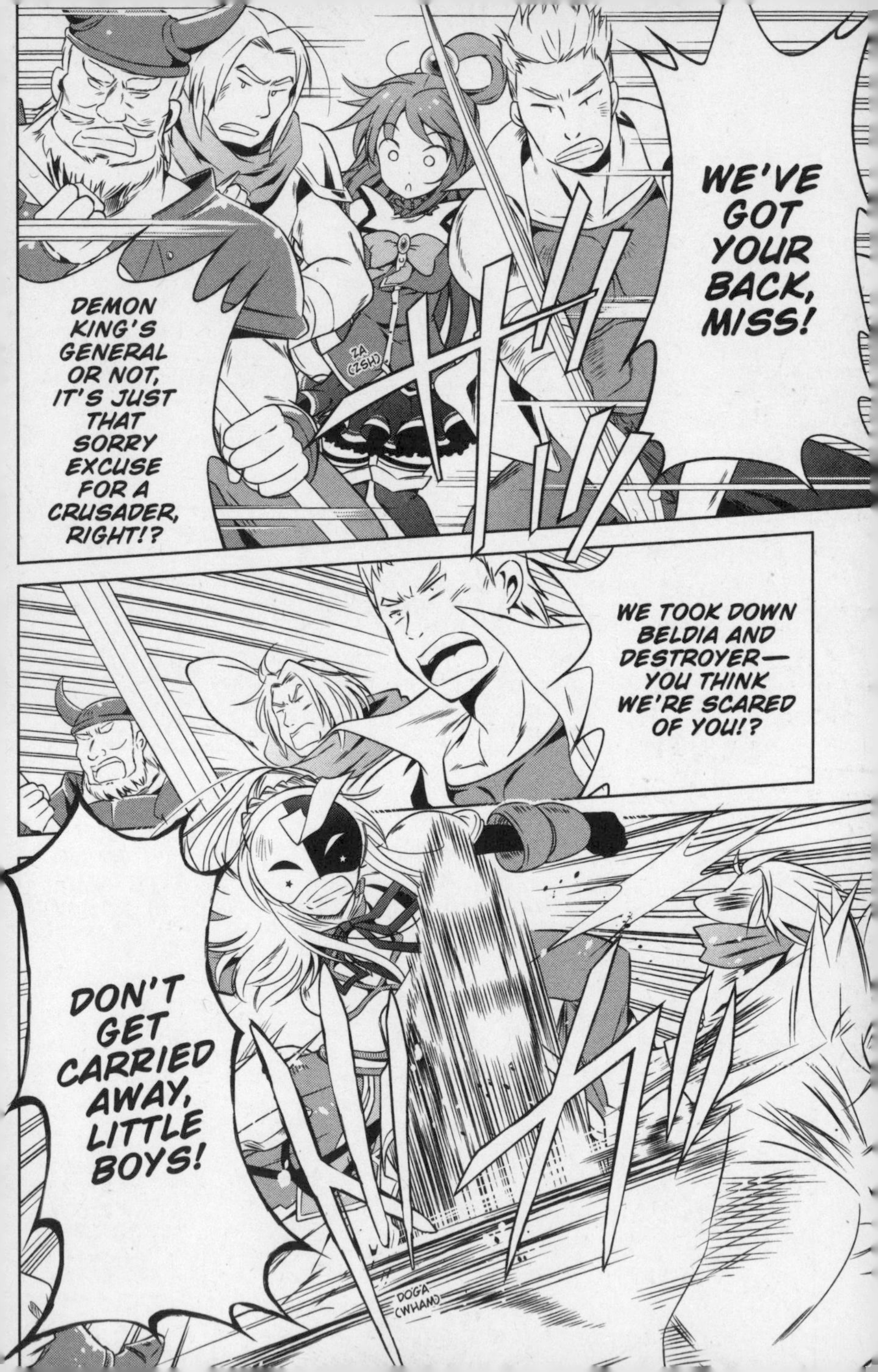
WE'VE GOT YOUR BACK, MISS!
ZA (ZSH)
DEMON KING'S GENERAL OR NOT, IT'S JUST THAT SORRY EXCUSE FOR A CRUSADER, RIGHT!?
WE TOOK DOWN BELDIA AND DESTROYER—YOU THINK WE'RE SCARED OF YOU!?
DON'T GET CARRIED AWAY, LITTLE BOYS!
DOGA (WHAM)

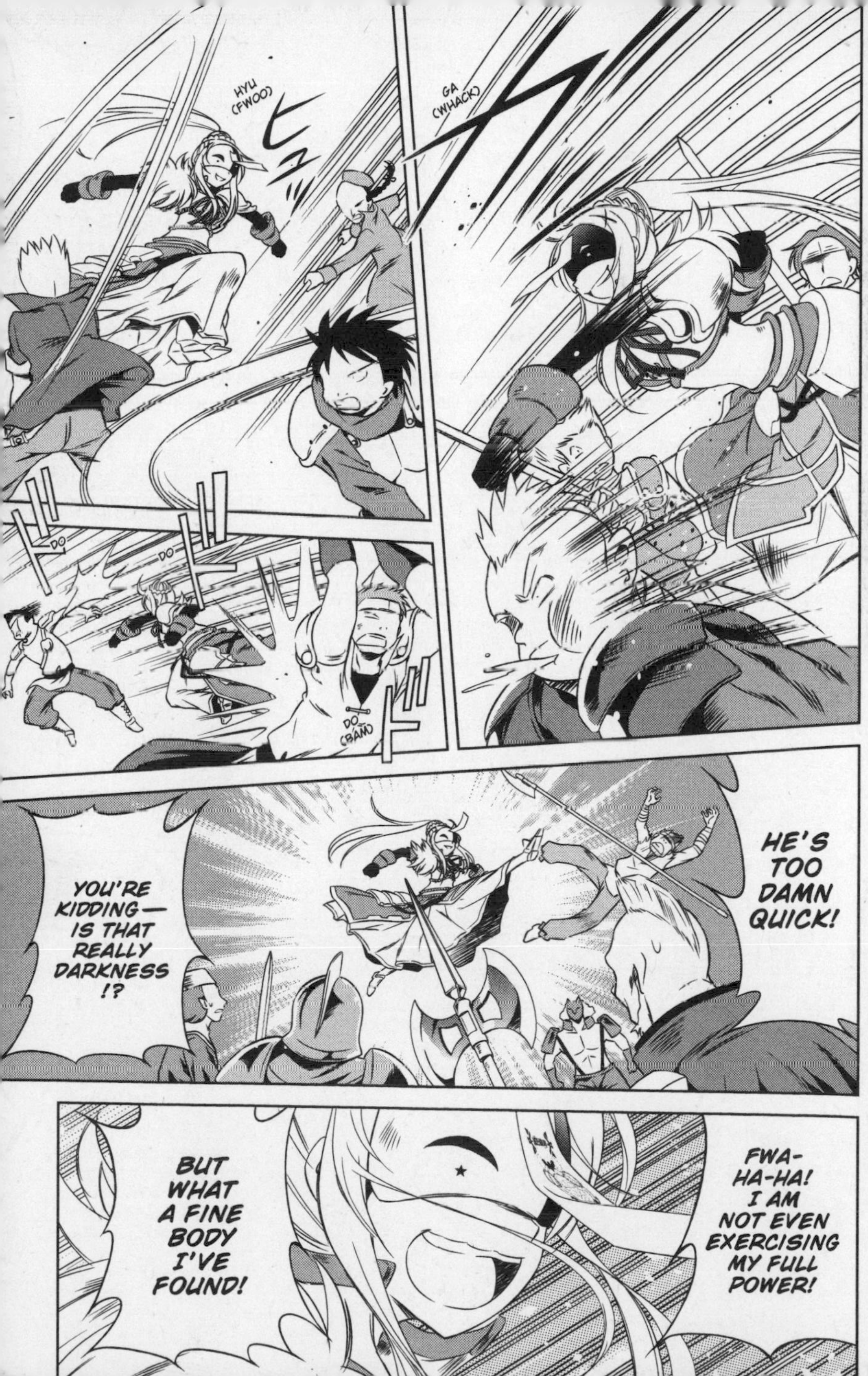
GA (WHACK)
HYU (FWOO)
DO
DO
DO (BAM)
HE'S TOO DAMN QUICK!
YOU'RE KIDDING— IS THAT REALLY DARKNESS !?
FWA-HA-HA! I AM NOT EVEN EXERCISING MY FULL POWER!
BUT WHAT A FINE BODY I'VE FOUND!

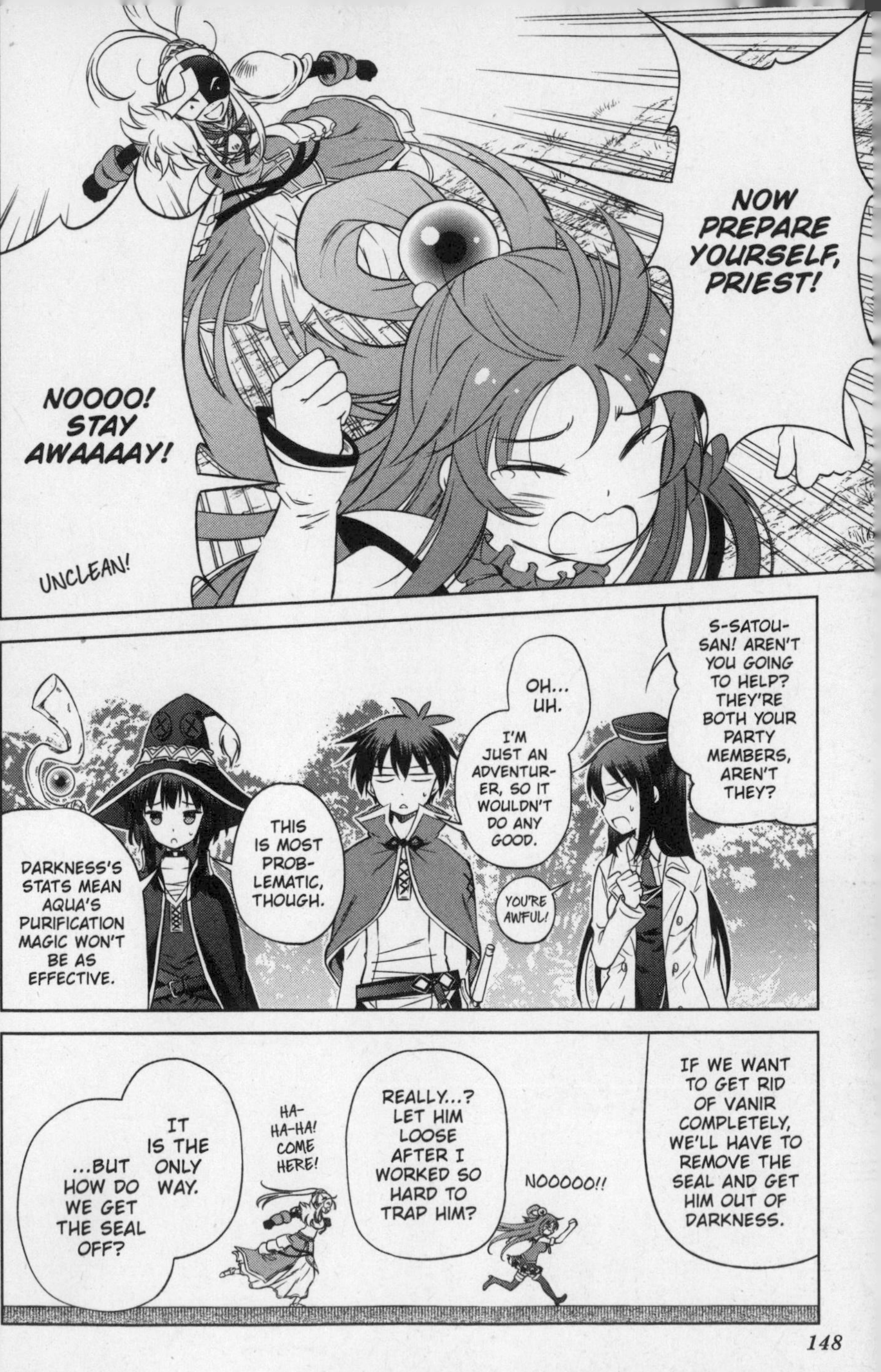
NOW PREPARE YOURSELF, PRIEST!
NOOOO! STAY AWAAAAY!
UNCLEAN!
S-SATOU-SAN! AREN'T YOU GOING TO HELP? THEY'RE BOTH YOUR PARTY MEMBERS, AREN'T THEY?
OH... UH.
I'M JUST AN ADVENTURER, SO IT WOULDN'T DO ANY GOOD.
YOU'RE AWFUL!
THIS IS MOST PROB-LEMATIC, THOUGH.
DARKNESS'S STATS MEAN AQUA'S PURIFICATION MAGIC WON'T BE AS EFFECTIVE.
IF WE WANT TO GET RID OF VANIR COMPLETELY, WE'LL HAVE TO REMOVE THE SEAL AND GET HIM OUT OF DARKNESS.
NOOOOO!!
REALLY...? LET HIM LOOSE AFTER I WORKED SO HARD TO TRAP HIM?
HA-HA-HA! COME HERE!
IT IS THE ONLY WAY.
...BUT HOW DO WE GET THE SEAL OFF?

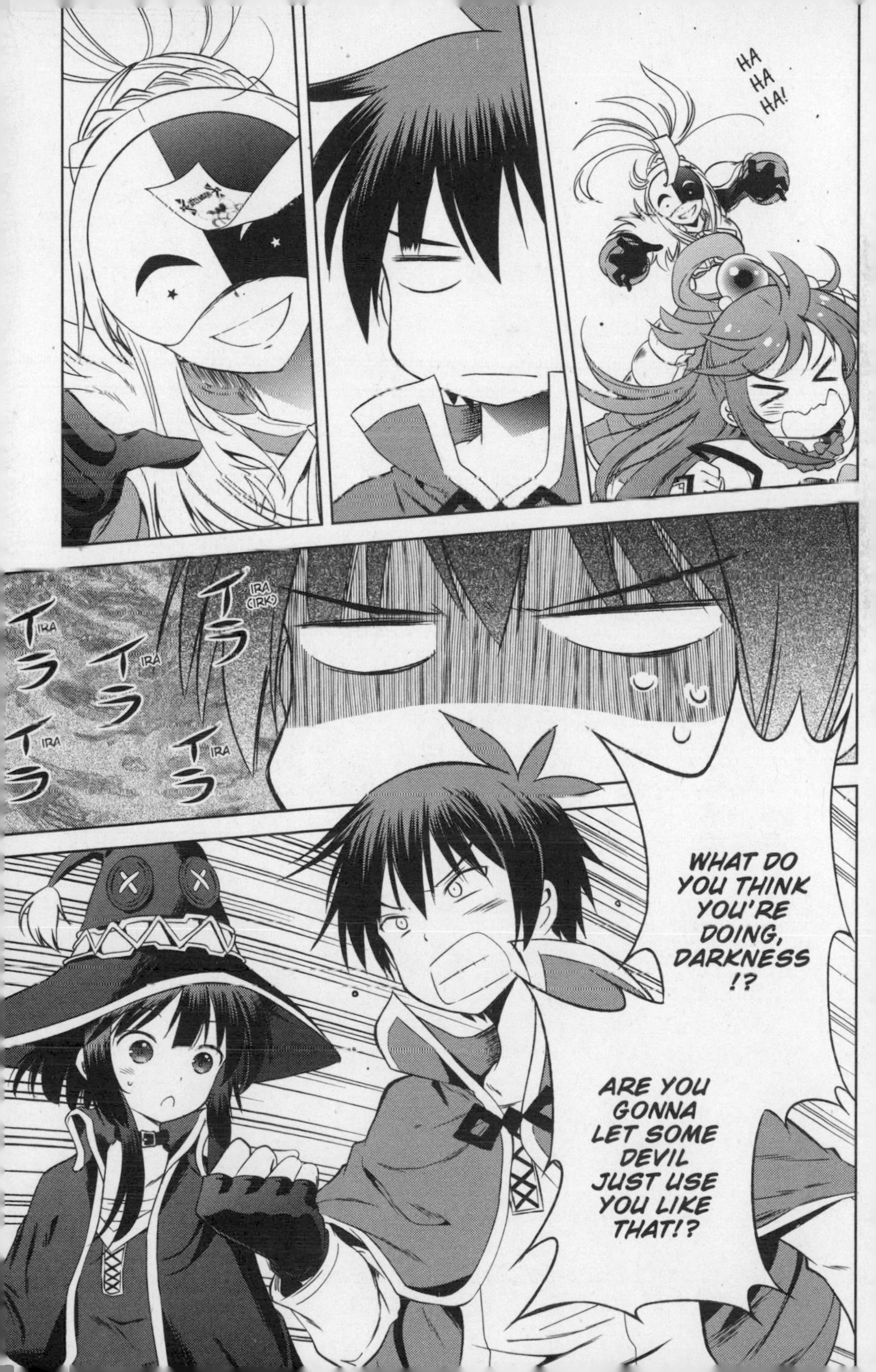
HA HA HA!
イラ IRA (IRK)
イラ IRA
イラ IRA
イラ IRA
イラ IRA
WHAT DO YOU THINK YOU'RE DOING, DARKNESS!?
ARE YOU GONNA LET SOME DEVIL JUST USE YOU LIKE THAT!?

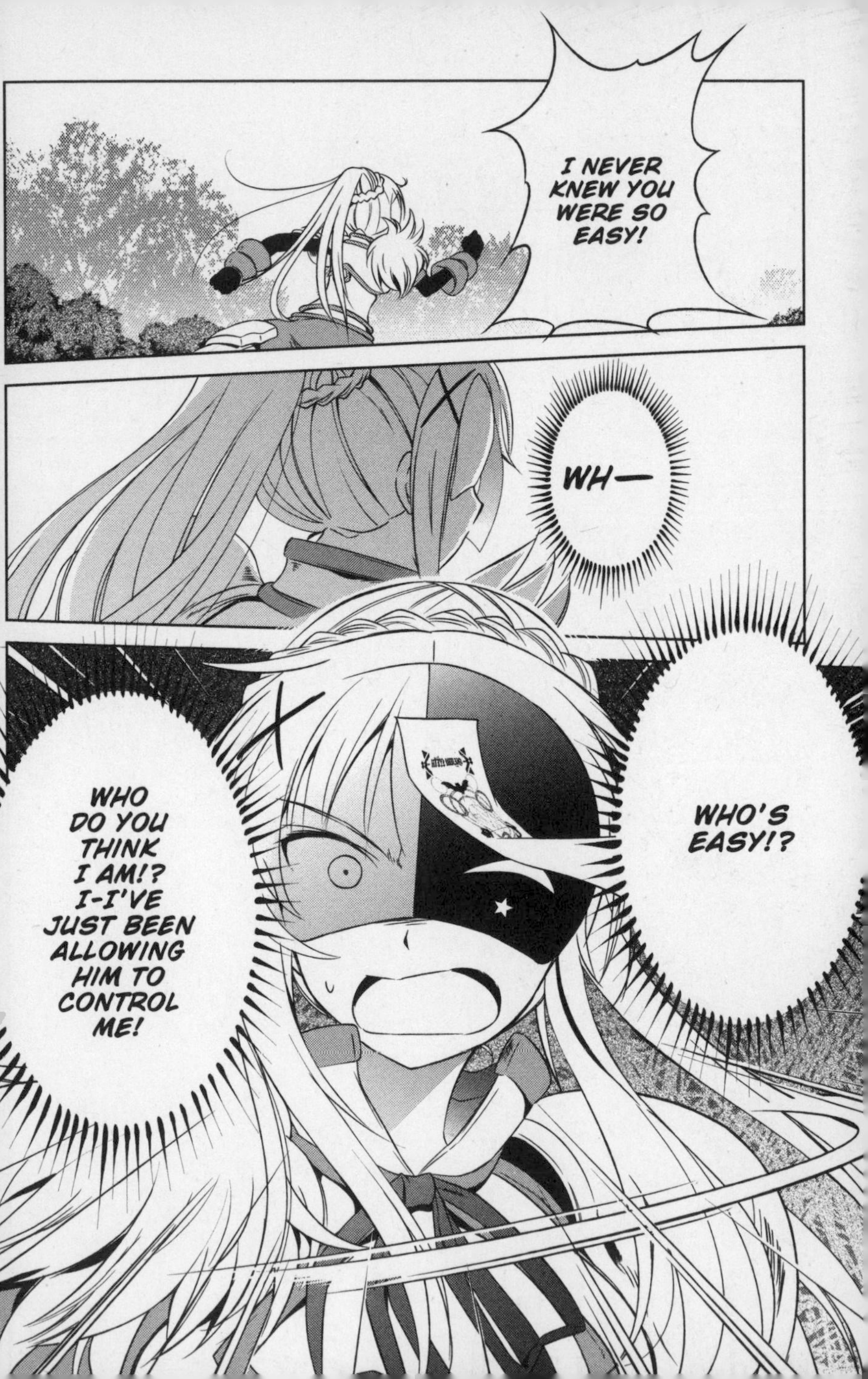
I NEVER KNEW YOU WERE SO EASY!
WH—
WHO'S EASY!?
WHO DO YOU THINK I AM!? I-I'VE JUST BEEN ALLOWING HIM TO CONTROL ME!

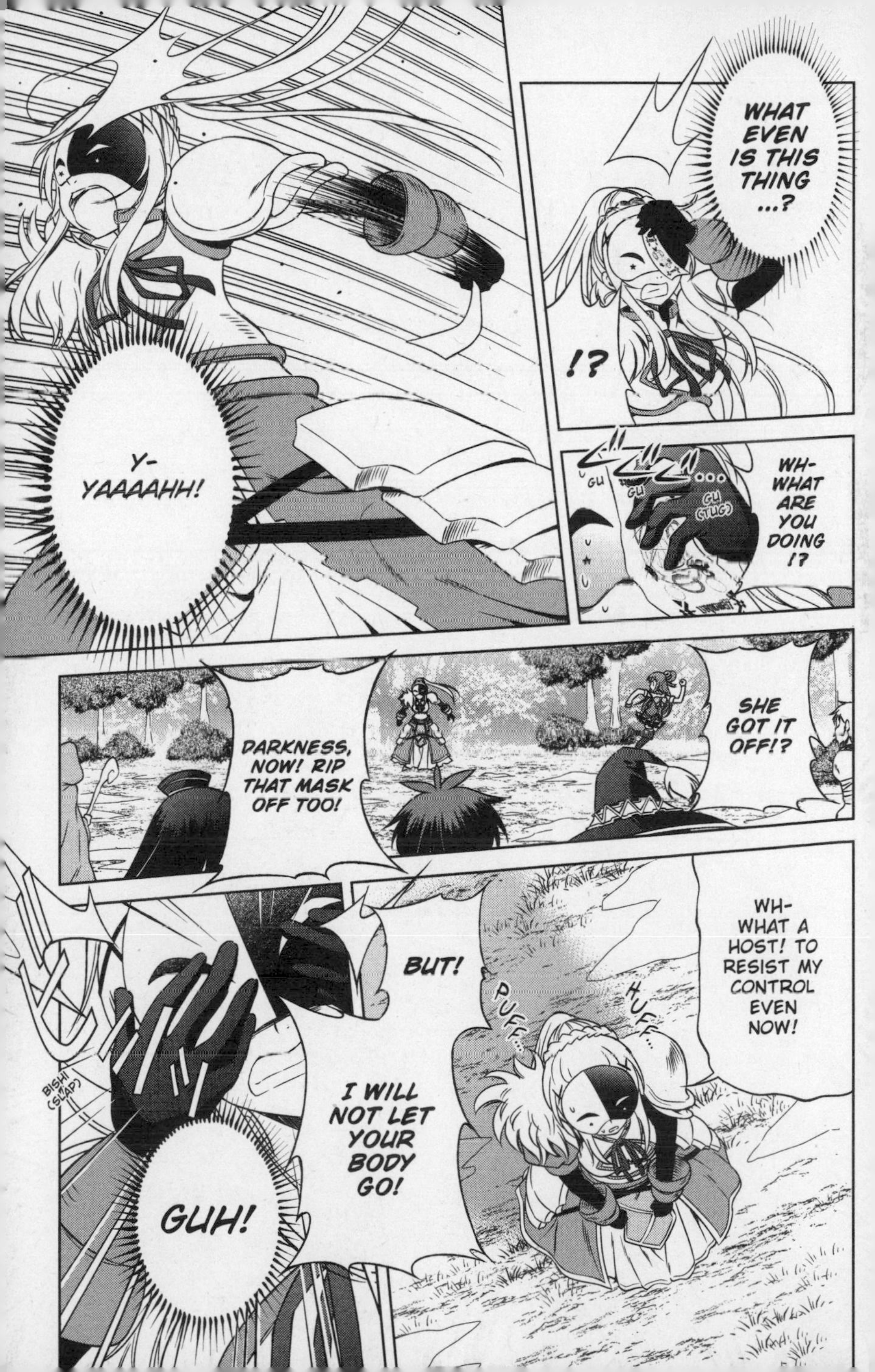
WHAT EVEN IS THIS THING ...?
!?
GU
GU
GU (TUG)
WH-WHAT ARE YOU DOING !?
Y-YAAAAHH!
SHE GOT IT OFF!?
DARKNESS, NOW! RIP THAT MASK OFF TOO!
WH-WHAT A HOST! TO RESIST MY CONTROL EVEN NOW!
HUFF...
PUFF...
BUT!
I WILL NOT LET YOUR BODY GO!
BISHI (SLAP)
GUH!

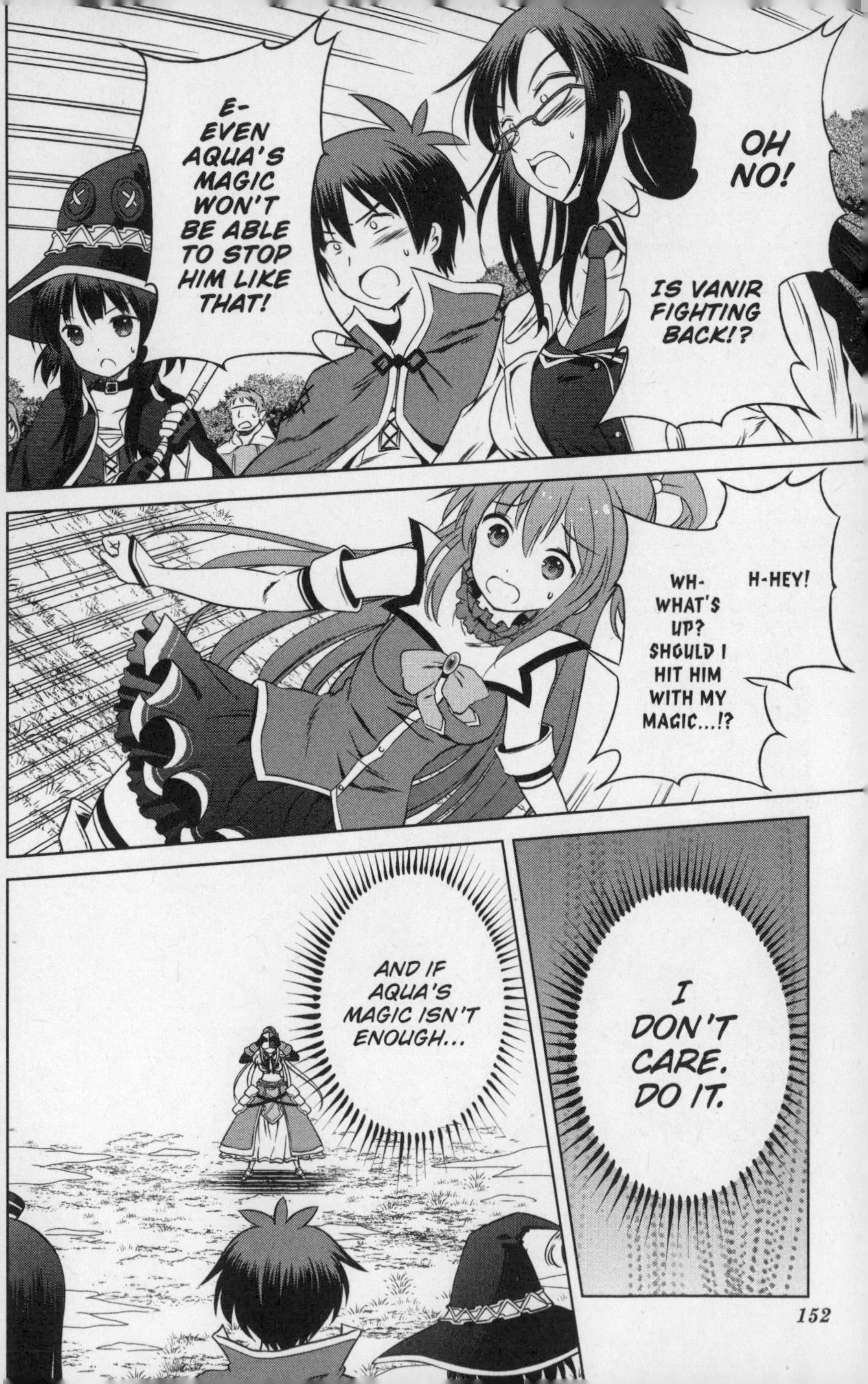
OH NO!
IS VANIR FIGHTING BACK!?
E-EVEN AQUA'S MAGIC WON'T BE ABLE TO STOP HIM LIKE THAT!
H-HEY!
WH-WHAT'S UP? SHOULD I HIT HIM WITH MY MAGIC...!?
I DON'T CARE. DO IT.
AND IF AQUA'S MAGIC ISN'T ENOUGH...

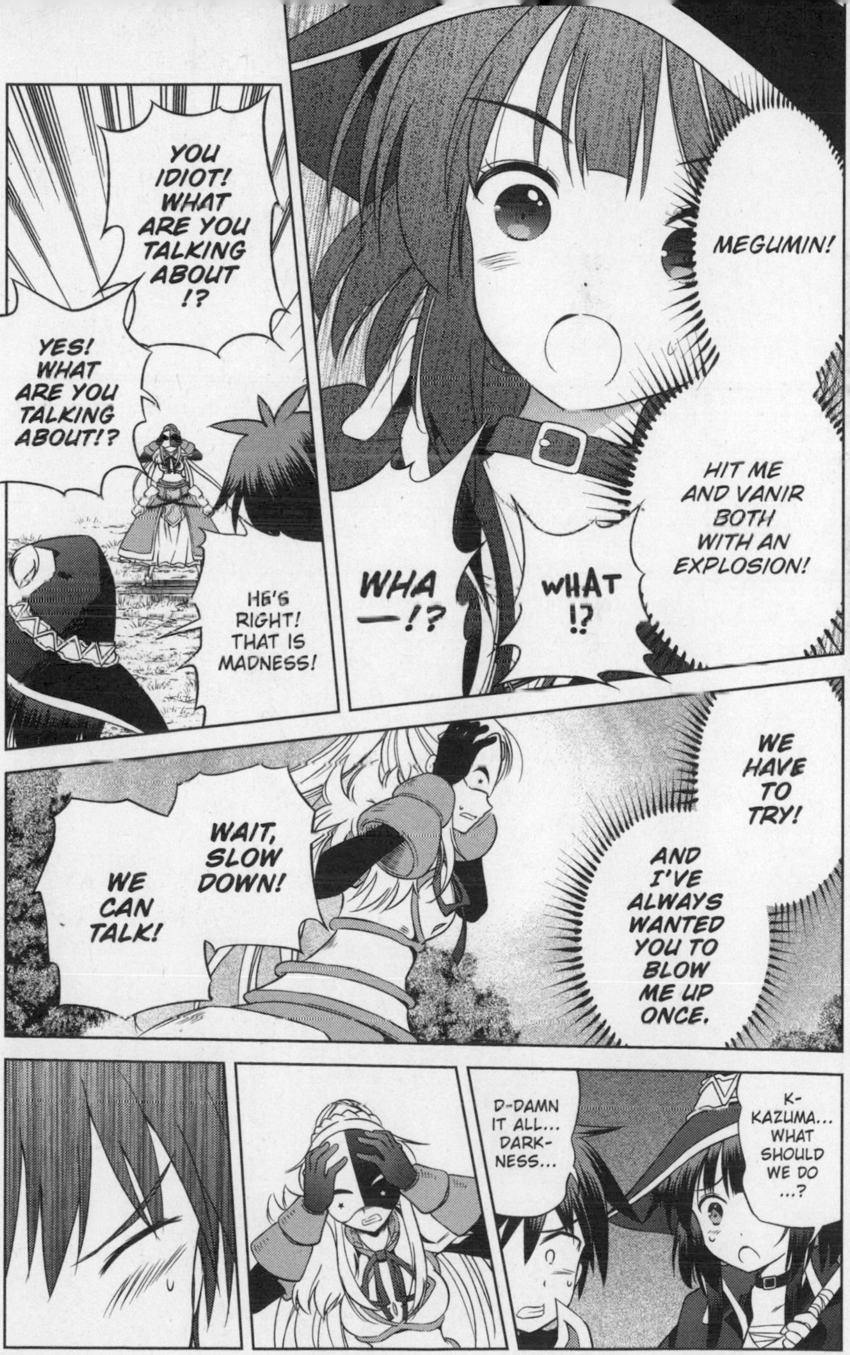
MEGUMIN!
HIT ME AND VANIR BOTH WITH AN EXPLOSION!
WHAT !?
WHA—!?
YOU IDIOT! WHAT ARE YOU TALKING ABOUT !?
YES! WHAT ARE YOU TALKING ABOUT!?
HE'S RIGHT! THAT IS MADNESS!
WE HAVE TO TRY!
AND I'VE ALWAYS WANTED YOU TO BLOW ME UP ONCE.
WAIT, SLOW DOWN!
WE CAN TALK!
K-KAZUMA... WHAT SHOULD WE DO ...?
D-DAMN IT ALL... DARK-NESS...

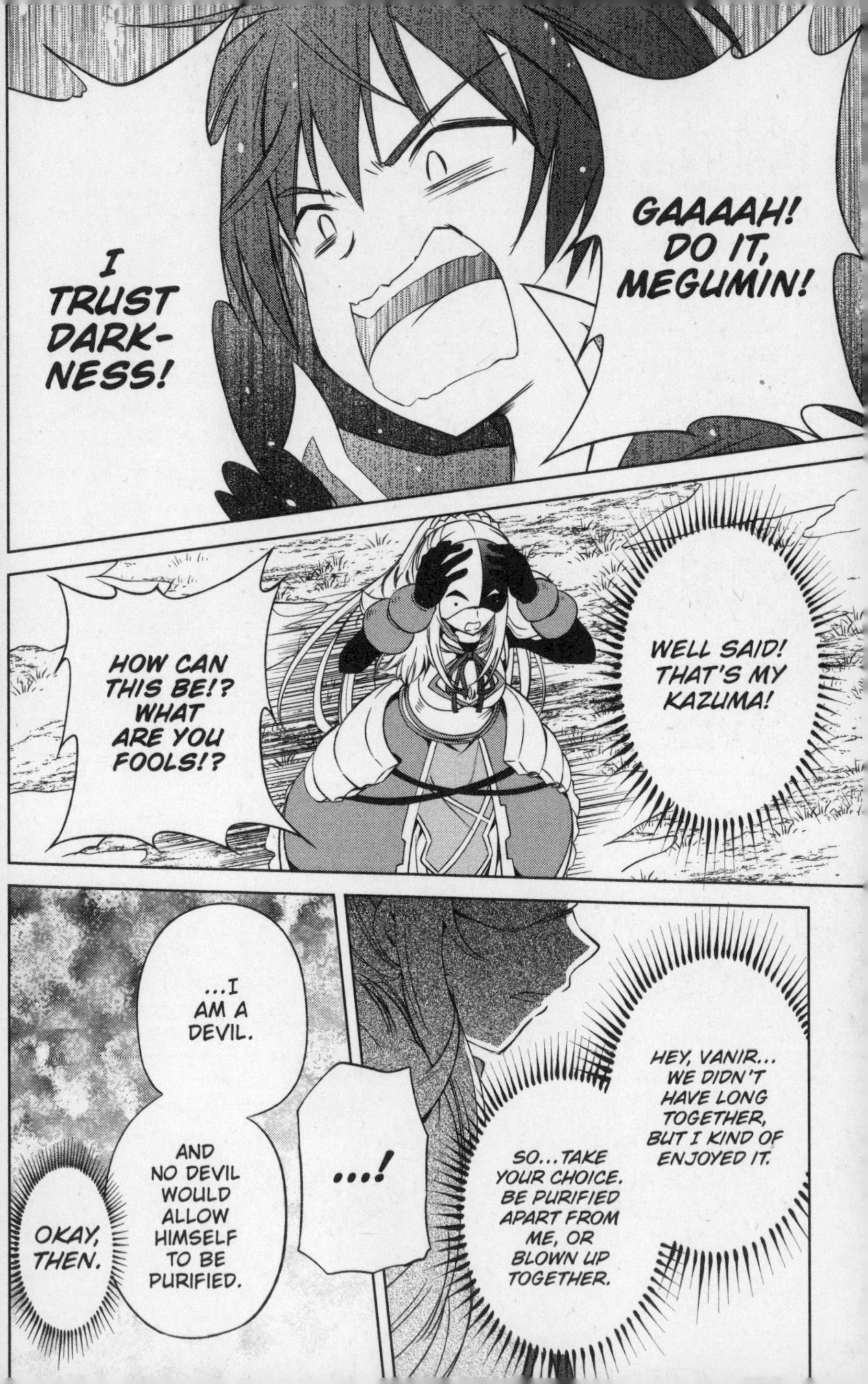
GAAAAH! DO IT, MEGUMIN!
I TRUST DARK-NESS!
WELL SAID! THAT'S MY KAZUMA!
HOW CAN THIS BE!? WHAT ARE YOU FOOLS!?
HEY, VANIR... WE DIDN'T HAVE LONG TOGETHER, BUT I KIND OF ENJOYED IT.
SO...TAKE YOUR CHOICE. BE PURIFIED APART FROM ME, OR BLOWN UP TOGETHER.
...!
...I AM A DEVIL.
AND NO DEVIL WOULD ALLOW HIMSELF TO BE PURIFIED.
OKAY, THEN.

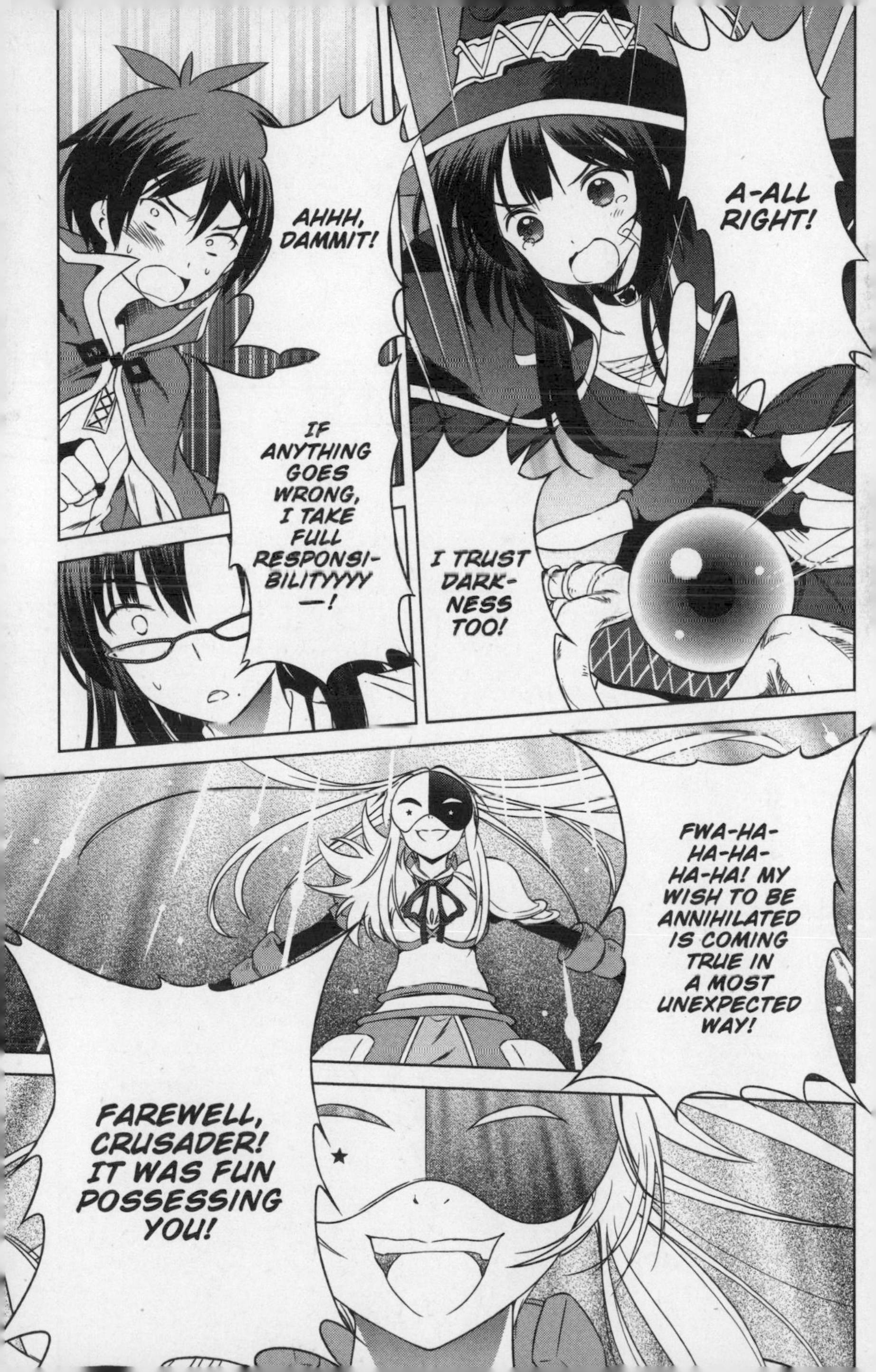
A-ALL RIGHT!
I TRUST DARKNESS TOO!
AHHH, DAMMIT!
IF ANYTHING GOES WRONG, I TAKE FULL RESPONSIBILITYYYY—!
FWA-HA-HA-HA-HA-HA! MY WISH TO BE ANNIHILATED IS COMING TRUE IN A MOST UNEXPECTED WAY!
FAREWELL, CRUSADER! IT WAS FUN POSSESSING YOU!

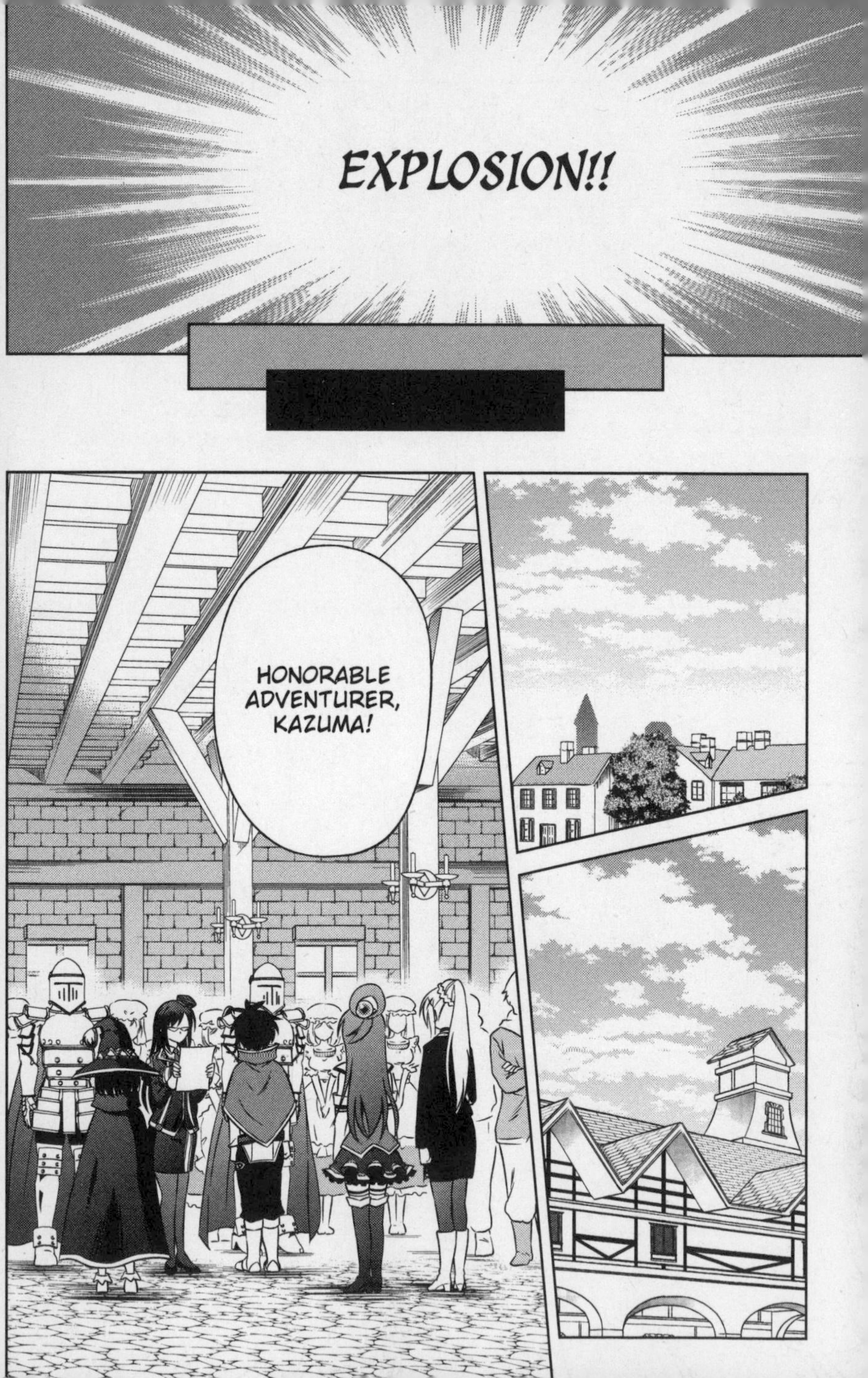
EXPLOSION!!
HONORABLE ADVENTURER, KAZUMA!

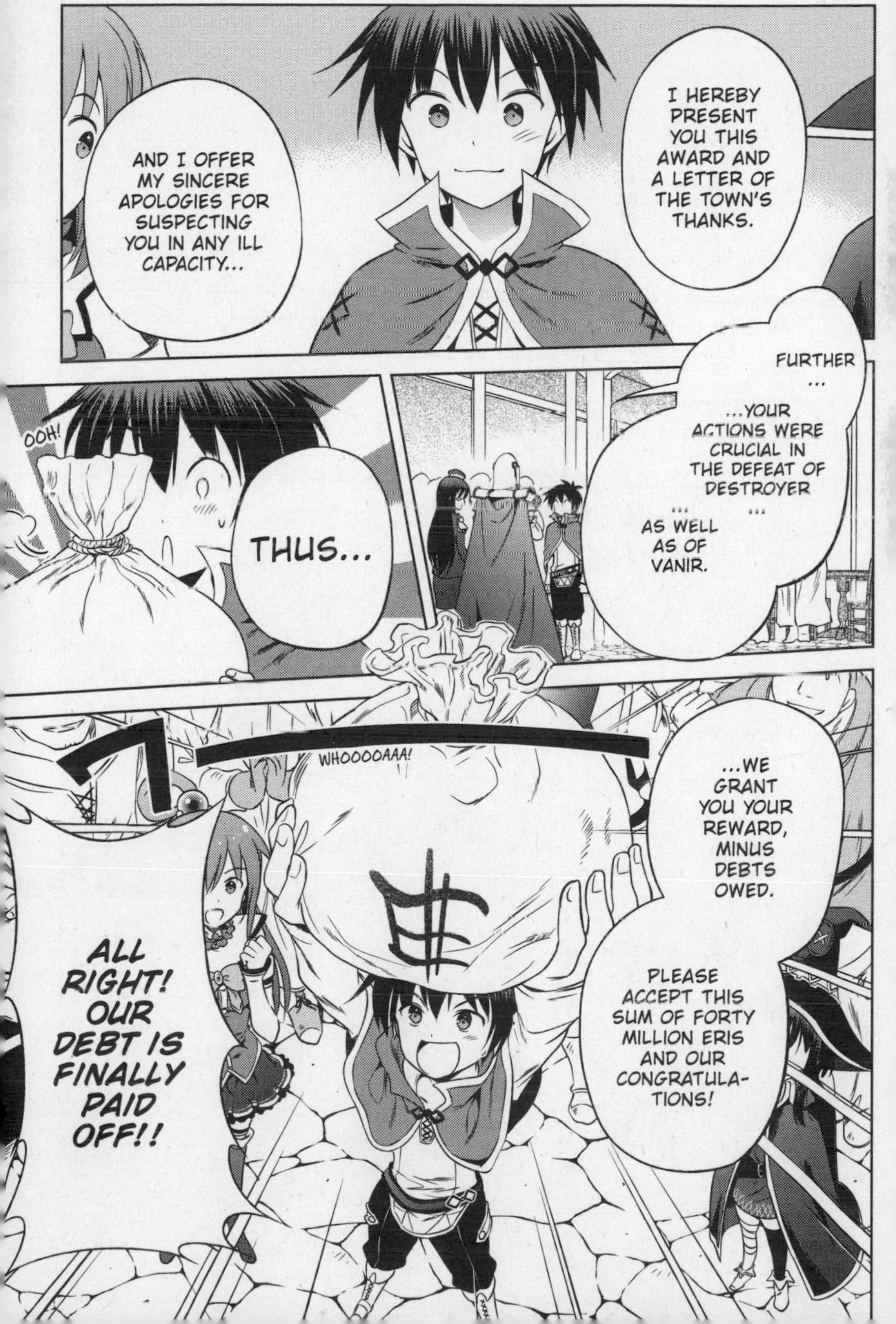
I HEREBY PRESENT YOU THIS AWARD AND A LETTER OF THE TOWN'S THANKS.
AND I OFFER MY SINCERE APOLOGIES FOR SUSPECTING YOU IN ANY ILL CAPACITY...
FURTHER ...
...YOUR ACTIONS WERE CRUCIAL IN THE DEFEAT OF DESTROYER ... ... AS WELL AS OF VANIR.
OOH!
THUS...
...WE GRANT YOU YOUR REWARD, MINUS DEBTS OWED.
PLEASE ACCEPT THIS SUM OF FORTY MILLION ERIS AND OUR CONGRATULA-TIONS!
WHOOOOAAA!
ALL RIGHT! OUR DEBT IS FINALLY PAID OFF!!

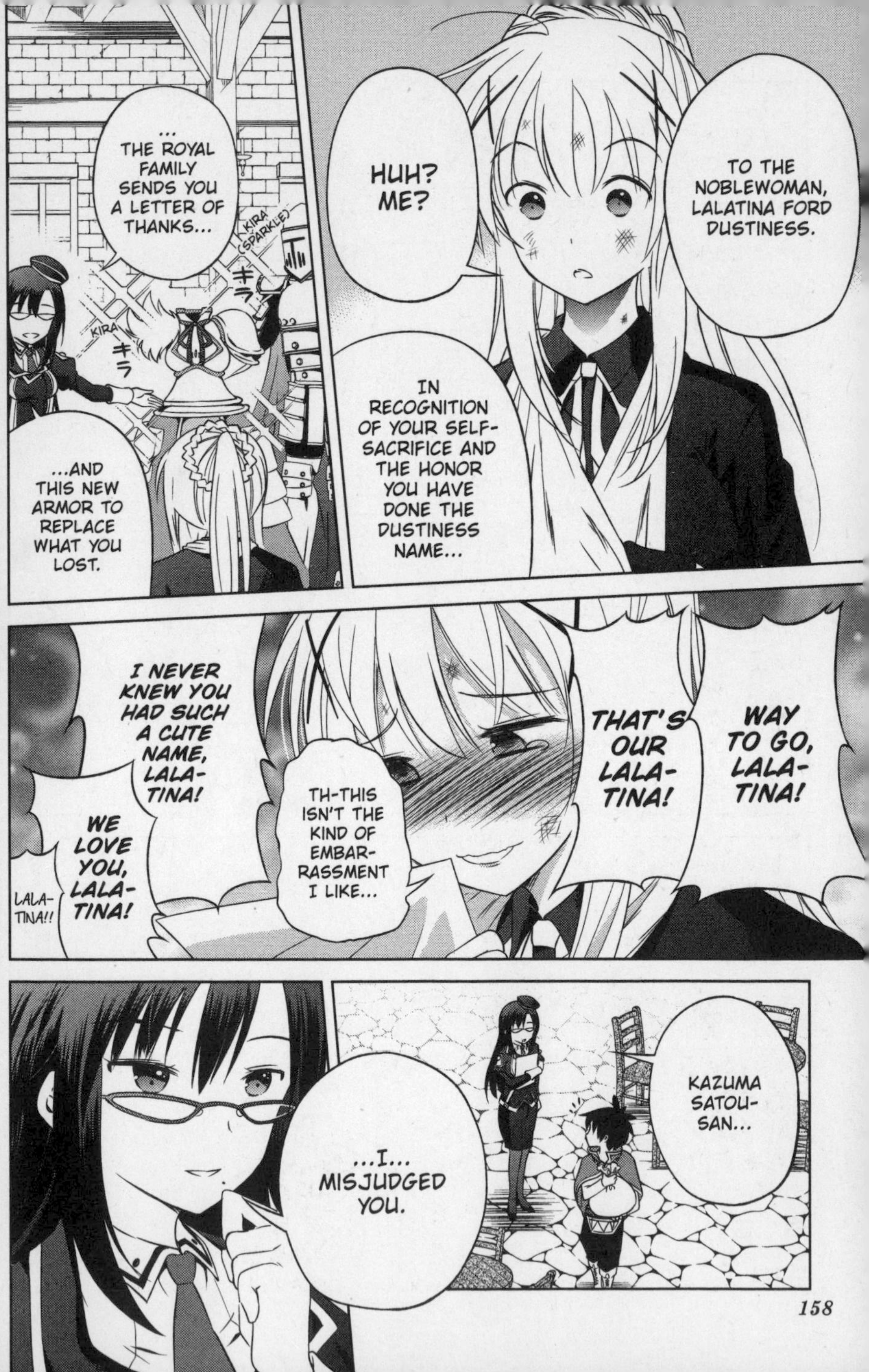
TO THE NOBLEWOMAN, LALATINA FORD DUSTINESS.
HUH? ME?
IN RECOGNITION OF YOUR SELF-SACRIFICE AND THE HONOR YOU HAVE DONE THE DUSTINESS NAME...
...THE ROYAL FAMILY SENDS YOU A LETTER OF THANKS...
KIRA (SPARKLE)
キラ
KIRA
キラ
...AND THIS NEW ARMOR TO REPLACE WHAT YOU LOST.
WAY TO GO, LALA-TINA!
THAT'S OUR LALA-TINA!
TH-THIS ISN'T THE KIND OF EMBAR-RASSMENT I LIKE...
I NEVER KNEW YOU HAD SUCH A CUTE NAME, LALA-TINA!
WE LOVE YOU, LALA-TINA!
LALA-TINA!!
KAZUMA SATOU-SAN...
...I... MISJUDGED YOU.

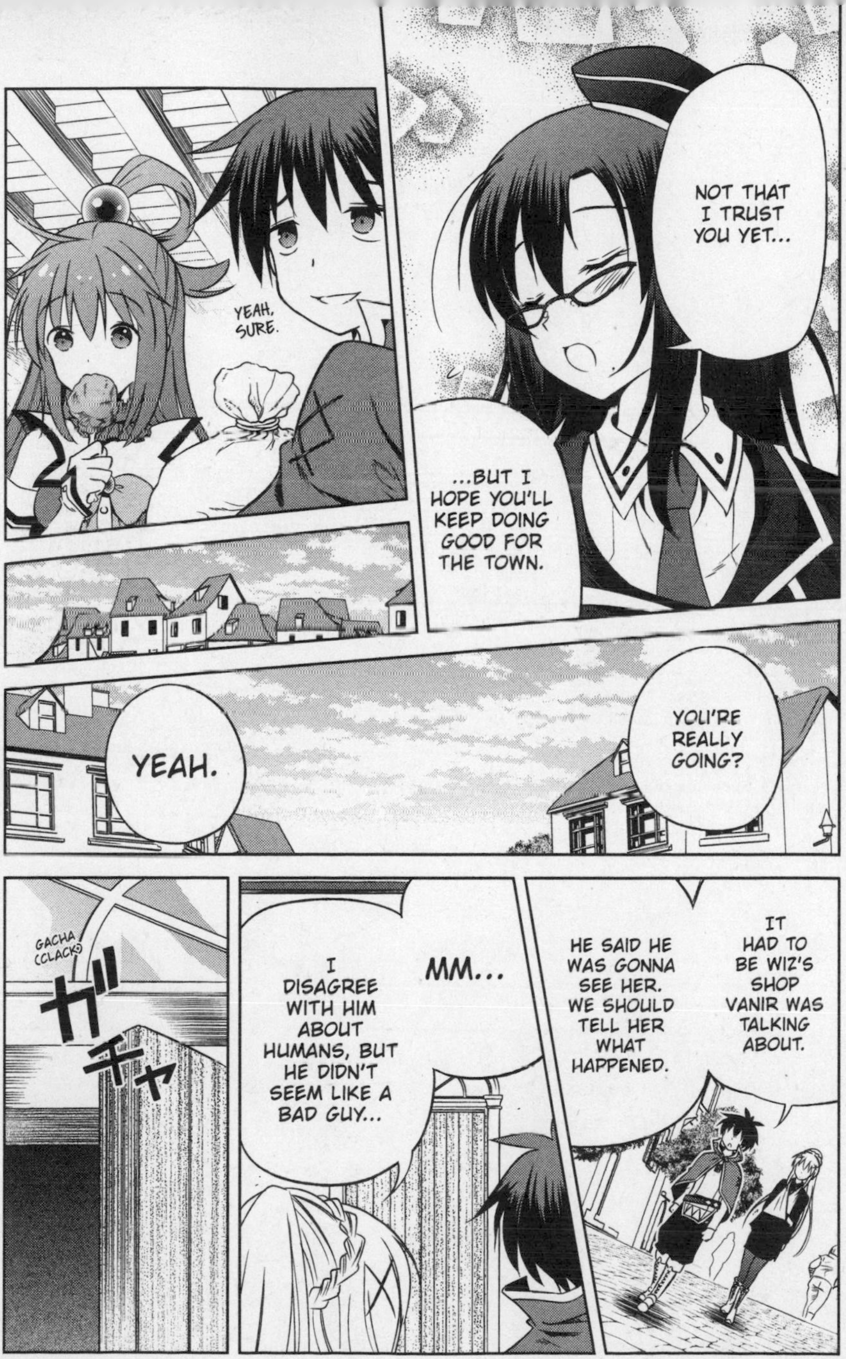

NOT THAT I TRUST YOU YET...
...BUT I HOPE YOU'LL KEEP DOING GOOD FOR THE TOWN.
YEAH, SURE.
YOU'RE REALLY GOING?
YEAH.
IT HAD TO BE WIZ'S SHOP VANIR WAS TALKING ABOUT.
HE SAID HE WAS GONNA SEE HER. WE SHOULD TELL HER WHAT HAPPENED.
MM...
I DISAGREE WITH HIM ABOUT HUMANS, BUT HE DIDN'T SEEM LIKE A BAD GUY...
GACHA (CLACK)
ガチャ

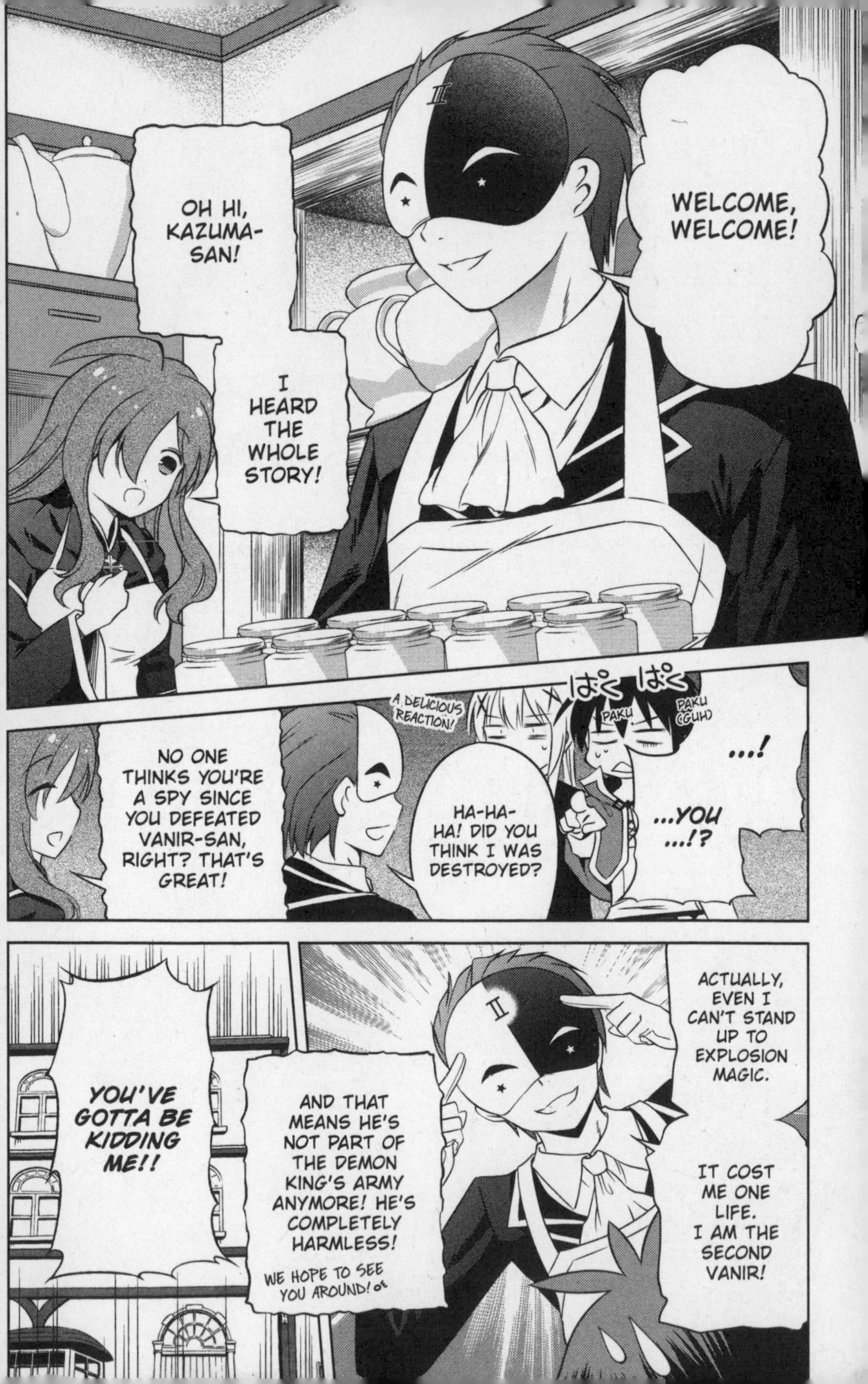
WELCOME, WELCOME!
OH HI, KAZUMA-SAN!
I HEARD THE WHOLE STORY!
...!
...YOU ...!?
ぱく ぱく
PAKU (GUH)
PAKU
A DELICIOUS REACTION!
HA-HA-HA! DID YOU THINK I WAS DESTROYED?
NO ONE THINKS YOU'RE A SPY SINCE YOU DEFEATED VANIR-SAN, RIGHT? THAT'S GREAT!
ACTUALLY, EVEN I CAN'T STAND UP TO EXPLOSION MAGIC.
IT COST ME ONE LIFE. I AM THE SECOND VANIR!
AND THAT MEANS HE'S NOT PART OF THE DEMON KING'S ARMY ANYMORE! HE'S COMPLETELY HARMLESS!
WE HOPE TO SEE YOU AROUND!
YOU'VE GOTTA BE KIDDING ME!!

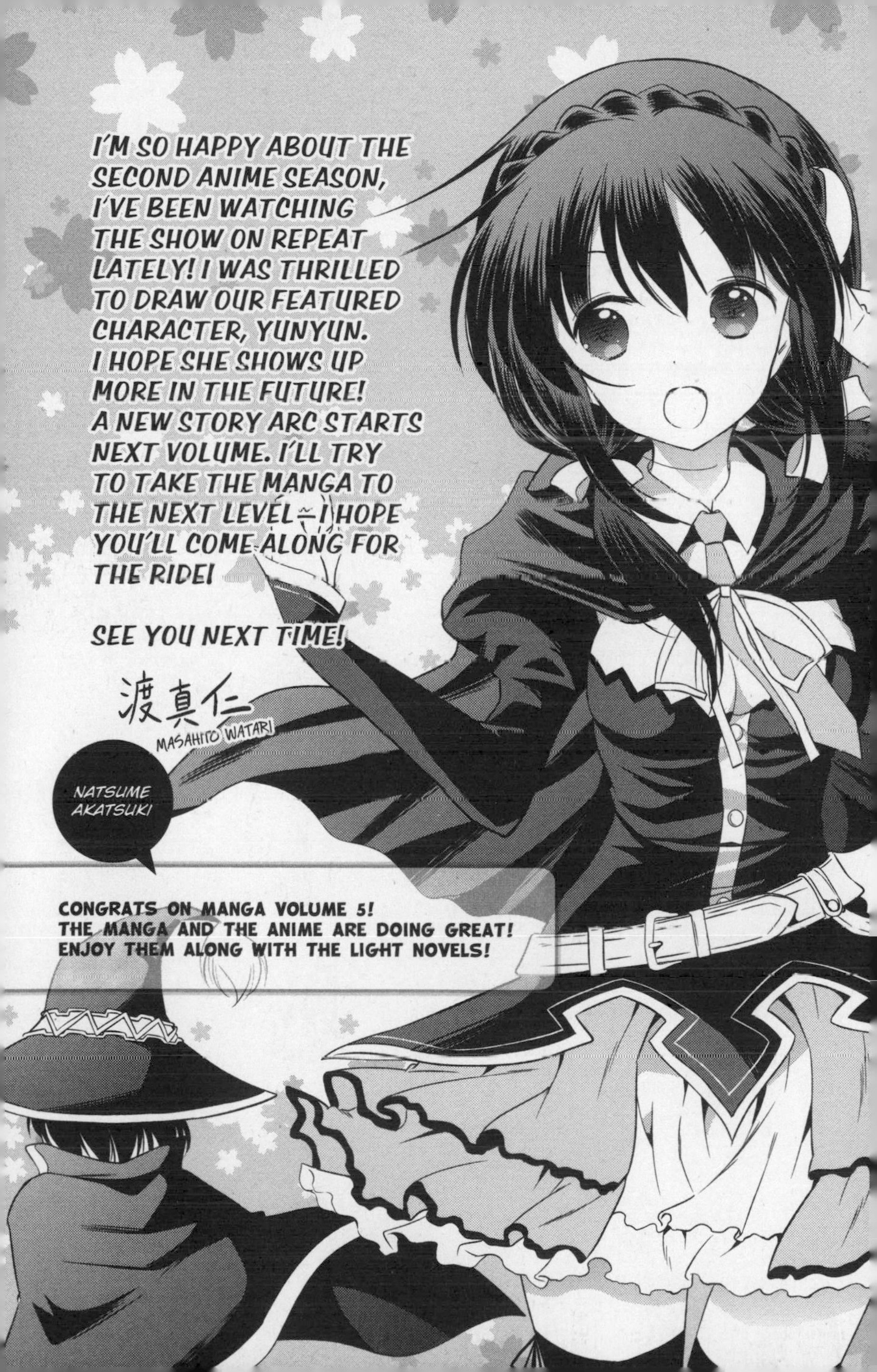
I'M SO HAPPY ABOUT THE SECOND ANIME SEASON, I'VE BEEN WATCHING THE SHOW ON REPEAT LATELY! I WAS THRILLED TO DRAW OUR FEATURED CHARACTER, YUNYUN. I HOPE SHE SHOWS UP MORE IN THE FUTURE! A NEW STORY ARC STARTS NEXT VOLUME. I'LL TRY TO TAKE THE MANGA TO THE NEXT LEVEL—I HOPE YOU'LL COME ALONG FOR THE RIDE!
SEE YOU NEXT TIME!
渡真仁
MASAHITO WATARI
NATSUME AKATSUKI
CONGRATS ON MANGA VOLUME 5!
THE MANGA AND THE ANIME ARE DOING GREAT!
ENJOY THEM ALONG WITH THE LIGHT NOVELS!

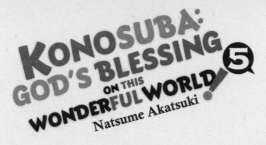

Translation: Kevin Steinbach ● **Lettering: Bianca Pistillo**

This book is a work of fiction. Names, characters, places, and incidents are the product of the author's imagination or are used fictitiously. Any resemblance to actual events, locales, or persons, living or dead, is coincidental.

KONO SUBARASHII SEKAI NI SYUKUFUKU WO! Volume 5
©MASAHITO WATARI 2017
©NATSUME AKATSUKI, KURONE MISHIMA 2017
First published in Japan in 2017 by Kadokawa Corporation, Tokyo. English translation rights arranged with KADOKAWA Corporation, Tokyo through Tuttle-Mori Agency, Inc., Tokyo.

English translation © 2017 by Yen Press, LLC

Yen Press
1290 Avenue of the Americas
New York, NY 10104

Visit us at yenpress.com
facebook.com/yenpress
twitter.com/yenpress
yenpress.tumblr.com
instagram.com/yenpress

First Yen Press Edition: November 2017

Yen Press is an imprint of Yen Press, LLC.
The Yen Press name and logo are trademarks of Yen Press, LLC.

The publisher is not responsible for websites (or their content) that are not owned by the publisher.

Library of Congress Control Number: 2016946112

ISBNs: 978-0-316-41281-0 (paperback)
      978-0-316-44648-8 (ebook)

10 9 8 7 6 5 4 3 2

WOR

Printed in the United States of America